Delhi University

Law (LLB) Entrance Exam

Latest Edition
Practice Kit

23 Tests

08 Mock Test
12 Sectional Test
03 Previous Year Paper

Based On Real Exam Pattern

✓ Thoroughly Revised and Updated

✓ Detailed Analysis of all MCQs

Title	: Delhi University Law (LLB) Entrance Exam
Author Name	: Mr. Rohit Manglik
Published By	: EduGorilla Community Pvt. Ltd.
Publishers Address	: 12/651, First Floor Opp. Arvindo Park, Near Jama Masjid, Indira Nagar, Lucknow, Uttar Pradesh-226016, India

Copyright EduGorilla

ISBN : 978-93-90893-00-3

Second Edition

Disclaimer EduGorilla

Compiled and created by EduGorilla Community Pvt. Ltd

Printed By EduGorilla Community Pvt. Ltd.

ROHIT MANGLIK
CEO, EduGorilla

Dear Applicants,

People say *"Success comes to those who work hard."* But I've seen people working hard for their exams day in and day out for marginal success. While others succeed in their examinations by putting in just half the work. So are they God Gifted? No! I believe that it's because they work *smart* and not just *hard*. Similarly, for your exams, you should strategize your preparation so as to increase the likelihood of success. Well with EduGorilla get ready to increase your *chances of selection* in your exam by *16x*.

EduGorilla helps you in not only working *hard* but also working in a *smart and strategic* manner. With EduGorilla's preparation package, you get a chance to make your exam preparation easy, and a fun learning path towards selection. Finding the right path to your preparations can be difficult if you don't know in which direction to head. Don't worry, we have you covered! EduGorilla will be your guide to success in your journey. With our Preparation Package, you can prepare strategically and beat the exam in just one attempt.

EduGorilla's Preparation Package includes-

- **Test Series**
- **Books**

Our preparation package is handcrafted as per the latest changes, expert opinions, and students' discretion. Thus, enabling you to get through each stage of the selection process for your exam.

Our Books are designed by the teachers and experts of the respective exam with a combined 150+ years of experience; to provide you with easy, efficient, and effective learning. Our books are smart, in the sense that not only do they give you the answers to the questions but also provide similar questions for practice.

EduGorilla's competent Test Series gives you real-time experience and confidence through which you can clear your offline or online exam in just one attempt. We currently host 83,000+ mock tests for 1,440+ competitive and academic exams.

Thus, EduGorilla misses no chance to assist you in your preparation and covers all stages of the exam, so that you don't have to look anywhere else.

We provide complete preparation packages for defense, banking, teaching, and other National & State-Level exams. Hence, it doesn't matter which exam you aspire to because you will reach your success.

ALL THE BEST !
Let EduGorilla be your Guide to Success.

Rohit Manglik,
Founder and CEO, EduGorilla

INTRODUCTION

EduGorilla focuses on guiding students to succeed in their examinations. With that in mind, our book, titled "Delhi University : Law (LLB) Entrance Exam", has been drafted through the collective efforts of our distinguished experts with 150+ years of combined experience. This book consists of questions that are created following the latest changes in the syllabus and exam pattern. We compiled the book on the basis of questions that are most likely to appear in the DU LLB : Law Entrance Exam. Through EduGorilla's "Delhi University : Law (LLB) Entrance Exam" your chances of success will increase 16x.

EduGorilla does this through our Complete Preparation Package. This package consists of well-conceptualized and structured content in the form of questions that are tailor-made according to your needs and will help you practice for exams in a smart way by pinpointing all the necessary information. It also provides hints and solutions, along with a smart answer sheet for your self-evaluation. You can assess your shortcomings and work accordingly on areas that may require more of your attention.

EduGorilla promises to help you succeed in your examination and accomplish your dream goals. We believe in our aspirants and see them at the top of the merit list. And the first step towards the top is to start preparing with us. EduGorilla's "Delhi University : Law (LLB) Entrance Exam" includes the following attributes.

➤ Well-Researched Content

➤ Top-Notch Quality

➤ Detailed Answers and Analysis

➤ Smart Answer Sheet

➤ Exam Relevant Questions

Therefore, EduGorilla fortifies your preparation and makes it durable enough to help you stand tall and beat the examination.

DU LLB : Law Entrance Exam
Scan QR code for Eligibility, Exam Pattern, Syllabus and more.

Book ID: 0740

TABLE OF CONTENTS

English Language & Comprehension

Q.1 Direction: In the following question, some part of the sentence may have errors. Find out which part of the sentence has an error and select the appropriate option. If a sentence is free from error, select 'No Error'.

The USA is aiming at (A) / double its bilateral trade with India (B) / by 2015. (C) / No error (D)

A. (A)	**B.** (B)	**C.** (C)	**D.** (D)

Q.2 Direction: In the given sentence, choose the part of the sentence that contains an error.

When few people own land and /(A) most people live in cities, it /(B) is quite common to have the highest degree of hunger in /(C) nations which are exporting food. /(D)

A. A	**B.** B	**C.** C	**D.** D

Q.3 In the following question, out of the four alternatives, select the alternative which will improve the underlined part of the sentence. In case no improvement is needed, select "No improvement".

Drunk driving is nothing <u>else than</u> pure madness.

A. else but	**B.** else not

C. else	**D.** No improvement

Q.4 In the following sentence has a blank space, and five words are given below. Click on the word which you consider the most appropriate to fit the blank.

His speculations in this regard, while intriguing, rely heavily on the fact of her general ________.

A. Obstreperous	**B.** Mendacity

C. Euphemism	**D.** Dichotomy

Q.5 Each of the following sentences has a blank space, and five words are given below. Click on the word which you consider the most appropriate to fit the blank.

To decipher the expected political behaviour of the subalterns in the wake of the current crisis ________ reverse migration-bound workers, one needs to go back to 2014.

A. Interceding	**B.** Obviating

C. Disparaging	**D.** Engulfing

Q.6 Select the most appropriate meaning of the underlined idiom.

When he lost his job, he had <u>his back against the wall</u>, as the money lenders came banging on his door.

A. Escaped from the place.

B. Be in a difficult situation.

C. Stood with back against the wall.

D. Hurt his back.

Q.7 Select the most appropriate meaning of the underlined idiom.

She eagerly took the project but soon realised that she had <u>bitten off more than she could chew</u>.

A. Take a big bite.

B. Become greedy.

C. Eat something tasteless.

D. Try to do something very difficult.

Q.8 In the following question, out of the four alternatives, select the alternative which is the best substitute of the phrase.

One who is unable to pay his debts

A. Misanthrope	**B.** Atheist

C. Insolvent	**D.** Recluse

Q.9 In the following question, out of the four alternatives, select the alternative which is the best substitute of the phrase.

An official pardon for people who have been convicted of political offenses

A. Draw	**B.** Amnesty

C. Octagon	**D.** Bureaucracy

Q.10 Direction: Four words are given, out of which one word is spelt incorrectly. Choose the incorrectly spelled word and click the button corresponding to it.

A. Rateable	**B.** Perversion

C. Pamphlet	**D.** Requittal

Q.11 Four words are given, out of which only one word is spelt correctly. Choose the correctly spelt word and click the button corresponding to it.

A. Enterpreneur	**B.** Entreperneur

C. Entreprenuer	**D.** Entrepreneur

Q.12 Direction: Select the correct passive form of the given sentence.

The mechanic repaired my bike.

A. The bike is repaired by my mechanic.

B. My bike has been repaired by the mechanic.

C. The bike was being repaired by my mechanic.

D. My bike was repaired by the mechanic.

Q.13 Direction: Choose the option that best transforms the sentence into its other voice:

The Smiths celebrated Christmas this year.

A. This year, Christmas was celebrated by the Smiths.

B. This year, the Smiths celebrated Christmas.

C. This year was celebrated Christmas by Smiths.

D. Christmas by the Smiths was celebrated.

Q.14 Janice and Dionne were visiting New York City when ___ noticed a man climbing an apartment building. (insert the proper pronoun).

A. She	**B.** Them

C. They   **D.** None of the above

Q.15 This type of noun expresses strong feelings or emotions.
A. Abstract   **B.** Concrete
C. Proper   **D.** Common

Q.16 Choose the correct answer from the options given below:
Sahil read the letter _______ carefully the second time to make sure he hadn't missed any detail.
A. most   **B.** more   **C.** much   **D.** many

Q.17 It has become his habit to ___ do his homework and then copies it from others.
A. always   **B.** seldom   **C.** often   **D.** never

Q.18 Directions: Choose the appropriate preposition for the given sentence:
Barring strong headwinds, the plane will arrive _________ schedule.
A. during   **B.** for   **C.** by   **D.** on

Q.19 Direction: Choose the appropriate preposition for the given sentence:
The US Open will be transmitted live _______ satellite.
A. via   **B.** on   **C.** within   **D.** towards

Q.20 Direction: A sentence with an underlined word/words is given below followed by four options. Select the option that is nearest in meaning to the underlined word/words.
The police officer tried to <u>intimidate</u> the witness but in vain.
A. Inform   **B.** Reward   **C.** Frighten   **D.** Persuade

Q.21 Which of the following is opposite in meaning to the underlined word?
The juice was <u>insipid</u> but it had to be consumed in order to take effect.
A. Incongruent   **B.** Despicable
C. Delicious   **D.** Insidious

Ques (22-25):Direction: Read the passage given below and answer the question that follows by selecting the most appropriate option.

It is easy to make a delicious-looking hamburger at home. But would this hamburger still look delicious after it sat on your kitchen table under very bright lights for six or seven hours? If someone took a picture or made a video of this hamburger after the seventh hour, would anyone want to eat it? These are the questions that fast food companies worry about when they produce commercials. Video and photoshoot often last many hours. Because of this, the menu items in fast-food commercials are probably not actually edible. As an example, the first step towards building the perfect commercial hamburger is the bun. The food stylist-a person employed by the company to make sure the products look perfect-sorts through hundreds of buns until he or she finds one with no wrinkles. Next, the stylist carefully rearranges the sesame seeds on the bun using glue and tweezers for maximum visual appeal. The bun is then sprayed with a waterproofing solution so that it will not get soggy from contact with other ingredients, the lights, or the humidity in the room. Next, the

food stylist shapes a meat patty into a perfect circle and paints the outside with a mixture of oil, molasses, and brown food coloring. Grill marks are either painted on or seared into the meat using hot metal skewers. Finally, the food stylist searches through dozens of tomatoes and heads of lettuce to find the best-looking produce. One leaf of the crispest lettuce and one center slice of the reddest tomato are selected and then sprayed with glycerin to keep them looking fresh. So the next time you see a **delectable** hamburger in a fast-food commercial, remember: you're actually looking at glue, paint, raw meat, and glycerin!

Q.22 According to the passage, a food stylist working on a hamburger commercial might use glue and tweezers for:
A. Make patty stays attached to the bun
B. Maximum visual appeal
C. Arrange the lettuce on the tomato
D. Hold the entire hamburger together

Q.23 Based on information in the passage, it is most important for the lettuce and tomato used in a fast-food hamburger commercial to:
A. Look fresh
B. Have a great taste
C. Be the perfect shape and size
D. Appear natural

Q.24 As used in the passage, which is the best synonym for 'delectable'?
A. Disgusting   **B.** Familiar
C. Fake   **D.** Delicious

Q.25 'She finds one with no wrinkles' implies that she was looking for something-
A. Unnatural   **B.** Perfect
C. Suitable   **D.** Beautiful

Analytical Abilities

Q.26 Leela introduces two girls to her friend as the daughters of the only sister of her father. Leela and the girls are _____.
[RRB/RRC Group D, 2018]
A. Cousins   **B.** Sisters
C. Nieces   **D.** Can not determine

Q.27 If P denotes ÷; Q denotes ×, R denotes + and S denotes – , then what is the value of 18 Q 12 P 4 R 5 S 6?
A. 33   **B.** 43   **C.** 53   **D.** 63

Q.28 Direction: Based on the first two statements answer about the third statement logically.
Class A has a higher enrollment than Class B.
Class C has a lower enrollment than Class B.
Class A has a lower enrollment than Class C.
If the first two statements are true, the third statement is-
A. True   **B.** False
C. Uncertain   **D.** Nothing can be said

Q.29 Direction: In the question below is a statement followed by two conclusions. Answer the question according to the given statements.

Statement:

Some pearls are jewels. Some Jewels are ornaments.

Conclusion:

I. Some jewels are pearls.

II. Some ornaments are jewels.

A. Only conclusion I follows

B. Only conclusion II follows

C. Neither conclusion I nor II follows

D. Both conclusions I and II follow

Q.30 Direction: In the question below is a statement followed by conclusions. Answer the question according to the statement and conclusion are given.

Statement: All the harmoniums are instruments. All the instruments are flutes.

Conclusion:

1. All the flutes are instruments.
2. All the harmoniums are flutes.

A. Only (1) conclusion follows

B. Only (2) conclusion follows

C. Either (1) or (2) follows

D. Neither (1) nor (2) follows

Q.31 Direction: In the question below is a statement followed by conclusions. Answer the question according to the statement and conclusion are given.

Statements: Some mangoes are yellow. Some tixo are mangoes.
Conclusions:
1. Some mangoes are green.
1. All Tixo are yellow.

A. Only 1 conclusion follows.

B. Only 2 conclusion follows.

C. Either 1 or 2 follows.

D. Neither 1 nor 2 follows.

Q.32 Five friends, K, L, M, O and P are sitting around a circular table facing the centre. P sits second to the left of K. M sits third to the right of P. L sits immediate right of M. Who among the following sits exactly between P and K?

A. L

B. M

C. O

D. None of these

Q.33 Arjun, Pooja, Rahul, Varun, Sanam and Zara are sitting in a row. Sanam and Zara are in the center. Arjun and Pooja are at the ends. Rahul is sitting to the left of Arjun. Sanam is sitting to the right of Varun. Who is to the right of Pooja?

A. Arjun   **B.** Varun   **C.** Sanam   **D.** Zara

Q.34 In an Exhibition seven cars of different companies - Cadillac, Ambassador, Fiat, Maruti, Mercedes, Bedford, and Fargo are standing facing to the east in the following order :

- Cadillac is next to the right of Fargo.
- Fargo is fourth to the right of Fiat.
- Maruti car is between Ambassador and Bedford.
- Fiat which is third to the left of Ambassador is at one end.

Which of the following groups of cars is to the right of Ambassador ?

A. Cadillac, Fargo and Maruti

B. Mercedes, Cadillac and Fargo

C. Maruti, Bedford and Fiat

D. Bedford, Cadillac and Fargo

Q.35 What comes next in the sequence: 1, 2, 6, 22, ___ ?

A. 82   **B.** 84   **C.** 86   **D.** 88

Q.36 Select the option that is related to the third term in the same way as the second term is related to the first term.

DEMOGRAPHY : EDOMHSPAYH :: BACKGROUND : ?

A. DNKCSHUOAB   **B.** DNKCHSUOAB

C. ABKCHSUODN   **D.** ABKCSHUODN

Q.37 Direction: Select the related letters from the given alternatives.

QTWZ : UPAV : : GJMP : ?

A. KNFL   **B.** CFQL   **C.** KFPL   **D.** KFQL

Q.38 Direction: Answer according to the analogous relation given:

Float : Sink:: Boat:?

A. Ship   **B.** War

C. Submarine   **D.** Missile

Q.39 Direction: Answer according to analogous relation given.

Country : President :: State : ?

A. Chief Minister   **B.** Prime Minister

C. Speaker   **D.** Governor

Q.40 Direction: Given below are two statements, one is labeled as Statement and other as Assumption.

Statement: The X-Airlines has decided to increase the passenger fare by 15 percent with immediate effect.

Assumption:

I. The demand for seats of X-Airlines may remain unchanged even after the hike of fare.

II. Other airline companies may also hike the passenger fares.

A. Only assumption I is implicit

B. Only assumption II is implicit

C. Either I or II is implicit

D. Neither I nor II is implicit

Q.41 Direction: Given below are two statements, one is labeled as Statement and other as Assumption.

Statement:

It's an important matter; the prime minister is not taking any decision with regard to declaring war against our hostile neighbour.

Assumption:

I. It is better if he decides the matter without any hurry.

II. This is a matter which should not be postponed and war should be declared immediately.

A. If only assumption I is implicit.
B. If only assumption II is implicit.
C. If either I or II is implicit.
D. If neither I nor II is implicit.

Q.42 Introducing Sonia, Aamir says, "She is the wife of only nephew of only brother of my mother." How Sonia is related to Aamir?

A. Wife
B. Sister
C. Sister-in-law
D. Data is inadequate

Q.43 If Rahim moves 20 metres in East direction and then turns to his left and then moves 15 metres and then he turns to his right and moves 25 metres. After this he turns to his right and moves 15 metres. Now, how far is he from starting point?

A. 40 meters
B. 50 meters
C. 25 meters
D. 45 meters

Q.44 Direction: The following questions consist of a statement followed by two arguments I and II. Choose the best answer from the given options.

Statement: Should all the drugs patented and manufactured in Western countries be first tried out on sample basis before giving a license for sale to general public in India?

Arguments:

I. Yes. Many such drugs require different doses and duration for Indian population and hence it is necessary.

II. No. This is just not feasible and hence cannot be implemented.

A. Only argument I is strong
B. Only argument II is strong
C. Either I or II is strong
D. Neither I nor II is strong

Q.45 Direction: The following question consists of a statement followed by two arguments I and II. Choose the best answer from the given options.

Statement: Should 'computer knowledge' be made a compulsory subject for all the students at the secondary school level?

Argument:

I. No, our need is 'bread' for everyone, we cannot follow western models.

II. Yes. We cannot compete in the international market without equipping our children with computers.

A. Only argument I is strong
B. Only argument II is strong
C. Either I or II is strong
D. Neither I nor II is strong

Q.46 In a certain code, FAVOUR is written as EBUPTS. How is DANGER written in that code?

A. CBFFDS
B. CBMHDS
C. EBFHDS
D. EBHHFS

Q.47 In a certain code 'BONE' can be written as ' 36 ' and 'BORN' can be written as '49'. How is 'BODY' written in that code?

A. 46
B. 50
C. 52
D. 45

Q.48 If 'DANGER' are coded as 'ADGNRE' then how would you code 'DAMAGE'?

A. ADAMEG
B. ADAMGE
C. ADAEMG
D. ADAMEH

Q.49 Direction: Two statements I and II are given. These statements may be either independent causes or may be effects of independent causes or a common cause. One of these statements may be the effect of the other statements. Read both the statements and decide which of the following answer choice correctly depicts the relationship between these two statements.

Mark answer:

I. The Central Government has recently declared to finish the rebate on farming.

II. The Central Government faced financial loss on account of giving rebate on farming for the last few years.

A. If statement I is the cause and statement II is its effect.
B. If statement II is the cause and statement I is its effect.
C. If both the statements I and II are independent causes.
D. If both the statements I and II are effects of independent causes.

Q.50 Direction: Two statements I and II are given. These statements may be either independent causes or may be effects of independent causes or a common cause. One of these statements may be the effect of the other statements. Read both the statements and decide which of the following answer choice correctly depicts the relationship between these two statements.

Mark answer:

I. Ram's father was ill.

II. Ram brought medicine after consulting the doctor.

A. If statement I is the cause and statement II is its effect.
B. If statement II is the cause and statement I is its effect.
C. If both the statements I and II are independent causes.
D. If both the statements I and II are effects of independent causes.

Legal Awareness & Aptitude

Q.51 Rule of Law means -
A. All persons are equal in the eyes of the law
B. Treating all unequally as equals
C. Working according to law
D. Distributing state largesse to everyone in equal proportion

Q.52 What does the legal term Caveat Emptor refer to?
A. Let the buyer beware
B. According to value
C. An unwelcome person
D. Beyond the powers

Q.53 Which of the following best describes the legal phrase amicus curiae?
A. Let the buyer beware
B. Friend of the court
C. At one's own risk

D. On what authority

Q.54 In which landmark judgment did the Supreme Court of India lay down guidelines against sexual harassment of women at the workplace?
A. Nilabati Behera vs. State of Orissa
B. Vishakha vs. State of Rajasthan
C. Maneka Gandhi vs. Union of India
D. Hussainara Khatoon vs. State of Bihar

Q.55 Which Landmark case of the Supreme Court talked about Speedy Trial?
A. Nandini Satpathi v. P.L. Dani
B. Hussainara khatoon v. Home Secretary, State of Bihar
C. Ahmed Khan v. Shah Bano Begum
D. Rajagopal v. State of Tamilnadu

Q.56 In which Landmark Legal case court explained the provision 'Procedure Established by Law'?
A. Sajjan singh v. State of Rajasthan
B. Minerva mills v. Union of India
C. Bacchan Singh v. the State of Punjab
D. Maneka Gandhi v. Union of India

Q.57 In which of the following cases did the Supreme Court direct the compulsory registration of all marriages in India?
A. Danial Latifi vs Union of India
B. Ashok Kumar vs Union of India
C. Seema vs Ashwini Kumar
D. Sharda vs Dharampal

Q.58 In which of the following cases did the Supreme Court allow Passive Euthanasia under exceptional circumstances?
A. Gian Kaur vs. State of Punjab
B. Aruna Shanbaug vs. Union of India
C. Sharda vs. Union of India
D. Seema vs. Ashwini Kumar

Q.59 In which one of the following judgments of the Constitutional Bench of the Supreme Court of India, the 'rarest of rare' principle in the award of death penalty was first laid down?
A. Bachan Singh vs. State of Punjab (1980)
B. Gopalanachari vs. State of Kerala (1980)
C. Dr. Upendra Baxi vs. State of UP (1983)
D. Tukaram vs. State of Maharashtra (1979)

Q.60 Direction: Give the meaning for the following maxim word given.
Assentio Mentium
A. The meeting of minds
B. In good faith
C. An argument directed at the person
D. Injury without damage

Q.61 Direction: Give the meaning for the following maxim word given.
Pacta sunt servanda
A. Agreements must be kept

B. Treaties are legally binding only to the contracting parties
C. Goods without an owner
D. With the intention of making a will

Q.62 Who of the following is credited with drafting the Indian Penal Code, 1860?
A. Sir James Stephen
B. Charles Wood
C. John Morley
D. Lord Macaulay

Q.63 The motive under section 81 of IPC should be:
A. Prevention of harm to person
B. Prevention of harm to property
C. Both (A) and (B)
D. None of These

Q.64 Andaman and Nicobar Islands come under the jurisdiction of which of the following High Courts?
A. Calcutta High Court
B. Madras High Court
C. Port Blair High Court
D. Delhi High Court

Q.65 Which State ordinarily exercises jurisdiction in respect of crimes committed onboard vessels?
A. The coastal State
B. The flag State
C. All States enjoy such jurisdiction
D. The International Tribunal for the Law of the Sea

Q.66 Under which law a minor is incapable of entering into a contract?
A. Indian Contract Act, 1872
B. Majority Act, 1875
C. Guardians and Wards Act, 1890
D. Contract Labour ((Regulation and Abolition) Act, 1970

Q.67 A person has designed a new type of scissors for cutting of clothes. Under which act can he seek the protection of his invention?
A. The Patents Act
B. The Copyrights Act
C. Consumer Protection Act
D. Arms Control Act

Q.68 Who of the following is the Chancellor of the NALSAR University of Law located in Hyderabad?
A. Governor of A.P.
B. The Union Law Minister
C. Chief Justice of A.P. High Court
D. Solicitor General of India

Q.69 Who is the Legal Advisor to the Government of a State in India?
A. The Solicitor General
B. The State Chief Legal Officer
C. The High Court
D. The Advocate General

Q.70 Which of the following principles is applicable for the purpose of reducing the multiplicity of proceedings?

A. Res getae

B. Res interregnum

C. Res judicata

D. Res ispa loquitor

Q.71 Which of the following is both a tort as well as a crime?

A. Defamation

B. Murder

C. Theft

D. None of these

Q.72 If the offence of Culpable Homicide is the genus, then murder is-

A. An offence

B. A crime

C. Specie

D. None of these

Q.73 The provision of 'Ordinance' has been taken in the Indian Constitution by:

A. Government of India Act from 1858

B. Government of India Act from 1935

C. Government of India Act from 1919

D. India Independence Act 1947

Q.74 Which case laid down the basic structure doctrine of the Constitution of India?

A. A K Kraipak v Union of India

B. Kesavananda Bharti v State of Kerala

C. A K Gopalan v State of Madras

D. None of these

Q.75 Social, economic and political Justice is-

A. An idea enshrined in the Preamble to the Constitution of India.

B. Guaranteed by Fundamental Rights in the Constitution of India.

C. A Directive Principle of State Policy taken into consideration while making enactments.

D. Guaranteed to the people by the writs issued by the High Courts and Supreme Court.

General Knowledge

Q.76 Who amongst the following gave the 'Periodic Law'?

A. Carlton McGee

B. Emil Fischer

C. Charles Darwin

D. Dmitri Mendeleev

Q.77 Which technology company has introduced the health monitoring device 'Halo Band'?

A. Microsoft

B. Apple

C. Google

D. Amazon

Q.78 Bluetooth technology allows:

A. Wireless communication between equipments

B. Signal transmission on mobile phones only

C. Landline to mobile phone communication

D. Satellite television communication

Q.79 We brought the concurrent list from which constitution?

A. Australian constitution

B. French constitution

C. Japanese constitution

D. South African constitution

Q.80 Which one among the following is not a Fundamental Right under the Constitution of India?

A. Right to equality

B. Right to freedom

C. Right to citizenship

D. Right against exploitation

Q.81 Part XVII of the Indian constitution deals with_________.

A. Special provisions for SC, ST

B. Election commission

C. Emergency provisions

D. Official language

Q.82 Which of the following lakes is present in the Nagaland?

A. Sangestar Tso lake

B. Gurudongmar lake

C. Shilloi lake

D. Loktak lake

Q.83 Against which dam was Narmada Bachao Andolan started?

A. Sardar Sarovar Dam

B. Bargi Dam

C. Tungabhadra Dam

D. Bhakra Nangal Dam

Q.84 Which state has the largest coastline?

A. Karnataka

B. Kerala

C. Tamil Nadu

D. Gujarat

Q.85 Which of the following cities is not a capital of India's neighbouring countries?

A. Naypyitaw

B. Kathmandu

C. Thimpu

D. Lahore

Q.86 The PURA (Providing Urban Amenities to Rural Areas) model was advocated by:

A. APJ Abdul Kalam

B. Manmohan Singh

C. Lal Krishna Advani

D. Rajiv Gandhi

Q.87 Planned economic development in India began in with the inception of the First Five Year Plan:

[SSC Sub Inspector (CPO), 2020]

A. 1958　　**B.** 1948　　**C.** 1951　　**D.** 1956

Q.88 ________was on the top priority in the First Five Year Plan in India.

A. Agriculture

B. Ports

C. Industries

D. Defence

Q.89 The net value of GDP after deducting depreciation from GDP is:

A. Net national product

B. Net domestic product

C. Gross national product

D. Disposable income

Q.90 The average income of the country is:

A. Per capita income

B. Disposable income

C. Inflation rate

D. Real national income

Q.91 Which of the following is indirect tax?

A. Income tax

B. Wealth tax

C. Corporation tax

D. Sales tax

Q.92 Which of the following tax will be abolished by the Goods and Services Tax?

A. Property tax

B. Corporation tax

C. VAT

D. All of the above

Q.93 According to budget 2017-18, which is the correct decreasing order of the government tax revenue? (A) Income Tax> Corporation Tax> Service Tax.

A. Income tax> Corporate tax> product tax

B. Income Tax> Corporation Tax> Service Tax.

C. Corporate tax> income tax> product tax

D. Corporate tax> product tax> income tax

Q.94 Which among the following does not belong to India's major large scale industries?

A. Cotton textile industry

B. Iron and steel industry

C. Jute industry

D. Khadi and village industry

Q.95 Who manufactures the largest quantity of jute goods in the world?

A. India

B. Bangladesh

C. Thailand

D. Myanmar

Q.96 Who issues one rupee notes in India?

A. SBI

B. CBI

C. Reserve Bank of India

D. Ministry of Finance

Q.97 Banks can avail refinance against loans made to industrial units from:

A. DICGC

B. NABARD

C. ECGC

D. IDBI

Q.98 At present most of the Indian Banks are falling under the:

A. Chain Banking System

B. Unit Banking System

C. Branch Banking System

D. None of the above

Q.99 Who is the first Indian to have won the Pulitzer Prize?

[SSC Sub Inspector (CPO), 2020]

A. Gobind Behari Lal

B. Sanghamitra Kalita

C. Jhumpa Lahiri

D. Geeta Anand

Q.100 Who was announced to be conferred the 57th Jnanpith Award on 7th December 2021?

A. Neelmani Phukan Jr.

B. Damodar Mauzo

C. Krishna Sobti

D. Amitav Ghosh

// Smart Answer Sheet //

Correct — Percentage of students who answered correctly. **Skipped** — Percentage of students who skipped.

Q.	Ans.	Correct / Skipped	Q.	Ans.	Correct / Skipped	Q.	Ans.	Correct / Skipped	Q.	Ans.	Correct / Skipped	Q.	Ans.	Correct / Skipped
1	B	47.32 % / 50.83 %	17	D	52.47 % / 38.9 %	33	B	25.67 % / 67.84 %	49	B	45.19 % / 35.96 %	65	B	25.79 % / 69.11 %
2	D	50.02 % / 34.23 %	18	D	80.76 % / 18.63 %	34	B	40.19 % / 32.3 %	50	A	13.49 % / 72.98 %	66	A	40.41 % / 58.4 %
3	A	78.6 % / 13.98 %	19	A	57.64 % / 37.72 %	35	C	48.66 % / 38.75 %	51	A	82.68 % / 11.33 %	67	A	60.37 % / 35.88 %
4	B	61.13 % / 30.04 %	20	C	59.51 % / 40.11 %	36	C	43.49 % / 46.94 %	52	A	59.76 % / 30.28 %	68	C	65.6 % / 30.93 %
5	D	44.56 % / 30.78 %	21	C	25.4 % / 73.82 %	37	D	46.78 % / 40.41 %	53	B	66.62 % / 33.37 %	69	D	69.54 % / 30.08 %
6	B	50.7 % / 45.17 %	22	B	66.52 % / 32.35 %	38	C	46.39 % / 45.26 %	54	B	56.95 % / 36.78 %	70	C	16.07 % / 77.91 %
7	D	58.3 % / 32.51 %	23	A	54.75 % / 42.35 %	39	D	55.36 % / 37.77 %	55	B	51.79 % / 45.11 %	71	A	61.26 % / 36.71 %
8	C	46.46 % / 50.11 %	24	D	40.95 % / 57.39 %	40	A	45.41 % / 45.3 %	56	D	46.87 % / 39.54 %	72	C	42.35 % / 33.72 %
9	B	85.18 % / 14.01 %	25	B	61.25 % / 31.82 %	41	C	55.88 % / 37.68 %	57	C	55.46 % / 38.66 %	73	B	43.61 % / 41.92 %
10	D	88.76 % / 10.5 %	26	A	62.86 % / 32.93 %	42	A	11.9 % / 73.84 %	58	B	12.14 % / 71.0 %	74	B	41.0 % / 55.91 %
11	D	82.78 % / 11.94 %	27	C	88.63 % / 10.42 %	43	D	64.2 % / 31.0 %	59	A	63.68 % / 30.59 %	75	A	69.47 % / 30.18 %
12	D	88.7 % / 11.16 %	28	B	44.29 % / 38.11 %	44	A	52.36 % / 32.78 %	60	A	63.37 % / 35.64 %	76	D	52.9 % / 30.13 %
13	A	69.14 % / 30.12 %	29	D	66.2 % / 33.03 %	45	B	40.18 % / 43.01 %	61	A	68.77 % / 31.15 %	77	D	49.67 % / 44.01 %
14	C	62.07 % / 35.27 %	30	B	12.46 % / 67.63 %	46	B	41.9 % / 30.26 %	62	D	68.19 % / 30.78 %	78	A	59.98 % / 38.09 %
15	A	89.11 % / 10.81 %	31	D	53.28 % / 31.47 %	47	A	48.55 % / 42.92 %	63	C	68.18 % / 30.97 %	79	A	58.94 % / 38.87 %
16	B	60.71 % / 32.52 %	32	C	46.08 % / 52.05 %	48	A	42.38 % / 56.69 %	64	A	50.87 % / 43.95 %	80	C	47.46 % / 51.79 %

Q.	Ans.	Correct	Skipped
81	D	49.46 %	47.4 %
82	C	83.04 %	13.42 %
83	A	46.82 %	41.23 %
84	D	44.95 %	52.26 %

Q.	Ans.	Correct	Skipped
85	D	50.79 %	44.86 %
86	A	47.65 %	51.83 %
87	C	58.53 %	40.63 %
88	A	55.25 %	32.23 %

Q.	Ans.	Correct	Skipped
89	B	60.31 %	32.6 %
90	A	58.64 %	40.23 %
91	D	47.02 %	34.59 %
92	C	65.51 %	30.67 %

Q.	Ans.	Correct	Skipped
93	C	68.82 %	30.83 %
94	D	68.38 %	31.34 %
95	A	68.89 %	30.53 %
96	D	18.54 %	76.66 %

Q.	Ans.	Correct	Skipped
97	D	41.85 %	33.67 %
98	C	50.88 %	48.57 %
99	A	32.68 %	67.27 %
100	B	13.59 %	73.61 %

//Hints and Solutions//

1. Replace 'double' with 'doubling' in part B.

We use a gerund (verb+ing form) after certain verbs/phrases that are followed by appropriate prepositions; desirous of, keen on, aiming at, hesitate in, etc.

Hence, the correct option is (B).

2. In option (D), 'nations that are exporting food' should be there in place of 'nations which are exporting food'.

When we use adjectives of a superlative degree in a sentence, we should use 'that' to refer to them. A superlative adjective is used to compare three or more nouns. It takes the comparison of nouns to the highest form. Example: Good, better, best. Best is a superlative adjective. Therefore, when using superlative adjectives in a sentence, we should use 'that' after it.

Example: She is the most beautiful girl that I have ever seen.

Hence, the correct option is (D).

3. Here, "else but" should be used instead of "else than". The adverb 'Else' should always be followed by 'but'.

Example: It is nothing else but stupidity to bunk classes.

Therefore, the correct sentence: Drunk driving is nothing else but pure madness.

Hence, the correct option is (A).

4. Mendacity: untruthfulness.

Obstreperous: noisy and difficult to control.

Euphemism: a mild or indirect word or expression substituted for one considered to be too harsh or blunt when referring to something unpleasant or embarrassing.

Dichotomy: a division or contrast between two things that are or are represented as being opposed or entirely different.

So the correct sentence is:

His speculations in this regard, while intriguing, rely heavily on the fact of her general mendacity.

Hence, the correct option is (B).

5. Engulfing: (of a natural force) sweep over (something) so as to surround or cover it completely.

Interceding: intervene on behalf of another.

Obviating: remove (a need or difficulty).

Disparaging: expressing the opinion that something is of little worth; derogatory

So the correct sentence is: To decipher the expected political behaviour of the subalterns in the wake of the current crisis engulfing reverse migrationbound workers, one needs to go back to 2014.

Hence, the correct option is (D).

6. The correct answer is option (B) i.e. Be in a difficult situation.

His back against the wall means to be in a difficult situation that seems difficult to resolve.

As the sentence explains that since he had lost his job, he could not pay his debt to the moneylender, and so he was in a difficult solution.

It does not refer to any escape or hurting his back or an accident of the wall falling.

Hence, the correct option is (B).

7. Bitten off more than she could chew means to try to do something too difficult to handle.

As the sentence explains that she agreed to do a project that she later realised was too difficult for her to accomplish.

Taking a big bite is nearly the same as becoming greedy. The sentence does not refer to either eating something tasteless or unable to chew the food.

Hence, the correct option is (D).

8. The correct answer is: Insolvent. The meaning of all words is:

Insolvent: Unable to pay debts owed

Misanthrope: A person who dislikes humankind and avoids human society

Atheist: A person who disbelieves or lacks belief in the existence of God

Recluse: A person who lives a solitary life and tends to avoid other people.

Hence, the correct option is (C).

9. The correct answer is Amnesty.

Amnesty: An official pardon for people who have been convicted of political offenses

Draw: A game in which no one wins

Octagon: A geometrical figure with eight sides

Bureaucracy: A system of government in which most of the important decisions are taken by state officials rather than by elected representatives.

Hence, the correct option is (B).

10. The correct answer is: Requittal. The correctly spelt word will be Requital.

Requital: The act of requiting

Rateable: Able to be rated or estimated

Perversion: Distortion or corruption of the original course, meaning, or state of something.

Pamphlet: A small booklet or leaflet containing information or arguments about a single subject.

Hence, the correct option is (D).

11. The correct answer is: Entrepreneur.

The given word 'Entrepreneur' is borrowed from the French language. The word 'entreprendre ' in French means undertake and it became 'Entrepreneur' in English.

Hence, the correct option is (D).

12. The correct answer is "My bike was repaired by the mechanic".

In Active Voice, a sentence emphasizes the subject, performing an action. In Passive Voice, a sentence emphasizes the action or the object of the sentence. The given sentence is in the active voice and 'The mechanic' is the subject and 'my bike' is the object. When we convert this sentence into passive voice, the subject 'The mechanic' of the active voice becomes the object and the object 'my bike' becomes the subject. The passive format "was + V3" should be used. This is the active and passive voice rule for the past simple tense.

Hence, the correct option is (D).

13. The correct answer is 'This year, Christmas was celebrated by the Smiths'.

In the given question the sentence 'The Smiths celebrated Christmas this year' is in 'Active voice' which is in the past indefinite and we know that after converted this sentence into 'Passive voice' the tense will same which also should be in past indefinite.

Example: Reema cleaned the floor (Active) The floor was cleaned by Reema (Passive) Past indefinite structure:

$Sub + V_2 +$ object (Active) Object $+$ was/were $+V_3 +$ by $+$ subject (Passive).

Hence, the correct option is (A).

14. 'They' is the correct proper pronoun for the sentence given. Janice and Dionne were visiting New York city when they noticed a man climbing an apartment building, is the correct sentence.

Hence, the correct option is (C).

15. The noun which expresses strong feeling or emotions is an abstract noun. A noun denoting an idea, quality, or state rather than a concrete object, e.g. truth, danger, happiness.

Sentence: "the website contains considerably more abstract nouns than hard facts".

Hence, the correct option is (A).

16. Complete sentence: Sahil read the letter more carefully the second time to make sure he hadn't missed any detail.

- The word 'second time' suggests that 'Sahil' has read the letter before.
- Therefore, the ways of reading the letter are being compared here. So, 'more' should be used here.

Hence, the correct option is (B).

17. Never is an adverb used to deny the occurrence of an action. An adverb is a word that modifies (describes) a verb (he sings loudly), an adjective (very tall), another adverb (ended too quickly), or even a whole sentence (Fortunately, I had brought an umbrella).

Hence, the correct option is (D).

18. The correct answer is 'on'. The preposition 'during' means throughout the course or duration of a period of time. The preposition 'for' is used for saying the particular time or date that something is planned to happen. The preposition 'by' is used for indicating a deadline or the end of a particular time period. The preposition 'on' means at the time of.

Hence, the correct option is (D).

19. The US Open will be transmitted live **via** satellite.

The preposition 'via' means travelling through a place en route to a destination.

Hence, the correct option is (A).

20. Intimidate: Refers to someone who scares someone, especially in order to make someone do what one wants.

Frighten: Refers to making someone very afraid and anxious

Example: The dinosaur frightened the children.

Thus, it is clear that 'frighten' is nearest in meaning to the underlined word 'intimidate'.

Hence, the correct option is (C).

21. The word 'insipid' refers to something that lacks flavor and is tasteless.

The word 'delicious' refers to something that is very tasty and very pleasant to the taste.

Hence, the correct option is (C).

22. Refer to this line of the passage "Next, the stylist carefully rearranges the sesame seeds on the bun using glue and tweezers for maximum visual appeal."

Therefore, a food stylist working on a hamburger commercial might use glue and tweezers for maximum visual appeal.

Hence, the correct option is (B).

23. The author claims that a food stylist looking for the perfect lettuce and tomato searches for the "crispest lettuce" and "the reddest tomato." The food stylist then sprays the lettuce and tomato with glycerin "to keep them looking fresh." From these sentences, we can understand that freshness is the most important quality when the food stylist deals with lettuce and tomatoes.

Hence, the correct option is (A).

24. Delicious is the best synonym for 'delectable' among the given options.

Delectable: Greatly pleasing to the taste

Delicious: Having a very pleasant taste or smell

Hence, the correct option is (D).

25. The food stylist—a person employed by the company to make sure the products look perfect—sorts through hundreds of buns until he or she finds one with no wrinkles.

Hence, the correct option is (B).

26. According to the given information:

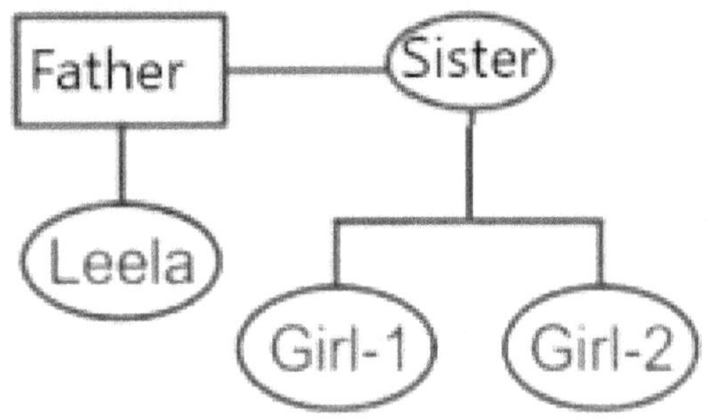

Leela and the girls are cousins.

Hence, the correct option is (A).

27. Symbols related to letters:-

P = ÷

Q = ×

R = +

S = -

We have to find the value of "18 Q 12 P 4 R 5 S 6"

So we will put the symbols given in the question,

18 × 12 ÷ 4 + 5 - 6

Now we will apply Bodmas rule ,

= 18 × 3 + 5 - 6

= 54 + 5 - 6

= 59 - 6

= 53

Hence, the correct option is (C).

28. In first statement, its given A has a higher enrollment than B and in the second statement B has a higher enrollment than C, therefore C has lower enrollment than A clearly. Therefore, statement C is false.

Hence, the correct option is (B).

29. From the following Statement we have these diagrams:

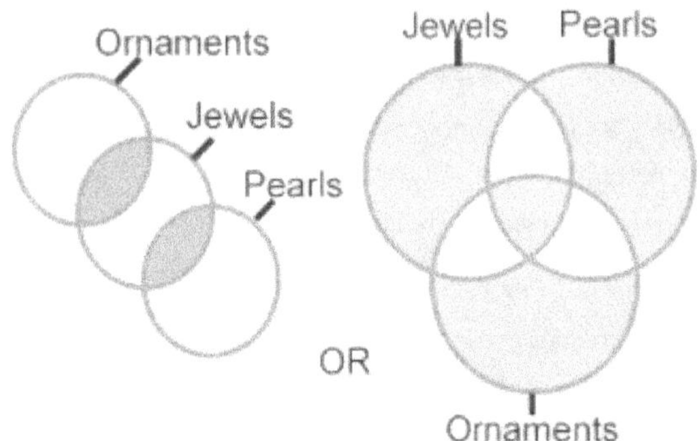

So, we can see that both the conclusions are followed.

Hence, the correct option is (D).

30. According to the statement and conclusion, we draw the figure as:

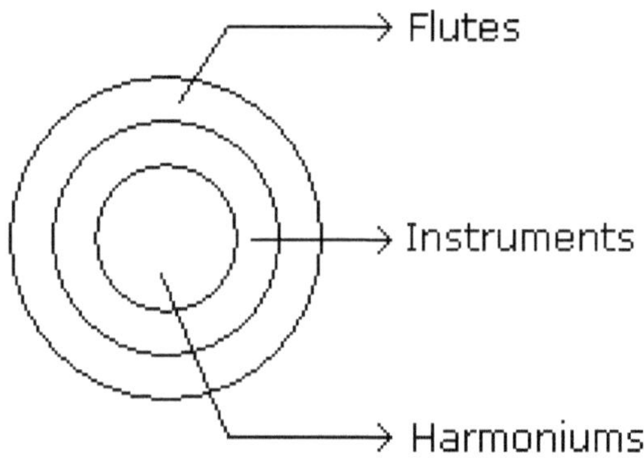

Therefore, only 2 follows according to the figure.

Hence, the correct option is (B).

31. We draw the following figures according to the statement given:

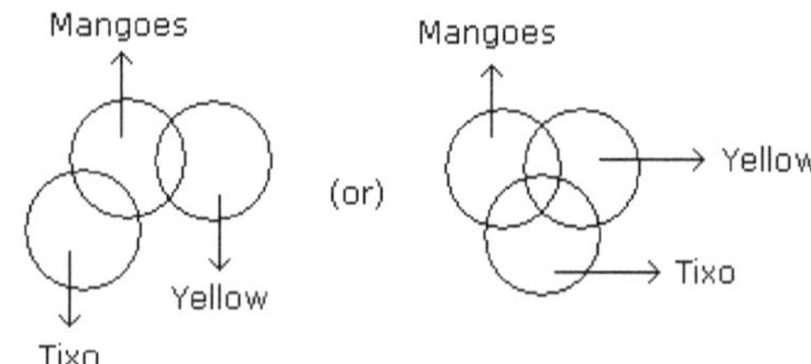

Therefore according to the figure neither 1 nor 2 follows.

Hence, the correct option is (D).

32. As per the given instructions:

I. P sits second to the left of K. M sits third to right of P.

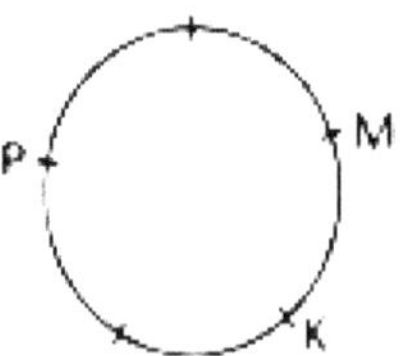

II. L sits immediate right of M.

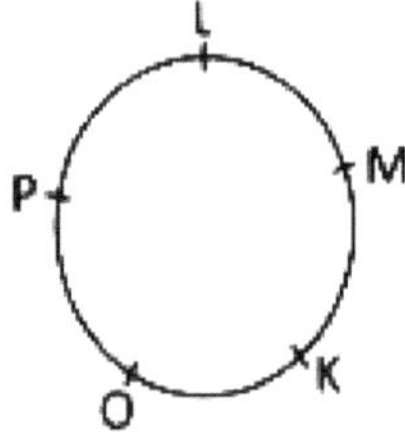

Clearly, O sits exactly between P and K.

Hence, the correct option is (C).

33. Right end and Pooja sits at the left end of the row.

Sanam and Zara are in the center. Sanam is sitting to the right of Varun. thus, Varun is sitting to the right of Pooja.

The final arrangement will be as shown,

Hence, the correct option is (B).

34.

Mercedes, Cadillac and Fargo cars are to the right of Ambassador.

Hence, the correct option is (B).

35. From the series given:

$1 \times 4 - 2 = 2$

$2 \times 4 - 2 = 6$

$6 \times 4 - 2 = 22$

$22 \times 4 - 2 = 86$

Hence, the correct option is (C).

36. The pattern is:

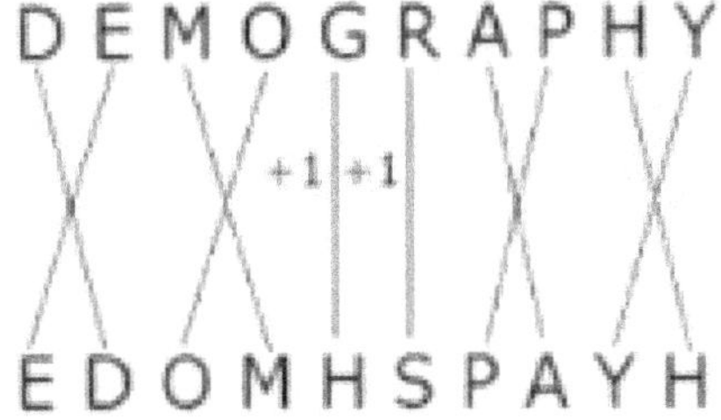

Similarly:

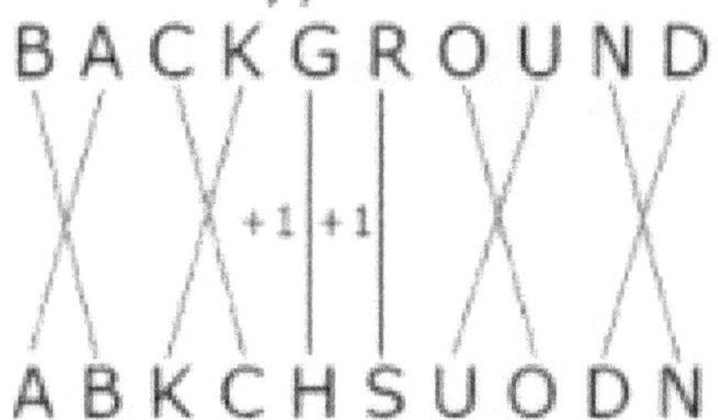

Hence, the correct option is (C).

37. The relation between the letters is as follows,

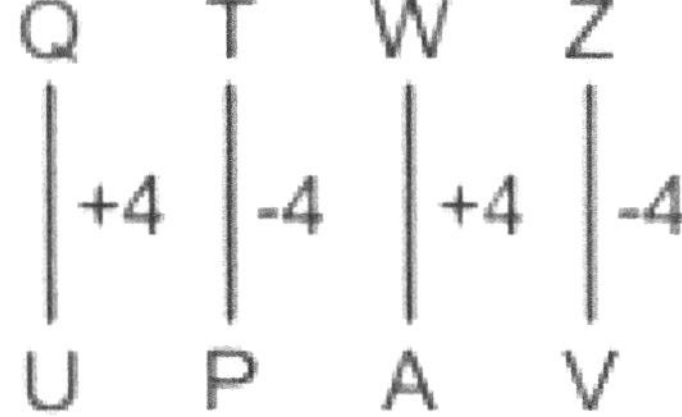

Similarly,

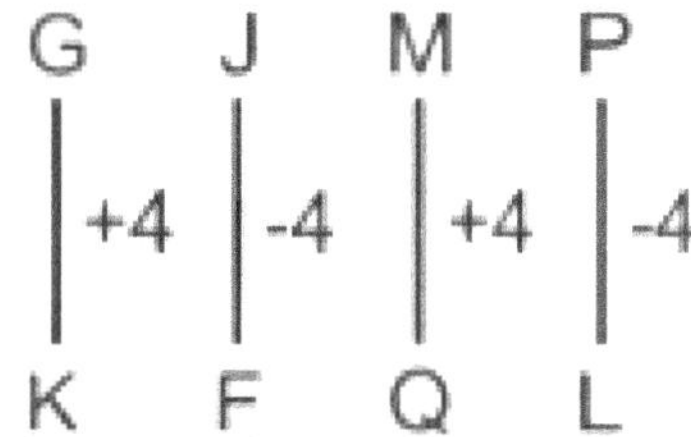

Therefore, KFQL is related to GJMP.

Hence, the correct option is (D).

38. Float means above water and sink means under water. In same way, the Boat floats on water, and the submarine moves underwater.

Hence, the correct option is (C).

39. President is the highest officer of the Country and Governor is the highest officer of State. Therefore Governor is the correct answer.

Hence, the correct option is (D).

40. Clearly, such decisions are taken only after making sure that it will not affect the company's business adversely. So, I is implicit. However, the impact of this increase on other airlines cannot be ascertained. So, II is not implicit.

Hence, the correct option is (A).

41. The opinion of the author of this statement is not clear from his words. It is sure that he is either favorable or against such an action of the Prime Minister. thus, either (I) or (II) but not both, is an assumption.

Hence, the correct option is (C).

42. Brother of the mother means maternal uncle. Therefore, only the nephew of Aamir's maternal uncle means Aamir himself. Therefore Sonia is the wife of Aamir.

Hence, the correct option is (A).

43. Rahim's Movement

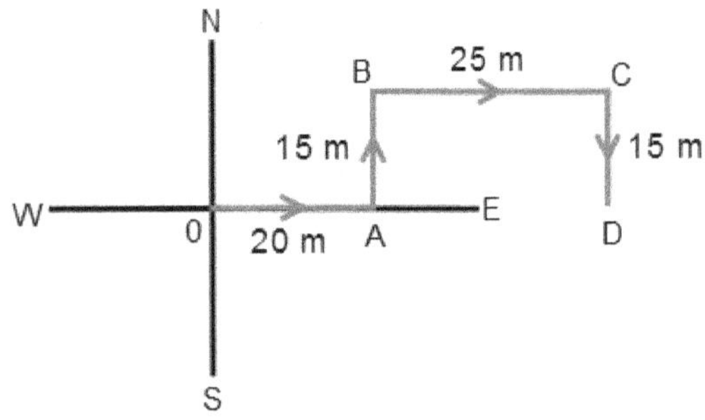

Therefore, the distance of Rahim from his starting point,

= 20 + 25

= 45 meters

Hence, the correct option is (D).

44. Clearly, health of the citizens is an issue of major concern for the Government. So, a product like drugs, must be first studied and tested in the Indian context before giving licence for its sale. So, only argument I holds strong.

Hence, the correct option is (A).

45. Nowadays, computers have entered all walks of life and children need to be prepared for the same. So, argument II is strong. Argument I holds no relevance.

Hence, the correct option is (B).

46. The first, third and fifth letters are each moved one step backward, while the second, fourth and sixth letters are each moved one step forward to obtain the corresponding letters of the code.

As,

F -1 = E

A +1 = B

V -1 = U

O +1 = P

U -1 = T

R +1 = S

On following the same above pattern,

DANGER will be coded as CBMHDS.

Hence, the correct option is (B).

47.

Alph abets	A	B	C	D	E	F	G	H	I	J	K	L	M

												1	1
Positi onal value	1	2	3	4	5	6	7	8	9	1 0	1 1	2	3
Positi onal value	2 6	2 5	2 4	2 3	2 2	2 1	2 0	1 9	1 8	1 7	1 6	1 5	1 4
Alph abets	Z	Y	X	W	V	U	T	S	R	Q	P	O	N

The pattern for the code is as follows,
BONE → B=2, O=15, N=14, E=5 → 2+15+14+5=36
Similarly,
BORN → B=2, O=15, R=18, N=14 → 2+15+18+14=49
In the same way,
BODY → B=2, O=15, D=4, Y=25 → 2+15+4+25=46
Hence, the correct option is (A).

48. The pattern for the code is as follows,

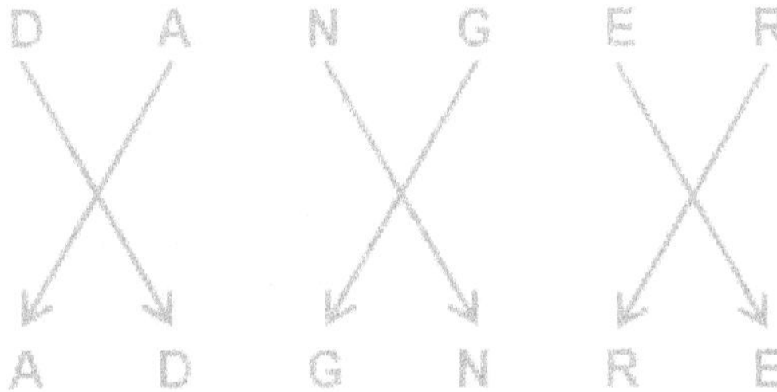

Similarly,

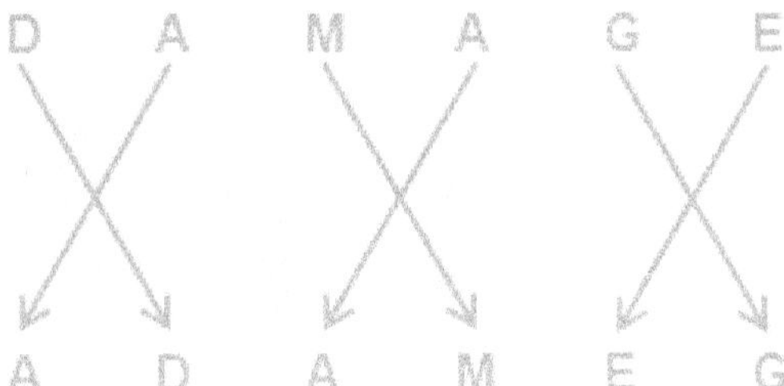

Hence, the correct option is (A).

49. As the Central Government faced financial loss on accounts of giving rebate on farming for the last few years, therefore, they declared to finish the rebate on farming. Therefore, II is the cause while I is the effect.

Hence, the correct option is (B).

50. As Ram's father was ill so he brought medicine on the advice of doctor. Therefore, Statement I is cause and II is the effect.

Hence, the correct option is (A).

51. Rule of law is as simply known as all persons are equal in the eyes of law. It also means that no man is above law and also that every person is subject to the jurisdiction of ordinary courts of law irrespective of their position and rank. The concept of rule of law further requires that no person should be subjected to harsh or arbitrary treatment.

Hence, the correct option is (A).

52. Caveat emptor is a Latin term that means "let the buyer beware." Similar to the phrase "sold as is," this term means that the buyer assumes the risk that a product may fail to meet expectations or have defects.

Hence, the correct option is (A).

53. An amicus curiae (literally, "friend of the court"; plural: amici curiae) is someone who is not a party to a case who assists a court by offering information, expertise, or insight that has a bearing on the issues in the case. Amicus parties try to "help" the court reach its decision by offering facts, analysis, or perspective that the parties to the case have not.

Hence, the correct option is (B).

54. In Vishakha vs. State of Rajasthan landmark judgment, the Supreme Court of India lay down guidelines against sexual harassment of women at the workplace.

Vishakha vs. State of Rajasthan is a case which deals with the evil of Sexual Harassment of a women at her workplace. It is a landmark judgment case in the history of sexual harassment which as being decided by the Supreme Court. Sexual Harassment means an uninvited/unwelcome sexual favor or sexual gestures from one gender towards the other gender. It makes the person feel humiliated, offended and insulted to whom it is been done.

Hence, the correct option is (B).

55. In the Hussainara khatoon case, the Supreme Court talked about the right to Speedy Trial. The Court recognized the right to a speedy trial and the right to legal aid services as basic and essential rights.

Hence, the correct option is (B).

56. During explaining the expression 'Procedure Established by Law' under Article 21, Supreme Court held that the procedure in Article 21 has to be fair, just and reasonable, not fanciful, oppressive or arbitrary. The 'Procedure established by law' is the same as the 'due process of law' as interpreted by the American Constitution.

Hence, the correct option is (D).

57. In Seema vs. Ashwini Kumar case, the Supreme court directed the compulsory registration of all marriages in India. The officials said the Supreme Court, in the Seema vs Ashwani Kumar case of 2006, had directed the states and the Centre that marriages of all persons who are citizens of India belonging to various religious denominations should be made compulsorily Legislation aimed at protecting women registerable. It had also said when the Centre enacts a comprehensive statute, it should be placed before the court for scrutiny.

Hence, the correct option is (C).

58. Aruna Shanbaug vs. Union of India case Supreme court allowed Passive Euthanasia under exceptional circumstances. Passive euthanasia occurs when the patient dies because the medical professionals either don't do something necessary to keep the patient alive or when they stop doing something that is keeping the patient alive. On 9 March 2018, the Supreme Court of India legalised passive euthanasia by means of the withdrawal of life support to patients in a permanent vegetative state.

Hence, the correct option is (B).

59. The Doctrine of Rarest of Rare was established in the case of Bacchan vs. State of Punjab. The Supreme Court, in this case, endeavoured to cut out a doctrine particularly for offences culpable with death to decrease the ambiguity for courts regarding when to go for the highest punishment of the land.

Hence, the correct option is (A).

60. Assento Mentium: Latin definition for a meeting of minds regarding the terms and conditions of the contract. It can be understood by the following illustration,

'While executing a contract deed for the sale of A's house there was "assentio mentium" between A (seller)and the B (purchaser) as to the terms and conditions of the contract.t means both were clear as to the object of the contract (the house) and the consideration being paid for it(a certain sum of money).

Hence, the correct option is (A).

61. Pacta sunt servanda means agreements must be kept.

Pacta sunt servanda, Latin for "agreements must be kept", is a brocard and a fundamental principle of law. In its most common sense, the principle refers to private contracts and prescribes that the provisions, i.e. clauses, of a contract are law between the parties to the contract, and therefore implies that neglect of their respective obligations is a violation of the contract.

Hence, the correct option is (A).

62. The code was drafted on the recommendations of first law commission of India established in 1834 under the Charter Act of 1833 under the Chairmanship of Lord Thomas Babington Macaulay. It came into force in British India during the early British Raj period in 1862.

Hence, the correct option is (D).

63. Necessity as a defense is defined under section 81 in the Indian Penal Code as: "Act likely to cause harm, but done without criminal intent, and to prevent other harm. Both preventions of harm to a person and prevention of harm to property comes under it.

Hence, the correct option is (C).

64. The Calcutta High Court is the oldest High Court in India. It has jurisdiction over the state of West Bengal and the Union Territory of the Andaman and Nicobar Islands.

Hence, the correct option is (A).

65. This type of jurisdiction ordinarily belongs to the flag State. The flag state of a merchant's vessel is the jurisdiction under whose laws the vessel is registered or licensed, and is deemed the nationality of the vessel. A merchant vessel must be registered and can only be registered in one jurisdiction, but may change the register in which it is registered.

Hence, the correct option is (B).

66. The Indian Contract Act, 1872 defines the term "Contract" under its section 2 (h) as "An agreement enforceable by law". In other words, we can say that a contract is anything that is an agreement and enforceable by the law of the land. It incapable of entering into a contract without force.

Hence, the correct option is (A).

67. Under the patents act, he can seek the protection of his invention. A patent is a legal document granting its holder the exclusive right to control the use of an invention, as set forth in the patent's claims, within a limited area and time by stopping others from, among other things, making, using or selling the invention without authorization.

Hence, the correct option is (A).

68. The National Academy of Legal Studies and Research (NALSAR) was established in 1998 by a Statute of the State of Andhra Pradesh. Chief justice of A.P. High court is the chancellor of Nalsar University of law located in Hyderabad.

Hence, the correct option is (C).

69. The Advocate General is the Legal Advisor to the Government of a State in India.

The advocate general is appointed by the governor. He must be a person who is qualified to be appointed a judge of a high court. In other words, he must be a citizen of India and must have held a judicial office for ten years or been an advocate of a high court for ten years.
As the chief law officer of the government in the state, the duties of the advocate general include the following:

- To give advice to the government of the state upon such legal matters which are referred to him by the governor.
- To perform such other duties of a legal character that is assigned to him by the governor.
- To discharge the functions conferred on him by the Constitution or any other law.

Hence, the correct option is (D).

70. Res judicata is applicable for the purpose of reducing the multiplicity of proceedings?

The doctrine of res judicata bars claims that have either been litigated or that could have been litigated from being litigated again. It also says that no person should be disputed twice for the same reason. It is the state that decides there should be an end to litigation. A judicial decision must be accepted as the correct decision.

Hence, the correct option is (C).

71. Defamation is the general term for a legal claim involving injury to one's reputation caused by a false statement of fact and includes both libel (defamation in written or fixed form) and slander (spoken defamation). The crux of a defamation claim is falsity. Therefore it is tort as well as crime.

Hence, the correct option is (A).

72. If we analyse the definition under Section 300 of the IPC, culpable homicide is considered as murder if: The act is committed with an intention to cause death. The act is done with the intention of causing such bodily injury for which the offender has knowledge that it would result in death. Therefore specie is the appropriate word for it.

Hence, the correct option is (C).

73. The provision of 'Ordinance' has been taken in the Indian Constitution by the Government of India Act from 1935, which gave the authority to the Governor-General to promulgate Ordinances.

An ordinance is an executive order issued by the president of India that holds the same force and effect as an act passed by the parliament. The president has the power to issue ordinances under Article 123 of the Indian Constitution. The president has the power to promulgate ordinances under article 123 of the Indian Constitution. Promulgating an ordinance is one of the most important powers that a president has, it not necessarily connected with an emergency but it can be issued by the president if he is convinced that an action is to be taken and that the parliament will not be able to enact on the same subject immediately but the circumstances render it necessary for him to take 'immediate action.

Hence, the correct option is (B).

74. The case of Kesavananda Bharati v State of Kerala (Kesavananda Bharati) is perhaps the most well-known constitutional decision of the Supreme Court of India (Supreme Court). While ruling that there is no implied limitation on the powers of Parliament to amend the Constitution, it held that no amendment can do violence to its basic structure (the "Basic Structure Doctrine"). Further, it established the Supreme Court's right of review and, therefore, established its supremacy on constitutional matters.

Hence, the correct option is (B).

75. Social, economic and political justice is an idea enshrined in the Preamble of the Constitution of India.

The expression 'Social and Economic Justice' involves the concept of 'Distributive Justice' which connotes the removal of economic inequalities and rectifying the injustice resulting from dealing or transaction between unequal in society. Social justice is concerned with the distribution of benefits and burdens.

Hence, the correct option is (A).

76. 'Periodic table' was given by Dmitri Mendeleev. The modern periodic table is developed after the periodic law and a periodic table was given by Mendeleev. The modern periodic law can be stated as "the physical and chemical properties of the elements are periodic functions of their atomic numbers".

Hence, the correct option is (D).

77. E-commerce and technology Major Amazon has launched 'Halo Band. Thus, officially venturing into the health monitoring segment.

The wrist band uses AI software to monitor personal wellness parameters. The device is said to have a three-dimensional scan feature for measuring body fat and voice detection to evaluate the user's emotion.

Hence, the correct option is (D).

78. Bluetooth is a wireless technology standard for exchanging data over short distances (using short-wavelength UHF radio waves in the ISM band from 2.4 to 2.485 GHz) from fixed and mobile devices and building personal area networks (PANs).

Hence, the correct option is (A).

79. Australian constitution: Concurrent List, freedom of trade, commerce and intercourse, and joint sitting of the two Houses of Parliament. The Australian Constitution has properly been described as 'the birth certificate of a nation'. It also provides the basic rules for the government of Australia. Indeed, the Constitution is the fundamental law of Australia binding everybody including the Commonwealth Parliament and the Parliament of each State.

Hence, the correct option is (A).

80. Citizenship in India is not a fundamental right and is the Part II of the Constitution (Article 5-11). Part III deals with the fundamental rights in the Indian Constitution. Right to Freedom comes under Article 19 of the Indian Constitution. Right against Exploitation comes under Article 23-24 of the Indian Constitution. Right to Equality comes under Article 14-18 of the Indian Constitution.

Hence, the correct option is (C).

81. Part XVII of the Indian constitution deals with the Official language. Parts of the constitution. It is nothing but a group of articles formed in a single format. In our constitution, there are 22 parts. Part XVII - Articles (343 to 351) Related to Official language.

Hence, the correct option is (D).

82.

Lakes	Place
Gurudongmar Lake	Sikkim
Sangestar Tso Lake	Arunachal Pradesh
Loktak Lake	Manipur
Shilloi Lake	Nagaland

Hence, the correct option is (C).

83. Narmada Bachao Andolan is the most powerful mass movement, started in 1985 , against the construction of huge dam on the Narmada river. Narmada Bachao Andolan (NBA) is an Indian social movement initiated by native tribals (Adivasis), farmers, environmentalists and human rights activists. The river flows through the states of Gujarat, Madhya Pradesh and Maharashtra. Sardar Sarovar Dam in Gujarat is one of the biggest dams on the river and was one of the first focal points of the movement.

Hence, the correct option is (A).

84. The length of the coastline in India is 7516.6 km.

Out of 7516.6 km, Mainland consists of 5422.6 km and Island Territories consists of 2094 km.

Gujarat has the largest coastline in India.

Andra Pradesh has the longest coastline in South India.

Gujarat is a state on the western coast of India with a coastline of 1,600 km.

Hence, the correct option is (D).

85. Lahore is one of the largest city of Pakistan but it is not the capital of Pakistan. The capital city of Pakistan is Islamabad. The above-stated cities Naypyitaw, Kathmandu and Thimpu are the capital cities of Myanmar, Nepal and Bhutan respectively.

Hence, the correct option is (D).

86. APJ Abdul Kalam proposed the concept of PURA in the VISION 2020 project. Its goal and objectives are to provide India with new heights and achievements, developed status, and economy. Ministry of Rural Development is implementing the PURA scheme on a pilot basis. The objective of PURA- Provision of livelihood opportunities and urban amenities in rural areas to bridge the rural-urban divide. It covers Sewerage, Construction, and maintenance of Village Streets, Drainage, Solid Waste Management, etc.

Hence, the correct option is (A).

87. First Five-Year Plan was launched from 1951 to 1956, under the leadership of Jawaharlal Nehru.

It was based on the Harrod-Domar model with a few modifications.

This plan was successful and achieved a growth rate of 3.6 % (more than its target of 2.1%\) The duration of the "Eleventh Five Year Plan" was from 2007 to 2012, under the leadership of Manmohan Singh. It was prepared by the C. Rangarajan.

The theme was towards faster and more inclusive development.

It achieved a growth rate of 8 % against a target of 9 % growth.

Hence, the correct option is (C).

88. The First Five Year Plan in India was from 1951 to 1956. The plan was based on the Harrod-Domar model. Gave priority to the agricultural development of the country. The First Five Year Plan was presented before the parliament by Jawaharlal Nehru. Economist K N Raj is known as the architect of this plan. It was quasi-successful for the government.

Hence, the correct option is (A).

89. After deducting the depreciation charges of plant and machinery from GDP, we get net value of GDP which is called NDP.Net domestic product (NDP) is an annual measure of the economic output of a nation that is adjusted to account for depreciation. It is calculated by subtracting depreciation from the gross domestic product (GDP).

Hence, the correct option is (B).

90. Per capita income is calculated by dividing the total national income by the total population of the year. Per capita income is a measure of the amount of money earned per person in a nation or geographic region. Per capita income for a nation is calculated by dividing the country's national income by its population.

Hence, the correct option is (A).

91. Income tax, wealth tax and corporation tax are all direct taxes and levied by the central government. Sales tax, Excise duty and custom duty are indirect taxes.

Hence, the correct option is (D).

92. GST is known as the Goods and Services Tax. It is an indirect tax that has replaced many indirect taxes in India such as the excise duty, VAT, services tax, etc. The Goods and Service Tax Act was passed in Parliament on 29th March 2017 and came into effect on 1st July 2017.

In other words, Goods and Service Tax (GST) is levied on the supply of goods and services. Goods and Services Tax Law in India is a comprehensive, multi-stage, destination-based tax that is levied on every value addition. GST is a single domestic indirect tax law for the entire country.

Hence, the correct option is (C).

93. According to budget 2017-18, the largest share of government's income is Corporation tax (19%), Income tax (16%) and Excise duty (14%). Direct taxes (personal income tax and corporate tax) accounted for 51.3% of total revenues in 2016-17 and the rest came from indirect taxes. In 2020-21, the figure stood at 56.4%, corporate tax at 28.1% and personal income tax at 28.3%

Hence, the correct option is (C).

94. Under the chairmanship of K.C. Pant, Deputy Chairman of Planning Commission, a committee was set up on strengthening the khadi and village industries sector. This does not belong to large-scale industry. Other industries are part of large-scale industries.

Hence, the correct option is (D).

95. India manufactures the largest quantity of jute goods in the world. This industry is located mainly in West Bengal, followed by Andhra Pradesh, Bihar, Jharkhand, Uttar Pradesh and Madhya Pradesh.

Hence, the correct option is (A).

96. one rupee notes are issues by the Ministry of Finance while other notes are printed by the RBI.

The Minister of Finance is the head of the Ministry of Finance of the Government of India. One of the senior-most offices in the Union Cabinet, the finance minister is responsible for the fiscal policy of the government.

Hence, the correct option is (D).

97. IDBI stands for Industrial Development Bank of India. It was formerly known Industrial Development Bank of India. It was established in 1964 to provide credit and other financial facilities for the development of Indian industry.

Hence, the correct option is (D).

98. Branch banking is the operation of storefront locations away from the institution's home office for the convenience of customers. Since the 1980s, branch banking in the U.S. has gone through significant changes in response to a more competitive and consolidated financial services market.

Hence, the correct option is (C).

99. The first Indian to win a Pulitzer Prize was Gobind Behari Lal, a journalist in the year 1937.

The Pulitzer Prize is an award for achievements in newspaper, magazine, online journalism, literature and musical composition within the United States. It was established in 1917 by provisions in the will of Joseph Pulitzer, who had made his fortune as a newspaper publisher, and is administered by Columbia University. Prizes are awarded yearly in twenty-one categories.

Hence, the correct option is (A).

100. On 7 December 2021, it was announced to confer the 57th Jnanpith Award 2022 to the famous Konkani novelist Damodar Mauzo.

In his writing career spanning nearly 50 years, he has composed story collections, novels, autobiographical works and children's literature.

Hence, the correct option is (B).

English Language & Comprehension

Q.1 Direction: In the given question choose the word which best expresses the meaning of the given word.

Vicissitude

A. Sorrows

B. Misfortunes

C. Changes

D. Surprises

Q.2 Direction: In the given question, choose the word opposite in meaning to the given word.

Hirsute

A. Shaggy   **B.** Bald   **C.** Erudite   **D.** Glorious

Q.3 Direction: In the sentence given below, replace the underlined part with its alternate meaning. If the sentence is correct as it is, mark (d) i.e. "None of these" as the answer.

Kiran was in high spirits when he was called upon the stage to deliver his speech.

A. was very cheerful

B. was highly depressed

C. was deeply engrossed in thoughts

D. None of these

Q.4 Direction: In the sentence given below, replace the underlined phrase to make the sentence grammatically correct. If the sentence is correct as it is, mark (d) i.e. "No correction required" as the answer.

The woman to who I sold my house was a criminal.

A. to whom I selled

B. to whom I sell

C. to whom I sold

D. No correction required

Q.5 Direction: Choose the correct alternative which can be substituted for the below given word/ sentence.

A person who talks in sleep is called as

A. Philatelist

B. Somnambulist

C. Somniloquist

D. Oneirocritic

Q.6 Direction: Choose the correct alternative which can be substituted for the below given word/ sentence.

The person who knows everything

A. Omnipresent

B. Omnipotent

C. Omniscient

D. Oblivious

Q.7 Direction: Pick the correct preposition from the given:

We arrived____ the station an hour late.

A. about   **B.** in   **C.** at   **D.** of

Q.8 Direction: Select the appropriate word which makes the sentence meaningful.

If there is some chance of succeeding, it would be unwise to _____ it at this stage.

A. craggy   **B.** grasp   **C.** abandon   **D.** clutch

Q.9 Direction: Select the appropriate word which makes the sentence meaningful.

Sachin Tendulkar is an ________ player.

A. eminent

B. imminent

C. emminent

D. emmeinent

Q.10 Which kind of adverb is the word in capitals?

"The newspaper boy delivers the newspaper DAILY to my house."

A. Adverb of Time/Frequency

B. Adverb of Place

C. Adverb of Degree

D. Adverb of Manner

Q.11 Which kind of adverb is the word in capitals?

"The volunteers helped the stranded CHEERFULLY."

A. Adverb of Time/Frequency

B. Adverb of Place

C. Adverb of Degree

D. Adverb of Manner

Q.12 Direction: Choose the appropriate meaning of the idiom/phrase:

Caught between two stools

A. Met with an accident

B. Difficulty in choosing between two alternatives

C. Struck in a calamity

D. None of these

Q.13 Direction: Choose the appropriate meaning of the idiom/phrase:

A sop to Cerberus

A. Bribery

B. Hush money

C. Ransom to an enemy

D. Money for compensation

Q.14 Find out that word, the spelling of which is wrong.

A. Resembelance

B. Recuperate

C. Recommend

D. Resource

Q.15 Find the correctly spelled word.

A. Kalidoscope

B. Kalaidoscope

C. Kaleidoscope

D. Kaliedoscope

Ques (16-18):Direction: In the following question, a sentence has been given in Active/Passive Voice. Out of the four alternatives suggested, select the one which best expresses the same sentence in Passive/Active Voice.

Q.16 Rahul will pass the message.

A. The message will passed by Rahul.
B. The message would be passed by Rahul.
C. The message will pass by Rahul.
D. The message will be passed by Rahul.

Q.17 Sita was reading the Gita.
A. The Gita was being read by Sita.
B. The Gita were being read by Sita.
C. Gita was being read by Sita.
D. The Gita was read by Sita.

Q.18 Someone has stolen his book.
A. His book is been stolen.
B. His book has been stolen.
C. His book is stolen.
D. His book has stolen.

Q.19 Direction: Pick the pronoun from the options to fill the blank in the sentence:

Bob is my dad, ___________ is a waiter.

A. he   **B.** she   **C.** her   **D.** him

Ques (20-21):Direction: Select the answer choice that identifies the noun in the sentence.

Q.20 The Trojans' rash decision to accept the wooden horse led to their destruction.
A. Their   **B.** Led
C. Accept   **D.** Destruction

Q.21 Sue's parents tried living in the north, but they could not adapt to the cold.
A. North   **B.** But   **C.** Not   **D.** Adapt

Ques (22-25):Direction: Read the passage given below carefully:

The idea of euthanasia, of hastening the death of someone from motives of compassion, covers two main situations. The first is where someone is close to death and can be kept alive briefly, with intensive medical care. The official reason for the use of every possible technique on patients, for whom there seems no hope, is that we never know that there is no hope of at least a brief recovery.

The second situation, in which it is proposed to end the life of someone who is not expected to die at once from natural causes, is more morally doubtful. In so far as the suggestion may be based on the notion of the 'quality of life' experienced by the patient, this is an inadequate approach to human beings. At one extreme we may be dealing with a birth that cannot be called 'human' at all: such a being likely to live at the most for only a few hours. Many feel that during this time it ought to be given ordinary nursing care. Bringing to an end of the life of say, a spastic child, by the deliberate refusal of the fullest medical care seems morally indefensible.

Read the question given below and choose the option you consider the most appropriate.

Q.22 Euthanasia means:
A. A place in Asia
B. Bringing about gentle and easy death
C. Enthusiasm
D. The youth in Asia

Q.23 One reason for trying all possible measures to save a person is:
A. Death is horrifying
B. There is the possibility of recovery
C. Doctors need to be compassionate
D. Science may invent more sophisticated machines later

Q.24 The people who argue for euthanasia advocate it saying:
A. The patient is not living a qualitative life
B. We must not spend quality resources on a sick person
C. We should not bother about the ailing
D. It can be defended morally

Q.25 The words '..................dealing with a birth that cannot be called 'human' at all' implies:
A. Humans have no control over birth and death
B. The person may survive only for a very brief period
C. Doctors are incapable of saving people
D. The patient may want to die

Analytical Abilities

Q.26 Direction: Study the following arrangement carefully and answer the questions given below :

8 C M @ N £ T 2 Y 6 S α Q $ 7 × W # Z 3 U E % A 4

How many symbols are there in the above series each of which is immediately preceded and also immediately followed by a vowel?
A. Nil   **B.** One   **C.** Two   **D.** Three

Q.27 Direction: Study the following arrangement carefully and answer the questions given below :

8 C M @ N £ T 2 Y 6 S α Q $ 7 × W # Z 3 U E % A 4

If all the vowels are dropped from the above series, which of the following would be the eighth element to the right of the thirteenth element from the left end?
A. 4   **B.** 8   **C.** %   **D.** C

Q.28 A man is facing west. He turns 45° in the clockwise direction and then another 180° in the same direction and then 270° in the anti-clockwise direction. Which direction is he facing now?
A. South   **B.** North-west
C. South-west   **D.** None of these

Q.29 A child is looking for his father. He went 90 metres in the east before turning to his right. He went 20 metres before turning to his right again to look for his father at his uncle's place 30 metres from this point. His father was not there. From there, he went 100 metres to his north before meeting his father in a street. How far did the son meet his father from the starting point?
A. 80 m   **B.** 100 m   **C.** 140 m   **D.** 180 m

Q.30 Which Pair does NOT belong with the others?
A. 34 – 43   **B.** 55 – 62   **C.** 62 – 71   **D.** 83 – 92

Q.31 Which Pair does NOT belong with the others?

A. 2 - 8   **B.** 3 - 27   **C.** 4 - 32   **D.** 5 - 125

Q.32 In a coding language, the letters of the English alphabet are arranged in such a manner that all the vowels are put in the end and the remaining letters are arranged from the first letter onwards. The rearranged alphabets are used to denote the position occupied by letters in the original alphabets. What is the code of META?

A. TEAM   **B.** PWLV   **C.** LWPV   **D.** QGYB

Q.33 In a certain system of coding, the word STATEMENT is written as TNEMETATS. In the same system of coding, what should be the code for the word POLITICAL?

A. LACITILOP   **B.** LCATILIOP

C. OPILITACL   **D.** None of these

Q.34 Directions: Choose the correct alternative from the given ones that will complete the series.

AD, EI, IN, OS, ?

A. UX   **B.** XY   **C.** WY   **D.** UT

Q.35 Directions: Choose the correct alternative from the given ones that will complete the series.

MN, QR, UV, ?

A. XY   **B.** WX   **C.** YX   **D.** YZ

Ques (36-37):Direction: In each of the following question, there is a certain relationship between two given words on one side of :: and one word is given on another side :: while another word is to be found from the given alternatives, having the same relation with this word as the words of the given pair bear. Choose the correct alternative.

Q.36 Tadpole : Frog :: Cub : ?

A. Hedgehog   **B.** Lion

C. Cat   **D.** Dog

Q.37 Fish : Scales :: Bear : ?

A. Feathers   **B.** Leaves   **C.** Fur   **D.** Skin

Q.38 Pointing towards a boy, Veena said, "He is the son of the only son of my grandfather." How is that boy related to Veena?

A. Uncle   **B.** Brother

C. Cousin   **D.** Data inadequate

Q.39 Introducing Reeta, Sarika said, "She is the only daughter of my father's only daughter." How is Sarika related to Reeta?

A. Aunt   **B.** Niece

C. Cousin   **D.** None of these

Ques (40-41):Direction: Two statements are given below followed by two conclusions numbered as I and II respectively. Consider the given statements as true even if they seem to be not. After reading all the conclusions conform which of the given conclusions logically follows, disregarding commonly known facts.

Q.40 Statements:

I. Some garlic are carrots.

II. Some carrots are onions.

Conclusions:

I. Some garlic are onions.

II. All onions are carrots.

A. If only conclusion I follow

B. If only conclusion II follow

C. If either conclusion I or II follow

D. If neither conclusion I nor II follows

Q.41 Statements:

I. All granites are marbles.

II. Some marbles are tiles.

Conclusions:

I. Some tiles are marbles.

II. No granite is a tile.

A. If only conclusion I follows

B. If only conclusion II follows

C. If either conclusion I or II follows

D. If neither conclusion I nor II follows

Q.42 Directions: In the question below is given a statement and followed by two arguments numbered I and II. Consider the arguments and decide which option is the correct answer.

Statements: The old order changed yielding place to new.

Conclusions:

Change is the law of nature.

Discard old ideas because they are old.

A. Only conclusion I follows

B. Only conclusion II follows

C. Either I or II follows

D. Neither I nor II follows

Q.43 Directions: In each of the following questions a statement is given, followed by two conclusions. Give answer :

Statements: The standard of education in private schools is much better than Municipal and Zila Parishad-run schools.

Conclusions:

I. The Municipal and Zila Parishad should make serious efforts to improve the standard of their schools.

II. All Municipal and Zila Parishad schools should be closed immediately.

A. Only conclusion I follow

B. Only conclusion II follow

C. Either I or II follow

D. Neither I nor II follow

Ques (44-45):Direction: Two statements I and II are given. These statements may be either independent causes or may be effects of independent causes or a common cause. One of these statements may be the effect of the other statements. Read both the statements and decide which of the following answer choice correctly depicts the relationship between these two statements. Mark answer:

Q.44 I. Many people visited the religious place during the weekend.

II. Few people visited the religious place during the weekdays.

A. If statement I is the cause and statement II is its effect

B. If statement II is the cause and statement I is its effect

C. If both the statements I and II are independent causes

D. If both the statement I and II are effects of some common cause

Q.45 I. The price of vegetables has been increased considerably during this summer.

II. There is a tremendous increase in the temperature during this summer thereby damaging crops greatly.

A. If statement I is the cause and statement II is its effect

B. If statement II is the cause and statement I is its effect

C. If both the statements I and II are independent causes

D. If both statements I and II are effects of independent causes

Q.46 Find the missing number?

4	3	7
6	4	2
9	?	3

A. 7   **B.** 3   **C.** 6   **D.** 8

Q.47 Find the missing number.

4	5	3	2	0
7	3	4	4	21
6	4	4	5	22
9	6	5	5	?

A. 34   **B.** 42   **C.** 44   **D.** 45

Q.48 Find the missing number?

3, 6, 5, 7, 8, 11, 15, ?

A. 17   **B.** 23   **C.** 22   **D.** 15

Q.49 K is 40 m South-West of L. If M is 40 m South-East of L, then M is in which direction of K?

A. East   **B.** West

C. North-East   **D.** South

Q.50 After walking 6 km, I turned to the right and then walked 2 km. After then I turned to the left and walked 10 km. In the end, I was moving towards the North. From which direction did I start my journey?

A. North   **B.** South   **C.** East   **D.** West

Legal Awareness & Aptitude

Q.51 Principles 1: Any person may use reasonable force in order to protect his property or person.

Principles 2: However, the force employed must be proportionate to the apprehended danger.

Facts: Krishna was walking on a lonely road. Maniyan came with a knife and said to Krishna, "Your life or your purse". Krishna pulled out his revolver. On seeing it, Maniyan ran. Krishna shot Maniyan in his legs. Decide (NLS 1990)

A. Krishna will not be punished, as there was danger to his property.

B. Krishna will not be punished, as the force he used was proportionate to the apprehended injury.

C. Krishna will be punished, as the force employed was disproportionate to the apprehended injury.

D. As Maniyan ran to escape there was no longer a threat to Krishna's property. So Krishna will be punished.

Q.52 Principles 1: Any person who interferes with the discharge of duties by a public servant is liable for punishment.

Principles 2: Nothing is an offense if the person who committed it was winnable to appreciate the consequences of his act, due to intoxication, provided such intoxication was administered against his will and without his consent. (NLS 1990)

Facts: Krishna got drunk of his own volition and on his way back home he assaulted a policeman. He is prosecuted for intimidating a public servant.

Is Mr. Krishna liable for punishment"?

A. Yes, Krishna is liable for punishment as he assaulted a policeman

B. No, Krishna is not liable for punishment as he was drunk

C. Yes, Krishna is liable for punishment as he got drunk of his own volition

D. None of the above

Q.53 Principle: A person commits cheating when he fraudulently induces another person to deliver the latter's property to him.

Facts: A falsely represented to B, a shop-owner that he was an officer from the Sales Tax Department. In the course of going through the vouchers, A expressed his interest to buy, a costly television on an installment basis. B readily agreed to hope that he would get a favorable assessment from A regarding his tax liability. A paid the first installment and took the T.V. and disappeared. The police somehow managed to arrest him and sought to prosecute 'A' for cheating. Decide.

A. Committed cheating, because he induced B to part with the TV, posing himself as a sales-tax officer

B. A committed cheating, because he did not pay the subsequent installment

C. A did not commit cheating, because B handed over the T.V. to him in order to get a favorable assessment

D. A commits the offense of Criminal Misappropriation

Q.54 The doctrine of "stare decisis" underpins the common law system. What is "stare decisis"?

A. Courts must adhere to statutes in all of their decisions

B. The reasoning behind the decision

C. To stand by what has gone before

D. Parliament can overturn decided cases

Q.55 What does the "sine qua non" rule, in terms of causation, mean?

A. Causation does not apply to some crimes
B. Necessary Legal causation
C. The "but for" rule, or factual causation
D. Effect of act

Q.56 What is meant by "Ex turpi causa non-oritur action"?

A. The victim of a crime has a right to sue the perpetrator in tort
B. A person cannot pursue a cause of action if it arises out of his own guilty act
C. A person cannot be guilty if he has no reason to commit the crime
D. Friends who commit crimes together cannot be tried together

Q.57 In which landmark legal case it was held that the preamble is not a part of the Indian Constitution?

A. Berubari Union(I), Re
B. Keshavnanada Bharti v. the State of Kerala
C. S.R Bommai v. Union of India
D. T.M.A Pai v. Union of India

Q.58 In which Landmark legal case the Supreme Court held that Parliament has the right to amend the Fundamental Rights enshrined in the Constitution?

A. Sajjan Singh v. State of Rajasthan
B. Minera mills v. Union Of India
C. Bacchan Singh vs the State of Punjab
D. Shankari Prasad v. Union of India

Q.59 In which landmark case the Supreme Court held that the Second marriage of Hindu man is invalid even if he converts to Islam before marriage?

A. Daniel latiffi vs. Union Of India
B. Sarla Mudgal vs. Union Of India
C. Roopa Hurrah vs. Ashok Hurrah
D. Ramchandra Saraswati vs. Neena Bajpai

Q.60 In which Landmark case Fundamental Rights were considered as Inviolable part of the Indian Constitution?

A. Golak Nath vs. the State of Punjab
B. Keshavnanada Bharti vs. Union Of India
C. S.R Bommai V. Union Of India
D. Prem Singh v. State of Haryana

Q.61 What is meant by "doli incapax"?

A. Incapable of crime
B. A new judgment
C. New bye-law
D. A good decision

Q.62 What is meant by per incuriam?

A. To bind all other courts
B. To stand by what has gone before
C. A case settled with a lack of care so that the decision is wrong
D. A case decided on facts alone as no law exists in the area

Q.63 The Fourth schedule of Indian Constitution deals with:

A. Allocation of seats in Rajya Sabha
B. Allocation of seats in Lok Sabha
C. Allocation of seats in State Assemblies
D. Allocation of Seats in State Vidhan Parishad

Q.64 Which of the following writs can be used against a person believed to be holding a public office he is not entitled to hold?

A. Mandamus
B. Quo Warranto
C. Habeas Corpus
D. Certiorari

Q.65 'Infancy' as an exception has been provided under:

A. Section 80
B. Section 81
C. Section 82
D. Section 84

Q.66 A hangman who hangs the prisoners pursuant to the order of the court is exempt from criminal liability by virtue of:

A. Section 77 of IPC
B. Section 78 of IPC
C. Section 79 of IPC
D. Section 76 of IPC

Q.67 The right of private defense is contained in:

A. Section 94 of IPC
B. Section 95 of IPC
C. Section 96 of IPC
D. None of these

Q.68 When is the communication of a proposal complete:

A. When it comes to the knowledge of the person to whom it is made
B. Only when the proposal, acceptance or revocation of the proposal is recorded in writing
C. When the other party gives his assent or dissent to the proposal
D. Only when a clear verbal communication of such proposal is made

Q.69 The codified law for the law of Contract in India is:

A. Indian Contract Act,1872
B. Indian Contract Act,1973
C. Indian Contract Act,1992
D. Indian Contract Act, 1901

Q.70 A void contract is a contract which:

A. Is not enforceable by law
B. Does not have reasonable terms
C. Declared void by the Indian contract act
D. Both (a) and (c)

Q.71 The remedy of compensation given in the case of breach of contract is given under which section of The Indian Contract Act?

A. Section 73
B. Section 115
C. Section 79
D. Section 69

Q.72 A friend of the Court is called as:

A. Amicus curiae
B. judgment Debtor
C. Judge
D. Witness

Q.73 The term enactment means:

A. By virtue of office
B. Act of Parliament
C. Liability of property
D. An interest in land

Q.74 The law relating to prisoners of war has been codified by:

A. Geneva Convention
B. Vienna Convention

C. Paris Convention   **D.** None of the above

Q.75 The maxim 'de minimus non-curat lex' means:

A. The law would not take action on small & trifling matter

B. Law does not ignore any act which causes the slightest harm

C. Law would not take action in serious matters

D. All the above

General Knowledge

Q.76 The first Indian communication satellite was ________.

A. Aryabhatta   **B.** Bhaskara-I

C. Apple   **D.** Chandrayaan-I

Q.77 The "Braille System" was invented by ______ and he is from ______.

A. Marie Curie, France

B. Hellen Keller, USA

C. Nicolas Appert, France

D. Louis Braille, Paris

Q.78 Which statement is not correct in the case of "Sovereign India"?

A. India is not dependent on any country

B. India is not a colony of any other country

C. India can give any part of its country to any other country

D. India is obliged to obey the UN in its internal affairs

Q.79 Which article of the Indian constitution gives an extensive original jurisdiction to the Supreme Court in regard to enforcement of Fundamental Rights?

A. Article 22   **B.** Article 32

C. Article 35   **D.** Article 37

Q.80 Which of the following geographical term related with the "piece of sub-continental land that is surrounded by water"?

A. Peninsula   **B.** Gulf

C. Strait   **D.** Island

Q.81 Which of the following countries are divided by the Radcliffe Line?

A. India and Pakistan

B. India and China

C. India and Bangladesh

D. India and Nepal

Q.82 A person who is not a member of the state legislature can be appointed as Chief Minister for how many months?

A. 2 months   **B.** 3 months

C. 4 months   **D.** 6 months

Q.83 The total amount of income from economic activities across the country in a year is called:

A. Disposable income   **B.** National income

C. Personal income   **D.** Private Income

Q.84 Who releases data of national income in India?

A. NSSO

B. CSO

C. NITI Aayog

D. None of the following

Q.85 Chalapathi Rao committee was meant for restructuring of:

A. State financial corporation in India

B. Commercial banks in India

C. Co-operative banks in India

D. Regional Rural banks in India

Q.86 In which of the following circumstances, the prime minister of India cannot participate in voting on a no-confidence motion against his / her government?

A. He/She leads a coalition government

B. He/she has a minority in Rajya Sabha

C. He/she is a member of the Rajya Sabha

D. He/she is forbidden by the speaker of Lok Sabha

Q.87 How many presidents of India so far were elected unopposed since 1952?

A. One   **B.** Two   **C.** Three   **D.** Four

Q.88 Which of the following canals is considered to be an important link between the developed countries and the developing countries?

A. Panama Canal   **B.** Suez Canal

C. Kiel Canal   **D.** Grand Canal

Q.89 Which of the following is a correct sequence of seaports of India from "South to North"?

A. Cochin →Thiruvananthapuram→Calicut→Mangalore

B. Calicut→ Thiruvananthapuram→ Cochin→ Mangalore

C. Thiruvananthapuram→ Cochin→ Calicut→ Mangalore

D. Thiruvananthapuram→ Calicut→ Mangalore→ Cochin

Q.90 Myanmar does not share its international boundary with__?

A. Laos   **B.** Thailand   **C.** Vietnam   **D.** India

Q.91 SBI's new training initiative "Strategic Training Unit" is located at:

A. New Delhi   **B.** Banglore

C. Hyderabad   **D.** Mumbai

Q.92 Which of the following is not a regulatory institution in the Indian financial system?

A. RBI   **B.** CIBIL   **C.** SEBI   **D.** IRDA

Q.93 What is called Tax heaven?

A. A country that gives tax exemptions to the foreign citizens that there will be no tax on investing the money in their country

B. Subsidy given by the government in taxes

C. Tax evasion in the domestic country

D. To impose equal taxes on domestic producers and foreign producers

Q.94 Which of the following is not imposed by the Central Government?

A. Agricultural tax   **B.** Corporation tax

C. Custom duty   **D.** Sales tax

Q.95 Which unit of the Hindustan Copper Ltd. is the first copper smelting unit in India?

A. Malanjkhand Copper Project (MP)

B. Khetri Copper Complex (Rajasthan)

C. Indian Copper Complex (Jharkhand)

D. Tajola Copper Project (Maharashtra)

Q.96 Central Pollution Control Board (CPCB) partnered with which Power-based company to install Air Quality Monitoring Stations?

A. NTPC Limited

B. Power Grid Corporation

C. Tata Power

D. NHPC Limited

Q.97 What is the name of the faceless assessment programme launched by the Central Board of Indirect Taxes and Customs?

A. Bharat Customs   B. Turant Customs

C. Efficient Customs   D. Clear Customs

Q.98 Who is the winner of Kamaladevi Chattopadhyay NIF Book Award 2021?

A. M. Mukundan   B. Dinyar Patel

C. Naveen Kumar   D. Jaya Srikumar

Q.99 Who has been given the Times Business Award 2022 for Eastern India's Leading READY-TO-EAT brand?

A. Vineta Suyal   B. Roshni Dixit

C. Rashmi Sahoo   D. Deepika Sharma

Q.100 Which film won the Jury Prize at Cannes Film Festival 2022?

A. Stars at Noon   B. Joyland

C. Close   D. Triangle of Sadness

// Smart Answer Sheet //

Correct Percentage of students who answered correctly. **Skipped** Percentage of students who skipped.

Q.	Ans.	Correct / Skipped
1	C	40.65 % / 45.59 %
2	B	61.04 % / 30.62 %
3	A	44.73 % / 50.33 %
4	C	59.9 % / 36.28 %
5	C	48.11 % / 45.11 %
6	C	88.51 % / 10.83 %
7	C	87.08 % / 10.94 %
8	C	40.74 % / 53.54 %
9	A	69.33 % / 30.32 %
10	A	59.0 % / 32.67 %
11	D	46.59 % / 44.33 %
12	B	55.43 % / 34.7 %
13	C	59.58 % / 39.58 %
14	A	69.25 % / 30.45 %
15	C	25.47 % / 70.1 %
16	D	66.5 % / 31.36 %
17	A	77.43 % / 15.43 %
18	B	88.98 % / 10.94 %
19	A	81.92 % / 13.2 %
20	D	67.65 % / 30.93 %
21	A	61.75 % / 32.55 %
22	B	86.37 % / 11.11 %
23	B	60.24 % / 36.7 %
24	A	47.95 % / 50.04 %
25	B	64.79 % / 33.31 %
26	B	83.55 % / 16.43 %
27	C	60.02 % / 34.38 %
28	C	66.87 % / 32.97 %
29	B	10.38 % / 86.53 %
30	B	81.31 % / 12.77 %
31	C	52.91 % / 34.59 %
32	D	42.63 % / 48.23 %
33	A	48.33 % / 33.06 %
34	A	27.17 % / 70.68 %
35	D	40.86 % / 57.18 %
36	B	59.94 % / 30.17 %
37	C	66.34 % / 32.73 %
38	B	41.73 % / 40.21 %
39	D	52.0 % / 42.62 %
40	D	55.11 % / 33.03 %
41	A	63.98 % / 32.06 %
42	A	57.15 % / 30.7 %
43	A	54.21 % / 44.04 %
44	D	65.41 % / 31.77 %
45	B	67.07 % / 30.94 %
46	C	85.21 % / 11.53 %
47	A	28.01 % / 67.97 %
48	C	41.12 % / 43.78 %
49	A	53.73 % / 33.53 %
50	B	48.53 % / 33.99 %
51	C	40.43 % / 39.33 %
52	C	56.67 % / 30.42 %
53	A	41.27 % / 53.71 %
54	C	46.77 % / 30.11 %
55	B	52.6 % / 47.08 %
56	B	68.56 % / 30.77 %
57	A	65.67 % / 33.86 %
58	D	49.14 % / 49.8 %
59	B	59.1 % / 32.72 %
60	A	56.09 % / 41.32 %
61	A	60.0 % / 30.74 %
62	C	83.73 % / 15.43 %
63	A	87.15 % / 11.85 %
64	B	82.52 % / 13.32 %
65	C	85.82 % / 11.43 %
66	B	54.8 % / 39.63 %
67	C	57.38 % / 31.72 %
68	A	79.6 % / 10.6 %
69	A	79.86 % / 13.3 %
70	C	79.54 % / 18.72 %
71	A	53.95 % / 30.26 %
72	A	89.92 % / 10.02 %
73	B	53.25 % / 41.5 %
74	A	79.4 % / 12.85 %
75	A	50.0 % / 31.98 %
76	C	80.31 % / 13.07 %
77	D	78.59 % / 14.67 %
78	D	40.88 % / 39.16 %
79	B	77.38 % / 19.71 %
80	D	55.41 % / 37.9 %

Q.	Ans.	Correct		Q.	Ans.	Correct		Q.	Ans.	Correct		Q.	Ans.	Correct		Q.	Ans.	Correct
		Skipped				Skipped				Skipped				Skipped				Skipped
81	A	80.09 %		85	D	59.69 %		89	C	67.03 %		93	A	55.73 %		97	B	56.15 %
		13.52 %				32.66 %				32.03 %				32.5 %				39.64 %
82	D	84.62 %		86	C	51.84 %		90	C	43.25 %		94	A	58.89 %		98	B	14.76 %
		13.71 %				44.73 %				50.24 %				32.97 %				76.28 %
83	B	86.88 %		87	A	80.85 %		91	C	13.87 %		95	A	16.44 %		99	C	26.44 %
		12.29 %				14.96 %				75.99 %				76.56 %				67.43 %
84	B	48.03 %		88	B	66.23 %		92	B	76.08 %		96	A	24.8 %		100	B	62.25 %
		51.56 %				32.28 %				19.64 %				67.91 %				31.72 %

//Hints and Solutions//

1. Vicissitude - One of the many changes and problems in a situation or your life, that you have to deal with

Change - To become different or to make somebody/something different

Sorrow - Deep distress, sadness

Misfortune - Bad luck or disaster

Surprises - The feeling that you have when something happens that you do not expect

Hence, the correct option is (C).

2. Hirsute - Hair

Bald - Having little or no hair on head

Shaggy - Covered with long, thick, untidy hair

Erudite - Having or showing great knowledge that is based on careful study

Glorious - Having or deserving fame or success

Hence, the correct option is (B).

3. 'in high spirits' means, he was in a very happy state of mind or was very cheerful.
Hence, the correct option is (A).

4. The woman to whom I sold my house was a criminal is the correct form of the sentence.

The word 'who' is used if it is answered for him.

The word 'whom' is used as a direct or indirect object of a verb or preposition. 'Whom' is used if it is answered for him.
Hence, the correct option is (C).

5. A person who talks in sleep is called a Somniloquist.

The word 'Somniloquist' is a Latin word. 'Somni' means sleep and 'liquid' means to talk.

Philatelist - A person who collects stamps.

Somnambulist - A person, who walks in sleep.

Oneirocritic - A person who interprets dreams.

Hence, the correct option is (C).

6. Omniscient - The person who knows everything.

Omnipresent - present everywhere.

Omnipotent - To have unlimited power.

Oblivious - Ignorant person (A person who is unaware of everything).
Hence, the correct option is (C).

7. We arrived at the station an hour late.

The preposition 'at' is used when referring to buildings as locations in a city. This can be confused with the preposition 'in'. Generally, 'in' is used with buildings to mean that something occurs inside the building. 'At', on the other hand, is used to express that something happens at the location.
Hence, the correct option is (C).

8. The appropriate word for the blank will be "abandon," which means to leave somebody/something that you are responsible for.

If there is some chance of succeeding, it would be unwise to abandon it at this stage.

Hence, the correct option is (C).

9. 'Eminent' means a person who is successful, well-known, outstanding, etc.

Sachin Tendulkar is an eminent player.

Hence, the correct option is (A).

10. Adverbs of time and definite frequency say when or how often something happens. Examples are- today, yesterday, in the afternoon, last night, last week, last year, two months ago, already, soon, still, finally, weekly, daily, every year, monthly, etc. Adverbs of time and definite frequency usually go in the end-position.
Hence, the correct option is (A).

11. Adverbs of manner describe how something happens. For example, it is possible to walk or run at different speeds. The words used to describe walking or running at different speeds (quickly or slowly for example) and joyful, cheerfully are excellent examples of adverbs of manner.
Hence, the correct option is (D).

12. 'Caught between two stools' means finding it difficult to choose between two alternatives. Or,

To fail due to difficulty in choosing between two alternatives.

Example in a sentence:

He tries to be both mother and father of his daughter but falls between two stools.
Hence, the correct option is (B).

13. A sop to Cerberus means a concession or bribe to conciliate a person otherwise liable to be troublesome.
Hence, the correct option is (C).

14. The incorrect spelling of "Resembelance" will be "Resemblance" that means the quality or state of resembling especially, correspondence in appearance or superficial qualities.
Hence, the correct option is (A).

15. Kaleidoscope is a correctly spelt word. It means a large number of different things.
Hence, the correct option is (C).

16. Rule to make the active voice of Simple Future Tense:

Object + shall/will + be + third form of verb + by + subject

The correct passive of the given sentence is-

The message will be passed by Rahul.
Hence, the correct option is (D).

17. The rule for the making of passive voice is-

Object + was/were + being + + third form of verb + by + subject

The correct passive will be-

The Gita was being read by Sita.
Hence, the correct option is (A).

18. The rule for making a passive voice for this type of sentences-

Object + has/have + been+ third form of verb

His book has been stolen.
Hence, the correct option is (B).

19. Bob is my dad. He is a waiter.

Dad is the male so we will use the 'He' for him.
Hence, the correct option is (A).

20. Destruction is a noun.

"Their" is a plural possessive pronoun modifying destruction.

"Led" and "Accept" are verbs.
Hence, the correct option is (D).

21. North is a noun here. North is one of the four compass points or cardinal directions. It is the opposite of south and is perpendicular to east and west.

"But" is a conjunction. "Not" is an adverb modifying the verb "Adapt".
Hence, the correct option is (A).

22. According to the passage, Euthanasia means hastening the death of someone from motives of compassion or bringing about gentle and easy death.
Hence, the correct option is (B).

23. According to passage "The official reason for the use of every possible technique on patients, for whom there seems no hope, is that we never know that there is no hope of at least a brief recovery."
Hence, the correct option is (B).

24. According to passage, "it is proposed to end the life of someone who is not expected to die at once from natural causes, is more morally doubtful. In so far as the suggestion may be based on the notion of the 'quality of life' experienced by the patient."
Hence, the correct option is (A).

25. From the line given in the passage, "At one extreme we may be dealing with a birth that cannot be called 'human' at all: such a being likely to live at the most for only a few hours." It implies that the person may survive only for a very brief period.
Hence, the correct option is (B).

26. 8 C M @ N £ T 2 Y 6 S α Q $ 7 × W # Z 3 U E % A 4

There is only one symbol (%) that satisfies the given condition.
Hence, the correct option is (B).

27. The new arrangement becomes:

8 C M @ N £ T 2 Y 6 S α Q $ 7 × W # Z 3 % 4

Note: In the case of opposite directions we add the positions and calculate the resultant position of an element from the given end of the series.

∴ 8th element to the right of the 13th element from the left end means (8 + 13) = 21st element from the left end, i.e., %.
Hence, the correct option is (C).

28.

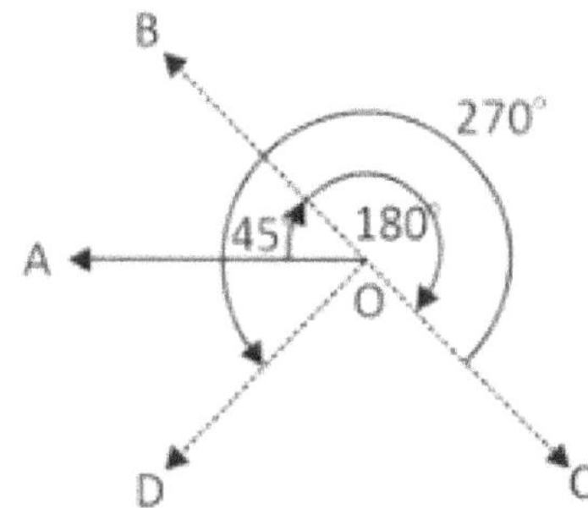

He is facing towards South-West.
Hence, the correct option is (C).

29.

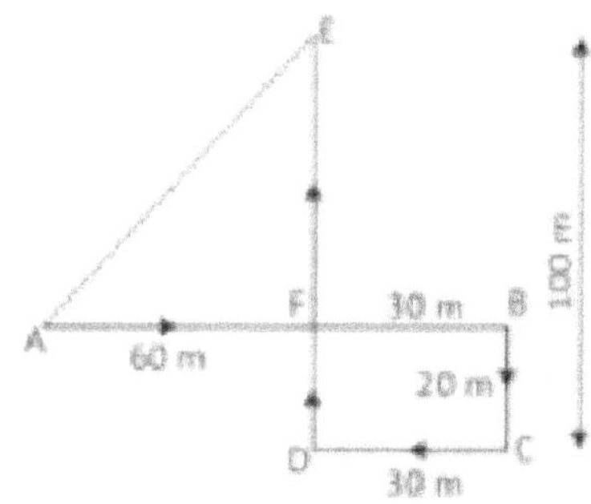

Clearly, $AB = 90\ m, BF = CD = 30\ m.$

So, $AF = AB - BF = 60\ m.$

Also $DE = 100\ m.$

$DF = BC = 20\ m.$

So, $EF - DE - DF = 80\ m$

So his distance from starting point $A = AE =$ $\sqrt{(AF^2 + EF^2)}$

$\Rightarrow \sqrt{(60)^2 + (80)^2} = \sqrt{3600 + 6400}$

$\Rightarrow \sqrt{10000} = 100\ m$

Hence, the correct option is (B).

30. In all other pairs, the second number is 9 more than the first.

But in the "55 - 62" pair the difference is only 7.
Hence, the correct option is (B).

31. In all other pairs, the second number is the cube of the first.

But in the pair of "4 - 32" it does not follow the same rule.
Hence, the correct option is (C).

32. The original and rearranged letter sequences are as shown:

A B C D E F G H I J K L M N O P Q R S T U V W X Y Z

B C D F G H J K L M N P Q R S T V W X Y Z A E I O U

Thus, the code for META is QGYB.
Hence, the correct option is (D).

33. The letters of the given word are written in a reverse order to obtain the code.

Reversing the order of letters in POLITICAL,

We get LACITILOP.
Hence, the correct option is (A).

34. $A - E - 1 - 0 - U =$ Vowels
$$D \xrightarrow{+5} 1 \xrightarrow{+5} N \xrightarrow{+5} S \xrightarrow{+5} X$$
Hence, the correct option is (A).

35.

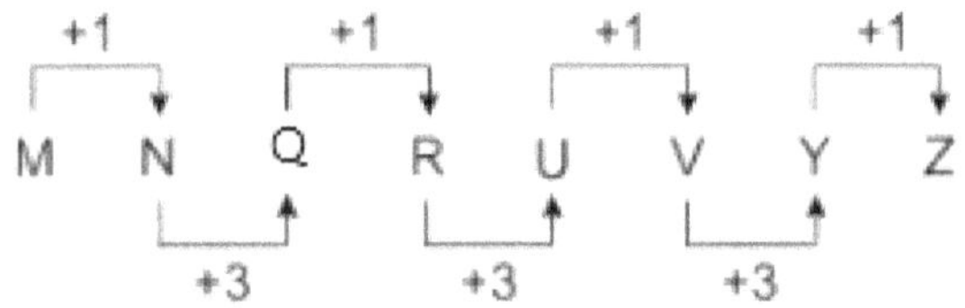

Hence, the correct option is (D).

36. The young one of the frog is called tadpole. Similarly, the young one of lion is called cub.
Hence, the correct option is (B).

37. The body of fish remains covered with scales externally. Similarly, the body of the bear remains covered with fur.
Hence, the correct option is (C).

38.

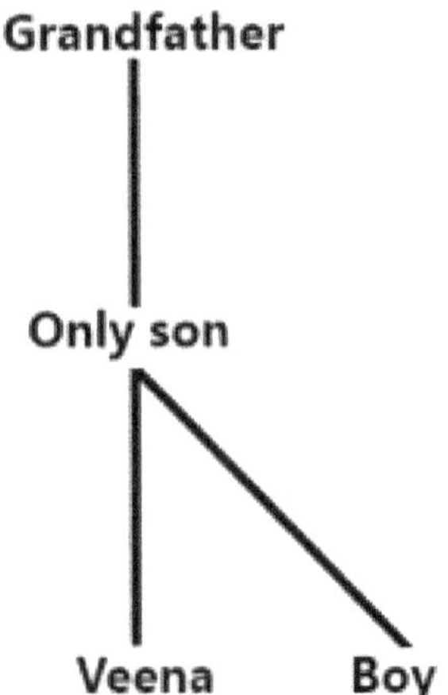

According to the diagram boy is the brother of Veena.

Hence, the correct option is (B).

39.

Sarika is mother of Reeta.

Hence, the correct option is (D).

40.

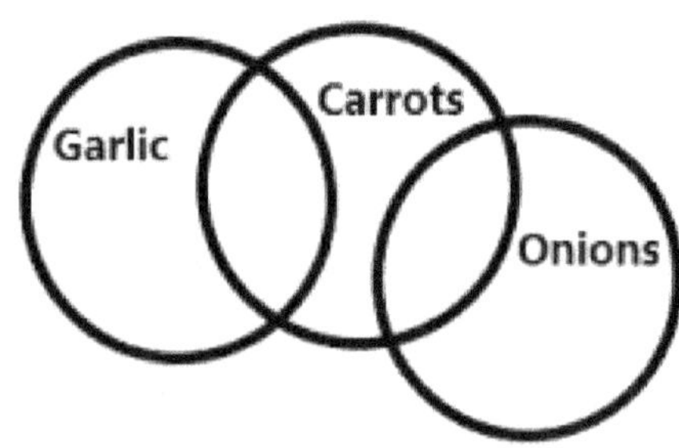

Hence, the correct option is (D).

41.

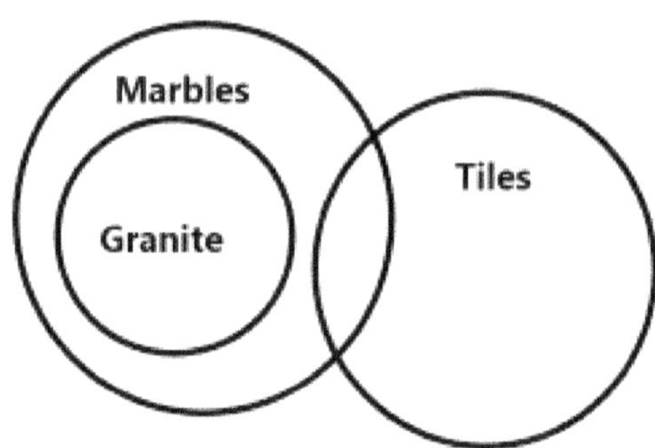

Hence, the correct option is (A).

42. Clearly, I directly follow from the given statement. Also, it is mentioned that old ideas are replaced by new ones, as thinking changes with the progressing time. So, II does not follow.
Hence, the correct option is (A).

43. Clearly, the solution to the problem is not to close down the Municipal and Zila Parishad-run schools but to strive to improve the standard of education of these schools. So, only I follow while II does not.
Hence, the correct option is (A).

44. Clearly, a lesser number of people are visiting a place during the weekdays and more people are visiting during the weekend, both imply events that go together, and must have happened due to a common cause such as, it being a holiday during the weekend.
Hence, the correct option is (D).

45. Damage of crops due to high temperature may have resulted in a short supply of vegetables and hence an increase in their prices. Thus, statement II is cause and I is its effect.
Hence, the correct option is (B).

46. Central Element = Difference of Left and Right elements

7 - 4 = 3

6 - 2 = 4

So,

9 - 3 = 6

Missing Element = 6
Hence, the correct option is (C).

47. Column-Wise

(First Column Element × 4th Column element) - (2nd column element + 3rd Column element) = Last Column Element

(4×2)-(5+3) = 0

(7×4)-(3+4) = 21

(6×5)-(4+4) = 22

(9×5)-(6+5) = 34
Hence, the correct option is (A).

48. First number + second number - 4 = Third Number

3 + 6 - 4 = 5

6 + 5 - 4 = 7

5 + 7 - 4 = 8

8 + 7 - 4 = 11

11 + 8 - 4 = 15

15 + 11 - 4 = 22

So,

Missing number = 22
Hence, the correct option is (C).

49.

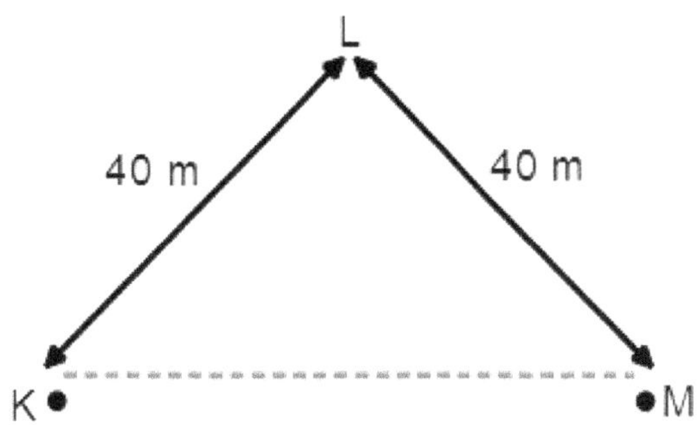

So, M is in the East of K.
Hence, the correct option is (A).

50.

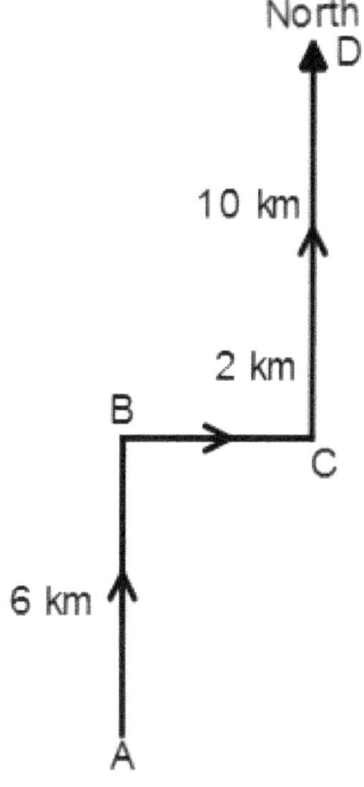

The journey was started from the South.
Hence, the correct option is (B).

51. Krishna will be punished, as the force employed was disproportionate to the apprehended injury.

The force employed was way more than the danger level as Maniyan started to run away from Krishna. As the threat was reduced and was continuously reducing, there was no need to shoot Maniyan in the Legs.

Hence, the correct option is (C).

52. The Defense of Intoxication is available in the Indian Penal Code when the said state is not caused by the voluntary Action. Krishna Drunk of his volition and hence his Act is punishable.
Hence, the correct option is (C).

53. Firstly, A falsely impersonated as a Sales Tax officer to buy a television, and secondly, he fraudulently induced B to sell that to him. He is liable for cheating.
Hence, the correct option is (A).

54. In common law legal systems, a precedent, or authority, is a principle or rule established in a previous legal case that is either binding on or persuasive for a court or other tribunal when deciding subsequent cases with similar issues or facts.
Hence, the correct option is (C).

55. The essential, crucial, or indispensable ingredient without which something would be impossible: "Her leadership was the sine qua non of the organization's success." From Latin, meaning "without which nothing."
Hence, the correct option is (B).

56. Ex turpi causa non-oritur action is a legal doctrine that states that a plaintiff will be unable to pursue a legal remedy if it arises in connection with his own illegal act.
Hence, the correct option is (B).

57. In Berubari Union(I), Re:- It was held that the preamble is not part of the constitution. This judgment was overruled by 13 Judge Bench in Keshvananda Bharti case and it was held that the 'Preamble is part of Indian Constitution'.
Hence, the correct option is (A).

58. Shankari Prasad Case V. Union of India, 1951 Shankari Prasad Vrs. Union of India is a landmark case in the basic structure of our constitution. In the cases, the power to amend the rights had been upheld on the basis of Article 368. Chief Justice Subba Rao writing for the majority six judges in the special bench of eleven, overruled the previous decisions.
Hence, the correct option is (D).

59. Sarla Mudgal v. Union of India:- The case is related to the offense of Bigamy, the conflict between the personal laws, and a strong need for a uniform civil code in the country. The court held that the second marriage of a Hindu man after being converted to Islam will be invalid if the first marriage has not been dissolved.
Hence, the correct option is (B).

60. In 1967, in Golak Nath vs. The State of Punjab, a bench of eleven judges (such a large bench constituted for the first time) of the Supreme Court deliberated as to whether any part of the Fundamental Rights provisions of the constitution could be revoked or limited by amendment of the constitution. Secondly, declared that the Fundamental Rights were transcendental and inviolable and the Parliament of India had no power to take away or abridge any of the Fundamental Rights guaranteed by the Constitution by way of the Constitutional amendments. Their lordship felt that the liberty of the Individual in the Indian Constitution is subject to various "reasonable restrictions" which are expressly mentioned in the Constitution and that no further limitations should be imposed on it at any time.
Hence, the correct option is (A).

61. Doli Incapax is a Latin term that means "incapable of doing harm". This term has been used to describe a presumption of innocence for children in Criminal law in most countries. The basis of this presumption lies in the theory of Criminal responsibility.
Hence, the correct option is (A).

62. Per incuriam - literally translated as "through lack of care" is a device within the common law system of judicial precedent. A finding of per incuriam means that a previous court judgment has failed to pay attention to relevant statutory provisions or precedents.
Hence, the correct option is (C).

63. Schedules are lists in the constitution that categorize and tabulate bureaucratic activity and government policy. The fourth Schedule deals with the allocation of seats in the Rajya Sabha.
Hence, the correct option is (A).

64. Quo warranto is a special form of legal action used to resolve a dispute over whether a specific person has the legal right to hold the public office that he or she occupies. Quo warranto is used to test a person's legal right to hold an office, not to evaluate the person's performance in the office.
Hence, the correct option is (B).

65. Provision of section 82 of IPC - Act of a child under seven years of age. Nothing is an offense that is done by a child under seven years of age.
Hence, the correct option is (C).

66. Section 78 of IPC - Act did pursuant to the judgment or order of the Court. Nothing which is done in pursuance of, or which is warranted by the judgment or order of, a Court of Justice, if done whilst such judgment or order remains in force, is an offence, notwithstanding the Court may have had no jurisdiction to pass such judgment or order, provided the person doing the act in good faith believes that the Court had such jurisdiction.
Hence, the correct option is (B).

67. Section 96 in the Indian Penal Code - Things are done in private defence.

Nothing is an offence that is done in the exercise of the right of private defence.
Hence, the correct option is (C).

68. The communication of a proposal is complete when it comes to the knowledge of the person to whom it is made. as against the proposer, when it is put in a course of transmission to him, so as to be out of the power of the acceptor; as against the acceptor, when it comes to the knowledge of the proposer.
Hence, the correct option is (A).

69. The Indian Contract Act, 1872, prescribes the law relating to contracts in India and is the key act regulating Indian contract law. The Act is based on the principles of English Common Law. It is applicable to all the states of India. It determines the circumstances in which promises made by the parties to a contract shall be legally binding. Under Section 2(h), the Indian Contract Act defines a contract as an agreement that is enforceable by law.
Hence, the correct option is (A).

70. A void contract is a formal agreement that is effectively illegitimate and unenforceable from the moment it is created. A void contract differs from a voidable contract, although both may indeed be nullified for similar reasons. A contract may be deemed

void if it is not enforceable as it was originally written.
Hence, the correct option is (C).

71. Section 73 of the Act provides that "When a contract has been broken, the party who suffers by such breach is entitled to receive, from the party who has broken the contract, compensation for any loss or damage caused to him thereby, which naturally arose in the usual course of things from such breach, or which the parties knew, when they made the contract, to be likely to result from the breach of it."
Hence, the correct option is (A).

72. An amicus curia means "friend of the court" is someone who is not a party to a case who assists a court by offering information, expertise, or insight that has a bearing on the issues in the case. The decision on whether to consider an amicus brief lies within the discretion of the court.
Hence, the correct option is (A).

73. The enactment of a law is the process in a legislature by which the law is agreed upon and made official.
Hence, the correct option is (B).

74. The Geneva Conventions and their Additional Protocols is a body of Public International Law, also known as the Humanitarian Law of Armed Conflicts, whose purpose is to provide minimum protections, standards of humane treatment, and fundamental guarantees of respect to individuals who become victims of armed conflicts.
Hence, the correct option is (A).

75. De minimis is a legal principle that allows for matters that are small scale or of insufficient importance to be exempted from a rule or requirement. It can be used by the courts as an exclusionary tool to dismiss trivial matters from litigation.
Hence, the correct option is (A).

76. The first Indian communication satellite was Apple.

The satellite successfully launched by Ariane-1, from French Guiana on June 19, 1981. APPLE was used in several communication experiments. India's first satellite, the Aryabhata, was launched by the Soviet Union on 19 April 1975 from Kapustin Yar using a Cosmos-3M launch vehicle.

Hence, the correct option is (C).

77. The "Braille System" was invented by Louis Braille and he is from Paris.

Braille, a universally accepted system of writing used by and for blind persons and consisting of a code of 63 characters. Each character made up of one to six raised dots arranged in a six-position matrix or cell.

Hence, the correct option is (D).

78. India is called a sovereign country because the Preamble of the Indian constitution defines India to be a 'Sovereign' country; meaning India has its own supreme law and not a matter of any additional state or nation. Moreover, India is independent of any kind of external intervention in its domestic operations.
Hence, the correct option is (D).

79. Article 32 has given original jurisdiction to the Supreme Court for matters regarding the enforcement of Fundamental Rights.

The Supreme Court is empowered to issue directions, orders, or writs, including writs in the nature of habeas corpus, mandamus, prohibition, quo warranto, and certiorari to enforce them. Article 32 also empowers an individual to approach directly to Supreme Court for enforcement of his fundamental rights.
Hence, the correct option is (B).

80. An island or isle is any piece of subcontinental land that is surrounded by water. Very small islands such as emergent land features on atolls can be called islets, skerries, cays, or keys.
Hence, the correct option is (D).

81. The Radcliffe Line was the boundary demarcation line between the Indian and Pakistani portions of the Punjab and Bengal provinces of British India. It was named after its architect, Sir Cyril Radcliffe, who, as the joint chairman of the two boundary commissions for the two provinces, received the responsibility to equitably divide 175,000 square miles (450,000 km2) of territory with 88 million people.
Hence, the correct option is (A).

82. A person can appoint as Chief Minister who is not a member of the state legislature for six months, within which, he should be elected to the state legislature, failing which he ceases to be the Chief Minister of the state.
Hence, the correct option is (D).

83. National income means the value of goods and services produced by a country during a financial year. Thus, it is the net result of all economic activities of any country during a period of one year and is valued in terms of money.
Hence, the correct option is (B).

84. The GDP figures in India are released by the Central Statistics Office (CSO), which comes under the Ministry of Statistics and Program Implementation (MOSPI).
Hence, the correct option is (B).

85. Chalapathi Rao Committee was constituted for the restructuring of Regional Rural Banks in India. The committee under the Chairmanship of Chalapathy Rao in 2003 recommended that the entire system of RRBs may be consolidated while retaining the advantages of the regional character of these institutions.

As part of the process, some sponsor banks may be eased out.

The sponsoring institutions may include other approved financial institutions as well, in addition to commercial banks.
Hence, the correct option is (D).

86. If PM is a member of Rajya Sabha, he can participate in procedures of both houses but can vote only in Rajya Sabha. Vote of No Confidence can be moved only in Lok Sabha so PM will not vote in it.
Hence, the correct option is (C).

87. N Sanjiva Reddy is the only president since 1952 who elected unopposed.

Apart from N Sanjiva Reddy First President Dr. Rajendra Prasad was elected unopposed for the period 1950 to 1952, but he faced opposition in further elections.
Hence, the correct option is (A).

88. Suez Canal considered being an important link between the developed countries and developing countries.

The Suez Canal is an artificial sea-level waterway in Egypt, connecting the Mediterranean Sea to the Red Sea through the Isthmus of Suez and dividing Africa and Asia.
Hence, the correct option is (B).

89. The correct sequence will be Thiruvananthapuram→ Cochin→ Calicut→ Mangalore.
Hence, the correct option is (C).

90. Myanmar is bound by China to the north and northeast, Laos to the east, Thailand to the east and southeast, India to the northwest, Bangladesh to the west and the Andaman Sea to the south.
Hence, the correct option is (C).

91. The Strategic Training Unit, located at Hyderabad will be headed by Smt. Mahapara Ali, Chief General Manager.

Training in the State Bank of India (SBI) is a proactive, planned and continuous process and forms an integral part of organizational development. It seeks to impart knowledge, improve skills and reorient attitudes for individual growth and organizational effectiveness.
Hence, the correct option is (C).

92. CIBIL is a Credit Bureau or Credit Information Company. This company is engaged in maintaining the records of all the credit-related activities of companies as well as individuals including credit cards and loans.

RBI, SEBI, and IRDA are the regulatory bodies.

Hence the correct option is (B).

93. A tax haven is generally an offshore country that offers foreign individuals and businesses little or no tax liability in a politically and economically static environment.

Hence the correct option is (A).

94. Agriculture comes under the jurisdiction of the state government, So state can impose a tax on it.

Hence the correct option is (A).

95. Malanjkhand Copper Project was established in 1982. The initial project has been set up by Hindustan Copper Ltd to exploit the copper ore through an open-pit mine.

Hence the correct option is (A).

96. NTPC Limited announced that it has signed an agreement with Central Pollution Control Board (CPCB) to provide financial support to install Air Quality Monitoring Stations.

NTPC will provide financial support of Rs 80 crore for installing and commissioning of 25 Continuous Ambient Air Quality Monitoring Stations (CAAQMS), across six states and three Union Territories. The data from these monitoring stations will be used as inputs for Air Quality Index.

Hence the correct option is (A).

97. Central Board of Indirect Taxes and Customs, CBIC has recently launched its flagship faceless assessment program Turant Customs.

The program has been launched in Bengaluru and Chennai. With this, the goods imported at Chennai would be assessed by the Customs officers at Bengaluru and vice versa. This is the first phase of the nationwide rollout of the facility. This step is expected to increase the ease of doing business in the country.

Hence the correct option is (B).

98. The biography of Dadabhai Naoroji, one of the founders of the Indian National Congress, has been named the winner of the Kamaladevi Chattopadhyay NIF Book Award 2021 by Dinyar Patel. 'Naoroji: Pioneer of Indian Nationalism' was selected from six shortlisted books.

Hence, the correct option is (B).

99. Director of Ruchi Foodline, Eastern India's leading food brand and Odisha's No.1 spices company, Rashmi Sahoo has been presented the Times Business Award 2022.

Hence, the correct option is (C).

100. Pakistani film 'Joyland', written and directed by the debutant Saim Sadiq, won the Jury Prize in the Un Certain Regard section of the 75th Cannes Film Festival.

Hence, the correct option is (B).

English Language & Comprehension

Ques (1-4):Direction: Read the passage carefully and give the answer to the given question based on it.

Despite the frustrating years of dragging children out of bed and persuading them to go to school, young children have an internal drive to learn about their world and become industrious and productive individuals. Their educational eagerness and curiosity can either be stifled or encouraged by parents, teachers and other adults. Aware parents can encourage their children's development of important life skills. Besides teaching them to read and write, school and home environments teach children cooperation and interdependence. Children also engage in important play rituals (like playing with dolls or cops and robbers) which prepare them for adolescence and adulthood. Supportive parents can promote crucial learning of life skills. Above all, school-age children struggle with feelings of inferiority and incompetence when they compare themselves with their peers. If they don't fit in, they might feel insignificant. Loving and accepting parents help these children develop the confidence to create a future where they can thrive and feel good about themselves.

Q.1 Most of the young children have an internal drive:

A. To learn the basics of fear

B. To learn the fundamentals of English

C. To teach manners to others

D. To learn about their world

Q.2 When the students compare themselves with their peers:

A. They feel inferiority

B. They feel superiority

C. They feel afraid of them

D. They notice something awkward

Q.3 The role parents can play to help their children is by:

A. Punishing them

B. Providing them extra food

C. Loving and accepting them

D. Taking them to zoo daily

Q.4 Some games prepare the children for:

A. Discipline

B. Adolescence and adulthood

C. Character

D. Their superiority

Ques (5-7):Direction: Choose the correct preposition for fill in the blanks.

Q.5 He struggled and gained a victory ___ his enemies.

A. with   **B.** at   **C.** over   **D.** between

Q.6 This passport is valid ___ five years.

A. to   **B.** for   **C.** of   **D.** In

Q.7 We travelled ___ a boat to reach Sri Lanka.

A. about   **B.** for   **C.** on   **D.** by

Q.8 Direction: Change the given sentence into active/passive voice.

Our task had been completed before sunset.

A. We completed our task before sunset.

B. We have completed our task before sunset.

C. We complete our task before sunset.

D. We had completed our task before sunset.

Q.9 Direction: Change the given sentence into an active or passive voice.

This shirt cannot be worn by me any longer.

A. I cannot wear this shirt any longer.

B. Wearing of this shirt any longer is not possible.

C. This shirt is too worn out any longer.

D. This worn out shirt cannot be worn any longer.

Q.10 'You must trust yourself' – Which one is a reflexive pronoun?

A. You   **B.** Must

C. Yourself   **D.** None of the above

Q.11 Which of the following is an indefinite pronoun?

A. Which   **B.** All   **C.** Mine   **D.** Whom

Q.12 Direction: Select the answer choice that identifies the noun in the sentence.

The works of many great poets have been placed on reserve.

A. Many   **B.** Great   **C.** Placed   **D.** Reserve

Q.13 Direction: Select the answer choice that identifies the noun in the sentence.

Mastering basic mathematics is an important goal for younger students.

A. Mastering   **B.** Important

C. Younger   **D.** Students

Q.14 Direction: Choose the appropriate meaning of the idiom:

Make up one's mind

A. To be prepared

B. To make someone happy

C. Make a decision

D. To criticize someone

Q.15 Direction: Choose the incorrect spelling from the words given below:

A. Brevity   **B.** Breakage

C. Breathless   **D.** Briliance

Q.16 Direction: Choose the incorrect spelling from the words given below:

A. Explaination   B. Exaggeration
C. Extermination   D. Expectation

Q.17 Direction: In the Question given below a statement consists of one/two blank. You have to choose the option which provides the correct word that fits in the blanks.

The government must now _______ its seriousness by moving away from the _______ policies of the past.

A.   ensconce, conscientious
B.   masquerade, equitable
C.   shelter, scrupulous
D.   demonstrate, flawed

Q.18 Direction: In the Question given below a statement consists of one/two blank. You have to choose the option which provides the correct word that fits in the blanks.

We are witnessing an industry that is_______ on poverty, mostly.

A. leading   B. superior   C. thriving   D. discord

Q.19 Choose the word or group of words that is most opposite in meaning to the word printed in bold.

Morbid

A. Healthy   B. Liberal
C. Progressive   D. Stale

Q.20 Choose the word or group of words that is most opposite in meaning to the word printed in bold.

Belittle

A. Expand   B. Prohibit   C. Inflate   D. Extol

Q.21 Choose the word or group of words that is most similar in meaning to the word printed in bold.

Garrulity

A. Credulity   B. Speciousness
C. Loquaciousness   D. None of these

Q.22 Direction: Choose the correct alternative which can be substituted for the given word/ sentence.

A person involving in an activity for pleasure and not money is called ___

A. Amateur   B. Follower
C. Altruist   D. Antiquarian

Q.23 Direction: Choose the correct alternative which can be substituted for the below given word/ sentence.

The life history of a person written by an author is called as

____

A. Autobiography   B. History
C. Bibliography   D. Biography

Q.24 Direction: In the following question, a sentence is divided into four parts you have to find out which part has an error and mark it as your answer.

Can you (1)/ repair my (2)/digital camera until (3)/ Wednesday (4).

A. (1)   B. (2)   C. (3)   D. (4)

Q.25 Direction: In the following question, a sentence is divided into four parts you have to find out which part has an error and mark it as your answer.

A free press is not (1)/ a privilege but the (2)/ organic necessity in (3)/ a free society. (4).

A. (1)   B. (2)   C. (3)   D. (4)

Analytical Abilities

Q.26 Direction: Find the next term in the series:

1, 4, 27, 256, ?

A. 625   B. 1024   C. 3125   D. 5625

Q.27 Direction: Find the missing term in the series:

A, D, ?, P. Y

A. G   B. H   C. I   D. J

Q.28 Directions: Study the following question carefully and choose the right answer:

1. Windows
2. Walls
3. Floor
4. Foundation
5. Roof
6. Room

A. 4, 1, 5, 6, 2, 3   B. 4, 2, 1, 5, 3, 6
C. 4, 3, 5, 6, 2, 1   D. 4, 5, 3, 2, 1, 6

Q.29 If you are facing north-east and move 10 m forward, turn left and move 7.5 m, then you are:

A.   north of your initial position
B.   south of you initial position
C.   12.5 m from the initial position
D.   Both A and C

Q.30 One day Ravi left home and cycled 10 km southwards, turned right and cycled 5 km and turned right and cycled 10 km and turned left and cycled 10 km. how many kilometers will he have to cycle to reach his home straight?

A. 10 km   B. 15 km   C. 20 km   D. 25 km

Ques (31-32):Directions: Read the following information carefully and answer the questions given beside.

Four friends – Ram, Laxman, Bharat and Shatrughan were having a conversation. They were expressing their thoughts in a coded language.

Ram says, "le po ki ba" when he wants to convey that "friends make life live". Laxman says, "te ki mo ba" when he wants to convey that "without friends life impossible". Bharat says, "lo mo se te" when he wants to convey that "without trouble gain impossible". Shatrughan says, "st ba po lo" when he wants to convey that "life make trouble joy".

Q.31 Which of the following is most probably the code for "life gives joy"?

A. st lo ba   B. ba fo st   C. le po st   D. ba fo go

Q.32 What is the code for "mission impossible"?

A. mo fi   B. te fi

C. fi se   **D.** Either A or B

Ques (33-34):Directions: Read the given information carefully and answer the questions given besides:

In a family of some persons, Sushant says that Manu is the daughter of my sister Rhea, who is the only daughter of Tahir. Arun is the child of Tahir and Ileana, who is the grandmother of Kiara. Roma is the mother of Trisha, who is the only sister of Kiara. Arun is unmarried.

Q.33 How is Arun related to Kiara?

A. Maternal Uncle   **B.** Maternal Aunt

C. Paternal Uncle   **D.** Paternal Aunt

Q.34 How is Kiara related to Tahir?

A. Dauther-in-law   **B.** Grand Daughter

C. Grand Son   **D.** Either option B or C

Q.35 Direction: Select the related word/letters/number from the given alternatives.

Chug : Train : : Bang : ?

A. House   **B.** Animal   **C.** Door   **D.** Man

Q.36 Direction: Select the related word/letters/number from the given alternatives.

HJIK : MONP : : PRQS : ?

A. UVWX   **B.** UWVX   **C.** UXWV   **D.** UWXV

Q.37 What will be the difference between the third last digit and fourth digit from the left end of the number '947823165' after arranging all its digits in ascending order?

A. 4   **B.** 5   **C.** 3   **D.** 7

Q.38 What will be the addition of the third digit from the right end and the fourth digit from the left end of the number '768395241' after arranging all its digits in descending order?

A. 8   **B.** 12

C. 17   **D.** None of these

Ques (39-41):Direction: Which number replaces the question mark?

Q.39

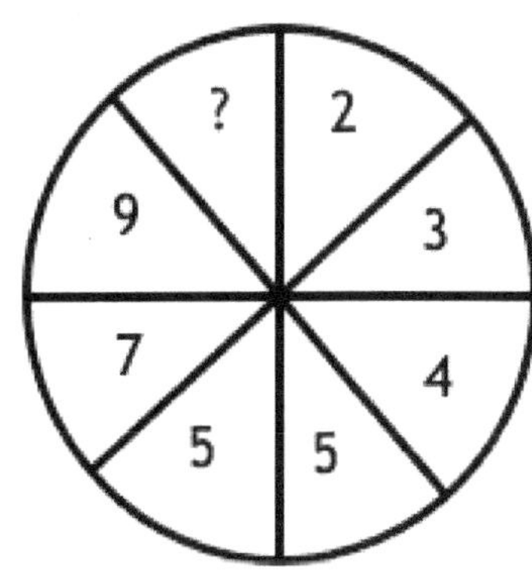

A. 1   **B.** 11   **C.** 14   **D.** 12

Q.40

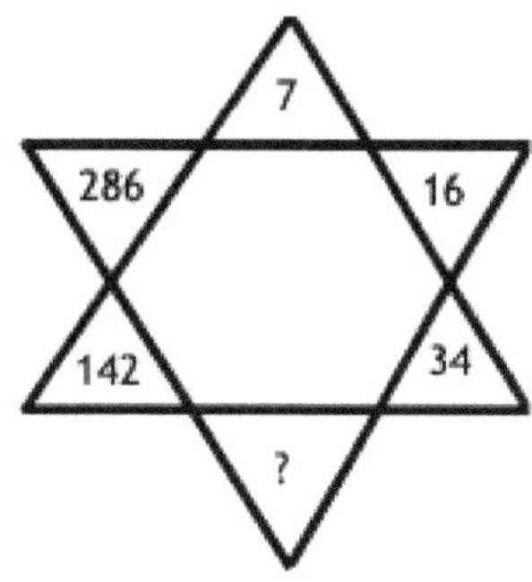

[NCERT National Talent Search Exam, 2020], [UPSSSC Forest Guard, 2015]

A. 70   **B.** 71   **C.** 17   **D.** 170

Q.41

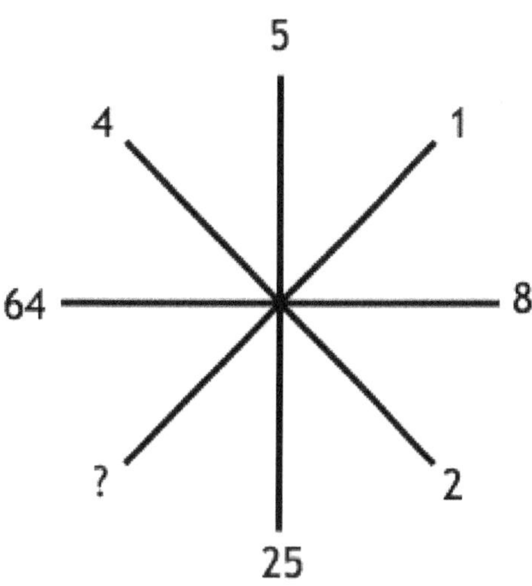

[UP Police Sub Inspector, 2021]

A. 1   **B.** 11   **C.** 2   **D.** 22

Ques (42-44):Direction: Statements are given below. Consider the given statements as true even if they seem to be not. After reading all the conclusions confirm which of the given conclusions logically follows, disregarding commonly known facts.

Q.42 Statements: Some actors are singers. All the singers are dancers.

Conclusions:

I. Some actors are dancers.

II. No singer is an actor.

A. Only (I) conclusion follows

B. Only (II) conclusion follows

C. Either (I) or (II) follows

D. Neither (I) nor (II) follows

Q.43 Statements:

I. No stain is steel.

II. Some steels are baskets.

Conclusions:

I. No stain is a basket.

II. Some baskets are not stains.

A. If only conclusion I follow

B. If only conclusion II follow

C. If either conclusion I or II follows

D. If Both conclusion I and II follow

Q.44 Statements:

I. Some bananas are flowers.

II. No flower is yellow.

Conclusions:

I. Some flowers are bananas.

II. No banana is yellow

A. If only conclusion I follow

B. If only conclusion II follow

C. If either conclusion I or II follow

D. If neither conclusion I nor II follow

Ques (45-48):Direction: Study the following figure and answer the questions given below.

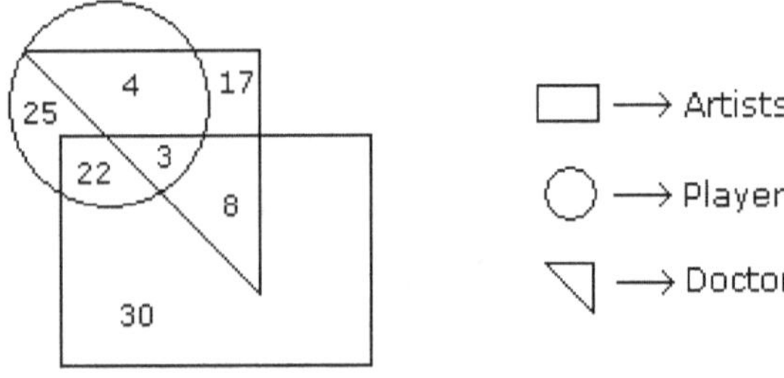

Q.45 How many doctors are neither artists nor players?

A. 17   **B.** 5   **C.** 10   **D.** 30

Q.46 How many doctors are both players and artists?

A. 22   **B.** 8   **C.** 3   **D.** 30

Q.47

How many artists are players?

A. 5   **B.** 8   **C.** 25   **D.** 16

Q.48

How many players are neither artists nor doctors?

A. 25   **B.** 17   **C.** 5   **D.** 10

Q.49 F is the brother of A, C is the daughter of A, K is the sister of F and G is the brother of C then who is the uncle of G?

A. F   **B.** K

C. C   **D.** None of these

Q.50 Sundar runs 20 m towards East and turns to the right and runs 10 m. Then he turns to the right and runs 9 m. Again he turns to the right and runs 5 m. After this, he turns to the left and runs 12 m and finally he turns to the right and 6 m. Now to which direction is Sundar facing?

A. East   **B.** West   **C.** North   **D.** South

Legal Awareness & Aptitude

Q.51 Writ of habeas corpus is a/an __________ ?

A. Constitutional remedy

B. Legislative remedy

C. Executive remedy

D. Quasi-judicial remedy

Q.52 Under the Constitution Protection and improvement of environment and safeguarding of forests and wildlife has been provided as a:

A. Fundamental Duty

B. Directive Principle

C. Fundamental Right

D. Duty of Environment Council of India

Q.53 Which important case led to the First Amendment of the Indian Constitution?

A. A.K Goplan v. State of Madras

B. Naiku v. State of Maharashtra

C. Jeevan Deep Singh v. State of Punjab

D. Champakam Dorairjan v. State of Madras

Q.54 Personation at an election is dealt with under:

A. Section 171 F of IPC

B. Section 172 F of IPC

C. Section 173 F of IPC

D. Section 174 F of IPC

Q.55 Bribery is dealt under:

A. Section 167E of IPC

B. Section 168E of IPC

C. Section 169E of IPC

D. Section 171E of IPC

Q.56 Public servant unlawfully engaging in trade is dealt under:

A. Section 166 of IPC   **B.** Section 167 of IPC

C. Section 168 of IPC   **D.** Section 169 of IPC

Q.57 Legal Principle: A contract to do an impossible act is void ab initio.

Facts of the Problem: Tarun enters into a contract with Karan to make his dead pet dog alive again through the use of magic. Karan agrees to pay him Rs. 20,000 for the act. Later, when Tarun tries to bring back the dog to life, Karan refuses to pay the money to him. Tarun sues Karan for damages due to non-payment of the agreed consideration by him. Decide the case?

A. The court would direct Karan to pay the agreed amount to Tarun.

B. The suit would fail as the contract was void ab initio.

C. The court would direct Karan to only pay compensation to Tarun for rescinding the contract.

D. The court would allow Tarun to perform his magic procedure to bring back the deade dog to life.

Q.58 Legal Principle: The notice for auction or sale of goods is only an invitation to offer, and not an offer in itself under the law of contract.

Facts of the Problem: Uday puts up an advertisement in front of his house for selling the house at the price of Rs. 50 lakhs. Saif sees that advertisement and goes to Uday with the money

to buy the house. Uday refuses to sell the house to Saif. Saif sues Uday for the breach of the contract. Decide?

A. Uday must sell his house to Saif at the advertised price.

B. Saif would be able to get damages from Uday for the breach of contract.

C. No legal remedy is available to Saif as the advertisement for the sale of the house was a mere invitation to offer.

D. The court could decide the right price for the sale of the house by Uday.

Q.59 Legal Principle: A contract enters into by the use of misrepresentation is voidable at the option of the other party.

Facts of the Problem: Lalit with an intention to deceive Rahul into buying his cement factory, falsely stated that his factory is capable of producing 2,000 kg of cement per day. However, in reality, the factory only has a production capacity of 500 kg/day. Rahul gets induced and agrees to buy the factory. Is it a valid contract?

A. The contract is a valid one and Rahul must buy the factory.

B. The contract is voidable at the option of Rahul due to misrepresentation by Lalit.

C. The contract is void due to false claims made by Lalit in relation to his factory.

D. The price of the contract could be reduced to commensurate with the reduced production capacity of the factory.

Q.60 Legal Principle: Any contract made for an unlawful consideration is void in law.

Facts of the Problem: Gagan enters into a contract with Nikhil to murder his wife, Preity for a sum of Rs. 5 lakhs. Gagan agrees to pay the amount to Nikhil in return of the murder. Is it a valid contract?

A. The contract is voidable at the option of Nikhil due to the risk involved in it.

B. The contract is void due to unlawful consideration.

C. The contract is valid and Nikhil must perform the act of murdering Preity.

D. The contract is uncertain as the manner of murdering Preity is not specified in it.

Q.61 In which case the 42nd Amendment Act was declared null and void by the Supreme Court?

A. Minerva mills vs Union of India

B. M.c Mehta vs Union of India

C. Kasturi vs the state of Rajasthan

D. Keshavnanda Bharati vs the State of Kerala

Q.62 Which case laid the guidelines for sexual harassment at the workplace?

A. Pooja vs state of M.P

B. Naz foundation vs state

C. Vishakha vs the state of Rajasthan

D. Subramanium swamy vs Union Of India

Q.63 In which of the following cases Section 66a of the IT act was struck down:

A. Shreya Singhal vs Union of India

B. Naz foundation vs NCT Delhi

C. Sneha Singhal vs Union of India

D. Lilavati vs the State of Maharashtra

Q.64 In which of the following cases Supreme court gave legal recognition to Third genders:

A. Yakub Abdul Razak Memon V State of Maharashtra

B. Sushil Ansal vs State Thr CBI

C. Novartis v Union of India & Others

D. National Legal Services Authority v Union of India

Q.65 Which case laid down the Basic structure doctrine?

A. Keshavnanada Bharati vs the State of Kerala

B. Adm Jabalpur vs union of India

C. S.b subbarao vs state of tamil nadu

D. Janaki das vs union of India

Q.66 What is meant by Consensus ad idem?

A. Disagreement of Minds

B. No contract between parties

C. Void agreement

D. The meeting of minds

Q.67 What is meant by Quid pro quo?

A. Nothing for nothing

B. Cheap bargain

C. Ilegal agreement

D. Something for something/ consideration

Q.68 What is Meant by Ubberrima fides?

A. Malafide Action

B. Wrongful confinement

C. Vicious injury

D. Utmost good faith

Q.69 What do you mean by Nudum Pactum?

A. Illegal object

B. The contract formed on alien barren land

C. A gratuitous or bare promise, devoid of any consideration

D. Malafide Practice

Q.70 What is meant by the doctrine of restitution?

A. Law doctrine gains based recovery

B. Law doctrine which bars recovery

C. Law doctrine which allows mercy petitions

D. Law doctrine based on death penalty

Q.71 "Iddat" is a period during which a Muslim woman is prohibited from marrying on the dissolution of marriage:

A. By Death of a husband

B. By Divorce

C. None of these

D. Both (A) and (B)

Q.72 Legal Principle: A contract with a minor would be void if the other party knew about the minority.

Facts of the Problem: Hitesh is a leading seller of computer hardware items in the city. He's sixteen years old son has Rohan as his best friend. Rohan is also of the same age. Hitesh knowing the age of Rohan entered into a contract with him for a set of laptops for a sum of Rs. 20 lakhs to him. When Hitesh sent the consignment of the laptops, Rohan refused to take them and dishonored the contract. Hitesh sues Rohan for the damages suffered by him. Decide the legal outcome of the situation?

A. Hitesh would be able to get compensation for the damages from Rohan.

B. Hitesh would not be able to get the damages but can force Rohan to buy the laptops from him.

C. Hitesh would not be able to get the damages as the contract is void.

D. The court could grant exemplary damages to Hitesh.

Q.73 Legal Principle: Nothing is an offense that is done by a person who is bound by law to do it.

Facts: 'A', a police officer, without a warrant, apprehends Rohan, who has committed murder and is running for cover.

Decide as a judge.

A. 'A' is not guilty of the offense of wrongful confinement.

B. 'A' cannot apprehend Rohan' without a warrant issued by a court of law.

C. 'A' is guilty of the offense of wrongful confinement.

D. 'A' may be guilty of the offense of wrongful restraint.

Q.74 Legal Principle: Nothing is an offense that is done by a child under seven years of age.

Facts: A, a child born on January 01, 2013, has killed another child 'B' on December 30, 2017.

Decide as a judge:

A. A has committed no offense

B. A has not committed the offense on the date of the killing of B

C. A has committed the offense as it is heinous crime

D. The killing of one child by another child is not an offense

Q.75 The Supreme Court of India formulated the doctrine of the eclipse in:

A. Bhikaji Narain Dhakras Vs State of M.P.

B. Bashesharnath Vs Income Tax Commissioner

C. State of W.B. Vs Anwar Ali Sarkar

D. Maneka Gandhi Vs Union of India

General Knowledge

Q.76 Which of the following term defined SONAR?

A. Sound Nautical Ranging

B. Sound Navigation and Ranging

C. Super Nautical Range

D. Sound Navigate Ray

Q.77 What is the name of India's first manned space flight?

A. Gaganyaan   **B.** Vayuyaan

C. Pushpakyaan   **D.** Gagan Viman

Q.78 Who decides the reasonableness of the restrictions placed on Fundamental rights in India?

A. Parliament   **B.** Courts

C. President   **D.** Prime minister

Q.79 It is not possible to obtain Indian citizenship by which of the following ways?

A. Naturalization

B. Birth

C. Depositing money in Indian Banks

D. Incorporation of new territory by India

Q.80 The President gives his resignation to the:

A. Chief Justice   **B.** Parliament

C. Vice President   **D.** Prime Minister

Q.81 Which of the following statements are correct regarding Union Public Service Commission?

A. Its recommendations are binding in nature

B. Its recommendations are advisory in nature

C. It is a non-government organization

D. None of these

Q.82 Who compiles and maintains the accounts of state governments?

A. State government

B. State Ministry of Finance

C. Union Cabinet

D. Comptroller and Auditor General of India

Q.83 What is the abbreviation of SSD disease, that was seen in the news?

A. Sandalwood Spike Disease

B. Sunflower Spike Disease

C. Shoe flower Straight Disease

D. Sweet potato Disease

Q.84 Duodenum, jejunum, and ileum are associated with which of the following?

A. Small intestine   **B.** Large intestine

C. Hypothalamus   **D.** Epididymis

Q.85 Which of the following geographical term related with a body of land surrounded by water on three sides?

A. Peninsula   **B.** Gulf

C. Strait   **D.** Island

Q.86 Which among the following cities of Madhya Pradesh is located on the banks of Shipra River?

A. Indore   **B.** Ujjain   **C.** Gwalior   **D.** Bhopal

Q.87 Which among the following dam is located across the Krishna river?

A. Mettur Dam

B. Dool Hasti Dam

C. Hirakud Dam

D. Nagarjuna Sagar Dam

Q.88 Which of the following regions of India is best suited to cotton cultivation?

A. Deccan Plateau   **B.** North East India

C. Indo-Gangetic Plain   **D.** East Coastal Plains

Q.89 Which among the following lakes are a part of the Great Lakes of North America?

1. Lake Erie

2. Lake Superior

3. Lake Michigan

4. Lake Ontario

5. Lake Winnipeg

Select the correct code from the options given below:

A. 2, 3 and 4   **B.** 2 and 4

C. 1, 2, 3, 4, and 5   **D.** 1, 2, 3, and 4

Q.90 Which Indian activist was presented with the prestigious Dan David Prize?

A. Gita Sen   **B.** Medha Patkar

C. Indira Jaising   **D.** Aruna Roy

Q.91 Unfair trade practices are included in:

A. FERA   **B.** FEMA

C. MRTP Act   **D.** Anti laundering act

Q.92 Unemployment occurs due to moving from one job to another job is known as:

A. Seasonal Unemployment

B. Frictional unemployment

C. Cyclical unemployment

D. Technical Unemployment

Q.93 Which is the first Urban Cooperative Bank (UCB), that is approved to convert into a Small Finance Bank?

A. Bharat Cooperative Bank

B. Shivalik Mercantile Cooperative Bank

C. Punjab And Maharashtra Cooperative Bank

D. Bombay Mercantile Cooperative Bank

Q.94 Which of the following industries is not a heavy industry?

A. Cotton textile   **B.** Cement

C. Iron and Steel   **D.** Ship building

Q.95 Which statement is correct for nominal GDP?

i. Nominal GDP is calculated based on current prices.

ii. Nominal GDP is calculated based on the base prices.

iii. Data on Nominal GDP shows an accurate picture of the economy as compared to real GDP.

A. Only ii and iii   **B.** only ii

C. only i   **D.** i and iii

Q.96 Which Ministry is responsible for calculating GDP in India?

A. Ministry of Finance

B. Ministry of Commerce and Industry

C. Ministry of Central Statistical and Program Implementation

D. Ministry of consumer Affairs

Q.97 What of the following taxes is applicable in the case of a supply of goods from Gujarat to Assam?

A. CGST   **B.** SGST   **C.** UTGST   **D.** IGST

Q.98 In the GST council meetings , the vote of the Central Government shall have a weightage of.

A. 1/3 of votes cast   **B.** 1/2 of votes cast

C. 2/3 of votes cast   **D.** None of these

Q.99 Which actress has won the "Best Actress in a Leading Role" Award at the 94th Oscars Awards 2022?

A. Nicole Kidman   **B.** Scarlett Johansson

C. Kristen Stewart   **D.** Jessica Chastain

Q.100 Which actor won best actor award at International Indian Film Academy (IIFA) Awards, 2022 ?

A. Varun Dhawan   **B.** Shahid Kapoor

C. Vicky Kaushal   **D.** Salman Khan

// Smart Answer Sheet //

Correct Percentage of students who answered correctly.   **Skipped** Percentage of students who skipped.

Q.	Ans.	Correct / Skipped
1	D	84.21 % / 12.73 %
2	A	81.88 % / 14.75 %
3	C	88.55 % / 10.01 %
4	B	83.42 % / 11.0 %
5	C	64.71 % / 32.67 %
6	B	83.81 % / 10.21 %
7	D	76.48 % / 20.3 %
8	D	84.77 % / 14.69 %
9	A	60.6 % / 35.27 %
10	C	49.1 % / 39.18 %
11	B	79.09 % / 13.64 %
12	D	86.89 % / 10.28 %
13	D	51.39 % / 39.08 %
14	C	85.23 % / 11.5 %
15	D	53.67 % / 46.09 %
16	A	81.59 % / 16.61 %
17	D	50.33 % / 36.84 %
18	C	42.62 % / 37.55 %
19	A	51.72 % / 38.59 %
20	D	61.69 % / 35.94 %
21	C	25.93 % / 70.12 %
22	A	50.28 % / 41.97 %
23	D	85.94 % / 11.01 %
24	C	49.73 % / 49.2 %
25	B	69.14 % / 30.37 %
26	C	63.65 % / 33.92 %
27	C	87.54 % / 11.62 %
28	B	46.51 % / 48.49 %
29	D	43.71 % / 54.9 %
30	B	68.06 % / 31.46 %
31	B	54.82 % / 44.46 %
32	D	20.42 % / 74.91 %
33	C	67.05 % / 30.87 %
34	D	40.87 % / 43.54 %
35	C	68.57 % / 30.8 %
36	B	42.96 % / 47.25 %
37	C	62.46 % / 34.05 %
38	D	45.32 % / 35.54 %
39	B	40.06 % / 30.75 %
40	A	46.23 % / 35.82 %
41	A	49.84 % / 35.57 %
42	A	62.25 % / 30.76 %
43	B	40.64 % / 48.51 %
44	A	66.28 % / 32.31 %
45	A	54.65 % / 44.69 %
46	C	61.39 % / 30.89 %
47	C	50.37 % / 46.23 %
48	A	57.72 % / 39.88 %
49	A	54.93 % / 34.54 %
50	C	51.04 % / 42.34 %
51	A	80.06 % / 10.22 %
52	B	49.26 % / 47.49 %
53	D	61.87 % / 31.86 %
54	A	27.28 % / 70.34 %
55	D	49.83 % / 31.11 %
56	C	49.86 % / 36.39 %
57	B	44.71 % / 34.8 %
58	C	44.51 % / 43.24 %
59	B	64.42 % / 30.41 %
60	B	40.66 % / 42.09 %
61	A	67.76 % / 30.39 %
62	C	45.96 % / 38.67 %
63	A	58.95 % / 32.13 %
64	D	65.53 % / 30.26 %
65	A	53.62 % / 33.5 %
66	D	57.79 % / 30.87 %
67	D	63.72 % / 30.74 %
68	D	52.56 % / 36.87 %
69	C	69.43 % / 30.48 %
70	A	49.82 % / 48.57 %
71	D	59.05 % / 31.08 %
72	C	58.06 % / 39.51 %
73	A	59.43 % / 37.1 %
74	A	69.67 % / 30.04 %
75	A	57.88 % / 35.62 %
76	B	79.35 % / 19.06 %
77	A	81.63 % / 17.58 %
78	B	44.18 % / 33.4 %
79	C	49.97 % / 48.42 %
80	C	85.94 % / 11.5 %

Q.	Ans.	Correct / Skipped
81	B	54.27 %
		42.83 %
82	D	66.17 %
		32.9 %
83	A	82.24 %
		11.78 %
84	A	85.38 %
		10.23 %

Q.	Ans.	Correct / Skipped
85	A	81.22 %
		15.55 %
86	B	85.61 %
		10.37 %
87	D	80.5 %
		15.44 %
88	A	83.95 %
		11.76 %

Q.	Ans.	Correct / Skipped
89	D	14.22 %
		73.32 %
90	A	85.15 %
		11.97 %
91	C	78.8 %
		18.01 %
92	B	87.25 %
		10.41 %

Q.	Ans.	Correct / Skipped
93	B	26.47 %
		72.43 %
94	A	76.84 %
		16.15 %
95	C	86.14 %
		10.61 %
96	C	81.79 %
		17.14 %

Q.	Ans.	Correct / Skipped
97	D	83.12 %
		15.33 %
98	A	86.88 %
		10.19 %
99	D	57.2 %
		30.56 %
100	C	83.45 %
		13.3 %

//Hints and Solutions//

1. According to the passage, young children have an internal drive to learn about their world and become industrious and productive individuals.
Hence, the correct option is (D).

2. According to the passage, "School-age children struggle with feelings of inferiority and incompetence when they compare themselves with their peers. If they don't fit in, they might feel insignificant."
Hence, the correct option is (A).

3. If we read the passage we can say that loving and accepting parents help children develop the confidence to create a future where they can thrive and feel good about themselves.
Hence, the correct option is (C).

4. According to the passage, children can engage in important play rituals like playing with dolls or cops and robbers which prepare them for adolescence and adulthood.
Hence, the correct option is (B).

5. The suitable preposition for the blanks is "over".

We use "over" for movement and position or talk about movement or position at a higher level than something else.
Hence, the correct option is (C).

6. The correct preposition for the blank will be "for:"

We use "for" with a period of time in the past, present or future.
Hence, the correct option is (B).

7. The correct prepostion for this question is "By".

By is used with a method of transport. LIke, by train, by car, by boat, by plane etc.
Hence, the correct option is (D).

8. The given sentence is in passive voice and it is in Past Perfect Tense.

To convert it into an active voice, we just remove been from the given sentence, and the object "our" will be changed into the subject "We".

Subject + had + third form of verb + Other agents

We had completed our task before sunset.
Hence, the correct option is (D).

9. Given sentence is in passive voice and Contains model verb.

Subject + Cannot + first form of verb + Other agents.

I cannot wear this shirt any longer.
Hence, the correct option is (A).

10. Reflexive pronouns are words like myself, yourself, himself, herself, itself, ourselves, yourselves and themselves. They refer back to a person or thing. We often use reflexive pronouns when the subject and the object of a verb are the same.
Hence, the correct option is (C).

11. An indefinite pronoun does not refer to any specific person, thing or amount. It is vague and "not definite". Some typical indefinite pronouns are- all, another, any, anybody, anyone, anything, each, everybody, everyone, everything, few, many, nobody, none, one, several, some, somebody, someone.
Hence, the correct option is (B).

12. In the given options "Reserve" is the only noun of the choices. "Many" and "Great" are adjectives modifying the noun poets. "Placed" is a verb.
Hence, the correct option is (D).

13. Students is a plural noun. "Mastering" is a gerund, i.e. a verb form functioning as a noun. "Important" is an adjective modifying the noun "goal". "Younger" is an adjective modifying the noun students.
Hence, the correct option is (D).

14. Make up one's mind means make a decision.

Example: She was not able to make up her mind in selecting a college.
Hence, the correct option is (C).

15. Correct Spelling of "Briliance" will be "Brilliance"

It means the quality or state of being brilliant, very bright, or intelligent.
Hence, the correct option is (D).

16. Correct Spelling of "Explaination" will be "Explanation".

It means the act or process of explaining or statement that makes something clear.
Hence, the correct option is (A).

17. The government must now demonstrate its seriousness by moving away from the flawed policies of the past.

Demonstrate - give a practical exhibition and explanation of (how a machine, skill, or craftworks or is performed).

Flawed - having or characterized by a fundamental weakness or imperfection.
Hence, the correct option is (D).

18. We are witnessing an industry that is thriving on poverty, mostly.

Thriving means prosperous and growing, flourishing.
Hence, the correct option is (C).

19. Morbid means showing interest in unpleasant things, for example, disease and death.

Healthy means showing good health

Liberal means accepting different opinions or kinds of behavior

Progressive means using modern methods and ideas

Stale means old and not fresh anymore

Hence, the correct option is (A).

20. Belittle means to make somebody or the things he/she does, seem unimportant or not very good.

Extol means praise enthusiastically

Expand means to become or to make something bigger

Prohibit means to say that something is not allowed by law

Inflate means to fill something with air

Hence, the correct option is (D).

21. Garrulity means use of too many words to express an idea.

Loquaciousness means talkativeness, garrulousness, gift of the gab, long tongue etc.

Credulity means a tendency to be too ready to believe that something is real or true.

Speciousness means having a false look of truth or genuineness.
Hence, the correct option is (C).

22. Amateur - A person involving in an activity for pleasure and not money

Follower – Believer, supporter, etc.

Altruist - A person unselfishly concerned for or devoted to the welfare of others

Antiquarian – Person interested in antiquities (ancient objects).

Hence, the correct option is (A).

23. The life history of a person written by an author is called Biography

Autobiography - The life history of a person written by himself is called an Autobiography

History - Study of past events

Bibliography - List of all of the sources used in research work
Hence, the correct option is (D).

24. Replace 'until' with 'by'.

The correct sentence should be:

Can you repair my digital camera by Wednesday?
Hence, the correct option is (C).

25. Replace 'the' with 'an' in part 2.

The correct sentence should be:

A free press is not a privilege but an organic necessity in a free society.
Hence, the correct option is (B).

26. $1^1 = 1$

$2^2 = 4$

$3^3 = 27$

$4^4 = 256$

$5^5 = 3125$
Hence, the correct option is (C).

27. These alphabets are first, fourth, ninth, sixteenth, and twenty-fifth terms of alphabets which are squares of all the natural numbers.
Hence, the correct option is (C).

28. Correct Sequence will be:

4. Foundation

2. Walls

1. Windows

5. Roof

3. Floor

6. Room
Hence, the correct option is (B).

29.

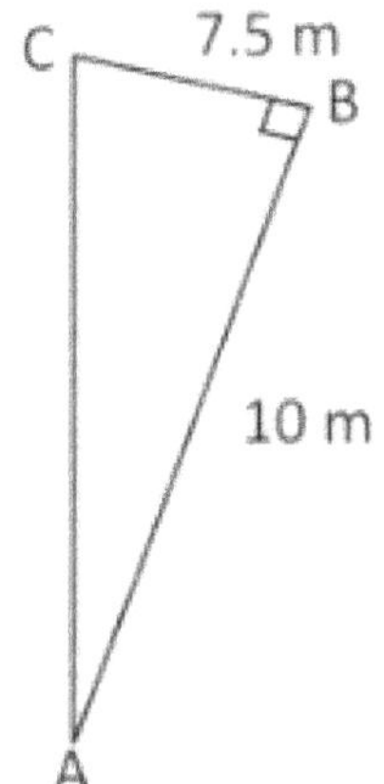

Clearly, the narrator starts from A, moves towards north-east a distance of $10\ m$ up to B, turns left (90 degree anti-clockwise) and moves 7.5 m up to C. Clearly, C lies to the north of A. Also, $\triangle ABC$ is right-angled at B. So,

$$AC^2 = AB^2 + BC^2 = (10)^2 + (7.5)^2$$

$$= 100 + 56.25 = 156.25$$

$$AC = \sqrt{(156.25)}m = 12.5\ m$$

Thus the narrator is $12.5\ m$ to the north of his initial position.
Hence, the correct option is (D).

30.

According to diagram, to reach his home straight way he has to make a distance of AE.

AE = AD + DE and AD = BC = 5

= AD + DE

= (5 + 10) km

= 15 km
Hence, the correct option is (B).

31.

Word	Code
life	ba
friends	ki
make	po
live	le
trouble	lo
gain	se
joy	st
without	mo/te
impossible	te/mo

From the following explanation, the code for 'life gives joy' is most probably coded as "ba fo st". Though the code of 'gives' is not given but checking the other options we can observe that 'gives' can be coded as 'fo'.
Hence, the correct option is (B).

32.

Word	Code
life	ba
friends	ki
make	po
live	le
trouble	lo
gain	se
joy	st
without	mo/te
impossible	te/mo

From the following explanation, the code for 'life gives joy' is most probably coded as "ba fo st". Though the code of 'gives' is not given but checking the other options we can observe that 'gives' can be coded as 'fo'.
Hence, the correct option is (D).

33.

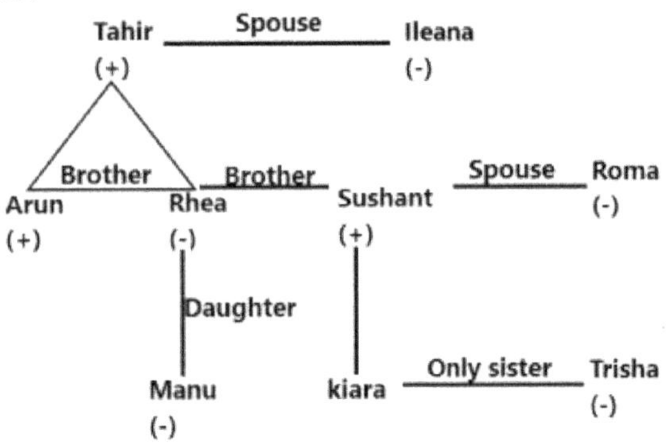

From the above image, it is clear that Arun is the maternal uncle of Kiara.
Hence, the correct option is (C).

34.

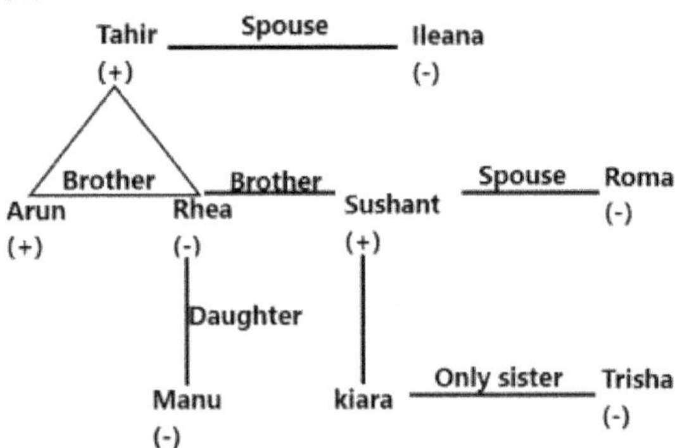

Kiara's gender is not known and therefore Kiara could be either the granddaughter or grandson of Tahir.
Hence, the correct option is (D).

35. "Chug" is the sound of "train". Same as "Bang" is the sound of "door."
Hence, the correct option is (C).

36.

$$H \quad J \quad I \quad K$$
$$+5\downarrow \quad +5\downarrow \quad +5\downarrow \quad +5\downarrow$$
$$M \quad O \quad N \quad P$$

SImilarly,

$$P \quad R \quad Q \quad S$$
$$+5\downarrow \quad +5\downarrow \quad +5\downarrow \quad +5\downarrow$$
$$U \quad W \quad V \quad X$$

Hence, the correct option is (B).

37. The given number:

947823165

After arranging all the digits of the given number in ascending order, we have:

123456789

The third last digit = 7

The fourth digit from the left end = 4

The difference between the third last digit and fourth digit from the left end = 7 − 4 = 3
Hence, the correct option is (C).

38. The given number:

7 6 8 3 9 5 2 4 1

After arranging all its digits in descending order, we get:

9 8 7 6 5 4 3 2 1

Now,

The third digit from the right end = 3

The fourth digit from the left end = 6

Now,

Addition of the third digit from the right end and the fourth digit from the left end = 3 + 6 = 9
Hence, the correct option is (D).

39. The numbers in the right half from the series:

2, 3, 4, 5

The numbers in the left half from the series:

5, 7, 9, 11
Hence, the correct option is (B).

40. 7 × 2 + 2 = 16;

16 × 2 + 2 = 34 and so on,

So, missing number

= 34 × 2 + 2

= 70
Hence, the correct option is (A).

41. The two ends of each line segment contain a number and its square.

So answer is = 1^2 = 1.
Hence, the correct option is (A).

42.

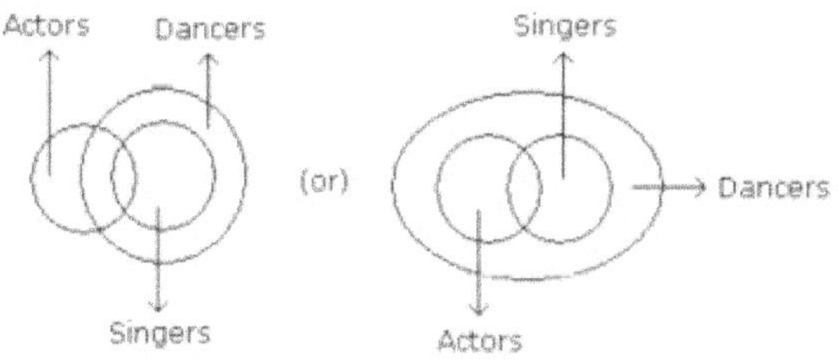

Hence, the correct option is (A).

43. According to the given statements, we can draw the following diagram:-

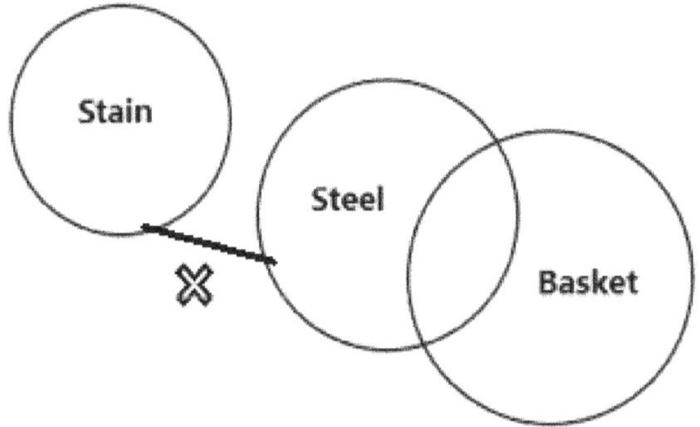

Now conclusion:

I. No stain is a basket, not follows because nothing has been said about this.

II. Some baskets are not stains, baskets that are steel can never be stained so conclusion II follows.

Hence, the correct option is (B).

44. Conclusion I is the immediate inference drawn from the first statement. For mediate inference, I + E = O. Therefore, from the pair of statements, the conclusion "some banana are not yellow" is valid. But this is not our conclusion.
Hence, the correct option is (A).

45. The number of doctors who are neither artists nor players is 17.
Hence, the correct option is (A).

46. The number of doctors who are both players and artists is 3.
Hence, the correct option is (C).

47. The number of artists who are players is,

= 22 + 3

= 25
Hence, the correct option is (C).

48. The number of players who are neither artists nor doctors is 25.
Hence, the correct option is (A).

49.

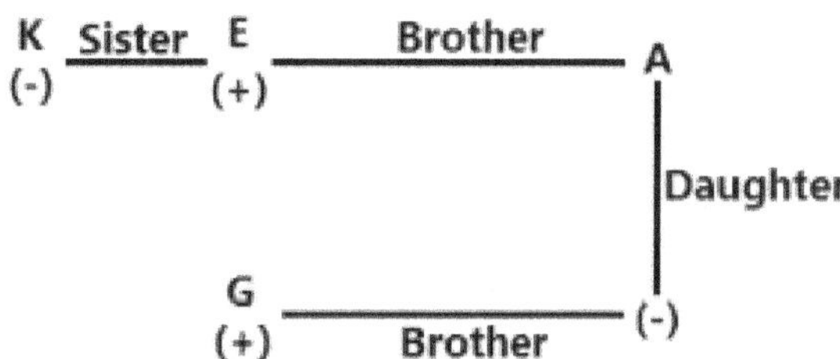

Hence, the correct option is (A).

50.

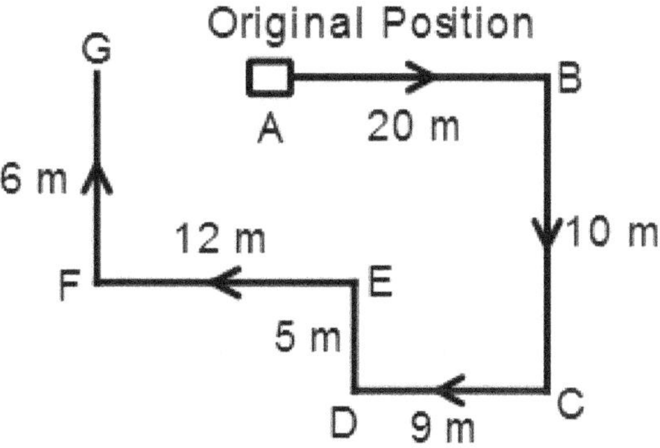

Therefore, it is clear that Sundar will face towards North.
Hence, the correct option is (C).

51. Habeas corpus writ is called "Bulwark or Barrier of Individual Liberty against Arbitrary Detention". A general rule of filing the petition is that - A person whose right has been infringed must

file a petition. But Habeas corpus is an exception and anybody on behalf of the detainee can file a petition. Habeas corpus writ is applicable to preventive detention also. This writ can be issued against both public authorities as well as individuals.
Hence, the correct option is (A).

52. Article 48(A), Protection and improvement of environment and safeguarding of forests and wildlife. "State shall endeavour to protect and improve the environment and to safeguard the forests and wildlife of the country." Article 48A was added by the Constitution (42nd Amendment) Act, 1976.
Hence, the correct option is (B).

53. State of Madras v. Champakam Dorairajan is a landmark decision of the Supreme Court of India. This judgement led to the First Amendment of the Constitution of India. It was the first major judgement regarding reservations in the Republic of India. In its ruling, the Supreme Court upheld the Madras High Court judgement, which in turn had struck down the Government Order (G.O) passed in 1927 in the [Madras Presidency]. The G.O had provided caste-based reservation in government jobs and college seats. The Supreme Court's verdict held that providing such reservations was in violation of Article 29 (2) of the Indian Constitution.
Hence, the correct option is (D).

54. Section 171 F of IPC- Punishment for undue influence or personation at an election. Whoever commits the offense of undue influence or personation at an election shall be punished with imprisonment of either description for a term which may extend to one year or with fine, or with both.
Hence, the correct option is (A).

55. Section 171E in The Indian Penal Code dealt with "Bribery".

According to 171E - Punishment for bribery—Whoever commits the offence of bribery shall be punished with imprisonment of either description for a term which may extend to one year, or with fine, or with both: Provided that bribery by treating shall be punished with fine only. Explanation.—"Treating" means that form of bribery where the gratification consists in food, drink, entertainment, or provision.
Hence, the correct option is (D).

56. Section 168 of Indian penal code - Public servant unlawfully engaging in trade. —Whoever, being a public servant, and being legally bound as such public servant not to engage in trade, engages in trade, shall be punished with simple imprisonment for a term which may extend to one year, or with fine, or with both.
Hence, the correct option is (C).

57. In the present case, the contract was to bring back a dead dog to life which is an impossible act. As the law says that a contract to do an impossible act is void ab initio; so, the contract between Tarun and Karan was void in law. Thus, Tarun's action of suing Karan for a void contract would fail in the court.
Hence, the correct option is (B).

58. In the instant case, the advertisement for the sale of the house by Udau was not an offer to the contract. It was merely an invitation to sell. The legal position is that the notice for auction or sale of goods is only an invitation to offer, and not an offer in itself under the law of contract. Thus, no contract is made between Saif and Uday for the sale of the house, and

consequently, no question of awarding any damages for the breach of the contract arises.
Hence, the correct option is (C).

59. In the instant situation, Lalit has misrepresented the production capacity of the cement factory to induce Rahul into buying the factory. Thus, the contract is voidable at the option of Rahul due to misrepresentation of Lalit. Section 18 of the Indian Contract Act, 1872 deals with it.
Hence, the correct option is (B).

60. In the present case, the contract is void as the consideration of the same i.e. murdering of Preity is unlawful. No obligations arise out of a void contract. Section 24 of The Indian Contract Act, 1872 states that a contract whose object or consideration is unlawful is void.
Hence, the correct option is (B).

61. The 42nd Amendment of the Constitution of India, officially known as The Constitution (Forty-second Amendment) Act, 1976, was enacted during the Emergency (25 June 1975 – 21 March 1977) by the Indian National Congress government headed by Indira Gandhi. This amendment brought about the most widespread changes to the Constitution in its history and is sometimes called a "mini-Constitution" or the Constitution of Indira. The radical changes brought in by Indira Gandhi were neutralized by holding them unconstitutional in Minerva Mills's judgment.
Hence, the correct option is (A).

62. Vishakha and others v State of Rajasthan was a 1997 Indian Supreme Court case where Vishakha and other women groups filed Public Interest Litigation (PIL) against State of Rajasthan and Union of India to enforce the fundamental rights of working women under Articles 14, 19, and 21 of the Constitution of India. Justice J.S Verma was also a member of the bench who laid out the guidelines in this case. Later after the Nirbhaya case in 2013, Justice Verma Committee was constituted to recommend amendments to the Criminal Law so as to provide for quicker trial and enhanced punishment for criminals accused of committing sexual assault against women. The Committee submitted its report on January 23, 2013.
Hence, the correct option is (C).

63. Supreme Court in a landmark judgment struck down section 66A of the Information Technology Act, 2000 which provided provisions for the arrest of those who posted allegedly offensive content on the internet upholding freedom of expression. Section 66A defines the punishment for sending "offensive" messages through a computer or any other communication device like a mobile phone or tablet and a conviction of it can fetch a maximum three years of jail and a fine.
Hence, the correct option is (A).

64. The Supreme Court, in National Legal Service Authority v. Union of India ("NALSA"), has given legal recognition to the transgender community by mandating that they be treated as the third gender, thereby doing away with the binary understanding of gender.
Hence, the correct option is (D).

65. The case of Kesavananda Bharati v. the State of Kerala is perhaps the most well-known constitutional decision of the

Supreme Court of India. While ruling that there is no implied limitation on the powers of Parliament to amend the Constitution, it held that no amendment can do violence to its basic structure (the "Basic Structure Doctrine"). Further, it established the Supreme Court's right of review and, therefore, established its supremacy on constitutional matters.
Hence, the correct option is (A).

66. There must be a meeting of the minds of both parties on the same subject for a valid contract.

EXAMPLE 1 - X contracts with B to sell his White house. B sends his acceptance for the same horse. A valid Contract is made.

EXAMPLE 2- X contracts with B to sell his White Horse. B sends his acceptance.
Hence, the correct option is (D).

67. Quid pro quo in Latin stands for "something for something," and is used to describe when two parties engage in a mutual agreement to exchange goods or services. In a quid pro quo agreement, one transfer is contingent upon a reciprocal transfer. As a term, quid pro quo is used similarly in business and legal contexts to convey that a good or service has been exchanged for something of equal value.
Hence, the correct option is (D).

68. Utmost good faith.

It is the name of a legal doctrine that governs insurance contracts. This means that all parties to an insurance contract must deal in good faith, making a full declaration of all material facts in the insurance proposal. This contrasts with the legal doctrine caveat emptor ("let the buyer beware").
Hence, the correct option is (D).

69. A gratuitous or bare promise, devoid of any consideration.

A nudum pactum in Latin literally means 'Bare or Naked Promise.' In common law, it refers to a promise that is not legally enforceable for want of consideration. An example of a nudum pactum would be an offer to sell something without a corresponding offer of value in exchange. While the offer may bind a person morally, since the offer has not been created with any consideration, it is gratuitous and treated as a unilateral contract. The offer is therefore revocable at any time by the offeror before acceptance by the offeree.
Hence, the correct option is (C).

70. The law of restitution is the law of gains-based recovery. It is to be contrasted with the law of compensation, which is the law of loss-based recovery. When a court orders restitution it orders the defendant to give up his/her gains to the claimant. If a minor has unjustly enriched himself equity demands that such property or goods be restored by a minor.

Example- X a minor makes a contract with D to sell his house and pays him 50000 rupees. The contract is held as void ab into by the court and the house is returned to X. X must return the Consideration for the house i.e. 50k back to D.
Hence, the correct option is (A).

71. In Islam, iddah or iddat is the period a woman must observe after the death of her husband or after a divorce, during which she may not marry another man.

Iddat is the period in which a Muslim woman has to observe after the dissolution of marriage. In this period a woman has to remain in seclusion and is abstain from marrying another person or, it can be also be said that during this period woman is prohibited from marrying again after the dissolution of her first marriage.
Hence, the correct option is (D).

72. In the present case, Hitesh entered into a contract with Rohan despite knowing that Rohan was a minor at the time of entering into the contract. Hitesh would not be able to get the required damages as the fact that Rohan is a minor, renders the contract void. Thus, not damages could be attained from a contract that is void ab initio.
Hence, the correct option is (C).

73. As a general rule, the police cannot arrest an accused without a warrant. However, there are certain exceptional circumstances enumerated in Law under which a policy can make an arrest without a warrant. Section 41 of the Code of Criminal Procedure envisages the circumstances under which an arrest can be made without a warrant. The section states that when any person is actually concerned or reasonably suspected to be concerned in a cognizable offense.
Hence, the correct option is (A).

74. A has committed no offense. According to section 82 of the IPC, a child below 7 years of age gets a complete defense from any kind of criminal liability. The reason for this is the principle of 'doli incapax', a child below the age of 7 cannot be held guilty for any offence because of the assumption that he cannot draw a distinction between 'right' and 'wrong'. It works under the assumption that a child below 7 lacks the ability to understand the nature and consequences of his act and therefore cannot form the required mens rea. This is a complete defense and cannot be taken away in any circumstances. No sort of evidence to prove that the child could understand the nature or consequences of his act will act as a rebuttal.

Hence, the correct option is (A).

75. The Apex Court for solving such problems formulated the doctrine of the eclipse in the landmark case of Bhikhaji v. State of M.P., AIR 1955 S.C. 781.

The case of the petitioners was that the passing of the Constitution and the grant of fundamental rights rendered the Act void under Art. 13(1) being inconsistent with the provisions of Arts. 19(1)(g) and 31(2), and reliance was placed on the decision.
Hence, the correct option is (A).

76. SONAR is defined as (Sound Navigation and Ranging) it is a technique that uses Sound Propagation (usually underwater, as in submarine navigation)(Basically used by the Indian Navy) to Navigate, communicate or Detect objects on or under the surface of the water, such as other vessels, submarine, etc.

There are two types of technology using by "SONAR" they are as follows

- Passive Sonar is essential to help to listen for the sound made by Vessels.

- Active Sonar helps to detect the emitting pulses of sounds and listening for Echoes.

Hence, the correct option is (B).

77. ISRO's Gaganyaan mission is India's maiden manned space mission.

Gaganyaan is an Indian crewed orbital spacecraft that will serve as the foundation for the country's human spaceflight programme. The spaceship will be able to carry three people, and an updated version will be able to rendezvous and dock with other spacecraft.

Hence, the correct option is (A).

78. Fundamental Rights guaranteed by the Constitution are not absolute and certain restrictions can be imposed by the state according to the procedure established by law. However, these restrictions must be reasonable and not arbitrary. The reasonableness of the restrictions is decided by courts.
Hence, the correct option is (B).

79. According to the Indian Citizenship Act 1955, the citizenship of India may be acquired only by the means of the following five methods: (1) by birth, (2) descent, (3) registration, (4) naturalization, (5) incorporation of territory.
Hence, the correct option is (C).

80. The President holds office for a term of 5 years from the date on which he enters upon his office. However, he can also resign from his office at any time by addressing the resignation letter to the Vice President.
Hence, the correct option is (C).

81. The role of the Union Public Service Commission is not only limited but also recommendations made by it are only of advisory nature and hence, not binding on the government of India.
Hence, the correct option is (B).

82. The Comptroller and Auditor Genera of India (CAG) compiles and maintains the accounts of state governments. He also acts as a guide, friend and philosopher of the Public Accounts Committee of the Parliament of India.
Hence, the correct option is (D).

83. As per a study conducted by the Bengaluru-based Institute of Wood Science & Technology (IWST), the Sandalwood Spike Disease (SSD) has returned.

The sandalwood trees of the country, especially of Karnataka, are heavily infected with SSD and facing a great threat. At present, there is no option but to cut down and remove the infected tree, to prevent the spread of the disease.
Hence, the correct option is (A).

84. The primary function of the small intestine is the absorption of nutrients and minerals from food. The small intestine has three distinct regions the duodenum, jejunum and ileum. The duodenum receives bile and pancreatic juice through the pancreatic duct. The jejunum is the midsection of the small intestine, connecting the duodenum to the ileum.
Hence, the correct option is (A).

85. A peninsula is a landform surrounded by water on most of its border while being connected to a mainland from which it extends. The surrounding water is usually understood to be continuous, though not necessarily named as a single body of water. Peninsulas are not always named as such; one can also be referred to as a headland, cape, island promontory, bill, point,

fork, or spit.
Hence, the correct option is (A).

86. Shipra River raises in the kakri bardi hills Vindhya Range north of Dhar district and flows north across the Malwa Plateau to join the Chambal River. It is a sacred river to Hindus. Also, the holy city of Ujjain is situated on its right bank where after every 12 years, the Kumbh Mela festival takes place.
Hence, the correct option is (B).

87. Nagarjuna Sagar Dam is located across the Krishna river. It is located in the state of Telangana. The height of the dam is 124 meters.
Hence, the correct option is (D).

88. Black soil is considered best for cotton cultivation. Black soil is mainly found in Deccan Plateau. So, most of the cotton cultivation is confined to this region, however, cotton also grows well in alluvial soils of the Satluj-Ganga plain and red and laterite soils of the peninsular region. About 70% of total cotton is produced in Gujarat, Maharashtra and Andhra Pradesh.
Hence, the correct option is (A).

89. The Great Lakes are a series of interconnected freshwater lakes in North America. The Great Lakes include:

Lake Superior, Lake Michigan, Lake Huron, Lake Erie, Lake Ontario
Hence, the correct option is (D).

90. India's renowned feminist scholar and activist Gita Sen has won the prestigious Dan David Prize, which annually awards three prizes of $ 1 million to inspiring individuals and organizations across the world.

The Dan David Foundation is headquartered at Tel Aviv University, Israel. Gita Sen is also the Director of the Public Health Foundation of India. She has worked hard in the fields of women's rights, reproductive and sexual health and poverty eradication.
Hence, the correct option is (A).

91. Monopolies and restrictive trade practices act (MRTP), 1969 was enacted to prevent the concentration of economic power to common detriment, control of monopolies, and prohibition of monopolistic and restrictive trade practices (MRTP) and matters connected therewith.
Hence, the correct option is (C).

92. Frictional unemployment is a type of unemployment that arises when workers are searching for new jobs or are transitioning from one job to another. It is part of natural unemployment and hence is present even when the economy is considered at full employment.
Hence, the correct option is (B).

93. The Reserve Bank of India has granted 'in-principle' approval to Shivalik Mercantile Cooperative Bank, to convert into a Small Finance Bank (SFB). It is the first Urban Cooperative Bank (UCB) to be granted such permission after the announcement of RBI, about voluntary conversion of UCBs into Small Finance Banks.
Hence, the correct option is (B).

94. Heavy industry is an industry that involves one or more characteristics such as large and heavy products, large and heavy

equipment and facilities or numerous processes. Some examples are-

Aerospace, Shipbuilding, Mining, Machine tool building, Locomotive manufacturing, Oil and gas, Steel production, Chemical production, etc.
Hence, the correct option is (A).

95. Nominal GDP is calculated on the basis of current prices. While real GDP is calculated on the base year prices and its data are more reliable or accurate as compared to Nominal GDP.
Hence, the correct option is (C).

96. The work of computing the GDP is done by the Central Statistical Organization (CSO) which is under the Ministry of Statistical and Program Implementation.
Hence, the correct option is (C).

97. Under GST, IGST is a tax levied on all Inter-State supplies of goods and/or services and will be governed by the IGST Act. IGST will be applicable on any supply of goods and/or services in both cases of import into India and export from India.
Hence, the correct option is (D).

98. The vote of the central government has a weightage of one-third of the total votes cast, and the votes of all the state governments taken together have a weightage of two-thirds of the total votes cast in that meeting.
Hence, the correct option is (A).

99. Jessica Chastain has won the "Best Actress in a Leading Role" Award at the 94th Oscars Awards 2022.

Jessica Chastain portrayed the role of Tammy Faye Bakker in the film The Eyes of Tammy Faye.

Hence, the correct option is (D).

100. Vicky Kaushal has won the best actor award for his movie Sardar Udham at the 22nd International Indian Film Academy Awards in Abu Dhabi, United Arab Emirates.

The International Indian Film Academy Awards, popularly known as IIFA, was held in Abu Dhabi during the first weekend of June.

Hence, the correct option is (C).

English Language & Comprehension

Q.1 Direction: In the following sentence a word in bold is given which is to be corrected.

There are not many men who are so famous that they are frequently referred to by their **short names** only.

A. initials
B. signatures
C. pictures
D. middle name

Q.2 Following is a set of four sentences. Choose the sentence which is most appropriate – grammatically, semantically & logically.

A. Sorry to keep you. How long are you waiting?
B. My apologies for delaying. How long have you been waiting?
C. Sorry to keep you. How long have you been waiting?
D. Sorry for the delay. Since how long are you waiting?

Q.3 Direction: Replace with appropriate word from the options to make it a meaningful sentence.

Sachin Tendulkar is an _imminent_ player.

A. Eminent
B. Iminent
C. Emminent
D. None of these

Q.4 Direction: Choose the word that can substitute the given sentence.

One who study the elections and trends in voting

A. Anthropologist
B. Psephologist
C. Plagiarist
D. Philologist

Q.5 Direction: Choose the word that can substitute the given sentence.

Someone who walks in sleep

A. Arsonist
B. Amateur
C. Somnambulist
D. Somniloquist

Q.6 Select the word with correct spelling:

A. Benefited
B. Benefitted
C. Benifitted
D. Benifited

Q.7

Find the mis-spelt word:

A. Annex
B. Aniversary
C. Animate
D. Animosity

Q.8 Direction: Select the correct active form of the given sentence.

The business may not have been developed by him.

A. He may not have been developed the business.
B. He might not have developed the business.
C. He may not have developed the business.
D. He may not develop the business.

Q.9 Direction: Select the correct passive form of the given sentence.

The frog made the nightingale practice day in and day out.

A. The nightingale is made to practice day in and day out by the frog.
B. The nightingale did made to practise day in and day out by the frog.
C. The nightingale was made to practise day in and day out by the frog.
D. The nightingale was made to practise by the frog day in and day out.

Q.10 Direction: From the four alternatives given below, choose the correct meaning of the idioms and phrases.

Call a spade a spade.

A. To be hypocritical
B. To lie
C. To snitch
D. To be frank

Q.11 Direction: From the four alternatives given below, choose the correct meaning of the idioms and phrases.

To bury the hatchet

A. To put aside differences
B. To put away a weapon
C. To bury a weapon
D. To hide something

Q.12 Select the most appropriate synonym of the given word.

Confinement

A. Dismal
B. Indicate
C. Declaim
D. Enclosure

Q.13 Select the most appropriate synonym of the given word:

Characteristic

A. Particular
B. Common
C. Usual
D. Ordinary

Q.14 Select the most appropriate ANTONYM of the given word.

OUTSPOKEN

A. Ambivalent
B. Candid
C. Equivocal
D. Secretive

Q.15 Select the most appropriate ANTONYM of the given word.

CONVENIENCE

A. Enjoyment
B. Assistance
C. Hindrance
D. Satisfaction

Q.16 Select the most appropriate word to fill in the blank.

The police used tear gas to ________ the crowd.

A. attack **B.** disburse **C.** collect **D.** disperse

Q.17 Select the most appropriate word to fill in the blank.

Ritu is an ______ reader. I always find her with a book.

A. irritated   B. avid
C. inattentive   D. erratic

Q.18 Choose the correct part of speech for the underlined word.

The coefficients decrease rapidly at first, but then decrease <u>slowly</u>.

A. Noun   B. Adverb
C. Adjective   D. Pronoun

Q.19 Choose the correct part of speech for the underlined word.

Be careful with that knife or you'll cut <u>yourself</u>.

A. Possessive Pronoun   B. Relative Pronoun
C. Reflexive Pronoun   D. Personal Pronoun

Q.20 Choose the correct part of speech for the underlined word.

He came in with four shopping bags and dumped them on the <u>table</u>.

A. Adjective   B. Noun
C. Adverb   D. Preposition

Q.21 Choose the correct part of speech for the underlined word.

Thieves <u>broke into</u> our office downtown and stole the computers.

A. Noun   B. Preposition
C. Verb   D. Pronoun

Q.22 Fill in the appropriate Adjective.

The brides were much _______ than the grooms.

A. young   B. younger   C. youngest   D. None

Ques (23-25):Direction: Read the passage carefully and answer the question that follow

It is notable that power major NTPC has joined hands with oil giant IOC to set up a series of electric vehicle (EV) charging stations in cities and along highways. There is much potential for India to emerge as a leader in small and public EVs, given high latent demand. The benefits in reducing demand for imported crude oil can be huge, apart from reducing carbon emissions and other air pollutants.

The most effective way to bring down carbon emissions and pollution from transport is to vastly expand and improve public transport — buses are just 2% of the vehicles on the road. That said, there is much scope to replace India's giant fleet of two-wheelers with electric bikes. India has over 170 million two-wheelers, and sales data from the last six years show that 79% of on-road vehicles here are two-wheelers. It would make perfect sense to boost the supply of EVs, especially two-wheelers, e-rickshaws, tempos and small cars, so as to complement and supplement public transport going forward.

Estimates suggest that by meeting a rising part of the incremental demand for mobility, EVs can lead to macroeconomic benefits, and sooner rather than later.

Assuming only about half a litre of petrol consumption per two-wheeler daily, or about 200 litres annually, the volumes would add up to over 30 billion litres. And the bill for which, at current prices, would amount to well over Rs 2 lakh crore.

In tandem, we need power reforms to rev up utility realisations and strengthen the grid. India also has an opportunity in supplying on-board electric batteries. Swapping services to provide charged batteries on the lease would step-up the diffusion of EVs. A power-electronics industry ecosystem would raise production and provide high-efficiency subsystems for EVs. India must not miss the bus on EVs.

Q.23 "There is much potential for India to emerge as a leader in small and public EVs, given high latent demand." What can be logically deducted from the given sentence?

I. Electric vehicles are less in developed countries as compared to India.

II. India has not yet adopted electric vehicles fully.

III. Indians are already demanding a huge number of electric vehicles.

A. Only III   B. Only II
C. Only I and III   D. All of I, II and III

Q.24 Which of the following is/are true with respect to the two-wheelers in India?

I. India has over 160 million two-wheelers.

II. 79% of on-road vehicles in India are two-wheelers.

III. People prefer two-wheelers to four-wheelers due to ease of use.

A. Only I   B. Only II
C. Only I and II   D. Only I and III

Q.25 What is the tone of the passage?

A. Sarcastic   B. Caustic
C. Cynical   D. Laudatory

Analytical Abilities

Q.26 Direction: According to the relation given complete the following series.

DEF, DEF$_2$, DE$_2$F$_2$, ______, D$_2$E$_2$F$_3$.

A. DEF$_3$ B. D$_3$EF$_3$ C. D$_2$E$_3$F   D. D$_2$E$_2$F$_2$

Q.27 Direction: Answer according to the logical relation given.

FISH: SCHOOL

A. Wolf : pack   B. Cow : farm
C. Herd: peacock   D. Elephant: jungle

Q.28 The decimal representation of the number 1011$_2$ in binary system is:

A. 5   B. 7   C. 9   D. 11

Q.29 Direction: In the question below there are two statements followed by two conclusions I and II. You have to take the two given statements to be true even if they seem to be at variance with commonly known facts and then decide which of the given conclusions logically follows from the given statements disregarding commonly known facts.

Statements:

I. Some hen are not bottle.

II. All home are hen.

Conclusions:

I. Some bottle are home.

II. All home are not bottle is a possibility.

A. Only I follows

B. Only II follows

C. Only I and II follows

D. None follows

Q.30 Direction: In the question below there are two statements followed by two conclusions I, and II. You have to take the two given statements to be true even if they seem to be at variance with commonly known facts and then decide which of the given conclusions logically follows from the given statements disregarding commonly known facts.

Statements:

I. Some scissor are paper.

II. Some glass are not scissor.

Conclusions:

I. All scissor are glass.

II. Some paper are glass.

A. Only I follows

B. Only II follows

C. Both I and II follows

D. None follows

Q.31 Direction: In the question below there are two statements followed by three conclusions I, II and III. You have to take the two given statements to be true even if they seem to be at variance with commonly known facts and then decide which of the given conclusions logically follows from the given statements disregarding commonly known facts.

Statements:

I. All coffee are tea.

II. Some juice are not coffee.

Conclusions:

I. Some tea are not juice.

II. No coffee is juice.

III. No juice is tea.

A. Only I follows

B. Only II and III follows

C. Only I and III follows

D. Only III follows

Q.32 If 'A' is replaced by '+', 'B' is replaced by '-', 'C' is replaced by '÷' and 'D' is replaced by 'x', find the value of the following expression.

9D8B7A60C5

A. 77   B. 84   C. 72   D. 69

Q.33 Six board members P, Q, R, S, T, and U are sitting on a circular table for conference. P is facing R and S is facing Q who is immediate left of U. S is between P and T. Who is immediate right T?

A. S   B. Q   C. R   D. T

Q.34 Arpith, Balu, Chendu and Dinesh are four friends playing carom. Arpith and Balu are partners. Dinesh faces towards the north. If Arpith faces towards the west, then in which direction will Chendu face?

A. North   B. West   C. East   D. South

Q.35 Direction: Logically answer with the best possible option given.

Carrot, food, vegetable

A.

B.
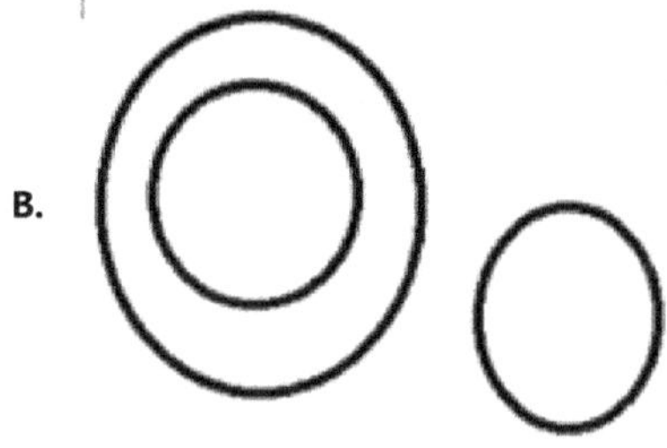

C.

D.
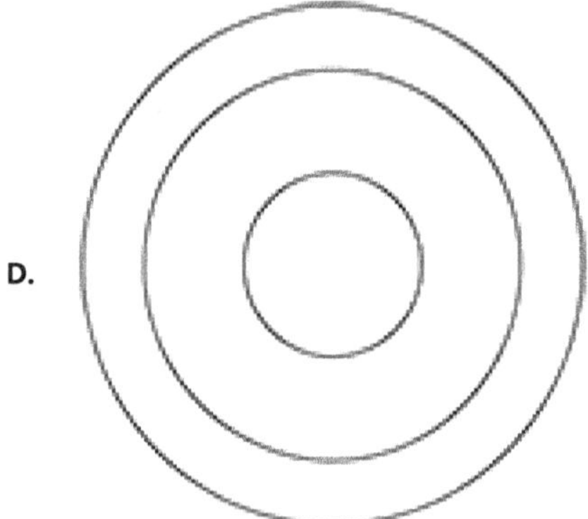

Q.36 What is the 31st term of the sequence: 1, 4, 7, 10, ... ?

A. 90   B. 91   C. 92   D. 93

Q.37 Direction: Answer the question mark according to sequence.

CORDEM : ZROGBQ : : ? : PXIVRO-

A. MWMUL   B. SULSUL

C. MUNMUM   D. SRSPQL

Q.38 Direction: Answer the blank according to the relation given:

TALE : LATE :: ? : CAFE-

A. FACE   **B.** CAEF   **C.** CEFA   **D.** FEAC

Q.39 Direction: Fill the left blank according to relation given:

CUP : LIP:: BIRD:?

A. BUSH   **B.** GRASS

C. FOREST   **D.** BEAK

Q.40 Direction: Each question given below consists of a statement, followed by two arguments numbered I and II. You have to decide which of the arguments is a 'strong' argument and which is a 'weak' argument.

Statement: Should India give away Kashmir to Pakistan?

Arguments:

I. No. Kashmir is a beautiful state. It earns a lot of foreign exchange for India.

II. Yes. This would help settle conflicts.

A. Only argument I is strong

B. Only argument II is strong

C. Either I or II is strong

D. Neither I nor II is strong

Q.41 Direction: Each question given below consists of a statement, followed by two arguments numbered I and II. You have to decide which of the arguments is a 'strong' argument and which is a 'weak' argument.

Statement: Should internal assessment in colleges be abolished?

Arguments:

I. Yes. This will help in reducing the possibility of favouritism.

II. No, teaching faculty will lose control over students.

A. Only argument I is strong

B. Only argument II is strong

C. Either I or II is strong

D. Neither I nor II is strong

Q.42 If A is the brother of B; B is the sister of C; and C is the father of D, how D is related to A?

A. Brother

B. Sister

C. Nephew

D. Cannot be determined

Q.43 If South-East becomes North and South becomes North-East and all the rest directions are changed in the same manner, the what will be the direction for West?

A. North-East   **B.** North-West

C. South-East   **D.** South-West

Q.44 Direction: The question consists of statement and two assumptions. The student must first determine whether each statement is true. Choose the appropriate option after reading the three statements carefully.

Statement:

The government may reduce the export duty on Basmati rice, in view of competition from Pakistan in the international market.

Assumption:

I. Reduction in export duty leads to increase in exports.

II. Pakistan is an exporter of Basmati rice.

A. Only I is implicit

B. Only II is implicit

C. Both I and II are implicit

D. Either I or II implicit

Q.45 Direction: In the question below is given one statement that followed by two assumptions numbered I and II. Consider the statement and decide which of the given assumptions is implicit.

Statement:

After every six months free medical health check-up camp is organized in the city Z. This time's camp will be seventh in continuation. The health awareness among people has improved over the last three years.

Assumption:

I. The medical health check-up camp has been the reason for improved health awareness.

II. With the improved health awareness among people, this camp will be the last camp required.

A. Only assumption I is implicit.

B. Only assumption II is implicit.

C. If either assumption I or II is implicit.

D. If neither I nor II is implicit.

Q.46 In a certain code language,"BORROW" is written as "769965" and "BOMB" is written as "7647". How is "WOMB" written in that code language?

A. 5647   **B.** 5674   **C.** 4674   **D.** 5685

Q.47 Which two signs should be interchanged to make the given equation correct?

$$51 + 18 - 5 \times 12 \div 3 = 137$$

A. - and ÷   **B.** + and ×   **C.** × and -   **D.** ÷ and ×

Q.48 If in a code language "ABACUS" is coded as "SUCABA" then the code for "TACKER" will be?

A. REKCAT   **B.** CATKER

C. ACERKT   **D.** KACERT

Q.49 Direction: Below in each of the questions are given two statements I and II. These statements may be either independent causes or may be effects of independent causes or a common cause. One of these statements may be the effect of the other statements.

Statement:

I. Importance of Yoga and exercise is being realized by all sections of the society.

II. There is an increasing awareness about health in the society particularly among middle ages group of people.

A. Statement I is the cause and statement II is its effect.

B. Statement II is the cause and statement I is its effect.

C. Both the statements I and II are independent causes.

D. Both the statements I and II are effects of independent causes.

Q.50 Direction: Below in each of the questions are given two statements I and II. These statements may be either independent causes or may be effects of independent causes

or a common cause. One of these statements may be the effect of the other statements.

Statement:

I. The university officers have decided to conduct last examination every year in March/April in order to announce the result at proper time.

II. In past the result was declared late by the University due to the lack of number of examiners.

A. Statement I is the cause and statement II is its effect.

B. Statement II is the cause and statement I is its effect.

C. Both the statements I and II are independent causes.

D. Both the statements I and II are effects of independent causes.

Legal Awareness & Aptitude

Q.51 Which of the following act is related to The Prohibition of Child Marriage?

A. The Prohibition of Child Marriage Act, 2005

B. The Prohibition of Child Marriage Act, 2006

C. The Prohibition of Child Marriage Act, 2007

D. The Prohibition of Child Marriage Act, 2010

Q.52 When is the communication of proposals, the acceptance of proposals and therevocation of proposals deemed to be made:

A. Only on clear verbal communication of such proposal, acceptance or revocation.

B. By any act or omission of the party by which he intends to communicate suchproposal, acceptance or revocation or has the effect of communicating it.

C. Only when the proposal, acceptance or revocation of the proposal is recorded inwriting.

D. Only when the proposal, acceptance or revocation of the proposal is received andunderstood by the other party receiving the information.

Q.53 According to Section 498 of IPC, if anyone enticing or taking away or detaining with criminal intent a married woman, what is the minimum punishment for the offense:

A. Punishment of two years and fine.

B. Punishment of three years and fine.

C. Punishment of four years and fine.

D. Punishment of six years and fine.

Q.54 According to Section 373 of IPC, if any person buys minor for purposes of prostitution, etc. what is the minimum punishment for the offence.

A. Punishment of ten years and fine.

B. Punishment of ten years only.

C. Punishment of eight years and fine.

D. Punishment of six years and fine.

Q.55 Children in conflict with law means?

A. All children under age of 16 years.

B. All children under the age of 18 years and is alleged or found to have committed an offence.

C. All children under the age of 18 years and have been found deserted or without a guardian.

D. All children under the age of 18 years who have been found working in contravention of Child Labour laws.

Q.56 Is a pronote executed in favour of a minor good in law?

A. Yes

B. No

C. Not in normal cases

D. Depends

Q.57 With which of the following issues did D.K. Basu v. State of West Bengal deal with?

A. Safeguards against sexual exploitation

B. Safeguards for arrested persons

C. Safeguards for children

D. Safeguards for unorganized workers

Q.58 In law, the term 'neighbour' means-

A. People who might be affected by your actions

B. People who stay in your locality

C. People who live adjoining to your residence

D. The word has not been given any particular definition

Q.59 In which of the following cases did the Supreme Court for the first time lay down that Fundamental Rights have primacy over the Directive Principles of State Policy?

A. Keshavananda Bharati vs State of Punjab

B. A.K. Roy vs Union of India

C. ADM Jabalpur vs Shiv Kant Shukla

D. Minerva Mills vs Union of India

Q.60 In which one of the following cases, the Constitutional validity of the Muslim Women (Protection of Rights of Divorce) Act 1986, was upheld by the Supreme Court?

A. Muhammad Ahmed Khan v. Shah Bano Begum

B. Danial Latifi v. Union of India

C. Mary Roy v. State of Kerala

D. Shankari Prasad v. Union of India

Q.61 Which of the following is entrusted with a statutory duty of laying down the standards of professional conduct and etiquette for advocates in India?

A. Supreme Court of India

B. Bar Association of India

C. Bar Council of India

D. Delhi Bar Council

Q.62 Original jurisdiction refers to-

A. Where an offender lives.

B. The types of law broken.

C. The area where the crime occurred.

D. The court where a trial case begins.

Q.63 Which Landmark constitutional case is known as the Mandal Case?

A. Indra Sawhney v. union of India

B. Ahmed Khan v. Shah Bano Begum

C. Hussainara khatoon v. Home Secretary, State of Bihar

D. Mithu v. State of Punjab

Q.64 In which Landmark Legal Case the Supreme court held the Right to Legal aid as a Fundamental Right?

A. Sheela Barse v. Union of India

B. Keshavnanada Bharti v. State of Kerala

C. S.R Bommai v. Union of India

D. T.M.A Pai v. Union of India

Q.65 In which case, the Supreme Court gave 'Doctrine of Prospective Overruling'?

A. Shankari Prasad v. Union of India

B. Sajjan Singh v. State of Rajasthan

C. GolakNath v. State of Punjab

D. Kesavananda Bharati v. State of Kerala

Q.66 Direction: Give the meaning of maxim term given.

Alibi

A. A friend of the court

B. From elsewhere

C. Equity follows the law

D. At another place

Q.67 Actus Non Facit Reum Nisi Mens Sit Rea:

A. The laws are adapted to those cases which occur more frequently

B. For a perpetual memorial for the matter

C. The act does not make one guilty unless there is a guilty intent

D. Alienation is preferred by law rather than accumulation

Q.68 On whose authority, prisoners are admitted to open-air jail:

A. Police

B. Judiciary

C. Jail Authorities

D. None of the above

Q.69 The aggregate of all operating, administrative and technical support agencies that perform criminal justice functions is called:

A. Social Justice System

B. Civil Justice System

C. Criminal Justice System

D. Consensus approach

Q.70 Which institution has resolved to clear all pending cases against sitting and former legislators in a time bound manner?

A. Bar Council of India

B. Insolvency and Bankruptcy Board of India

C. National Administrative Tribunal

D. Supreme Court of India

Q.71 Where is the headquarters of 'International Commission of Jurists' located?

A. Paris   **B.** Geneva   **C.** Rome   **D.** Nairobi

Q.72 Which bill is passed in Rajya Sabha to bring a law that punishes those who attack Health workers or Doctors?

A. Epidemic Diseases Amendment Bill, 2020

B. National Commission for Allied and Healthcare Professions Bill, 2020

C. Indian Medicine Central Council (Amendment) Bill, 2020

D. Healthcare Service Personnel and Clinical Establishments Bill, 2019

Q.73 Which constitutional body has recently made observations on Rs. 223 crore expenditure made by Indian Air Force?

A. Supreme Court of India

B. Election Commission of India

C. Finance Commission

D. Comptroller and Auditor General

Q.74 Which body has ordered to provide dry ration to all sex workers in the country without insisting on ration card?

A. National Commission on Women

B. Supreme Court of India

C. National Administrative Tribunal

D. National Human Rights Commission

Q.75 Jamnagar-based cluster of Ayurveda institutes, that was seen in news, are located in which state?

A. Gujarat   **B.** Assam

C. Madhya Pradesh   **D.** Maharashtra

General Knowledge

Q.76 The world's first railway steam engine was invented by ________.

A. Otto Hahn   **B.** James Watt

C. Henri Becquerel   **D.** Ernest Rutherford

Q.77 In the context of India's space research, 'Vyommitra' is the name of:

A. India's first manned Mars mission

B. An Indian spacecraft

C. An Indian robot

D. A newly found asteroid

Q.78 Which one of the following is India's heaviest rocket and referred to as 'Bahubali'?

A. PSLV - C - 37   **B.** RLV - TD

C. GSLV MK - III   **D.** PSLV - XL

Q.79 In which of the following article, the provision of Uniform Civil Code is mentioned?

A. Article 41   **B.** Article 44

C. Article 46   **D.** Article 49

Q.80 Which of the following is NOT a federal feature of the Indian Constitution?

A. Flexibility of Constitution

B. Supremacy of Constitution

C. Written Constitution

D. Bicameralism

Q.81 In accordance with the Indian Constitution, Protection of Life and Personal Liberty is granted under which Article?

A. Article 20

B. Article 21

C. Article 22

D. Article 23

A. D   **B.** C   **C.** B   **D.** A

Q.82 Through which of the following north east states in India , the tropic of cancer passes?

A. Tripura & Nagaland

B. Tripura & Mizoram

C. Meghalaya & Mizoram

D. Assam & Tripura

Q.83 Hirakud Dam, one of world's longest earthen dams is located in which among the following states?

A. Andhra Pradesh   **B.** Odisha

C. Karnataka   **D.** West Bengal

Q.84 The Konyak, Gaddi and Tharu tribes / ethnic people are found in which of the following states respectively?

A. Kerala, Haryana, Bihar

B. Nagaland, Himachal Pradesh, Tamil Nadu

C. Nagaland, Jammu & Kashmir, Uttarakhand

D. Assam, Punjab, Karnataka

Q.85 Which of the following forest types occupies the maximum area in India?

A. Tropical moist deciduous

B. Montane wet temperate forest

C. Tropical wet evergreen

D. Tropical rainforest

Q.86 Which among the following works as central processing agent in RTGS?

A. Reserve Bank of India

B. Institute for Development & Research in Banking Technology

C. Indian Financial Network

D. Indian Banks Association

Q.87 How many currencies are used in the Real Effective Exchange Rate (REER) that is both trade and export weighted indicator?

A. 6   **B.** 18   **C.** 36   **D.** 72

Q.88 Liquidity Adjustment Facility (LAF) is used by RBI to bring changes in which of the following?

1. CRR and SLR

2. Repo and Reverse Repo rates

3. Bank rate

Choose the correct option from the codes given below:

A. 1, 2, 3   **B.** 1 and 2   **C.** 1 Only   **D.** 2 Only

Q.89 What is India's share in the world carpet export market?

A. 30%   **B.** 50%   **C.** 40%   **D.** 20%

Q.90 Which among the following are a tools for central bank to achieve the monetary policy?

1. Bank Rate

2. Reserve Ratios

3. Open Market Operations

4. Intervention in forex market

5. Moral Suasion

Choose the correct option from the choices given below:

A. 1, 2, 3 and 4 only   **B.** 1, 2, 3 and 5 only

C. 1, 2 and 5 only   **D.** All the above

Q.91 FINO stands for________.

A. Financial Investment Network and Operations

B. Farmers Investment in National Organization

C. Farmers Inclusion News and Operations

D. Financial Inclusion Network and Operations

Q.92 Which of the following "tax" is levied at every stage of production?

A. VAT   **B.** Income tax

C. Custom duty   **D.** None of the above

Q.93 What kind of tax system is found in India?

A. Progressive

B. Degressive

C. Proportional

D. None of the following

Q.94 The number of structures in India's GST model is?

A. 6   **B.** 4   **C.** 3   **D.** 5

Q.95 Which state of India currently has the highest Per Capita Income?

A. Goa   **B.** Delhi

C. Maharashtra   **D.** Punjab

Q.96 Which is not added in the calculation of National income of India?

A. The value of goods and services

B. The sold value of the old fridge

C. Services rendered by the housewives

D. Both (B) & (C)

Q.97 Which Indian state has the largest production of cotton mill cloth, as per 2010-11?

A. Gujarat   **B.** Maharashtra

C. Punjab   **D.** Tamil Nadu

Q.98 Which is the Indian state with the highest number of powerlooms?

A. Gujarat   **B.** Madhya Pradesh

C. Maharashtra   **D.** Tamil Nadu

Q.99 Who has won the 1st prize for the Amazon Smbhav Entrepreneurship Challenge 2022?

A. Mukush Ambani   **B.** Ratan Tata

C. Gautam Adani   **D.** Subhash Ola

Q.100 The fifth Romain Rolland Book Prize - Romain Rolland Book Prize 2022 has been awarded to which Bengali translation of the French novel?

A. The Immoralist by Andre Gide

B. The Meursault Investigation

C. The Stranger by Albert Camus

D. The Lover by Marguerite Duras

// Smart Answer Sheet //

Correct Percentage of students who answered correctly. **Skipped** Percentage of students who skipped.

Q.	Ans.	Correct / Skipped	Q.	Ans.	Correct / Skipped	Q.	Ans.	Correct / Skipped	Q.	Ans.	Correct / Skipped	Q.	Ans.	Correct / Skipped
1	A	41.73 % / 31.55 %	17	B	49.42 % / 31.45 %	33	C	23.25 % / 73.63 %	49	B	51.78 % / 32.83 %	65	C	40.21 % / 33.27 %
2	B	59.37 % / 31.39 %	18	B	55.05 % / 42.29 %	34	D	53.36 % / 41.7 %	50	B	64.35 % / 32.93 %	66	D	54.33 % / 32.15 %
3	A	56.56 % / 34.62 %	19	C	44.04 % / 40.37 %	35	D	49.8 % / 48.99 %	51	B	49.7 % / 44.18 %	67	C	53.72 % / 38.12 %
4	B	51.55 % / 39.15 %	20	B	46.27 % / 50.66 %	36	B	53.71 % / 38.51 %	52	B	48.28 % / 47.92 %	68	C	62.21 % / 34.69 %
5	C	41.6 % / 52.81 %	21	B	43.65 % / 38.1 %	37	B	66.58 % / 31.56 %	53	A	67.54 % / 31.22 %	69	C	48.42 % / 38.36 %
6	B	42.02 % / 37.95 %	22	B	47.26 % / 40.75 %	38	A	80.78 % / 11.46 %	54	A	16.36 % / 79.43 %	70	D	51.27 % / 35.63 %
7	B	81.36 % / 16.53 %	23	B	57.17 % / 34.44 %	39	D	65.17 % / 31.37 %	55	B	66.6 % / 31.81 %	71	B	79.61 % / 14.62 %
8	C	80.32 % / 17.47 %	24	C	40.55 % / 38.57 %	40	A	64.18 % / 33.72 %	56	A	50.57 % / 42.87 %	72	A	69.65 % / 30.13 %
9	C	50.16 % / 32.5 %	25	D	89.47 % / 10.53 %	41	A	53.55 % / 31.33 %	57	B	61.53 % / 37.5 %	73	D	64.2 % / 31.18 %
10	D	89.2 % / 10.75 %	26	D	21.9 % / 72.35 %	42	D	59.53 % / 32.31 %	58	A	47.35 % / 42.37 %	74	B	27.22 % / 70.61 %
11	A	55.66 % / 40.18 %	27	A	51.19 % / 45.58 %	43	C	60.45 % / 36.47 %	59	D	53.19 % / 41.82 %	75	A	30.4 % / 68.32 %
12	D	54.36 % / 41.85 %	28	D	68.89 % / 30.48 %	44	A	40.08 % / 43.96 %	60	A	58.05 % / 37.5 %	76	B	77.45 % / 19.64 %
13	A	50.7 % / 38.4 %	29	B	59.66 % / 33.99 %	45	A	56.31 % / 31.0 %	61	C	65.87 % / 30.68 %	77	C	85.65 % / 10.96 %
14	D	67.86 % / 31.23 %	30	D	61.64 % / 32.22 %	46	A	48.68 % / 32.28 %	62	D	47.75 % / 32.14 %	78	C	85.63 % / 11.51 %
15	C	78.11 % / 19.67 %	31	A	12.53 % / 71.89 %	47	C	42.73 % / 31.47 %	63	A	45.83 % / 51.53 %	79	B	43.25 % / 32.59 %
16	D	56.47 % / 42.45 %	32	A	42.6 % / 46.99 %	48	A	60.85 % / 30.85 %	64	A	65.58 % / 32.53 %	80	A	67.87 % / 31.42 %

Q.	Ans.	Correct		Q.	Ans.	Correct		Q.	Ans.	Correct		Q.	Ans.	Correct		Q.	Ans.	Correct
		Skipped				Skipped				Skipped				Skipped				Skipped
81	C	58.89 %		85	A	52.63 %		89	C	53.42 %		93	B	64.21 %		97	A	62.11 %
		32.67 %				35.46 %				30.13 %				32.77 %				35.54 %
82	B	41.9 %		86	B	55.29 %		90	D	17.69 %		94	B	60.08 %		98	C	44.28 %
		37.24 %				33.62 %				72.37 %				32.98 %				31.28 %
83	B	53.03 %		87	C	69.41 %		91	D	56.22 %		95	A	44.07 %		99	D	47.86 %
		38.17 %				30.06 %				43.08 %				36.93 %				50.97 %
84	C	44.58 %		88	D	51.13 %		92	A	68.32 %		96	D	42.11 %		100	B	60.03 %
		42.36 %				46.95 %				31.02 %				42.28 %				38.11 %

//Hints and Solutions//

1. In place of short name, it must be initials. The correct sentence is: There are not many men who are so famous that they are frequently referred to by their **initials** only.

Hence, the correct option is (A).

2. My apologies for delaying. How long have you been waiting? is the correct sentence grammatically and logically. Always a question is asked after a sentence that is incomplete in the message of the sentence.

Hence, the correct option is (B).

3. 'Eminent' means a person who is successful, well-known, outstanding, etc.

'Imminent' means about to happen or likely to occur, possible, etc.

Use of Imminent in a sentence:

Imminent - The earthquake is imminent, so be prepared to face it.

Hence, the correct option is (A).

4. Psephologist- One who studies election trends

Anthropologist- A social scientist who specializes in anthropology

Plagiarist- someone who uses another person's words or ideas as if they were his own

Philologist- A humanist specializing in classical scholarship.

Hence, the correct option is (B).

5. Somnambulist- Someone who walks about in their sleep

Arsonist- a criminal who illegally sets fire to property

Amateur- someone who pursues a study or sport as a pastime

Somniloquist- someone who talks while asleep.

Hence, the correct option is (C).

6. The correct spelling for the word is benefitted. The word means something eased out or improved. Another word for profit is also its meaning.

Hence, the correct option is (B).

7. The misspelled word is Aniversary. The correct word is Anniversary. Anniversary means an important year or a special event. Rest all words have correct spelling.

Hence, the correct option is (B).

8. The correct answer is 'He may not have developed the business.' The given sentence is in passive form. Find the subject and object of the sentence and exchange their places; make changes in their cases as well if subject and object are pronouns. If 'have been+ v3 is used in the passive form, 'have + v3 ' will be used in the active form. (have developed) 'May not' remains unchanged. At last line up the remaining part.

Hence, the correct option is (C).

9. The correct answer is 'The nightingale was made to practise day in and day out by the frog'. The instructions given below should be followed while changing an assertive sentence to passive voice.

Find the subject and object of the sentence and exchange their places; make changes in their cases as well if subject and object are pronouns.

Use preposition 'by' before the agent. (by the frog) 'By + agent' generally comes at the end of the sentence.

Use an appropriate helping verb in passive form according to the tense of the active form. (Simple past tense) Here, 'was' is used.

Always use the third form of the main verb in passive form. (Made)

The verb 'made' works as a causative verb in the given sentence.

I It is followed by the bare infinitive $(V_{\text{base form}})$ in the active voice and infinitive (to $+V_{\text{base form}}$) in the passive voice.

Examples: I made him wash the dishes. (Active)

He was made to wash the dishes by me. (Passive)

Hence, the correct option is (C).

10. The correct answer is- 'to be frank.' 'Call a spade a spade' is an idiom and it means 'to say the truth about something, even if it is not polite or pleasant' So that we can say according to the context of the given idiom 'Call a spade a spade' the best appropriate answer is 'to be frank'.

Hence, the correct option is (D).

11. The correct answer is 'to put aside differences.' The meaning of the idiom is- To stop an argument and become friends again.

Hence, the correct option is (A).

12. The correct answer is, 'Enclosure'. The most appropriate synonym of 'confinement' is 'enclosure'.

Confinement- The action of confining or state of being confined.

Enclosure- An area that is sealed off with an artificial or natural barrier.

Dismal- Depressing; Dreary.

Indicate- Point out; show.

Declaim- Utter or deliver words or a speech in a rhetorical or impassioned way, as if to an audience.

Hence, the correct option is (D).

13. The word 'Characteristic' is a noun and it means 'a' feature or quality belonging typically to a person, place, or thing and serving to identify them'. According to this, we can say 'particular' is the best synonym of the word 'Characteristic'.

Example: Unfortunately a big nose is a family characteristic.

Hence, the correct option is (A).

14. Outspoken- Speaking, or spoken, freely, openly, or boldy

Secretive- Having an inclination to secrecy

Ambivalent- Simultaneously experiencing or expressing opposing or contradictory feelings, beliefs, or motivations

Candid- Impartial and free from prejudice

Equivocal- A word or expression capable of different meanings.

Hence, the correct option is (D).

15. The word 'Convenience' means the state of being able to proceed with something without difficulty. The antonyms of the word 'Convenience' are "hindrance, restriction, inconvenience". From the antonym of the given word, we can say that the word 'Hindrance' is the opposite in meaning. The word 'Hindrance' means a thing that provides resistance, delay, or obstruction to something or someone.

Hence, the correct option is (C).

16. The correct answer is 'disperse'. The given sentence means that the police used tear gas to move apart the crowd. Tear gas is commonly used by law enforcement to control riots and crowds. Other meanings of the words are:

Disperse- To make somebody move apart or go in different directions.

Attack- to use violence to try to hurt or kill somebody.

Disburse- to pay money to somebody from a large amount that has been collected for a purpose.

Collect- to bring things together from different people or places.

Hence, the correct option is (D).

17. The correct answer is 'avid'. The given sentence means that Ritu reads a lot of books. It means that she is very enthusiastic about reading books.

Avid- Very enthusiastic about something (often a hobby).

Irritated- Annoyed or angry.

Inattentive- Not paying attention to something/somebody.

Erratic- Not happening at regular times.

Hence, the correct option is (B).

18. The correct answer is 'Adverb'. An adverb is a word or phrase that modifies or qualifies an adjective, verb, or other adverb or a word group, expressing a relation of place, time, circumstance, manner, cause, degree, etc. Generally, Adverbs are formed by adding (-ly) to an adjective.

Hence, the correct option is (B).

19. The correct answer is 'Reflexive Pronoun'. Here, in the given sentence 'yourself' is a 'Reflexive Pronoun'. Reflexive Pronoun: These are words ending in -self or -selves that are used when the subject and the object of a sentence are the same. The nine English reflexive pronouns are myself, yourself, himself, herself, oneself, itself, ourselves, yourselves, and themselves.

Hence, the correct option is (C).

20. The correct answer is 'Noun'. Here, in the given sentence 'table' is a common noun. It means 'a noun that is the name of a group of similar things, such as "table" or "book", and not of a single person, place, or thing'.

Example: He lived in a room with only two chairs, a bed, and a table.

Hence, the correct option is (B).

21. The correct answer is 'Preposition'. Here, in the given sentence 'broke into' is a phrasal verb. It means 'to enter a building illegally, usually by damaging a door or window, esp. for the purpose of stealing something'.

Hence, the correct option is (B).

22. From the sentence, younger is the appropriate word from the options given. Younger is the comparative degree of adjective used for the sentence.

Hence, the correct option is (B).

23. Statement I: Electric vehicles are less in developed countries as compared to India.

Nothing has been indicated regarding the number of electric vehicles in developed countries. This makes a statement I invalid.

Statement II: India has not yet adopted electric vehicles fully.

This is correct. Since there is scope for adoption of a huge number of EVs, India has the potential to emerge as a global leader in this sector but it has not yet achieved so. Thus, statement II is valid.

Statement III: Indians are already demanding a huge number of electric vehicles.

The demand for electric vehicles in India is still latent, i.e., existing but not yet developed or manifested. This, hence, makes statement III invalid.

Hence, the correct option is (B).

24. That said, there is much scope to replace India's giant fleet of two-wheelers with electric bikes. India has over 170 million two-wheelers, and sales data from the last six years show that 79% of on-road vehicles here are two-wheelers.

Statement I: India has over 160 million two-wheelers.

If the number is over 170 million, it would also be over 160 million.

So, a statement I is valid.

Statement II: 79% of on-road vehicles in India are two-wheelers.

This fact is given in the passage. Hence, statement II is valid.

Statement III: People prefer two-wheelers to four-wheelers due to ease of use.

Nothing regarding the preference of Indians for two-wheelers has been mentioned in the passage. This, hence, makes statement III invalid.

Hence, the correct option is (C).

25. Sarcastic, caustic and cynical are tones that correspond to negative passages. However, the given passage is not negative in nature. Therefore, options (A), (B), and (C) are eliminated.

The tone of this passage is positive and optimistic. The author supports as well as justifies the subject.

Hence, the correct option is (D).

26. In this series, the letters remain the same, i.e. DEF.

Here the subscript numbers follow the series: 1,1,1; 1,1,2; 1,2,2; 2,2,2; 2,2,3.

Therefore, the next letter series will be $D_2E_2F_2$.

Hence, the correct option is (D).

27. A group of fish is called a school and a group of wolves is called a pack.

Hence, the correct option is (A).

28. Covert Binary to Decimal:

For binary number with n digits;

$$D_{n-1} \ldots . . D_3 D_2 D_1 D_0$$

$$\text{Decimal} = D_0 \times 2^0 + D_1 \times 2^1 + D_2 \times 2^2 + \cdots$$

$$(1011)_2$$

$$= 1 \times 2^0 + 1 \times 2^1 + 0 \times 2^2 + 1 \times 2^3$$

$$= 1 + 2 + 0 + 8$$

$$= 11$$

Hence, the correct option is (D).

29. The least possible Venn diagram is as shown below,

Conclusions:

I. Some bottle are home. → False (It is possible, but not definite)

II. All home are not bottle is a possibility. → True (The possibility as shown below).

Hence, the correct option is (B).

30. The least possible Venn diagram is as shown below,

Conclusion:

I. All scissor are glass. → False (Some glass are not scissor)

II. Some paper are glass. → False (It is possible, but not definite)

Hence, the correct option is (D).

31. The least possible Venn diagram is as shown,

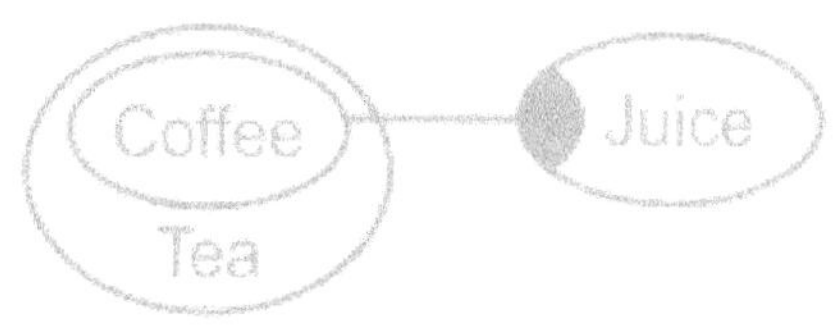

Conclusion:

I. Some tea are not juice. → True (All coffee are tea, and some juice are not coffee).

II. No coffee is juice. → False (It is possible, but not definite).

III. No juice is tea. → False (It is possible, but not definite).

Hence, the correct option is (A).

32.

Letter	A	B	C	D
Meaning	+	−	÷	×

Given expression: 9D8B7A60C5

Expression after applying given replacements: $9 \times 8 - 7 + 60 \div 5$

$$\Rightarrow 9 \times 8 - 7 + 60 \div 5$$

$$\Rightarrow 9 \times 8 - 7 + 12$$

$$\Rightarrow 72 - 7 + 12$$

$$\Rightarrow 84 - 7$$

$$\Rightarrow 77$$

Hence, the correct option is (A).

33. Six board members P, Q, R, S, T, and U.

1) P is facing R.

2) S is facing Q who is immediate left of U.

3) S is between P and T.

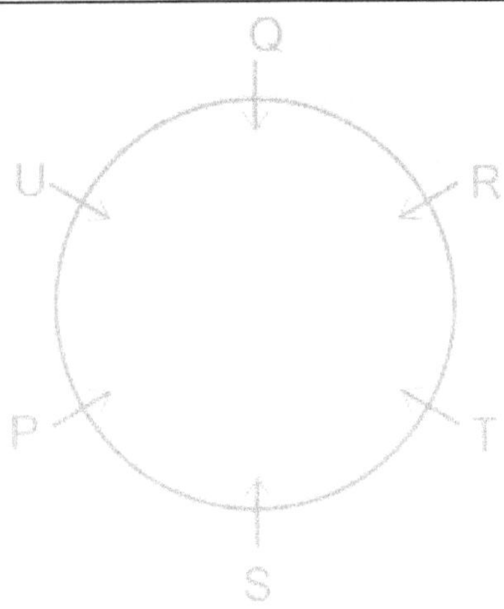

Therefore, R is immediate right of T.

Hence, the correct option is (C).

34. Below table shows the sitting arrangement of four friends:

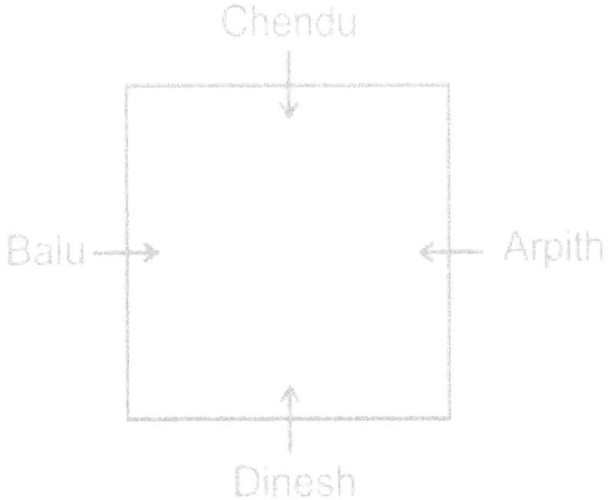

Chendu is facing the south.

Hence, the correct option is (D).

35. All carrots are vegetables and all vegetables are types of food.

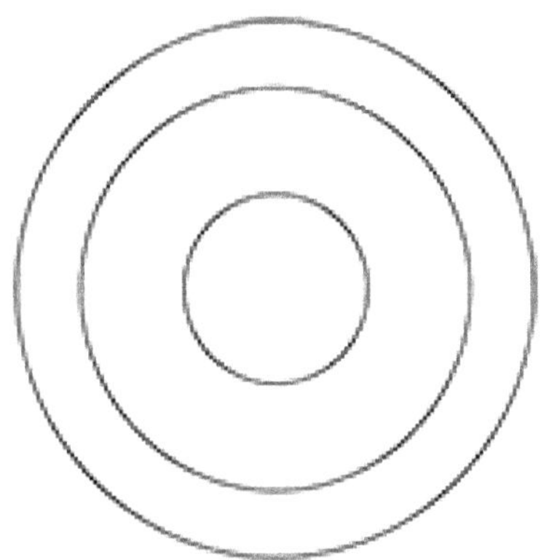

Hence, the correct option is (D).

36. Given Sequence: $1, 4, 7, 10, \ldots, a_{31}$

Here, $a_1 = 1, d = 4 - 1 = 3, n = 31$

We know,

$$a_n = a_1 + (n-1)d$$
$$a_{31} = 1 + (31 - 1)3$$
$$= 91$$

Hence, the correct option is (B).

37. The 1st 3rd and 5th Letters of the first group are each moved three steps backward while the second fourth and sixth letters are each moved three steps forward to obtain the corresponding letters of the second group. Therefore, the correct option is: SULSUL.

Hence, the correct option is (B).

38. TALE $\Rightarrow$ LATE

[First and third letter interchanged their positions.]

Thus,

FACE $\Rightarrow$ CAFE.

Hence, the correct option is (A).

39. Cup is used to drink something with the help of lips. Similarly birds collects grass with the help of beak to make her nest.

Hence, the correct option is (D).

40. Clearly, India cannot part with a state that is a major foreign exchange earner to it. So, argument I holds strong. Further, giving away a piece of land unconditionally and unreasonably is no solution to settle disputes. So, argument II is vague.

Hence, the correct option is (A).

41. Abolishing the internal assessment would surely reduce favouritism on personal grounds because the teachers would not be involved in examination system so that they cannot extend personal benefits to anyone. So, argument I holds strong. But it will not affect the control of teaching faculty on students because still the teachers would be teaching them. So, argument II is vague.

Hence, the correct option is (A).

42. If D is Male, the answer is Nephew.

If D is Female, the answer is Niece.

As the sex of D is not known, therefore, the relation between D and A cannot be determined.

Note: Niece - A daughter of one's brother or sister, or of one's brother-in-law or sister-in-law. Nephew - A son of one's brother or sister, or of one's brother-in-law or sister-in-law.

Hence, the correct option is (D).

43. If South-east becomes North and North East becomes West, therefore, the whole figure moves through 135^0. Hence, West will be South-East.

See, Actual figure is rotating 135^0 anticlockwise.

So, When West will be rotated by same degree anticlockwise. It will hold the place of south-East.

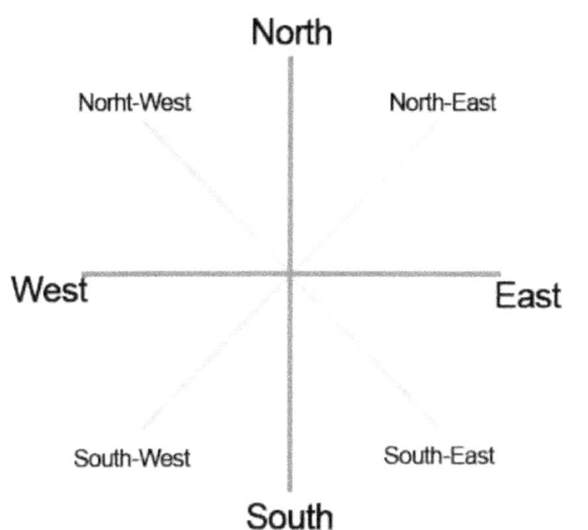

Hence, the correct option is (C).

44. To be a front runner in the competition, one has to increase its exports. So it is implicit that the government has reduced export duty under the assumption that the reduction in export duty may help to increase the export quantity.

II is a conclusion, that can be drawn from the statement but is not an assumption.

Hence, the correct option is (A).

45. It is certain that the last six sessions of health lessons were efficient in imparting information regarding health. But it is not mentioned that such camps are not needed anymore.

Hence, the correct option is (A).

46. Here each letter is coded with a specific number as:

'B' is 7

'O' is 6

'R' is 9

'W' is 5

'M' is 4

And,

'B' is 7

'O' is 6

'M' is 4

'B' is 7

Using the above letter codes we get, 'WOMB' is '5647'.

Hence, the correct option is (A).

47. Given,

$$51 + 18 - 5 \times 12 \div 3 = 137$$

A) $-$ and $\div$

$$\Rightarrow 51 + 18 \div 5 \times 12 - 3$$

$$\Rightarrow 51 + 3.6 \times 12 - 3$$

$$= 91.2 \neq 137$$

B) $+$ and $\times \rightarrow$

$$\Rightarrow 51 \times 18 - 5 + 12 \div 3$$

$$\Rightarrow 270 - 5 + 4$$

$$= 269 \neq 137$$

C) $\times$ and $-$

$$\Rightarrow 51 + 18 \times 5 - 12 \div 3$$

$$\Rightarrow 51 + 90 - 4$$

$$\Rightarrow 137 = 137$$

D) $\div$ and $\times$

$$\Rightarrow 51 + 18 - 5 \times 12 \div 3$$

$$\Rightarrow 69 - 5 \times 4$$

$$\Rightarrow 69 - 20$$

$$= 49 \neq 137$$

Hence, the correct option is (C).

48.

Alphabets	A	B	C	D	E	F	G	H	I	J	K	L	M
Positional value	1	2	3	4	5	6	7	8	9	10	11	12	13
Positional value	26	25	24	23	22	21	20	19	18	17	16	15	14
Alphabets	Z	Y	X	W	V	U	T	S	R	Q	P	O	N

The pattern followed,

Similarly,

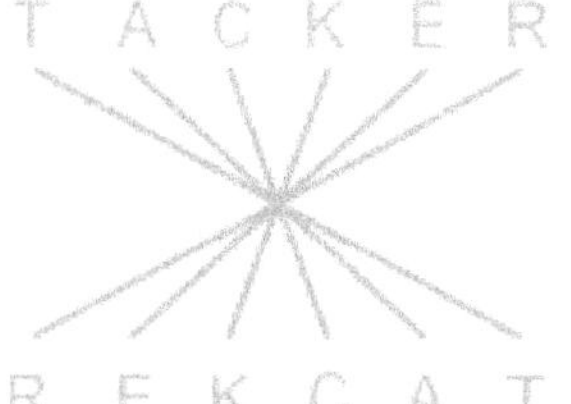

Therefore, TACKER is coded as REKCAT.

Hence, the correct option is (A).

49. As the awareness about health in the society is increasing particularly among middle-aged group of people, the importance of Yoga and exercise is being realized by all sections of the society.

Hence, the correct option is (B).

50. Since in the past the result was declared late by university, it has decided to conduct the examination in March/April in order to announce the result at proper time.

Hence, the correct option is (B).

51. The correct answer is The Prohibition of Child Marriage Act, 2006. The Prohibition of Child Marriage Act 2006 came into force on 1st November 2007 in India. In October 2017, Supreme Court of India gave a landmark judgement criminalising sex with a child bride, hence removing an exception in India's criminal jurisprudence which had until then accorded legal protection to men who raped their minor wives.

Hence, the correct option is (B).

52. The communication of proposals, the acceptance of proposals and the revocation of proposals deemed to be made only by any act or omission of the party by which he intends to communicate such proposal, acceptance or revocation or has the effect of communicating it. The communication of a proposal is complete when it comes to the knowledge of the person to whom it is made. The communication of an acceptance is complete, as against the proposer, when it is put in a course of transmission to him, so as to be out of the power of the acceptor; as against the acceptor, when it comes to the knowledge of the proposer.

Hence, the correct option is (B).

53. The correct answer is a Punishment of two years and a fine. Whoever takes or entices away any woman who is and whom he knows or has reason to believe to be the wife of any other man, from that man, or from any person having the care of her on behalf of that man, with the intent that she may have illicit intercourse with any person, or conceals or detains with that intent any such woman, shall be punished with imprisonment of either description for a term which may. extend two years, or with fine, or with both. It is a Non-cognizable offense, Bailable which is triable by Any Magistrate. The offence is compoundable by the husband of a woman and the woman.

Hence, the correct option is (A).

54. The correct answer is a Punishment of ten years and a fine. Whoever buys, hires, or otherwise obtains possession of any person under the age of eighteen years with the intent that such person shall be at any age be employed or used for the purpose of prostitution or illicit intercourse with any person or for any unlawful and immoral purpose, or knowing it to be likely that such person will at any age employed or used for any such purpose, shall be punished with imprisonment of either description for a term which may extend to ten years, and shall also be liable to fine. It is a cognizable offence and Non-bailable in nature which is triable by the court of session.

Hence, the correct option is (A).

55. The Juvenile Justice (Care and Protection) Act, 2015 discuss two types of children. First, Children in Conflict with Law meaning those children who are under 18 years of age and have been found doing an offence or is alleged of an offence.

Hence, the correct option is (B).

56. Any person capable of contracting can execute a valid pronote. A minor cannot execute a promissory note and a promissory note executed by a minor is not enforceable. However, a minor can be a promisee and be entitled to receive the money on demand of a pronote.

Hence, the correct option is (A).

57. D.K. Basu vs. State of West Bengal (AIR 1997 SC 610) This is a landmark judgment given by the Apex court in the case of an increasing number of custodial deaths in India. The court observed that custodial death is a matter of concern and it is more aggravated as it is committed by the protector of the citizens. Therefore this case deal with safeguard for persons.

Hence, the correct option is (B).

58. A neighbour was identified as someone who was so closely and directly affected by the act that one ought to have them in contemplation as being so affected when directing one's mind to the acts or omissions in question.

Hence, the correct option is (A).

59. In Minerva Mills vs Union of India case the Supreme Court for the first time lay down that Fundamental Rights have primacy over the Directive Principles of State Policy.

Minerva Mills Ltd. vs Union Of India is a landmark decision of the Supreme Court of India that applied and evolved the basic structure doctrine of the Constitution of India. In the Minerva Mills case, the Supreme Court provided key clarifications on the interpretation of the basic structure doctrine.

Hence, the correct option is (D).

60. The case follows its pursuit from the famous case of Mohd. Ahmed Khan vs Shah Bano Begum, commonly referred as the Shah Bano case. Shah Bano, a 62 -year-old Muslim mother of five from Indore, Madhya Pradesh, was divorced by her husband in 1978. She filed a criminal suit under Section 125 of the CrPC, ultimately in the Supreme Court of India, she won the right to alimony from her husband. However, she was subsequently denied the alimony when the Indian Parliament reversed the judgment bypassing the Muslim Women (Protection of Rights on Divorce) Act, 1986 which diluted the judgment of the Supreme Court and, in reality, denied even utterly destitute Muslim divorcees the right to alimony from their former husbands.

Hence, the correct option is (A).

61. The Bar Council of India is a statutory body established under section 4 of the Advocates Act 1961 that regulates the legal practice and legal education in India. Its members are elected from amongst the lawyers in India and as such represents the Indian bar. In other words, it is entrusted with a statutory duty of

laying down the standards of professional conduct and etiquette for advocates in India.

Hence, the correct option is (C).

62. Original jurisdiction of a court refers to a matter for which the particular court is approached first or where a trial case begins. In the case of the Supreme Court in India, its original jurisdiction is covered under Article 131. It involves the following cases:

Any dispute between the Indian Government and one or more States.

Any dispute between the Indian Government and one or more States on one side and one or more States on the other side.

Any dispute between two or more States.

Article 32 of the Constitution provides original jurisdiction to the SC for matters regarding the enforcement of Fundamental Rights.

The SC can issue writs, directions, or orders including writs in the nature of mandamus, habeas corpus, quo warranto, prohibition and certiorari.

The SC also has the power to direct the transfer of a criminal or civil case from the High Court in one State to the High Court in another State.

Hence, the correct option is (D).

63. Indra Sawhney v. Union of India case is also known as Mandal Commission Case. The court has held that barring any extraordinary situations reservation should not exceed 50 percent. Indra Sawhney, the petitioner in this case, made three principal arguments against the Order:

The extension of reservation violated the Constitutional guarantee of equality of opportunity.

Caste was not a reliable indicator of backwardness.

The efficiency of public institutions was at risk.

Hence, the correct option is (A).

64. In sheela Barse v. Union of India the court held that the right to legal aid is a fundamental right under article 14 and Article 21 of the constitution. Various fundamental rights under Article, 14, 19, 20, 21 and 22 of the Constitution of India impliedly deal with the rights of prisoners. Article 14 deals with right to equality which provides equality before law and equal protection of law to all persons.

Hence, the correct option is (A).

65. Golaknath v. State of Punjab was the major landmark under the doctrine of "prospective overruling". The law declared by the Court applies to the cases arising in the future only and its applicability to the cases which have attained finality is saved because the repeal would otherwise work hardship to those who had trusted to its existence.

Hence, the correct option is (C).

66. Alibi means a claim or a piece of evidence when an act, typically a criminal one, is alleged to have taken place. In a criminal action, a defense that the defendant was somewhere other than the scene of the crime when the crime was committed.

Hence, the correct option is (D).

67. An act does not make one guilty without a guilty mind. This Latin phrase is often given as the pinnacle of the English common law criminal justice system and is usually in the context of mens rea. It states that for any act to be illegal in nature it must be done with a guilty mind.

Hence, the correct option is (C).

68. According to the jail authority prisoners are admitted to open-air jail. The principal rule is that an inmate eligible for open-air prison has to be a convict. Good conduct in prison and at least five years spent in a controlled jail are the rules followed by the Rajasthan open prisons.

Hence, the correct option is (C).

69. The criminal justice system is a series of government agencies and institutions. Goals include the rehabilitation of offenders, preventing other crimes, and moral support for victims. The primary institutions of the criminal justice system are the police, prosecution and defense lawyers, the courts and prisons.

Hence, the correct option is (C).

70. India's apex judicial body, the Supreme Court of India has recently resolved to ensure that the pending criminal cases against sitting and former legislators would be completed in a time-bound manner.

The Supreme Court said that more than 4000 cases against legislatures are pending across the country, of which nearly 2500 pertain to sitting legislatures.

Hence, the correct option is (D).

71. 'International Commission of Jurists' is an international human rights non-governmental organization, headquartered at Geneva, Switzerland

ICJ was recently in the news as it has announced that the Foreign Contribution (Regulation) Amendment Bill, 2020 passed by the Indian Parliament was incompatible with international law. It also opined that the provisions of the bill would impose arbitrary obstacles in human rights promotion.

Hence, the correct option is (B).

72. The Epidemic Diseases Amendment Bill, 2020 has been recently passed in the Rajya Sabha, to bring a law, that punishes those who attack Health workers or Doctors who are fighting the coronavirus outbreak or a similar situation. It provides for up to five years in jail for the act.

Hence, the correct option is (A).

73. The Comptroller and Auditor General (CAG) has pointed out that the upgrade of 90 medium-lift Mi-17 helicopters of the Indian Air Force (IAF), which was proposed in 2002, is still not achieved even after a period of 18 years.

Due to this nonachievement, these helicopters are flying with limited capability. The CAG has also stated that an expenditure of Rs. 223 crore for upgrading these helicopters was "not justified" by Indian Air Force.

Hence, the correct option is (D).

74. The Supreme Court of India has ordered all the states and UTs to provide dry ration to all sex workers in the country.

The apex court has also insisted that the ration should be provided without insisting on ration card or any other identity proof. The top court has pronounced this order on observing the hardships faced by sex workers due to the COVID pandemic.

Hence, the correct option is (B).

75. The Bill named 'The Institute of Teaching and Research in Ayurveda Bill, 2020', was passed by a voice vote in Rajya Sabha.

It seeks to grant the status of an 'Institution of national importance' to the Jamnagar-based cluster of Ayurveda institutes in Gujarat: Institute of Post Graduate Teaching and Research in Ayurveda, Gulabkunwerba Ayurveda Mahavidyalaya and Institute of Ayurveda Pharmaceutical Sciences.

Hence, the correct option is (A).

76. James Watt was the inventor of the first steam engine. He developed the first design of the steam engine in 1763.

The steam engines he developed were used to pump water out of mills. This design was later put into locomotives.

Hence, the correct option is (B).

77. In the context of India's space research, 'Vyommitra' is the name of an Indian robot.

Vyommitra, a half-humanoid is being developed by the Indian Space Research Organisation (ISRO). It will go to space in the first test flight of the human space mission, Gaganyaan.

Hence, the correct option is (C).

78. GSLV MK - III is India's heaviest rocket and referred to as 'Bahubali'.

GSLV Mk-III weighs 3,423kg and is the heaviest launcher in India. It is taller than a 13-story building (43 meters, to be precise) and even then, it is the shortest Indian launcher.

Hence, the correct option is (C).

79. Uniform Civil Code:

It provides equal status to all the citizens, promote gender parity, accommodate the aspirations of the young population to support the national integration. It also states that the state has to secure for the citizens a Uniform Civil Code throughout the territory of India. In simple language, it promotes one country one rule.

Article 44: It is made to secure for all citizens a uniform civil code throughout the country.

Hence, the correct option is (B).

80. A flexible constitution is one that can be amended in the same manner as the ordinary laws are made. For example, the British Constitution. A rigid constitution on the other hand is one that requires a special procedure for its amendment. For example, the US Constitution. However, flexibility of the Constitution is NOT a federal feature. Rather, it is a unitary feature of the Constitution.

Hence, the correct option is (A).

81.

Article	Description
Article 19	It guarantees six freedoms to every citizen. 1. Speech and expression 2. Assembly 3. Association or Unions 4. Movement throughout the territory of India 5. Residence 6. Profession
Article 20	Protection with respect to the conviction for offenses.
Article 21	**Protection of life and personal liberty**
Article 21 A	Right to education
Article 22	Protection against arrest and detention in certain cases
Article 23	Prohibition of traffic in human beings and forced labor
Article 24	Prohibition of employment of children in factories, etc

Hence, the correct option is (C).

82. Tropic of Cancer passes through eight Indian states: Rajasthan, Gujarat, Madhya Pradesh, Chhattisgarh, Jharkhand, West Bengal, Tripura and Mizoram.

Tripura, state of India. It is located in the northeastern part of the subcontinent. It is bordered to the north, west, and south by Bangladesh, to the east by the state of Mizoram, and to the northeast by the state of Assam.

Hence, the correct option is (B).

83. Hidden Worlds And Stories Of Progress At Hirakud Dam, Odisha. Hirakud is the longest earthen Dam in the world and stands across the mighty river, Mahanadi, in the Sambalpur region of Odisha. It was the first major multipurpose river valley project after India's Independence in 1947.

Hence, the correct option is (B).

84. Konyak are a one of the groups among the Nagas and have the largest population among the Naga tribes. They live in Nagaland and Arunachal Pradesh in India where they are also

known as Wancho Konyak. Gaddi are a tribe living mainly in the Indian states of Himachal Pradesh and Jammu & Kashmir. Most of them rear Sheeps / Goats. Tharus are recognized as an official nationality by the Government of Nepal and they claim that they are direct descendants of Lord Buddha. In India, they are abundant in Uttarakhand and northern Uttar Pradesh.

Hence, the correct option is (C).

85. The Eastern Highlands mainly consist of tropical moist deciduous forests. It extends across portions of Andhra Pradesh, Chhattisgarh, Jharkhand, Madhya Pradesh, Maharashtra, Orissa, and Telangana states. These forests are found in region where rainfall is between 100 cm to 200cm.

Hence, the correct option is (A).

86. Institute for Research and Development in Banking Technology:

The Institute for Development & Research in Banking Technology (IDRBT) is an institution exclusively focused on banking technology. Established by the Reserve Bank of India (RBI) in 1996, the institution works at the intersection of banking and technology. It is located in Hyderabad, India.

Hence, the correct option is (B).

87. The external account is a major source of worry for policymakers as well as markets in India. India runs a large current account deficit—the difference between exports and imports of goods and services—which is funded by the inflow on the capital account—inflows as investment, both direct and portfolio.

Hence, the correct option is (C).

88. RBI's LAF helps banks to adjust their daily liquidity mismatches. There are two components of LAF viz. repo (repurchase agreement) and reverse repo. When banks need liquidity to meet its daily requirement, they borrow from RBI through repo. The rate at which they borrow fund is called the repo rate. When banks are flush with fund, they park with RBI through the reverse repo mechanism at reverse repo rate. LAF basically is the adjustment of repo and reverse repo rates.

Hence, the correct option is (D).

89. India is the world's largest producer and exporter of handmade carpets in terms of value and volume. Around 75–85 percent of carpets manufactured in India are exported. India is responsible for around 40 percent of the worldwide export of handmade carpets. Exports of handmade carpets from India stood at US$ 1.47 billion in 2018-19.

Hence, the correct option is (C).

90. RBI releases monetary policy once in 2 months. The following are a tools for central bank to achieve the monetary policy:

1. Bank Rate

2. Reserve Ratios

3. Open Market Operations

4. Intervention in forex market

5. Moral Suasion

Hence, the correct option is (D).

91. Financial inclusion means that individuals and businesses have access to useful and affordable financial products and services that meet their needs – transactions, payments, savings, credit and insurance – delivered in a responsible and sustainable way.

Being able to have access to a transaction account is a first step toward broader financial inclusion since a transaction account allows people to store money, and send and receive payments.

Hence, the correct option is (D).

92. VAT is levied on the every stage of production.

value-added tax (VAT) is a type of indirect tax levied on goods and services for value added at every point of production or distribution cycle, starting from raw materials and going all the way to the final retail purchase, Because the consumer bears the entire tax, VAT is also a consumption tax.

Hence, the correct option is (A).

93. There are three rates of income tax are applicable in India i.e. 5%, 10%, 20% and 30% which is progressive in nature initially but later on it becomes Proportional which is called degressive rate.

degressive tax: any tax in which the rate decreases as the amount subject to taxation increases. revenue enhancement, tax, taxation - charge against a citizen's person or property or activity for the support of government. Based on WordNet 3.0, Farlex clipart collection.

Hence, the correct option is (B).

94. The GST council has set the four-tier structure at 0%, 5%, 12%, 18% and 28%. The Government has decided in an attempt to keep inflation in check to exclude essential items such as basic food commodities from tax. However, a 5% tax will be applicable for common commodities. Most of the standard services will fall under the 12%, and 18% tax slab and the luxury items will fall under the 28% slab.

Hence, the correct option is (B).

95. The figures for the FY 2016-17 issued in May 2017 shows that an average person in Delhi earns more than Rs 3 lakh, which is three times the national average. Delhi succeeded Goa in this regard.

Goa has highest NSDP per capita among 33 Indian states and union territories. NSDP per capita of Goa is estimated at Rs 467,998 in 2018-19 at current prices. Ranking of Delhi is two with per capita income around of 365,529 INR.

Hence, the correct option is (A).

96. In the calculation of national income, the value of goods and services produced in a year Is added, while the value of old sold goods and the services of the Housewife are not added.

Symbolically: National Income = Total Rent + Total Wages + Total Interest + Total Profit. goods and services produced in a country during a year is obtained, which is called total final product. This represents Gross Domestic Product (GDP).

Hence, the correct option is (D).

97. Gujarat is the leading state with production of cotton mill cloth with 33% share followed by Punjab with 11.1% share and Maharashtra with 9.9% share.

A cotton mill is a building that houses spinning or weaving machinery for the production of yarn or cloth from cotton, an important product during the Industrial Revolution in the development of the factory system.

Hence, the correct option is (A).

98. Maharashtra is the leading Indian state with the highest number of powerlooms followed by Tamil Nadu, Madhya Pradesh, Gujarat, Uttar Pradesh.

Among all; Maharashtra has highest number of powerlooms amounting to approximately 8 lakhs of powerloom, Tamilnadu is second with 5 lakh units, and Gujarat ranks third with 4 to 4.

Hence, the correct option is (C).

99. Subhash Ola has won the 1st prize for the Amazon Smbhav Entrepreneurship Challenge 2022.

His enterprise "Geniusenergy Critical Innovation Private Limited" has won the Start-up of the Year award.

Hence, the correct option is (D).

100. The fifth Romain Rolland Book Prize - Romain Rolland Book Prize 2022 has been awarded to the Bengali translation of the French novel "Meursault, contre-enquete" (The Meursault Investigation).

Hence, the correct option is (B).

English Language & Comprehension

Q.1 Direction: In the following question, out of the four alternatives, select the word best expresses the meaning of the given word.

Exiguous

A. Bombastic **B.** Petite

C. Conventional **D.** Erroneous

Q.2 Direction: In the following question, out of the four alternatives, select the word opposite in meaning to the given word.

Astute

A. Feasible **B.** Aloof

C. Gregarious **D.** Foolish

Ques (3-4):Direction: In the following question, some part of the sentence is underlined. Which of the options given below the sentence should replace the part underlined to make the sentence grammatically correct?

Q.3 They felt humiliated because they realised that they **had cheated**.

A. have been cheated **B.** had been cheated

C. had been cheating **D.** were to be cheated

Q.4 We met him immediately after the session in which he **had been given** a nice speech.

A. would be giving **B.** has been given

C. will have given **D.** had given

Ques (5-6):Direction: Choose the correct alternative which can be substituted for the below given word/ sentence.

Q.5 Wrap or cover for warmth

A. Encourage **B.** Muffle

C. Divulge **D.** Expose

Q.6 Keen interest or enthusiasm

A. Lassitude **B.** Lethargy

C. Avidity **D.** Soporific

Ques (7-8):Direction: Fill in the blank with an appropriate preposition.

Q.7 The teacher set some homework _____ the end of the lesson.

A. about **B.** in **C.** of **D.** at

Q.8 Unfortunately, we had to cancel it owing _____ the bad weather.

A. in **B.** to **C.** of **D.** about

Ques (9-10):Direction: In the following question, the sentence given with a blank is to be filled in with an appropriate word.

Select the correct alternative out of the four and indicate it by selecting the appropriate option.

Q.9 Even many setbacks in his endeavours never made him falter in his _____.

A. Wish **B.** Supposition

C. Ambitions **D.** Question

Q.10 This letter is to _____ you with the problems faced by the society members.

A. Acquaint **B.** Illustrate

C. Convince **D.** Demonstrate

Q.11 Direction: Fill in the blank with the correct word.

People can see through _____ and, these days, they identify what is fake and exploitative sooner than they did earlier.

A. Inanity **B.** Gimmicks

C. Paradigm **D.** Liturgy

Ques (12-15):Direction: Read the passage carefully and answer the question that follows by choosing the correct alternative out of the given four options.

Nasiruddin was the cleverest man in Khorasan. One of his neighbours was a merchant. He was a great miser. One day the merchant saw Nasiruddin praying inside his house. He was praying in a loud voice asking God to be kind to him and send him 9999 dinars, not a dinar more, or a dinar less. If God sent him even one dinar more, he would return all the money. The merchant could not understand Nasiruddin's prayer. He decided to find out the truth. He put 10,000 dinars in a bag and threw it into Nasiruddin's house. Nasiruddin found the bag and counted the money carefully. He profusely thanked God for giving him 10,000 dinars, when he had asked for only 9999 dinars. The merchants heard Nasiruddin. He realized that Nasiruddin was going to keep the money. He went to Nasiruddin's house. He called him a liar and demanded that his 10,000 dinars be returned to him. Nasiruddin refused, he claimed that he was not a fool to believe that anyone would throw away 10,000 dinars just to test someone's honesty. It was his money given by God in answer to his prayer. The merchant decided to take the matter to the judge. Nasiruddin said that he had no clean clothes to wear. The merchant gave him some of his own clothes to wear. Then they went to see the judge.

The merchant told the judge what had happened. Nasiruddin argued that the merchant was mad. Ever since he lost a lot of money a few months back, he had been talking like a mad man. The judge asked Nasiruddin whether he could prove his charge. He said, "Just now he told you that I stole his money. Next, he is going to tell you that these clothes which I am wearing are also his." The merchant shouted angrily. "Of course, these clothes are mine.

The judge thought for a few minutes. Then he said, "The case is false. Nasiruddin has not stolen his neighbour's money. The merchant is mad. He should be sent to a mental hospital."

Q.12 Nasiruddin was praying in a loud voice because:

A. He wanted to show that he was the cleverest man in Khorasan

B. He wanted to show that he was a holy man

C. He wanted his neighbour to hear his prayer

D. He was in debts and hoped that god would answer his prayers

Q.13 The merchant threw the bag of money into Nasiruddin's house because:

A. He was a miser

B. He found Nasiruddin's prayer interesting

C. He wanted to surprise Nasiruddin by helping him

D. He wanted to catch Nasiruddin red-handed stealing the money

Q.14 When Nasiruddin found the bag of money he thought?

A. God had answered his prayer

B. Someone had been foolish enough to leave the money by mistake

C. His neighbour had thrown it into his house to help him

D. His neighbour had thrown it into his house to see what he would do

Q.15 When the judge heard the case of Nasiruddin, he thought that the merchant:

A. was telling lies

B. was mad

C. was telling the truth, which he could not prove

D. could be telling the truth

Ques (16-17):Direction: In the following question, out of the four alternatives, select the alternative which best expresses the meaning of the Idiom/Phrase.

Q.16 A bad patch

A. A potholed road.

B. A medical bandage.

C. A period of difficulty.

D. Shoddy repair work.

Q.17 A dime a dozen

A. A very expensive proposition

B. Something which appears cheap but which will prove expensive in the long run

C. Something which appears attractive but has zero value

D. Very common and of no particular value

Q.18 Four words are given in the question, out of which only one word is correctly spelt. Find the correctly spelt word.

A. Occasionally   B. Quarentine

C. Reminiscense   D. Withdrawel

Q.19 Four words are given in the question, out of which only one word is correctly spelt. Find the correctly spelt word.

A. Accountansy   B. Asthetics

C. Commomorate   D. Austere

Ques (20-21):Direction: In the question, a sentence has been given in active/passive voice. Out of the given four alternatives, suggest the one which best expresses the given sentence in passive/active voice.

Q.20 Please shut the door and go to sleep.

A. The door is to be shut and you are to go to sleep

B. Let the door be shut and you be asleep

C. You are requested to shut the door and go to sleep

D. The door is to be shut and you are requested to sleep

Q.21 The boy laughed at the beggar.

A. The beggar was laughed by the boy.

B. The beggar was being laughed by the boy

C. The beggar was being laughed at by the boy.

D. The beggar was laughed at by the boy.

Q.22 Which is the subjective pronoun in the sentences?

We cannot go to the movie until my mom gives permission to go.

A. my   B. we   C. until   D. can

Q.23 Which is the relative pronoun in the sentence?

The success is only for those who believe in hard working.

A. is   B. for   C. who   D. in

Q.24 Which word is a compound noun?

We know our art teacher will not take our class.

A. not   B. art teacher

C. class   D. know

Q.25 Which word is a singular noun?

Each day in my life having a same routine.

A. same   B. my   C. each   D. life

Analytical Abilities

Q.26 Direction: A series is given with one term missing. Select the correct alternative from the given ones that will complete the series.

80Y54, 40W46, 20U40, 10S36, ?

A. 5Q34   B. 5Q30   C. 5P30   D. 5P34

Q.27 Direction: In the given series one word/one term is missing. Select the correct alternative from the given ones that will complete the series.

Pig, Mead, Poise, Snarls,?

A. Garnets   B. Permuted

C. Bouffant   D. Heaths

Q.28 BRIDGE is written as DTKFIG in a certain code. How will STORY be written in that code?

A. UVPTA   B. VLXWT

C. UWXLA   D. UVQTA

Q.29 If NATIONALS can be written UZOONJTKB, how can DOMISTICS be written?

A. CDIOMTES   B. NNEURJTBJ

C. NNEURJBTJ   D. NNERUJTBJ

Ques (30-31):Direction: Study the following information and answer the question given below.

In the figure shown below, the rectangle represents managers, the triangle represents women, and the circle represents singers.

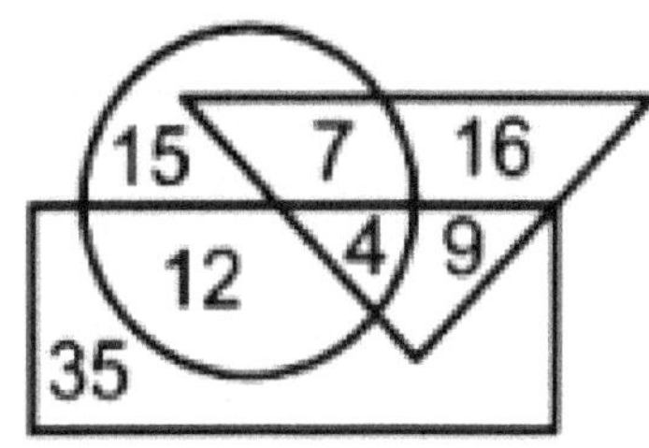

Q.30 How many women are managers?

A. 29   **B.** 32   **C.** 13   **D.** 12

Q.31 How many singers are neither women nor managers?

A. 15   **B.** 12   **C.** 17   **D.** 27

Ques (32-33):Direction: In the following question statements are given and these statements are followed by conclusions. You have to take the given statements to be true even if they seem to be at variance from commonly known facts. Read the conclusions and then decide which of the given conclusions logically follows from the given statements, disregarding commonly known facts.

Q.32 Statements:

All the bottles are boxes.

All the boxes are bags.

Some bags are trays.

Conclusions:

I. Some bottles are trays.

II. Some trays are boxes.

III. All the bottles are bags.

IV. Some trays are bags.

A. Only (III) and (IV) follow

B. Only (I) and (II) follow

C. Only (II) and (III) follow

D. Only (I) and (IV) follow

Q.33 Statements:

Some cars are jeeps.

All the boxes are jeeps.

All the pens are cars.

Conclusions:

I. Some cars are boxes.

II. No pen is jeep.

III. Some boxes are cars.

A. Only (I) and (II) follow

B. Only (I) and (III) follow

C. Only (II) and (III) follow

D. None of three

Q.34 Samir is taller than Sanjana, but shorter than Sushila .Sona is as tall as Samir, but shorter than Sandeep, who is not as tall as Sushila. Who is the tallest?

A. Sanjana   **B.** Sushila   **C.** Sandeep   **D.** Samir

Q.35 Six children A, B, C, D, E, and F are standing in a row. B is between F and D. E is between A and C. A does not stand next to either F or D. C does not stand next to D. Which pair is sitting at Extreme end of the line?

A. B and A   **B.** D and C   **C.** B and D   **D.** D and A

Ques (36-37):Direction: In the question are given two statements I and II. These statements may be either independent causes or may be effects of independent causes or a common cause. One of these statements may be the effect of the other statements. Read both the statements and decide which of the following answer choice correctly depicts the relationship between these two statements.

Q.36 Statements:

I. The literacy rate in the district has been increasing for the last four years.

II. The district administration has conducted extensive training programme for the workers involved in the literacy drive.

A. Statement I is the cause and statement II is its effect

B. Statement II is the cause and statement I is its effect

C. Both the statements I and II are independent causes

D. Both the statements I and II are effects of independent causes

Q.37 Statements:

I. Standard of living among the middle-class society is constantly going up for part of few years.

II. Indian Economy is observing remarkable growth.

A. Statement I is the cause and statement II is its effect

B. Statement II is the cause and statement I is its effect

C. Both the statements I and II are independent causes

D. Both the statements I and II are effects of independent causes

Q.38 Direction: In the following question, one statement is given followed by two conclusions I and II. You have to consider the statements to be true, even if they seem to be at variance from commonly known facts. You have to decide which of the given conclusions, if any, follow from the given statements.

Statement:

Self-discipline is the key to order in society.

Conclusions:

I. Disturbances in society are due to people without self-discipline.

II. There is nobody with self-discipline in society.

A. Both conclusions I and II follow

B. Neither conclusion I nor II follows

C. Only conclusion I follows

D. Only Conclusion II follows

Q.39 Direction: Two statements are followed by two conclusions I and II. You have to consider the statements to be true even if they seem to be at variance from commonly known facts. You have to decide which of the given conclusions, if any, follow from the given statements.

Statements:

The constitution assures fundamental rights.

Parliament has the right to amend the constitution.

Conclusions:

I. The Parliament includes fundamental rights in the constitution.

II. The Parliament did not assure fundamental rights.

A. Only conclusion I follows

B. Only conclusion II follows

C. Both conclusions I and II follow

D. Neither of the above

Ques (40-41):Direction: One statement is given followed by two assumptions, I and II. You have to consider the statement to be true, even if it seems to be at variance from commonly known facts. You are to decide which of the given assumptions can definitely be drawn from the given statement.

Q.40 Statement:

Some people are uneducated and therefore, superstitious.

Assumptions:

I. Education increases rational thinking.

II. Some people don't go to schools.

A. Only assumption II is implicit

B. Both assumptions I and II are implicit

C. Neither assumption I nor II is implicit

D. Only assumption I is implicit

Q.41 Statement:

Read this notice before entering into the stadium.

Assumptions:

I. People are literate.

II. No blind person comes to the stadium.

A. Only assumption I is implicit

B. Only assumption II is implicit

C. Neither I nor II is implicit

D. Both I and II are implicit

Ques (42-43):Direction: The question given below is followed by two arguments numbered I and II. You have to decide which of the argument is a strong argument and which is a weak argument.

Q.42 Statement: Should loyalty be the only criterion for promotion in any organization?

Arguments:

I. Yes. Without loyal men, no organization can function.

II. No. It leads to hypocrisy and partiality.

A. Only I is strong

B. Only II is strong

C. Either I or II is strong

D. Both I and II are strong

Q.43 Statement: Should a total ban be put on trapping wild animals?

Arguments:

I. Yes, trappers are making a lot of money.

II. No, bans on hunting and trapping are not effective.

A. Only I is strong

B. Only II is strong

C. Neither I nor II is strong

D. Both I and II are strong

Q.44 Direction: The below question is based on the following information:

M % N means M is the son of N.

M @ N means M is the sister of N.

M $ N means M is the father of N.

Which of the following shows the relation that R is the granddaughter of S?

A. R @ B % F % S

B. B $ F $ S % R

C. R % B $ F $ S

D. S % B $ F $ R

Q.45 Pointing to a woman, Abhinav said, "Her granddaughter is the only daughter of my brother." How is the woman related to Abhinav?

A. Sister

B. Grandmother

C. Sister-in-law

D. Mother

Q.46 A child is looking for his father. He went 90 m in the east before turning to his right. He went 20 m before turning to his right again to look for his father at his Uncle's place 30m from this point. He didn't find his father. From there, he went 100 m to his north before meeting his father in a street. How far did the son meet his father from the starting point?

A. 150 m

B. 200 m

C. 100 m

D. 50 m

Q.47 Mr. X goes 45 m to the North – East of his house. Then he goes 45 m to the South – East of his house and then again 45 m to the South – West. Now he turns towards his house. In which direction is he going now?

A. South – West

B. North – West

C. South – East

D. North – East

Ques (48-49):Direction: In the question select the related word from the given alternatives.

Q.48 Road: Car::Sky:?

A. Train

B. Airplane

C. Bus

D. Boat

Q.49 Breeze : Cyclone : : Drizzle : ?

A. Earthquake

B. Storm

C. Flood

D. Downpour

Q.50 In the following question, find the odd number from the given alternatives.

A. 111

B. 315

C. 552

D. 644

Legal Awareness & Aptitude

Q.51 Mala fide means:

A. In good faith

B. In bad faith

C. In utmost good faith

D. Man of Faith

Q.52 En Ventre Sa Mere is a person in being for the purpose of:

A. Punishment of abortion

B. Acquisition of property

C. Creation of partnership

D. Claiming compensation in torts

Q.53 Actio personalis moritur cum persona means:

A. A personal right of action dies with the person

B. Personal Care of citizens

C. An action directed toward a Criminal for reformation.

D. An action is not given to him who is not injured

Q.54 Autrefois convict means:

A. No person can be punished twice for the same offense

B. One who repeats the same offense can be punished twice

C. Neither (A) nor (B)

D. Automatically Convict on the basis of Presumption of Law

Q.55 What is the result of successful prosecution?

A. Acquittal

B. Discharge

C. Convention

D. Charge sheeting

Q.56 Who among the following was the first Chief Information Commissioner of India?

A. Wajahat Habibullah

B. Irfan Habib

C. Tahir Mahmood

D. Najma Heptullah

Q.57 The retired judge of High Court is not permitted to practice as a lawyer in:

A. Supreme Court

B. Any court in India

C. High Courts

D. The High Court where he retired from

Q.58 Who appoints the judges of district courts?

A. Governor

B. Chief Minister

C. Law Minister

D. President

Q.59 Which of the following comes under the jurisdiction of both the High Court and the Supreme Court?

A. Disputes between the states interse

B. Protection against the vipolation of the Constitution

C. Protection of fundamental rights

D. Disputes between centre andthe State

Q.60 Which one of the following statements about the Chief Justice of India (CJI) is not correct?

A. He appoints the Chief Justice of all High Courts

B. The CJI administers 'the oath' of office to the President

C. When both the office of the President and Vice President fall vacant simultaneously, the CJI discharges the duties of the President

D. The CJI can hold his office till he attains the age of 65 years

Q.61 Who was the first woman judge to be appointed to the Supreme Court of India?

A. Justice Smt Gyan Sudha Mishra

B. Justice Smt M. Fathima Beevi

C. Justice Smt Leila Seth

D. Justice Smt Ranjana Desai

Q.62 Which of the following acts does not fall under the categories of fraud?

A. International false statement of facts

B. Active concealment of facts

C. Innocent false statement

D. Promise made without intention to perform

Q.63 An agreement to do an impossible act is:

A. Avoidable agreement

B. Void agreement

C. Valid agreement

D. Illegal agreement

Q.64 Which one is not true about the Attorney General of India?

A. He is the legal advisor to the Government of India

B. His tenure and salary is decided by the President

C. He has the voting right in the proceeding of the Parliament

D. He appears before high courts and Supreme Court in cases involving union government.

Q.65 A nominal sum given as a token for striking a sale is called:

A. Earnest money

B. Advance

C. Interest

D. Solatium

Q.66 A, enters a house with the intention of committing theft. But moved by the poverty of the house holder he drops a rupee note and left the place. In this case:

A. A will be liable for criminal trespass

B. A will not be liable for criminal trespass

C. No offence

D. None of the above

Q.67 Principle: An abettor is liable for the crime of abetment only with regard to the crime which reasonably resulted from his abetment.

Facts: A instigates B to burn Z's house. B sets fire to the house and at the same time commits theft of property there.

A is responsible for abetting which of the following crimes?

A. Theft

B. Arson

C. Both

D. Neither

Q.68 Principle: Nothing is an offence which is done by a child above seven years of age and under twelve, who has not attained sufficient maturity of understanding to judge of the nature and consequences of his conduct on that occasion.

Facts: A is a nine year old boy who is jealous of his friend B's many toys. One day while playing at B's house, he steals one of the B's smaller toys. Has he committed theft?

A. Yes

B. No

C. Only if B really attached to the toy

D. Cannot be determined

Q.69 In which of the following cases Section 66(A) of the IT Act was struck down?

A. Shreya singhal vs Union of India

B. Naz foundation vs NCT Delhi

C. Sneha Singhal vs Union of India

D. Lilavati vs State of Maharashtra

Q.70 In which of the following cases Supreme court gave legal recognition to Third genders?

A. Yakub Abdul Razak Memon vs State of Maharashtra
B. Sushil Ansal vs State Thr CBI
C. Novartis vs Union of India & Others
D. National Legal Services Authority vs Union of India

Q.71 In which case the 42nd Amendment Act were declared as null and void by the Supreme Court?
A. Minerva mills's vs union of India
B. M.c Mehta vs union of India
C. Kasturi vs state of Rajasthan
D. Keshavnanda bharati vs state of kerala

Q.72 Under section 498A of IPC cruelty includes:
A. Harassment of the woman
B. Physical cruelty only
C. Mental cruelty only
D. Cruelty by the wife

Q.73 Section 64 of IPC provides for:
A. Nature & maximum limit of imprisonment for non-payment of fine
B. Nature & minimum limit of imprisonment for non-payment of fine
C. Nature but does not prescribe any limit of imprisonment for non-payment of fine
D. Limit of imprisonment for non-payment of fine but does not prescribe the nature of imprisonment

Q.74 Accident as an exception has been dealt with in:
A. Section 77
B. Section 78
C. Section 80
D. Section 82

Q.75 Who was the President of the drafting committee of the Indian Penal Code?
A. Lord William Bentinck
B. Lord Thomas Babington Macaulay
C. Lord Curzon
D. Lord Irwin

General Knowledge

Q.76 Who is considered the "father of Wi-Fi"?
A. Terence Percival
B. Graham Daniels
C. John Deane
D. Vic Hayes

Q.77 Which is the first private space company to send astronauts into space?
A. Blue Origin
B. Tesla
C. SpaceX
D. Orbital

Q.78 India's first COVID-19 vaccine to get approval for children above 12 Years was ________.
A. Covaxin
B. Sputnik
C. ZyCoV-D
D. Covishield

Q.79 In December 2021, SpaceX has launched 52 Starlink internet satellites into orbit from California base. Which rocket has been used to launch these sattelites?
A. Voyger Cassini
B. Falcon-9
C. Falcon-7
D. Rover-4

Q.80 Which among the following is the official language of the Union Territory of Lakshadweep?
A. Tamil
B. Malayalam
C. Great Andamanese
D. Sinhala

Q.81 The amendment of the constitution can be initiated in which of the following?
1. Lok Sabha
2. Rajya Sabha
3. State Assemblies

Select the correct option from the codes given below:
A. Only 1
B. Only 1 or 2
C. Only 1 or 3
D. 1 or 2 or 3

Q.82 The Paddy fields of India are located in the areas of annual rainfall:
A. 120 cm
B. 140 cm
C. 100 cm
D. 80 cm

Q.83 Fertility of soil can be improved by ________.
A. Adding living earthworms
B. Adding dead earthworms
C. Removing dead earthworms
D. Removing living earthworms and adding dead earthworms

Q.84 Urban Cooperative Banks are also called:
A. Short-term co-operatives
B. Secondary Cooperative Banks
C. Primary Cooperative Banks
D. Long-term co-operatives

Q.85 The oldest public bank in India is ________.
A. Bank of India
B. State Bank of India
C. Bank of Hindustan
D. Allahabad Bank

Q.86 When depreciation is deducted from GNP, the net value is:
A. Net national product
B. Net domestic product
C. Gross national product
D. Disposable income

Q.87 Which statement is correct for nominal GDP?
i. Nominal GDP is calculated based on current prices.
ii. Nominal GDP is calculated based on the base prices.
iii. Data on Nominal GDP shows an accurate picture of the economy as compared to real GDP.
A. Only ii, iii
B. Only ii
C. Only i
D. Only i, iii

Q.88 If 'Tata Company' imports a product from abroad, then which tax will be levied on it?
A. VAT
B. Custom duty
C. Income tax
D. Corporation tax

Q.89 Which of the following tax is imposed by the Central Government but the state government collects it?
A. VAT
B. Income tax
C. Corporation tax
D. Stamp Duty

Q.90 Which is called as the heavy engineering industry?

A. Heavy Electricals

B. Heavy Machinery

C. Glass

D. Iron and steel

Q.91 Which is the largest shipbuilding unit in India?

A. Cochin shipyard

B. Hindustan shipyard

C. Goa shipyard

D. Garden Reach shipyard

Q.92 Inflation is measured in India on the basis of which 'Index'?

A. Wholesale Price Index

B. Consumer Price Index for urban workers

C. Consumer Price Index for agricultural workers

D. National income deflation

Q.93 Planning commission constituted a high level committee for financial sector reforms in August 2007 under the Chairmanship of:

A. K.V. Kamath

B. Raghuram Govinda Rajan

C. Bimal Jalan

D. None of these

Q.94 The Mid Day Meal Scheme was launched on:

A. August 15, 2000

B. August 15, 1992

C. August 15, 1995

D. August 15, 2001

Q.95 In the World, in the production of cotton, India ranks:

A. Second

B. First

C. Third

D. Fourth

Q.96 Which of the following provisions can be passed with the simple majority of the Parliament?

A. Removal of Chief Justice of Supreme Court

B. Constitution of State Legislative Council

C. Salaries and allowances of Members of Parliament

D. Fundamental Rights

Q.97 When the name of the State is changed or a new State is created, the Constitution of India is required to be amended by Parliament by a:

A. Simple majority as under Articles 107 and 108 of Constitution

B. Majority of total numbers of both the Houses under Article 368

C. Special majority under Article 368 of Constitution

D. Special majority after obtaining opinion of the concerned State, under Article 3 of the Constitution

Q.98 In which of the following case, a special majority is used in the Parliament?

A. Removal of Vice President

B. For removing Speaker & Deputy Speaker of the Lok Sabha

C. Acquisition and Termination of Citizenship

D. For Removal of Chairman or Vice-Chairman of the Legislative Council

Q.99 Who has won the 2022 Scripps National Spelling Bee?

A. Vikram Raju

B. Harini Logan

C. Ekansh Rastogi

D. Shijay Sivakumar

Q.100 Which state has won the World No Tobacco Day Award 2022?

A. Jharkhand

B. Odisha

C. Gujarat

D. Madhya Pradesh

// Smart Answer Sheet //

Correct Percentage of students who answered correctly. **Skipped** Percentage of students who skipped.

Q.	Ans.	Correct	Skipped
1	B	60.8 %	31.39 %
2	D	53.78 %	40.12 %
3	B	40.32 %	57.19 %
4	D	47.68 %	49.74 %
5	B	54.53 %	34.4 %
6	C	12.81 %	68.76 %
7	D	40.63 %	49.73 %
8	B	69.03 %	30.77 %
9	C	55.97 %	41.21 %
10	A	10.19 %	83.32 %
11	B	54.47 %	43.61 %
12	C	45.81 %	44.0 %
13	B	68.2 %	31.45 %
14	D	65.48 %	30.13 %
15	B	42.7 %	37.14 %
16	C	59.17 %	31.62 %
17	D	41.0 %	37.38 %
18	A	89.2 %	10.7 %
19	D	57.43 %	33.98 %
20	C	63.01 %	36.42 %
21	D	52.41 %	38.95 %
22	B	69.71 %	30.18 %
23	C	65.58 %	33.05 %
24	B	21.25 %	74.35 %
25	D	52.64 %	32.85 %
26	A	42.97 %	51.75 %
27	A	21.03 %	77.78 %
28	D	47.65 %	38.99 %
29	B	45.36 %	31.27 %
30	C	42.78 %	43.88 %
31	A	58.18 %	36.81 %
32	A	66.92 %	33.07 %
33	D	44.72 %	39.74 %
34	B	41.13 %	50.74 %
35	D	43.55 %	34.29 %
36	B	29.79 %	68.57 %
37	A	47.22 %	32.82 %
38	C	65.4 %	33.37 %
39	D	32.74 %	67.15 %
40	D	49.76 %	35.56 %
41	A	46.23 %	31.82 %
42	B	62.88 %	33.85 %
43	C	58.07 %	30.47 %
44	A	49.38 %	31.52 %
45	D	16.44 %	82.35 %
46	C	66.66 %	30.39 %
47	B	53.91 %	37.64 %
48	B	46.03 %	36.66 %
49	D	80.85 %	11.58 %
50	D	51.65 %	45.83 %
51	B	57.99 %	35.2 %
52	B	46.64 %	47.81 %
53	A	22.06 %	72.37 %
54	A	13.95 %	78.23 %
55	C	42.55 %	48.13 %
56	A	59.08 %	37.86 %
57	D	40.77 %	52.26 %
58	A	60.24 %	37.72 %
59	C	29.8 %	67.29 %
60	A	57.46 %	41.38 %
61	B	51.32 %	41.06 %
62	C	45.37 %	49.75 %
63	B	31.57 %	68.07 %
64	C	67.85 %	31.34 %
65	A	58.86 %	37.81 %
66	A	68.85 %	30.86 %
67	B	55.87 %	34.78 %
68	B	51.3 %	37.3 %
69	A	53.91 %	36.3 %
70	D	65.43 %	33.51 %
71	A	28.45 %	68.33 %
72	A	12.59 %	85.34 %
73	C	40.17 %	59.41 %
74	C	18.27 %	75.08 %
75	B	40.9 %	50.07 %
76	D	51.75 %	46.91 %
77	C	52.45 %	40.67 %
78	C	65.19 %	34.8 %
79	B	42.01 %	47.21 %
80	B	46.36 %	30.35 %

Q.	Ans.	Correct		Q.	Ans.	Correct		Q.	Ans.	Correct		Q.	Ans.	Correct		Q.	Ans.	Correct
		Skipped				Skipped				Skipped				Skipped				Skipped
81	B	60.87 %		85	B	53.12 %		89	D	47.53 %		93	B	56.47 %		97	C	52.48 %
		35.65 %				40.97 %				31.67 %				31.64 %				36.81 %
82	C	77.63 %		86	A	52.55 %		90	B	54.11 %		94	C	50.57 %		98	C	47.83 %
		21.59 %				42.36 %				42.58 %				30.31 %				34.52 %
83	A	52.67 %		87	C	58.59 %		91	A	40.32 %		95	B	45.36 %		99	B	78.9 %
		41.71 %				36.64 %				33.56 %				31.2 %				10.02 %
84	C	14.24 %		88	B	41.26 %		92	A	56.54 %		96	D	58.13 %		100	A	45.91 %
		84.13 %				37.31 %				42.67 %				41.47 %				48.13 %

//Hints and Solutions//

1. The meanings of the words are:

Exiguous - small

Petite - small

Bombastic - pompous

Conventional - old

Erroneous - wrong

Hence, the correct option is (B).

2. The meanings of the words are:

Astute - having or showing an ability to accurately assess situations or people and turn this to one's advantage.

Hence, the word opposite in meaning would be foolish.

Feasible - possible and practical to do easily or conveniently

Aloof - not friendly to other people; distant

Gregarious - liking to be with other people

Hence, the correct option is (D).

3. They felt humiliated because they realised that they **had been** cheated.

Hence, the correct option is (B).

4. We met him immediately after the session in which he **had given** a nice speech.

Hence, the correct option is (D).

5. The word 'Muffle' is a verb and it means 'to make a sound quieter and less clear'.

Muffle- to wrap up so as to conceal or protect

Example: The house has double-glazed windows to muffle the noise of aircraft.

Hence, the correct option is (B).

6. The word 'Avidity' is a noun and it means 'the quality of being extremely eager or interested'

Example: He studied Indian history with avidity.

Hence, the correct option is (C).

7. The teacher set some homework **at** the end of the lesson.

The preposition 'at' is used when referring to buildings as locations in a city. This can be confused with the preposition 'in'. Generally, 'in' is used with buildings to mean that something occurs inside the building. 'At', on the other hand, is used to express that something happens at the location.

Hence, the correct option is (D).

8. Unfortunately, we had to cancel it owing **to** the bad weather.

Use the preposition 'to' when indicating that there is movement from one place to another. In other words, the preposition 'to'

with verbs such as drive, walk, go, hike, fly, sail, etc. We're flying to San Francisco on Thursday for a meeting.

Hence, the correct option is (B).

9. 'To falter' is to lose strength. The blank must contain a noun that conveys the meaning of the sentence. As even the setbacks did not make him lose his strength, that means he must be very strong in his desire to achieve through his endeavours, 'ambition' becomes apt here. 'Wish', 'suppositions' are too vague as words to aptly fit the blank.

Hence, the correct option is (C).

10. The sentence makes it understood that the person gets to know about the problems from the letter. The meanings of the words are:

Acquaint - make someone aware of or familiar with

Illustrate - serve as an example of

Convince - cause (someone) to believe firmly in the truth of something

Demonstrate - clearly show the existence or truth of (something) by giving proof or evidence

Hence, the correct option is (A).

11. The meanings of the words are:

Inanity - A nonsensical remark or action

Gimmicks - A trick or device intended to attract attention, publicity, or trade

Paradigm - A typical example or pattern of something

Liturgy - A form of public worship

Thus, option (B) fits here in the best way and conveys the meaning that people can see through tricks and identify them.

People can see through **gimmicks** and, these days, they identify what is fake and exploitative sooner than they did earlier.

Hence, the correct option is (B).

12. After reading the whole story it becomes obvious that Nasiruddin wanted his neighbour to hear him so that he could lure him into his scheme.

Hence, the correct option is (C).

13. The neighbour threw the bag of money into Nasiruddin's house as an act out of curiosity because he was unable to understand the interesting prayer.

Hence, the correct option is (B).

14. Nasiruddin was a clever man who knew that his neighbour was a miser merchant. So he intentionally said the prayer loudly for the merchant to hear. Thus when he got the bag of money he knew that it was sent to him by his neighbour to see what he would do since. This is because during his prayer Nasiruddin asked for exactly 9999 dinars and not a dinar more or less. He had also mentioned that he would return if the bag had one dinar more or less. So when he received the bag of 10000 dinars from his neighbour he knew that it was thrown to his house to see what he would do.

Hence, the correct option is (D).

15. The last part of the passage clearly mentions that the judge without any hesitation termed the merchant mad.

Hence, the correct option is (B).

16. 'A bad patch' is an idiom and it means 'If you have or go through a bad patch or a rough patch, you have a lot of problems for a time.'

Example: I'm going through a very bad patch just now.

Hence, the correct option is (C).

17. 'A dime a dozen' is an idiom and it means 'Very common and of no particular value'.

Example: Don't bother to buy one of these—they're a dime a dozen.

Hence, the correct option is (D).

18. Occasionally is the correctly spelt word.

The correct spellings of the other options are as follows:

- Quarantine
- Reminiscence
- Withdrawal

Hence, the correct option is (A).

19. The correct spellings are:

Accountancy

Aesthetics

Commemorate

The correctly spelt word is 'Austere',

Hence, the correct option is (D).

20. You are requested to shut the door and go to sleep.

Given sentence is an Imperative sentence and started with Please that means sentence contains a request in it.

Rule:

Please /kindly → You are requested to. You are requested + rest of sentence.

Hence, the correct option is (C).

21. Given sentence is in Past indefinite (Past simple) tense and it is in the active voice. To change it into Passive voice Object (the boy) will become subject and subject (The beggar) will be object. We also use helping verb of past simple tense was with V3 form of the main verb. Keep it in mind that the preposition at must be retained with the verb.

Rule :

Subject + (was /were) + V3 + Other Agents.

Hence, the correct option is (D).

22. "We" is the first person plural pronoun. "We" is used as the subject of a verb. A speaker or writer uses "We" to refer both to himself or herself and to one or more other people as a group. You can use "We" before a noun to make it clear which group of people you are referring to.

Hence, the correct option is (B).

23. "Who" is a subject pronoun, like I, he, she, we, and they. "Whom" is an object pronoun, like me, him, her, us, and them. When the pronoun is the object of a verb or preposition, the object form is the one you want.

Hence, the correct option is (C).

24. Compound nouns are sometimes one word, like toothpaste, haircut, or bedroom. These are often referred to as closed or solid compound nouns. Sometimes compound nouns are connected with a hyphen: dry-cleaning, daughter-in-law, and well-being are some examples of hyphenated compound nouns.

Hence, the correct option is (B).

25. If you look at one object and name it, you have an example of a singular noun. For example, there is one lamp on my bookcase and one chair at my desk. In these examples the nouns lamp, bookcase, chair, and desk are all singular because they indicate only one.

Hence, the correct option is (D).

26. Given Series: 80Y54, 40W46, 20U40, 10S36, ?

The logic followed for the first numbers:

First Numbers: 80, 40, 20, 10

$80 \div 2 = 40$

$40 \div 2 = 20$

$20 \div 2 = 10$

$10 \div 2 = \mathbf{5}$

The logic followed for the letter:

Letters are: Y, W, U, S,

$$Y \xrightarrow{-2} W \xrightarrow{-2} U \xrightarrow{-2} S \xrightarrow{-2} Q$$

The logic followed for the second numbers:

Second numbers: 54, 46, 40, 36

$54 - 46 = 8$

$46 - 40 = 6$

$40 - 36 = 4$

$36 - \mathbf{34} = 2$

So, the next term will be 5Q34.

Hence, the correct option is (A).

27. Here, the number of letters in a word increases by one in the series.

Pig is a three-letter word.

Mead is a four-letter word.

Similarly,

Poise, Snarls are five and six-letter words respectively.

Hence, the next word in the series will be a seven-letter word.

Garnets are a seven-letter word.

Hence, the correct option is (A).

28.

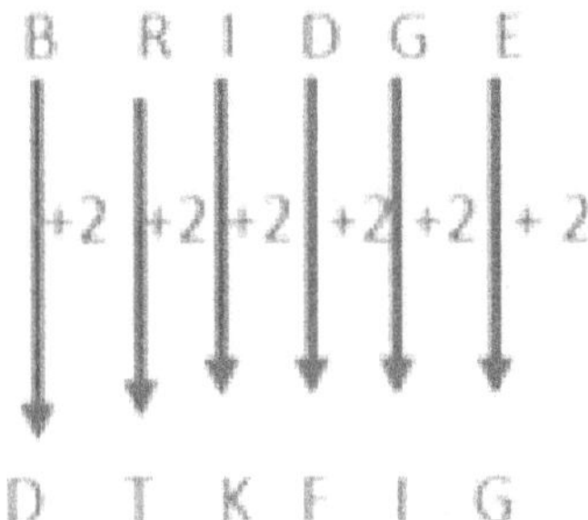

Similarly,

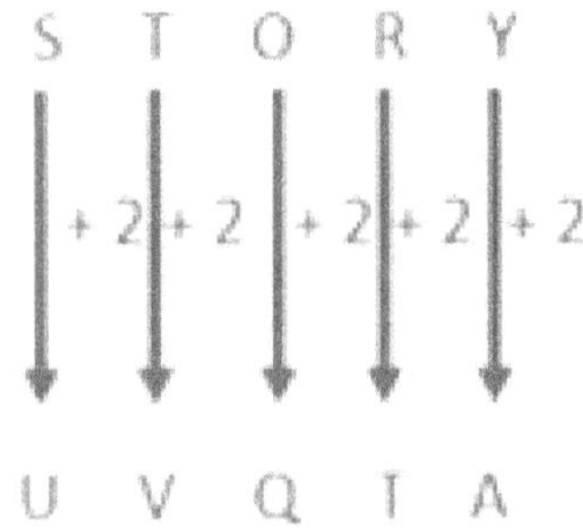

So, "STORY" will be coded as "UVQTA".

Hence, the correct option is (D).

29. The pattern is as follows,

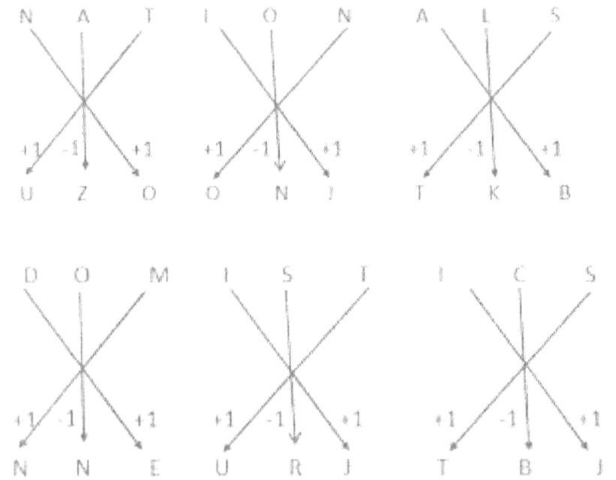

So, DOMISTICS can be written as NNEURJTBJ.

Hence, the correct option is (B).

30. According to the given information, the Venn diagram is as follows:

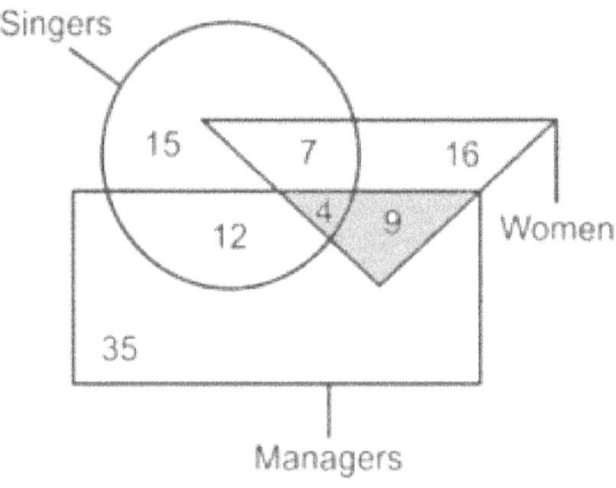

Women who are only managers = 9

Women who are managers as well as singers = 4

So, women who are manager = 9 + 4 = 13

Hence, the correct option is (C).

31.

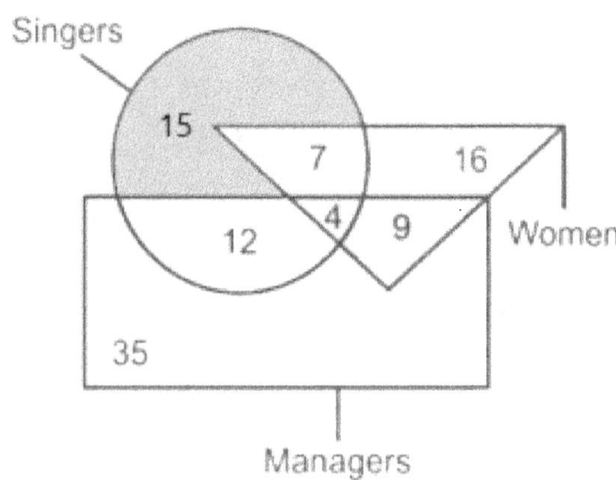

Hence, there are 15 singers who are neither managers nor women.

Hence, the correct option is (A).

32.

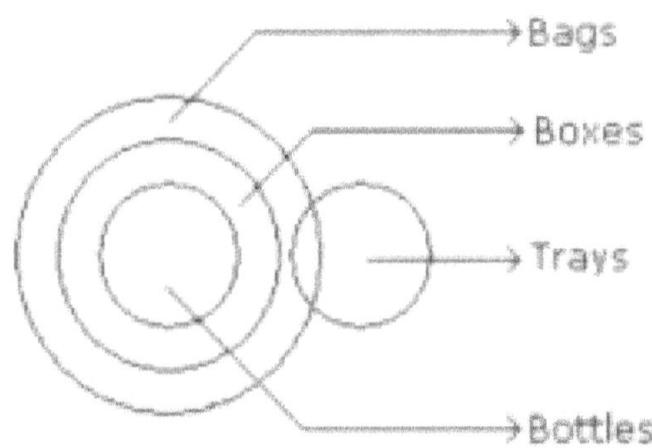

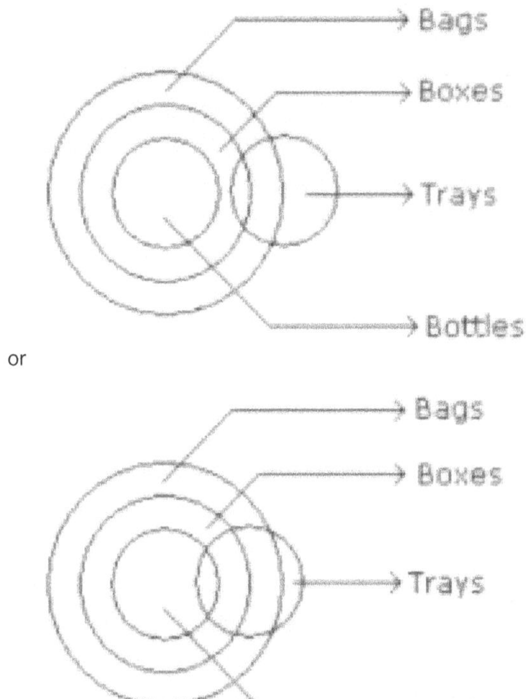

or

or

Hence, the correct option is (A).

33.

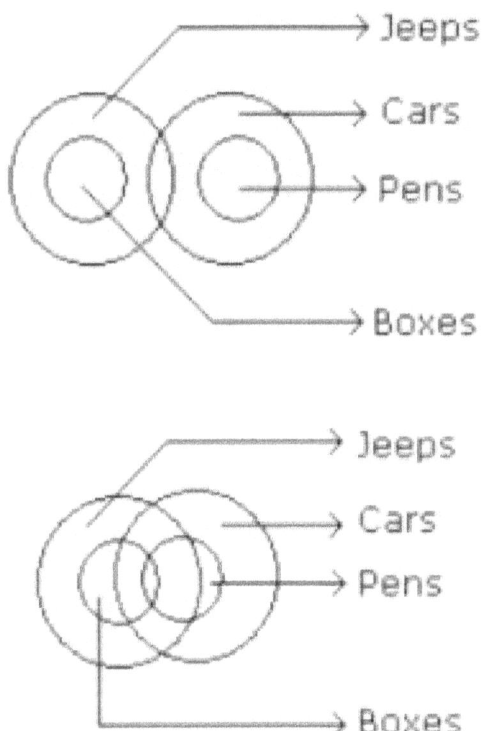

or

Hence, the correct option is (D).

34. Samir is taller than Sanjana, but shorter than Sushila

Sushila> Samir >Sanjana

Sona is as tall as Samir, but shorter than Sandeep, who is not as tall as Sushila.

Sandeep >Sona= Samir

Sandeep<Sushila

Combining all the inequalities

Sushila>Sandeep >Sona= Samir >Sanjana

So, Sushila is the tallest.

Hence, the correct option is (B).

35. B is between F and D = FbyD   B   FbyD

E is between A and C = AbyC   E   AbyC

A does not stand next to F or D, and C does not stand next to D so,

"D B F C E A" will be the standing arrangement,

where D and A are sitting Extreme end of the line.

Hence, the correct option is (D).

36. As the district administration has conducted extensive training programme for the workers involved in the literacy drive, therefore, the literacy in the district has been increasing for the last four years.

Hence, the correct option is (B).

37. Since the standard of living among the middle class society is constantly going up so Indian Economy is observing remarkable growth.

Hence, the correct option is (A).

38. Conclusion I:

Disturbances in the society are due to people without self-discipline.

We see that the question sentence states that discipline is key to ORDER in the society so people without discipline must be the source of the disturbance. Hence, it follows.

Conclusion II:

There is nobody with self-discipline in the society.

There is no given statement in the argument about all the people in the society that points or establishes this fact. Thus, this conclusion does not follow.

Hence, the correct option is (C).

39. Let us examine the conclusions:

1. There is no information in the statements to show who included the fundamental rights in the constitution. Thus, we cannot say for sure if the Parliament included the fundamental rights. Thus this conclusion does not follow.

2. Since the Parliament has the right to amend the constitution, in some cases, thus the Parliament can also assure the fundamental rights. Thus the second conclusion also does not follow.

Hence, the correct option is (D).

40. The statement tells us that uneducated people are superstitious. Here it has been assumed that education decreases superstitious thinking by increasing rational thinking.

While the statement tells us that lack of education causes superstitious thinking, it doesn't tell us anything about schools. People could go to school and still remain uneducated, while some may never go to school but educate themselves. So from the given statement, we can only talk about education and the lack of it, but not about people going to schools.

Hence, the correct option is (D).

41. Let us analyze both the statement and the assumptions:

Statement: Read this notice before entering the stadium.

Assumptions:

I. People are literate.

Implicit because if people are not literate they cannot read the notice. And, the message is intended to be read before entering the stadium.

II. No blind person comes to the stadium.

It is not implicit as there is no information provided in the statement to support it. Blind people cannot see does not mean they DO NOT come to the stadium.

Hence, the correct option is (A).

42. The argument I not strong here because loyalty is no proper reason for promotion in any organization, there are other criteria that can be analyzed for a promotion like an experience efficiency, etc. And focusing singularly on the loyalty of an employee while judging them for a promotion can lead to hypocrisy and partiality in the organization. So, argument II is strong here.

Hence, the correct option is (B).

43. The ban should be imposed not for the reason that trappers are making money, but for protecting our natural environment. Argument II is not strong as there is no information provided in favor of it. We cannot say that bans are not effective.

Hence, the correct option is (C).

44.

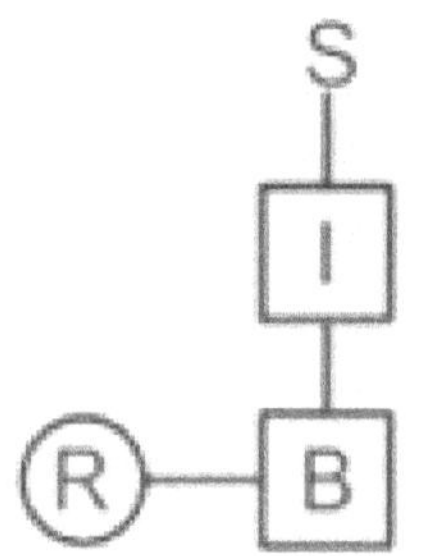

R @ B ⇒ R is the sister of B

B % F ⇒ B is the son of F

Hence, ⇒ R is the daughter of F

F % S ⇒ F is the son of S

So, R is the granddaughter of S.

Hence, the correct option is (A).

45. Following symbols are used:

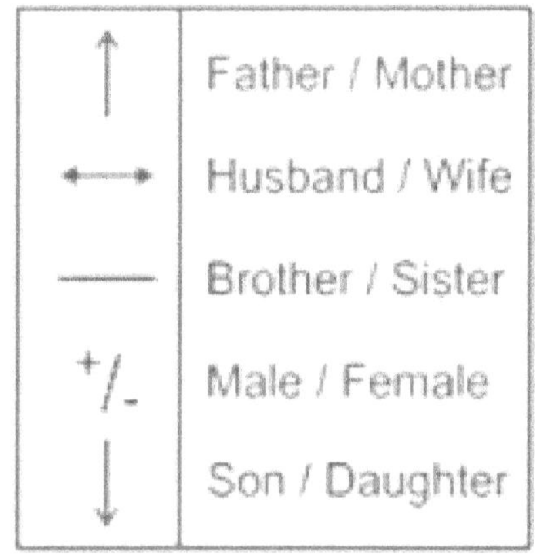

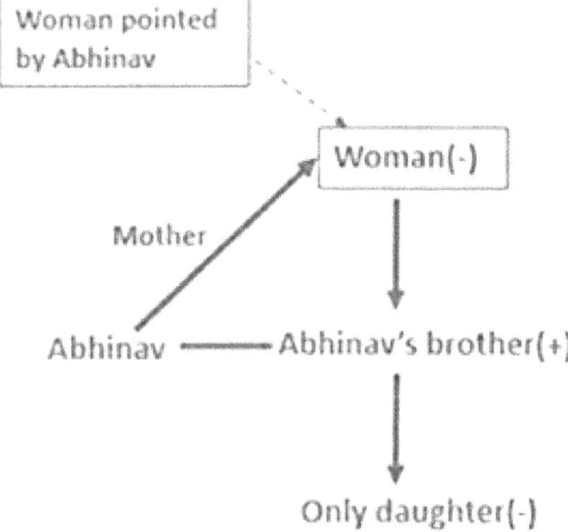

Clearly that woman is mother of Abhinav.

Hence, the correct option is (D).

46. We can trace the route taken by child as follows:

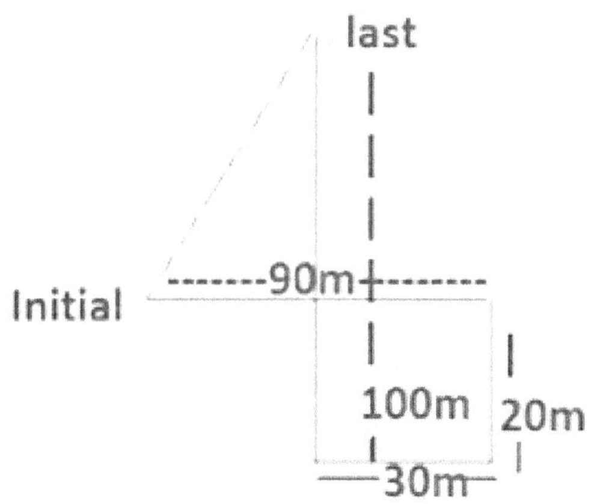

We have to find the diagonal distance between Initial and last point.

Here, perpendicular will be 80 m and base will be 60 m.

And, using Pythagoras theorem,

$$H^2 = P^2 + B^2$$

Diagonal distance between Initial and last point
$= \sqrt{80^2 + 60^2} = 100$ m

Hence, the correct option is (C).

47. The route taken by Mr. X can be illustrated as:

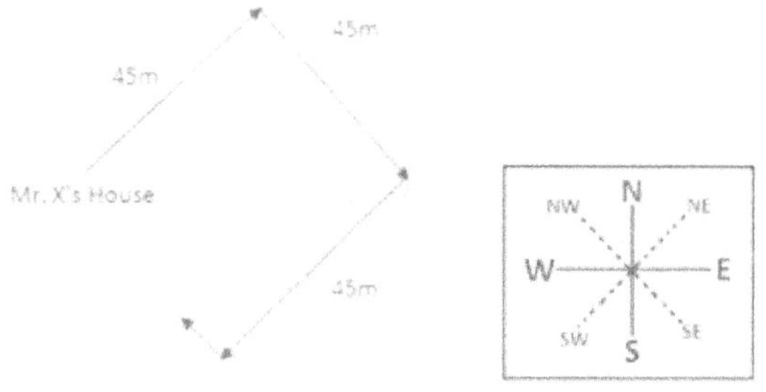

So, Mr. X is now moving in the Northwest direction.

Hence, the correct option is (B).

48. First is mode of travel for the second. Car is used in road transportation and Airplane is used in air transport.

Hence, the correct option is (B).

49. Breeze is a gentle flow of wind whereas cyclone is a violent flow of wind.

In the same way, drizzle is the light liquid precipitation whereas downpour is a heavy rainfall.

Hence, the correct option is (D).

50. $111 \div 3 = 37$

$315 \div 3 = 105$

$552 \div 3 = 184$

644 is not divisible by 3.

Hence, the correct option is (D).

51. Bad faith (Latin: mala fides) is double-mindedness or double-heartedness in duplicity, fraud, or deception. It may involve intentional deceit of others or self-deception.

Hence, the correct option is (B).

52. En Ventre Sa Mere means in the mother's womb. For example, 'child en ventre sa mere' means a child in the mothers womb. It refers to an unborn child and is usually used while referring to that child's rights. In law, a child is for all beneficial purposes considered as born while in ventre sa mere. For example, for the purpose of inheritance, a child is treated as having been in existence at the time of the decedent's death if the child is en ventre sa mere at the time of a decedent's death and is subsequently born alive.

Hence, the correct option is (B).

53. Actio personalis moritur cum persona is a Latin expression meaning "a personal right of action dies with the person". Some legal causes of action can survive the death of the claimant or plaintiff, for example, actions founded in contract law. However, some actions are personal to the plaintiff, defamation of character being one notable example. Therefore, such an action, where it relates to the private character of the plaintiff, comes to an end on his death, whereas an action for the publication of a false and malicious statement that causes damage to the plaintiff's personal estate will survive to the benefit of his or her personal representatives.

Hence, the correct option is (A).

54. The fundamental right which is guaranteed under Article 20(2) of the Constitution of India incorporates the principles of "autrefois convict" or Double jeopardy which means that person must not be punished twice for the offence. Doctrine against Double Jeopardy embodies in English common law's maxim 'Nemo debet bis vexari, si constat curice quod sit pro una iti eadem causa" (no man shall be punished twice if it appears to the court that it is for one and the same cause). It also follows the "audi alterum partem rule" which means that no person can be punished for the same offence more than ones. And if a person is punished twice for the same offence it is termed Double jeopardy.

Hence, the correct option is (A).

55. Prosecution means when a charge is framed against a person by the court of law and when such charge is proved the person is convicted. the opposite of conviction is an acquittal.

Hence, the correct option is (C).

56. He became IAS Officer in 1978. Also, he has served as the first chief information commissioner of India. The commissioner and other officials are appointed by the President. It's basically regarded as a statutory body. Its main objective is to deliver information to the center by the respective officers.

Hence, the correct option is (A).

57. As per provisions of Article-220, after retirement a Judge of High Court can practice as a lawyer in Supreme Court or in a High Court where he or she was not a judge. He or she is not permitted to practice in High Court where he retired from.

Hence, the correct option is (D).

58. As per provisions of Article-233 appointment posting and promotion of District Judges shall be made by Governor of of concerned state in consultation with the High Court exercising jurisdiction in relation to such state.

Hence, the correct option is (A).

59. Both Supreme Court and High Courts are conferred with power to protect the fundamental rights. Supreme Court under Article-32 and High Courts under Article-226 can issue writs in case of violation of fundamental rights.

Hence, the correct option is (C).

60. Chief Justice of India does not appoint Chief Justice of High Court. Rather, Chief Justice of High Court is appointed by President of India in consultation with Chief Justice of India and Governor of the concerned state.

Hence, the correct option is (A).

61. M. Fathima Beevi (born 30 April 1927) is a former judge of the Supreme Court of India. Appointed to the apex Court in 1989, she became the first female judge to be a part of the Supreme court of India, and the first Muslim woman to be appointed to any of the higher judiciaries in the country.

Hence, the correct option is (B).

62. As per Section 17 of the Indian Contract Act, 1872 the following acts constitute fraud:

(1) Making a false statement which a person does not himself believe to be true.

(2) The concealment or revealing of wrong statement of facts must be with the intention to deceive the person to enter into the contract.

(3) The other party must suffer a loss due to this statement.

An innocent false statement comes under the category of misrepresentation under Section 18 of the Act.

Hence, the correct option is (C).

63. Under section 56 of the Contract Act also known as Doctrine of Frustration, an agreement to do an act impossible in itself is void. A contract to do an act which, after the contract is made, becomes impossible, or, by reason of some event which the promisor could not prevent, unlawful, becomes void when the act becomes impossible or unlawful.

Hence, the correct option is (B).

64. The Attorney General of India is the Indian government's chief legal advisor and its primary lawyer in the Supreme Court of India. They can be said to be the advocate from the government's side. They are appointed by the President of India on the advice of the Union Cabinet under Article 76 (1) of the Constitution and hold office during the pleasure of the President. They must be a

person qualified to be appointed as a Judge of the Supreme Court (They must have been a judge of some high court for five years or an advocate of some high court for ten years or an eminent jurist, in the opinion of the President and must be a citizen of India).

Hence, the correct option is (C).

65. Earnest money is a deposit made to a seller indicating the buyer's good faith in an arrangement. Often used in real estate transactions, earnest money allows the buyer additional time when seeking financing. Earnest money is typically held jointly by the seller and buyer in a trust or escrow account.

Hence, the correct option is (A).

66. A actually entered the house without the permission of the owner and also had a 'mens rea' or an intention of committing theft, hence he is liable for criminal trespass irrespective of whether he left after leaving money.

Hence, the correct option is (A).

67. The principle clearly states that abettor is liable for the crime of abetment only with the crime which resulted from his abetment. The facts state that A instigates B for Arson(burning) Z's house. B set the fire but he also committed theft which B did himself without any abetment but A. Hence A is liable only for Arson not for the theft of property.

Hence, the correct option is (B).

68. A has not committed theft as while stealing he was not mature to understand the nature and consequences of the act. He has stolen toys just out of jealousy, he was unaware of the nature of the act.

Hence, the correct option is (B).

69. Supreme Court in a landmark judgment struck down section 66(A) of the Information Technology Act, 2000 which provided provisions for the arrest of those who posted allegedly offensive content on the internet upholding freedom of expression. Section 66A defines the punishment for sending "offensive" messages through a computer or any other communication device like a mobile phone or tablet and a conviction of it can fetch a maximum of three years of jail and a fine.

Hence, the correct option is (A).

70. The Supreme Court, in National Legal Service Authority vs Union of India ("NALSA"), has given legal recognition to the transgender community by mandating that they be treated as the third gender, thereby doing away with the binary understanding of gender.

Hence, the correct option is (D).

71. The 42nd Amendment of the Constitution of India, officially known as The Constitution (Forty-second Amendment) Act, 1976, was enacted during the Emergency (25 June 1975 – 21 March 1977) by the Indian National Congress government headed by Indira Gandhi. This amendment brought about the most widespread changes to the Constitution in its history and is sometimes called a "mini-Constitution" or the Constitution of Indira. The radical changes brought in by Indira Gandhi were neutralized by holding them unconstitutional in Minerva mills's judgment.

Hence, the correct option is (A).

72. Section 498A husband or relative of husband of a woman subjecting her to cruelty.—Whoever, being the husband or the relative of the husband of a woman, subjects such woman to cruelty shall be punished with imprisonment for a term which may extend to three years and shall also be liable to fine.

Hence, the correct option is (A).

73. Sentence of imprisonment for non-payment of a fine.—In every case, of an offense punishable with imprisonment as well as a fine, in which the offender is sentenced to a fine, whether with or without imprisonment, and in every case of an offence punishable [with imprisonment or fine, or] with fine only, in which the offender is sentenced to a fine,]

Hence, the correct option is (C).

74. IPC Section 80- Accident in doing a lawful act

Nothing is an offence which is done by accident or misfortune, and without any criminal intention or knowledge in the doing of a lawful act in a lawful manner by lawful means and with proper care and caution.

Hence, the correct option is (C).

75. The first draft of the Indian Penal Code was prepared by the First Law Commission, chaired by Lord Thomas Babington Macaulay. The draft was based on the simple codification of the law of England, while at the same time borrowing elements from the Napoleanic Code and Louisiana Civil Code of 1825.

Hence, the correct option is (B).

76. Vic Hayes has been called the "Father of Wi-Fi" because he chaired the Institute of Electrical and Electronics Engineers (IEEE) committee that created the 802.11 standards in 1997. The 802.11 standards were established in 1997.

The Commonwealth Scientific and Industrial Research Organisation (CSIRO) credits the following inventors for creating Wi-Fi: Dr. John O'Sullivan, Dr. Terry Percival, Mr. Diet Ostry, Mr. Graham Daniels, and Mr. John Deane.

Hence, the correct option is (D).

77. California-based American aerospace manufacturing and space transportation services firm SpaceX has become the first private company to send astronauts into space.

- The firm is owned by the tech-billionaire Elon Musk.
- The Crew Dragon spacecraft of SpaceX carried two astronauts of NASA Doug Hurley and Bob Behnken to the International Space Station (ISS).

Hence, the correct option is (C).

78. India's first COVID-19 vaccine to get approval for children above 12 Years was ZyCoV-D.

India's drug regulator recently approved Zydus Cadila's three-dose COVID-19 DNA vaccine for emergency use in adults and children aged 12 years and above, bringing in the sixth vaccine authorised for use in the country.

Hence, the correct option is (C).

79. A SpaceX rocket carried 52 Starlink internet satellites into orbit from California on 18 December 2021. The two-stage Falcon 9 rocket lifted off from coastal Vandenberg Space Force Base.

The Falcon's first stage returned and landed on a SpaceX drone ship in the ocean. The mission was the 34th launch for Starlink, a constellation of nearly 2,000 satellites in low Earth orbit.

Hence, the correct option is (B).

80. Official Languages of Lakshadweep are Malayalam and English, while there are two spoken languages also viz. Jeseri and Dhivehi.

Hence, the correct option is (B).

81. A constitution amendment bill can be introduced in any house of the parliament. A bill for the purpose of amendment of the constitution can NOT be introduced in any state legislature.

Hence, the correct option is (B).

82. The Paddy fields of India are located in areas of annual rainfall 100 cm. Paddy has become an important crop of Punjab and Haryana. It requires high humidity with annual rainfall above 100 cm.

Hence, the correct option is (C).

83. The fertility of soil can be improved by adding living earthworms. Worms help to increase the amount of air and water that gets into the soil. They break down organic matter, like leaves and grass into things that plants can use. When they eat, they leave behind castings that are a very valuable type of fertilizer. Earthworms are like free farm help.

Hence, the correct option is (A).

84. Urban Co-operative Banks (UCBs) occupy an important place among the Non-Agricultural Credit Society. They cater to the credit needs of people residing in urban areas. Primary Cooperative Banks which are otherwise known as Urban Cooperative Banks are registered as Cooperative Societies under the Cooperative Societies Acts of the concerned States or the Multi-State Cooperative Societies Act function in urban areas and their business is similar to that of Commercial Banks.

Hence, the correct option is (C).

85. State Bank of India, Bank of Calcutta was founded on 2 June 1806. Bank of Calcutta and the two other Presidency banks such as the Bank of Bombay and the Bank of Madras had merged and became Imperial Bank of India n 1921. The Imperial Bank of India is renamed as State Bank of India in 1955.

Hence, the correct option is (B).

86. NNP (Net national product) is the net value of GNP after the depreciation of plant and machinery is deducted. NNP at market price is calculated by deducting indirect taxes and subsidies from NNP at factor cost. NNP at factor cost is the value of the NNP when the value of goods and services are taken at the production point.

Hence, the correct option is (A).

87. Nominal GDP is calculated on the basis of current prices. While real GDP is calculated on the base year prices and its data are more reliable or accurate as compared to Nominal GDP.

Hence, the correct option is (C).

88. Customs duty refers to the tax imposed on goods when they are transported across international borders. In simple terms, it is the tax that is levied on import and export of goods. The government uses this duty to raise its revenues, safeguard domestic industries, and regulate movement of goods.

Hence, the correct option is (B).

89. The right to impose stamp duty lies with Central Government, but the state government has the right to collect it. The revenue generated from the Stamp duties and Excise duties on medical and toilet materials is imposed by the Central Government but collected and kept by the respective state government.

Hence, the correct option is (D).

90. Heavy Machinery is also called the heavy engineering industry. The major plants are located at Ranchi, Visakhapatnam and Durgapur.

Hence, the correct option is (B).

91. Cochin Shipyard Ltd (CSL) is the largest shipbuilding and maintenance facility in India. It is part of a line of maritime-related facilities in the port-city of Kochi, in the state of Kerala, India. Of the services provided by the shipyard are building platform supply vessels and double-hulled oil tankers.

Hence, the correct option is (A).

92. In India, Consumer Price Index (CPI) and Wholesale Price Index (WPI) are two major indices for measuring inflation. In the United States, CPI and PPI (Producer Price Index) are two major indices.

The Wholesale Price Index (WPI) was the main index for the measurement of inflation in India till April 2014 when RBI adopted the new Consumer Price Index (CPI) as the key measure of inflation.

Hence, the correct option is (A).

93. The Raghuram Govinda Rajan Committee on Financial Sector Reforms was a committee constituted by the Government of India in 2007 for proposing the next generation of financial sector reforms in India.

Hence, the correct option is (B).

94. National Programme of Mid Day Meal in Schools. With a view to enhance enrolment, attendance, retention and simultaneously to improve the nutritional status of children, a Centrally Sponsored Scheme 'National Programme of Nutritional Support to Primary Education (NP-NSPE)' was launched on August 15, 1995.

Hence, the correct option is (C).

95. Each year, India produces an average of 5,770 thousand metric tonnes of cotton making it the world's highest producer.

The United States is a key producer and exporter of cotton. It produces approximately 3,999 thousand metric tonnes a year.

Hence, the correct option is (B).

96. Laws related to Fundamental Rights, abolition or creation of new states and acquisition & termination of the citizenship can be changed by simple majority of the Parliament.

Hence, the correct option is (D).

97. Article 368 clearly states that if any change is to be made under the 7th schedule, then it has to be adopted by a special majority. Both houses of Parliament have to pass the Bill with a two-thirds majority.

Hence, the correct option is (C).

98. The parliament in the exercise of its power granted in Art. 11 of the Indian Constitution has passed the Indian Citizenship Act, 1955, making provisions for acquisition and termination of citizenship after the commencement of the Constitution.

Hence, the correct option is (C).

99. History was made when Harini Logan, 14, won the first-ever spell-off at the 2022 Scripps National Spelling Bee. The San Antonio, Texas, native received a trophy and a check for $50,000.

Hence, the correct option is (B).

100. Recognising its efforts in controlling tobacco consumption, the World Health Organization (WHO) has selected Jharkhand for the World No Tobacco Day (WNTD) Award-2022.

State Tobacco Control Cell of the Health Department received the award on the occasion of World No Tobacco Day in New Delhi on May 31.

Hence, the correct option is (A).

English Language & Comprehension

Q.1 Direction: In the sentence given below, replace the phrase underlined to make the sentence grammatically correct. If the sentence is correct, choose the option "No correction".

At an early age, she <u>had made her mark</u> as a criminal lawyer.

A. made her mark

B. makes her mark

C. has been making her mark

D. No correction

Q.2 Direction: Choose the word or group of words that is most similar in meaning to the given word.

Aesthetic

A. Mediocre   **B.** Prevalent

C. Ugly   **D.** Beautiful

Q.3 Direction: Choose the word or group of words that is most similar in meaning to the given word.

Imbecile

A. Sane   **B.** Astute   **C.** Foolish   **D.** Aid

Ques (4-7):Direction: Read the passage carefully and give the answer to the question based on it.

Emanating from the Indian kitchens every morning are the appetizing aromas of crushed spices, lentils, curry leaves and vegetables and working with her deft fingers and loving heart is the woman of the house creating 'the great Indian home cooked meal'.

This is where the 'dabbawallas' sensed a business opportunity way back in 1980 – the idea of delivering home cooked meals to office-goers and their workplace and returning empty meal boxes to their homes before their return in the evening.

Today 'dabbawallas' have become integral part of Mumbai's cultural mosaic. About 5000 of these delivery men crisscross the streets, lanes and by lanes of Mumbai, on foot, bicycle and local train, every morning to deliver about 2,00,000 home cooked meal boxes to office goers at their workplaces. What amazes business strategists across the world is the unique process of near faultless delivery, which even convinced Forbes magazine to give them the highly-prized Sigma Six Rating for quality assurance, a feat achieved by companies such as Motorola and General Electrics.

"The success of the system depends on teamwork and time management that would be the envy of every modern manager. Such is the dedication and commitment of the barely literate and barefoot delivery men who form links in the extensive delivery chain, that there is no system of documentation at all."

They do not rely on any high technology databases or computers for communication. Instead, they use colors and code markings for identification. "Each container carries an indelible ink alphanumeric coding of some ten characters signifying the various transfer and delivery stages, as well as the individuals who are to be involved in the process."

One of the major reasons for the success of this delivery service is the high level of personal involvement, relationship orientation, and continuous communication with their clients and amongst themselves.

Memorizing about 35 addresses from where they must pick up the boxes it becomes critical for the dabbawalla to keep the flow of information continuous as any miscommunication might result in the unpardonable error of serving a non-vegetarian meal to a pure vegetarian, an act blasphemous enough to wash away all the good deeds of the person in a single stroke.

Q.4 According to the passage, which qualities of the dabbawallas of Mumbai would make even modern manager envy?

A. Teamwork and time management

B. Dedication and commitment

C. Six sigma rating

D. Faultless delivery system

Q.5 According to the passage, what is the major reason for the success of dabbawallas in Mumbai?

A. Six sigma rating by Forbes

B. High level of personal involvement and communication with the clients

C. Ability to memorize 3 addresses

D. Taste of the home-cooked food

Q.6 Choose the word which is most nearly the same in meaning as the word "indelible" as used in the passage.

A. Memorable   **B.** Stirring

C. Inerasable   **D.** None of these

Q.7 Which of the following is false according to the passage?

A. Dabbawallas are integral part of Mumbai's culture

B. Dabbawallas rely on high technology databases or computers for communication

C. Forbes magazine to give them the highly-prized Sigma Six Rating for quality assurance

D. The success of this delivery service is the high-level of personal involvement

Q.8 Direction: In the following question choose the word which is the exact opposite of the given word.

Relinquish

A. Abdicate   **B.** Deny

C. Possess   **D.** None of these

Q.9 Direction: In the following question choose the word which is the exact opposite of the given word.

Quiescent

A. Active

B. Dormant

C. Weak

D. Unconcerned

Q.10 Direction: In the following question choose the word which is the exact opposite of the given word.

Zenith

A. Acme   B. Top   C. Nadir   D. Pinnacle

Q.11 Direction: Choose the word from the given alternative which best describes the meaning of the given word.

Development

A. Nurturing

B. Neglecting

C. Ignoring

D. None of these

Q.12 Direction: Choose the word from the given alternative which best describes the meaning of the given word.

Vernal

A. Dirty

B. Luxuriant

C. Springlike

D. Prone

Q.13 Direction: Choose the correct alternative which appropriately describes the given idioms and phrases.

Come off with flying colors

A. Without hope

B. Be highly successful

C. Bitterly hostile

D. None of these

Q.14 Direction: Choose the correct alternative which appropriately describes the given idioms and phrases.

Be in a tight corner

A. In a very difficult situation

B. In an easy situation

C. Stand in a corner

D. To keep at a distance

Q.15 What will be the correct one-word substitution for the given sentence in bold?

Extreme old age when a man behaves like a fool

A. Imbecility

B. Youth

C. Dotage

D. Superannuation

Q.16 What will be the correct one-word substitution for the given sentence in bold?

One who promotes the idea of absence of government of any kind, when every man should be a law unto himself

A. Anarchist

B. Belligerent

C. Iconoclast

D. Agnostic

Q.17 Direction: Find out that word, the spelling of which is wrong.

A. Abdominal

B. Clinical

C. Machenical

D. Technical

Q.18 Direction: Find out that word, the spelling of which is wrong.

A. Confedation

B. Camaraderie

C. Cataclysm

D. Carboniferous

Q.19 Direction: Select the correct passive voice of the given sentence.

God helps those who help themselves.

A.   Those who help themselves help God.

B.   Those who help God help themselves.

C.   Those who are helped by themselves are helped by God.

D.   Those who help themselves are helped by God.

Q.20 Direction: Choose the correct passive voice of the given sentence from the given alternatives.

The children could use the place always.

A.   The place can be used by children.

B.   The place is used by children always.

C.   The place could always be used by the children.

D.   The place has been used by children always.

Q.21 Direction: Choose the correct pronouns to complete the sentences.

Some of these clothes are ___, and the rest of ___ belong to Zack.

A. yours / it

B. my / them

C. mine / them

D. me / they

Q.22 Direction: Fill in the blank with an appropriate phrasal verb.

Harry was _____ to make a quick announcement at the meeting.

A. Called on

B. Call in

C. Calling against

D. Call for

Q.23 What will be the correct one-word substitution for the given sentence in bold?

Government by a small group of all powerful persons

A. Oligarchy

B. Monarchy

C. Democracy

D. Anarchy

Q.24 Direction: Choose the correct alternative which appropriately describes the given idioms and phrases.

Goes to dogs

A. Goes mad

B. Is insulted

C. Is ruined

D. Becomes brutal

Q.25 Direction: Choose the correct word from the given alternative for the given blank in the sentence.

Two students didn't do _______ mathematics homework.

A. their

B. them

C. those

D. None of these

Analytical Abilities

Q.26 P, Q, R and S are playing a game of carrom. P, R, and S, Q are partners. S is to the right of R who is facing west. Then Q is facing:

A. North   B. South   C. East   D. West

Q.27 A person starts from point A goes 4 km towards East then he takes his left and goes 4 km, at last, he takes his right and goes 3 km, reached point B, Now in which direction point B with respect to point A.

A. North-West
B. North-East
C. North
D. West

Ques (28-29):Directions: Select the missing number from the given alternatives:

Q.28

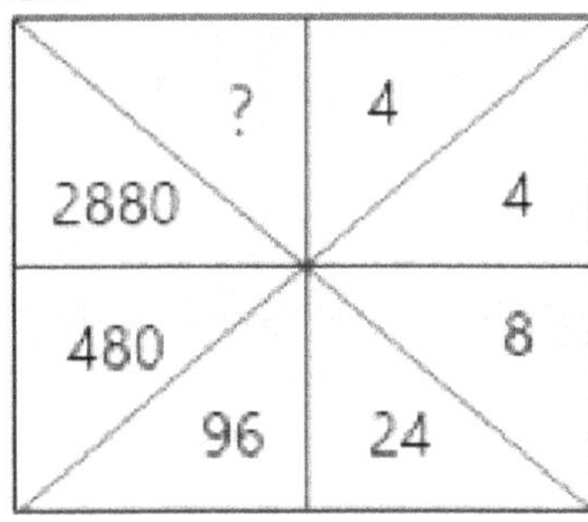

A. 20160   **B.** 20600   **C.** 21060   **D.** 23040

Q.29

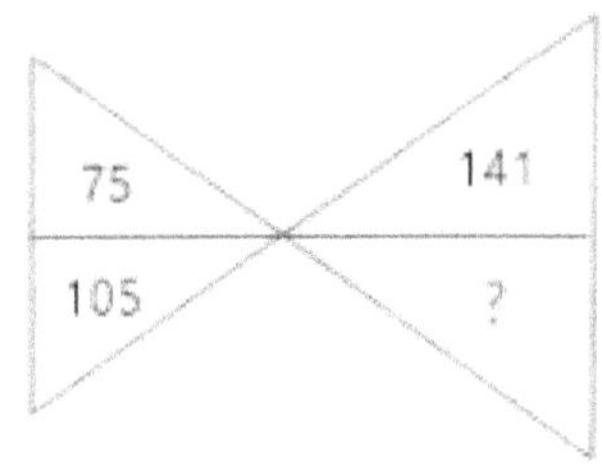

A. 75°   **B.** 39°   **C.** 45°   **D.** 120°

Q.30 One morning Sujata started to walk towards the Sun. After covering some distance she turned to the right then again to the right and after covering some distance she again turns to the right. Now in which direction is she facing?

A. North
B. South
C. North-East
D. South-West

Q.31 Pointing to a photograph Lata says, "He is the son of the only son of my grandfather." How is the man in the photograph related to Lata?

A. Brother
B. Uncle
C. Cousin
D. Data is inadequate

Q.32 Pointing to a photograph. Bajpai said, "He is the son of the only daughter of the father of my brother." How Bajpai is related to the man in the photograph?

A. Nephew
B. Brother
C. Father
D. Maternal Uncle

Q.33 Veena who is the sister-in-law of Ashok is the daughter-in-law of Kalyani. Dheeraj is the father of Sudeep who is the only brother of Ashok. How Kalyani is related to Ashok?

A. Mother-in-law
B. Aunt
C. Wife
D. None of these

Ques (34-36):Direction: The below question is consists of two-word pairs. Look at the first pair and decide how the two words relate to each other. Then select one of the words below so the second pair of words have the same relationship.

Q.34 Trouble : Safety :: Freedom : ?

A. Independence
B. Patient
C. Liberty
D. Slavery

Q.35 Sickness : Health :: Happiness : ?

A. Medicine
B. Sorrow
C. Comfort
D. Misery

Q.36 Stone : Hard :: Feather : ?

A. Soft   **B.** White   **C.** Bird   **D.** Fly

Q.37 In a certain code, THEN is coded as VFGL. How the WORD may be coded?

A. UQPF   **B.** YMTB   **C.** YMVB   **D.** VQFP

Q.38 If DELHI can be coded as CCIDD, how would you code BOMBAY?

A. AJMTVT
B. AMJXVS
C. MJXVSU
D. WXYZAX

Q.39 In a certain code language, COMPUTRONE is written as PMOCTUENOR. How are ADVANTAGES written in that code?

A. SEGATNAVAD
B. AVDATNSEGA
C. AVDATASEGN
D. NAVDASEGAT

Q.40 What will come at the place of the question mark?

2816, ? , 176, 44, 11

A. 704   **B.** 1408   **C.** 352   **D.** 2640

Q.41 7, 10, 8, 11, 9, 12, ... What number should come next?

A. 7   **B.** 10   **C.** 12   **D.** 13

Q.42 Direction: The diagram given below represents those students who play Cricket, Football and Kabaddi.

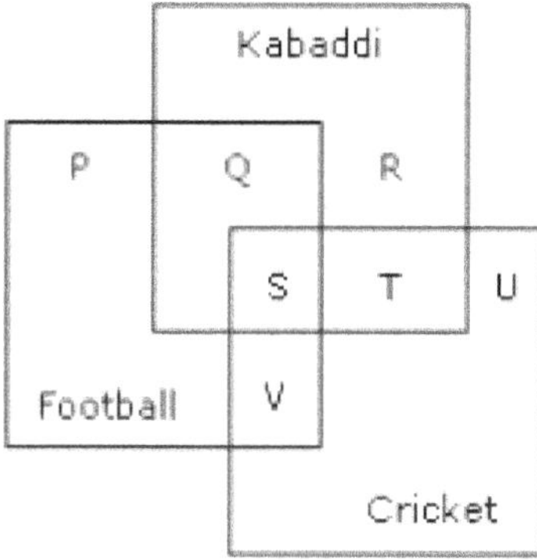

Study the diagram and identify the students who play all three games.

A. P + Q + R
B. V + T
C. S + T + V
D. S

Ques (43-45):Direction: In the following figure small square represents the persons who know English, triangle to those who know Marathi, a big square to those who know Telugu, and a circle to those who know Hindi. In the different regions of the figures from 1 to 12 are given.

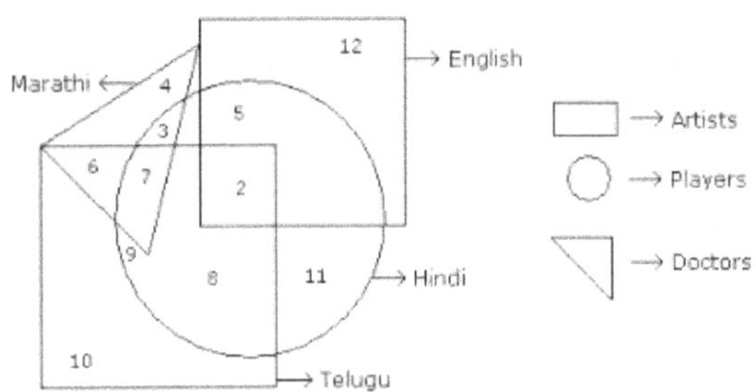

Q.43 How many persons can speak English and Hindi both languages only?

A. 5 **B.** 8 **C.** 7 **D.** 18

Q.44

How many persons can speak Marathi and Telugu both?

A. 10 **B.** 11
C. 13 **D.** None of these

Q.45 How many persons can speak all the languages?

A. 1 **B.** 8 **C.** 2 **D.** None

Ques (46-47):Direction: Statement and conclusion are given below read them carefully and find out that the conclusion follows the statement or not, and according to that choose your answer from the given option.

Q.46 Statements: All the actors are girls. All the girls are beautiful.

Conclusions:

I. All the actors are beautiful.

II. Some girls are actors.

A. Only I conclusion follows
B. Only II conclusion follows
C. Either I or II follows
D. Both I and II follow

Q.47 Statements: All the windows are doors. No door is a wall.

Conclusions:

I. Some windows are walls.

II. No wall is a door.

A. Only (I) conclusion follows
B. Only (II) conclusion follows
C. Either (I) or (II) follows
D. Both (I) and (II) follow

Ques (48-49):Direction: Two statements I and II are given. This statement may be either independent causes or may be effects of independent causes or a common cause. One of these statements may be the effect of the other statements. Read both the statements and decide which of the following answer choice correctly depicts the relationship between these two statements. Mark answer:

Q.48 I. The private medical colleges have increased the tuition fees in the current year by 200 percent over the last year's fees to meet the expenses.

II. The Government medical colleges have not increased their fees in spite of price escalation.

A. Statement I is the cause and statement II is its effect
B. Statement II is the cause and statement I is its effect
C. Both statements I and II are independent causes
D. Both statements I and II are effects of independent causes

Q.49 I. The local cooperative credit society has decided to stop giving loans to farmers with immediate effect.

II. A large number of credit society members have withdrawn a major part of their deposits from the credit society.

A. Statement I is the cause and statement II is its effect
B. Statement II is the cause and statement I is its effect
C. Both statements I and II are independent causes
D. Both statements I and II are effects of independent causes

Q.50 Direction: Arrange the given words in a logical order.

1. Probation
2. Interview
3. Selection
4. Appointment
5. Advertisement
6. Application

A. 5,6,2,3,4,1 **B.** 5,6,3,2,4,1
C. 5,6,4,2,3,1 **D.** 6,5,4,2,3,1

Legal Awareness & Aptitude

Q.51 Principle: Whoever causes death by doing an act with the intention of causing death commits culpable homicide; punishable under Indian Penal Code.

Facts: Bandipur is a protected area wherein hunting is totally forbidden. Kannan, a poacher, stealthily entered this area and he shot at a deer. He missed the target and the bullet hits the forest guard relaxing nearby, whom Kannan had not seen. The forest guard was killed. Decide whether Kannan is guilty of culpable homicide.

A. Kannan is liable for Culpable Homicide
B. Kannan is not liable for Culpable Homicide
C. Kannan is liable for Murder
D. Kannan is liable for Culpable Homicide as well as under Wildlife Protection Act

Q.52 Principle: Law does not take notice of trifles.

Facts: A proposes to his neighbor B that they both should go together for a morning walk. B agrees to the proposal and it is decided that both of them would meet at a particular point 6 A.M. from where they would set off for the morning walk. In spite of the agreement, B does not turn up. A waited for him at 6 a.m. every day, for a continuous period of seven days. Thereafter he files a suit against B claiming damages for the agony and mental torture suffered by him. Decide.

A. B is guilty of breach of contract and is liable to pay damages
B. There is the intention to enter into legal relations and the court will ask B to pay compensation
C. The matter is too small and the court will refuse to go into it
D. None of the above

Q.53 In which of the following cases Section 66a of IT act was struck down:
A. Shreya Singhal vs Union of India
B. Naz foundation vs NCT Delhi
C. Sneha Singhal vs Union of India
D. Lilavati vs State of Maharashtra

Q.54 The court laid down basic guidelines for power of President's Rule in:
A. S.R Bommai vs union of India
B. Minerva mills vs union of India
C. Sushil Mittal vs union of India
D. Vidya Bharati vs the state of Himachal Pradesh

Q.55 In which case SC upheld the constitutional validity of section 139AA of the Income Tax Act which made mandatory linkage of IT returns with AADHAAR subject to the outcome of the main case related to AADHAAR.
A. Subramanium swamy vs union of India
B. Biswam som vs Union of India
C. Puttuswamy vs union of India
D. Rajbala vs state of Haryana

Q.56 Which case led to the imposition of emergency and was a landmark case regarding election disputes, the primary issue was the validity of clause 4 of the 39th Amendment Act?
A. MC Mehta vs Union Of India
B. Sunil Narain vs Indira Gandhi
C. Raj Narain vs Indira Gandhi
D. Sushil Gandhi vs Indira Gandhi

Q.57 The consent is not a valid consent under section 90:
A. If given under a fear of injury or misconception of fact
B. If given by a person of unsound mind
C. If given by a child below 12 years of age
D. All of the above

Q.58 Criminal breach of trust is dealt under:
A. Section 406 of IPC
B. Section 407 of IPC
C. Section 408 of IPC
D. Section 409 of IPC

Q.59 What is meant by the Legal Maxim "jus naturale"?
A. Nature's fury
B. Natural justice
C. Natural Law
D. Naturalization of Citizenship

Q.60 What is meant by the Legal Maxim "jus cogens"?
A. Law of community
B. International law
C. Compelling law
D. Law coherent with Municipal Law

Q.61 What is meant by the Legal Maxim "jus in bello"?
A. Justice is in balance
B. Balance of scales in jurisprudence
C. Law of war
D. Just cause of a party

Q.62 What is meant by the term "mare clausum"?

A. Clauses hidden in contract
B. Closed competition in Mercantile law
C. Closed Sea
D. Competition clause in Mercantile law

Q.63 What is meant by the term "non compos mentis"?
A. Body recovered from the crime scene which is not fully decomposed
B. Not in possession of one's mind
C. Not in a good frame of mind
D. Body not in a decomposed state of condition

Q.64 Whether Narco-analysis or Polygraph test without consent is:
A. Permitted in all cases
B. Prohibited in all cases
C. within the discretion of the court
D. within the discretion of investigating officer

Q.65 A writ by which the decision of the lower court is quashed by higher Court because it was based on the irregular procedure is known as _______ ?
A. Mandamus
B. Prohibition
C. Certiorari
D. Quo Warranto

Q.66 "Directive Principle of State Policy is the conscience of the Constitution which embody the social philosophy of the constitution" was said by:
A. Granville Austin
B. K.C. Wheare
C. A.V. Dicey
D. B.R. Ambedkar

Q.67 How many articles were there originally in the Constitution of India?
A. 395
B. 397
C. 403
D. 410

Q.68 How does the Constitution of India describe India as?
A. A federation of States and Union Territories
B. A Union of States
C. Bharatvarsh
D. A federated nation

Q.69 What is consent under the Indian Contract Act, 1872:
A. When acceptance of proposal is made by the party to whom the proposal is made
B. When the acceptance is made by another person other than the person to whom the proposal is made
C. When they agree upon the same thing in the same sense
D. When both the parties agree upon a thing in the way it is understood by them

Q.70 Contingent contract means:
A. A suit entrusted to any person to abide by the result of any game or other uncertain event on which may wager is made
B. A contract to do or not to do something, if some event, collateral to such contract, does or does not happen
C. Agreements that are not certain, or capable of being made certain
D. Every agreement, by which any party thereto is restricted absolutely from enforcing his rights under or in respect of any contract

Q.71 X owes Rs. 10,000 to Y under a contract. It is agreed between X, Y & Z that Y shall henceforth accept Z as his debtor instead of X for the same amount. Old debt of X is discharged and a new debt from Z to Y is contracted. This is:

A. Alteration of contract

B. Rescission of contract

C. Novation of contract

D. Change in contract

Q.72 A person has designed a new type of scissors for cutting clothes. Under which act can he seek the protection of his invention?

A. The Patents Act

B. The Copyrights Act

C. Consumer Protection Act

D. Arms Control Act

Q.73 The term Hiba means:

A. The children of the same mother

B. The witness who makes statements adverse to the party calling and examining him

C. Perfect gift

D. The killing of a human being by another human being

Q.74 Sharda Act deals with:

A. Widow Remarriage

B. Child Marriage

C. Inter-caste Marriage

D. Polygamy

Q.75 Who among the following had moved the objectives resolution which formed the basis of the Preamble of the Constitution of India in the Constituent Assembly on December 13, 1946?

A. Dr. B.R. Ambedkar

B. Dr. Rajendra Prasad

C. Sardar Vallabhbhai Patel

D. Pt. Jawaharlal Nehru

General Knowledge

Q.76 Who is the inventor of the stethoscope?

A. Rene Laennec

B. John Logie Baird

C. Hippocrates

D. Alexander Fleming

Q.77 The term Log4Shell related to __________.

A. Cybersecurity

B. Nanotechnology

C. Robotics

D. Biotechnology

Q.78 In which of the following states, the Sharavati Project is located?

A. Andhra Pradesh

B. Karnataka

C. Tamil Nadu

D. Madhya Pradesh

Q.79 Which of the following state does not share a boundary with Myanmar?

A. Assam

B. Arunachal Pradesh

C. Nagaland

D. Manipur

Q.80 Who is known as the Father of the Green Revolution?

A. Dr. M S Swami Nathan

B. Norman Borlaug

C. Verghese Kurien

D. None of these

Q.81 What is the core objective of the World Bank-supported STRIVE project in India?

A. Elimination of Malaria

B. Elimination of HIV/ AIDS

C. Skill Development

D. Rural Infrastructure Development

Q.82 Which article of the Indian Constitution provides for Vice-President of India?

A. Article 61

B. Article 62

C. Article 63

D. Article 65

Q.83 Which of the following writs guarantee personal freedom?

A. Quo-Warranto

B. Prohibition

C. Habeas Corpus

D. Mandamus

Q.84 Which of the following Article promotes the formation of village panchayats?

A. Article 39

B. Article 40

C. Article 41

D. Article 42

Q.85 The Reserve Bank of India (RBI) is conducting an OMO for purchase of Rs 10,000 crore worth government securities. What does OMO stand for?

A. Open Money Operations

B. Open Market Operations

C. Overview of Market Operations

D. Overview of Money Operations

Q.86 If RBI reduces the cash reserve ratio, what will happen to the credit creation?

[UPSSSC Preliminary Eligibility Test, 2021]

A. There will be no impact

B. It will decrease

C. It will increase

D. None of these

Q.87 Cocos plate lies between:

A. Central America and Pacific Plate

B. North America and Pacific Plate

C. South America and Pacific Plate

D. None of Above

Q.88 The great Victoria Desert is located in:

A. Canada

B. West Africa

C. Australia

D. North America

Q.89 What is the true meaning of "Secular"?

A. All religions are equal in the eyes of the government

B. Special importance to a religion related to minorities

C. One religion is promoted by the government

D. None of these

Q.90 Which of the following is not a method to calculate the Gross Domestic Product (GDP)?

A. Product method

B. Income method

C. Expenditure method

D. Diminishing cost method

Q.91 The value of national income adjusted for inflation is called:

A. Per capita income

B. Disposable income

C. Inflation rate

D. Real national income

Q.92 Which of the following relationships is indicated by a Laffer curve?

A. Relationship between money supply and price level in different stages of inflation

B. The above a certain tax rate, an increase in tax rate causes a reduction in tax revenue

C. A positive relationship between tax revenue and public expenditure

D. A negative relationship between high rates of income tax and people in tax net

Q.93 Which of the following best describes "tax expenditure"?

A. It is the expenditure incurred by the government during the collection of tax

B. It is the concessions and exemptions provided to the taxpayers by the government

C. It is the expenditure made by the government from the income accrued through taxes

D. None of these

Q.94 On which of the following rates Reserve Bank of India provides loan to scheduled commercial banks?

A. Repo Rate

B. Reverse Repo rate

C. Credit Rate

D. Bank rate

Q.95 Which among the following does not belong to the list of leading sugarcane-producing States?

A. Uttar Pradesh

B. Andhra Pradesh

C. Madhya Pradesh

D. Maharashtra

Q.96 Who has been conferred with the Param Vishisht Seva Medal for his distinguished service of exceptional order at a defence investiture ceremony?

A. Manoj Pande

B. Joginder Jaswant Singh

C. Bipin Rawat

D. Dalbir Singh Suhag

Q.97 Who wins the Palme d'Or at 75th Cannes Film Festival?

A. The Square

B. The Roads Not Taken

C. Boy from Heaven

D. Triangle of Sadness

Q.98 Which film won the Golden Conch Award at MIFF 2022 ?

A. Turn Your Body to the Sun

B. Prince in a Pastry Shop

C. Brother Troll

D. None of the above

Q.99 Who among these has been awarded the 12th Bharat Ratna Dr Ambedkar Award 2022?

A. Janhvi Kapoor

B. Sara Ali Khan

C. Harshaali Malhotra

D. Nora Fatehi

Q.100 Name of the participant who received the Best National Costume award at the Mrs World 2022 pageant.

A. Hardeep Kaur

B. Harnaaz Sandhu

C. Navdeep Kaur

D. Pooja Sharma

// Smart Answer Sheet //

Correct — Percentage of students who answered correctly. **Skipped** — Percentage of students who skipped.

Q.	Ans.	Correct / Skipped
1	A	41.36 % / 44.75 %
2	D	76.3 % / 17.09 %
3	C	77.35 % / 12.34 %
4	A	45.76 % / 42.91 %
5	B	58.03 % / 36.43 %
6	C	13.4 % / 76.9 %
7	B	10.4 % / 70.13 %
8	C	83.33 % / 12.25 %
9	A	62.3 % / 30.24 %
10	C	18.6 % / 67.21 %
11	A	80.4 % / 19.35 %
12	C	43.41 % / 49.5 %
13	B	89.94 % / 10.03 %
14	A	77.52 % / 18.02 %
15	C	23.31 % / 76.63 %
16	A	42.78 % / 53.17 %
17	C	84.54 % / 11.12 %
18	A	16.18 % / 78.7 %
19	D	89.39 % / 10.03 %
20	C	84.97 % / 13.87 %
21	C	64.43 % / 30.36 %
22	A	84.19 % / 14.15 %
23	A	82.58 % / 10.95 %
24	C	59.16 % / 37.32 %
25	A	82.22 % / 17.66 %
26	A	41.21 % / 32.78 %
27	B	41.87 % / 35.13 %
28	A	66.1 % / 31.53 %
29	B	54.09 % / 33.97 %
30	A	52.82 % / 35.05 %
31	A	44.34 % / 55.13 %
32	D	44.49 % / 50.23 %
33	D	40.63 % / 38.85 %
34	D	80.18 % / 16.9 %
35	B	58.18 % / 38.19 %
36	A	65.6 % / 34.35 %
37	B	83.99 % / 15.05 %
38	B	54.93 % / 44.76 %
39	B	68.97 % / 30.29 %
40	A	64.62 % / 31.83 %
41	B	44.84 % / 32.58 %
42	D	20.01 % / 78.15 %
43	A	89.71 % / 10.27 %
44	C	77.83 % / 19.07 %
45	D	69.36 % / 30.51 %
46	D	63.35 % / 33.67 %
47	B	54.16 % / 32.21 %
48	C	51.1 % / 33.44 %
49	B	68.6 % / 30.83 %
50	A	52.1 % / 32.49 %
51	B	30.06 % / 68.78 %
52	C	55.29 % / 40.92 %
53	A	26.27 % / 68.11 %
54	A	86.9 % / 12.55 %
55	B	16.46 % / 77.84 %
56	C	32.94 % / 67.0 %
57	D	27.54 % / 67.53 %
58	A	49.8 % / 30.05 %
59	C	86.1 % / 13.06 %
60	C	42.51 % / 31.3 %
61	C	60.34 % / 31.47 %
62	C	79.88 % / 10.98 %
63	B	60.33 % / 33.83 %
64	B	86.65 % / 13.15 %
65	C	89.53 % / 10.04 %
66	A	81.72 % / 12.09 %
67	A	86.8 % / 12.24 %
68	B	86.67 % / 10.05 %
69	C	81.26 % / 14.13 %
70	B	47.47 % / 52.05 %
71	C	40.87 % / 32.7 %
72	A	77.67 % / 20.41 %
73	C	89.39 % / 10.3 %
74	B	87.39 % / 10.53 %
75	D	88.88 % / 10.91 %
76	A	41.23 % / 56.48 %
77	A	56.21 % / 41.11 %
78	B	87.77 % / 10.73 %
79	A	76.67 % / 17.11 %
80	B	84.11 % / 14.67 %

Q.	Ans.	Correct
		Skipped
81	C	22.46 %
		74.01 %
82	C	76.05 %
		20.75 %
83	C	55.5 %
		33.92 %
84	B	88.29 %
		11.69 %

Q.	Ans.	Correct
		Skipped
85	B	84.99 %
		12.06 %
86	C	48.38 %
		39.57 %
87	B	32.57 %
		67.19 %
88	C	48.2 %
		49.52 %

Q.	Ans.	Correct
		Skipped
89	A	68.83 %
		31.16 %
90	D	21.52 %
		76.06 %
91	D	50.99 %
		34.96 %
92	B	31.5 %
		67.04 %

Q.	Ans.	Correct
		Skipped
93	B	57.46 %
		38.55 %
94	D	56.82 %
		37.32 %
95	C	85.2 %
		12.1 %
96	A	58.69 %
		39.62 %

Q.	Ans.	Correct
		Skipped
97	D	66.28 %
		33.19 %
98	A	62.61 %
		33.6 %
99	C	83.77 %
		11.03 %
100	C	61.95 %
		30.25 %

//Hints and Solutions//

1. 'At an early age, she made her mark as a criminal lawyer.' is the correct form. In the sentence, 'At an early age' stands for an uncertain period which is signifying her age. Thus, here the past perfect cannot be used, the simple past should be used.
Hence, the correct option is (A).

2. Aesthetic - Concerned with beauty or art

Beautiful - Very pretty or attractive

Mediocre - Of not very high quality

Prevalent - Most common in a particular place at a particular time

Ugly - Unpleasant to look at or listen to
Hence, the correct option is (D).

3. Imbecile - A stupid person

Foolish - Silly, not sensible

Sane - Mentally normal, not crazy

Astute - Very clever, good at judging people or situations

Aid - A person or thing that helps you
Hence, the correct option is (C).

4. According to the line given in the passage, the success of the system depends on teamwork and time management that would be the envy of every modern manager.
Hence, the correct option is (A).

5. According to the line given in the passage, "One of the major reasons for the success of this delivery service is the high level of personal involvement, relationship orientation and continuous communication with their clients and amongst themselves."
Hence, the correct option is (B).

6. Indelible - That cannot be removed or washed out

Inerasable - Incapable of being erased

Memorable - Worth remembering or easy to remember

Stirring - To move a liquid, to move or make somebody move slightly
Hence, the correct option is (C).

7. Dabbawallas do not rely on any high technology databases or computers for communication. Instead, they use colors and code markings for identification."

Other given options are correct according to the passage.
Hence, the correct option is (B).

8. Relinquish - To stop having or doing something

Possess - To have or own something

Abdicate - To give up being King or Queen

Deny - To refuse to admit or accept something
Hence, the correct option is (C).

9. Quiescent - In a state or period of inactivity or dormancy

Active - Involved in activity

Dormant - Not active for some time

Weak - Having little strength or energy

Unconcerned - Not interested in something or not worried about it
Hence, the correct option is (A).

10. Zenith - The highest point that the sun or moon reaches in the sky, directly above you

Nadir - The worst moment of a particular situation

Acme - The highest point of development or the most outstanding example of something

Top - The highest part or point of something

Pinnacle - The most important or successful part of something
Hence, the correct option is (C).

11. The correct synonym of the given word is 'nurturing'.

Development: The process of creating something more advanced; a more advanced product.

Nurturing: to look after and protect somebody/something while he/she/it is growing and developing.

Hence, the correct option is (A).

12. Vernal - Of, in, or appropriate to spring

Springlike - Typical of spring

Dirty - Covered or marked with an unclean substance

Luxuriant - Rich and profuse in growth; lush.

Prone - Likely or liable to suffer from, do, or experience something unpleasant or regrettable.

Hence, the correct option is (C).

13. The idiom, "come off with flying colors" means to be highly successful,

Use in a sentence-

He studied very hard for the exams and when the results were announced, he came off with flying colors.

Hence, the correct option is (B).

14. Be in a tight corner means in a very difficult situation.

Use in a sentence-

Rahul is in a tight corner after he fails the exam and sports together.

Hence, the correct option is (A).

15. Dotage - Extreme old age when a man behaves like a fool

Imbecility - Stupid or insane behaviour

Youth - The period between childhood and adult age

Superannuation - Regular payment made into a fund by an employee towards a future pension

Hence, the correct option is (C).

16. Anarchist - One who promotes the idea of the absence of government of any kind, when every man should be a law unto himself

Belligerent - Hostile and aggressive.

Iconoclast - A person who attacks or criticizes cherished beliefs or institutions

Agnostic - A person who believes that nothing is known or can be known of the existence or nature of God

Hence, the correct option is (A).

17. The correct spelling of "Machenical" will be "Mechanical".

Mechanical means connected with or produced by machines or done like a machine, as if you are not thinking about what you are doing

Hence, the correct option is (C).

18. The correct spelling of "Confedration" will be "Confederation."

Confederation means an organization of smaller groups which have joined together.

Hence, the correct option is (A).

19. Given sentence is in the simple present tense and it is in active voice.

Rule for making the passive voice of this sentence will be-

Object + is/am/are + third form of verb + by + subject

Those who help themselves are helped by God.

Hence, the correct option is (D).

20. The given sentence contains one of Model verb (will, shall, can, may, might, could, might, must, would). It is in active voice

Rule for making passive voice-

Object + model verb + be + third form of main verb + by + subject

The place could always be used by the children.

Hence, the correct option is (C).

21. The correct pronoun for the given blank will be - mine / them

Some of these clothes are mine, and the rest of them belong to Zack.

Hence, the correct option is (C).

22. Harry was **called on** to make a quick announcement at the meeting.

Called on - officially ask someone to do something.

Hence, the correct option is (A).

23. Oligarchy - A small group of people having control of a country or organization.

Monarchy - A form of government with a monarch at the head.

Democracy - A system of government by the whole population or all the eligible members of a state, typically through elected representatives.

Anarchy - A state of disorder due to absence or non-recognition of authority or other controlling systems.

Hence, the correct option is (A).

24. Goes to dog describes something on the downgrade, something that is worse than it used to be, something that is deteriorating.

Example- Our favorite restaurant has gone to the dogs lately.

Hence, the correct option is (C).

25. The correct word from the given alternatives will be "their".

Two students didn't do their mathematics homework.

Hence, the correct option is (A).

26. In carrom, playing partners are facing each other and sits opposite to each other.

It is given that, P and R are partners. Q and S are partners. R is facing west therefore his partner P will be facing east. S is in the right of R means S is facing south direction. Therefore, with the given information, we can draw the following diagram:

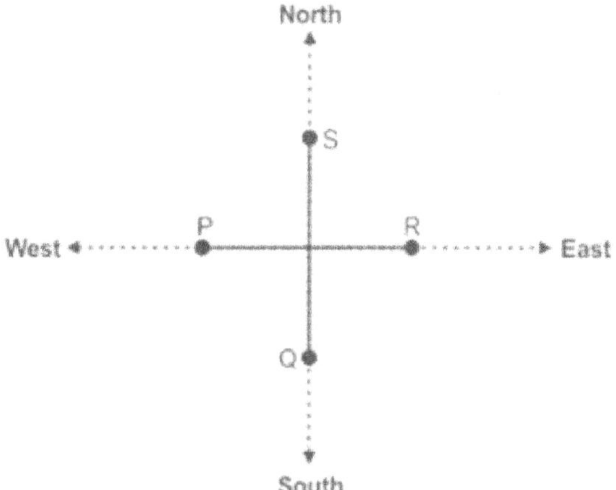

Thus, Q will be facing in the north direction.

Hence, the correct option is (A).

27.

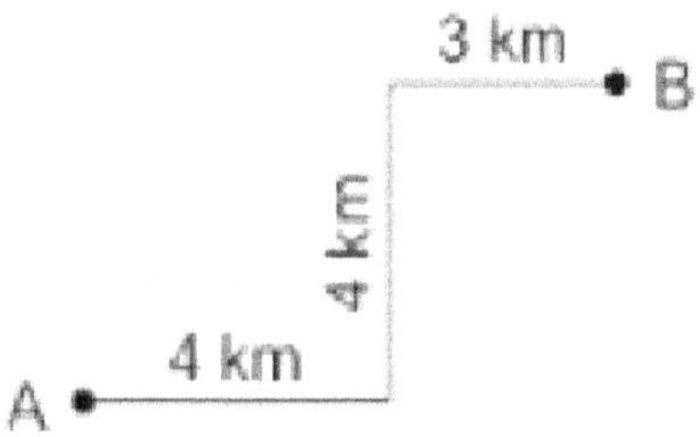

We can clearly observe from the figure that point B is North-East of point A.
Hence, the correct option is (B).

28. 4 × 1 = 4,

4 × 2 = 8,

8 × 3 = 24,

24 × 4 = 96,

96 × 5 = 480,

480 × 6 = 2880,

2880 × 7 = 20160
Hence, the correct option is (A).

29. Sum = 75° + 105°

= 180°

Now, 141° + ? = 180°

= 180° – 141°

= 39°
Hence, the correct option is (B).

30.

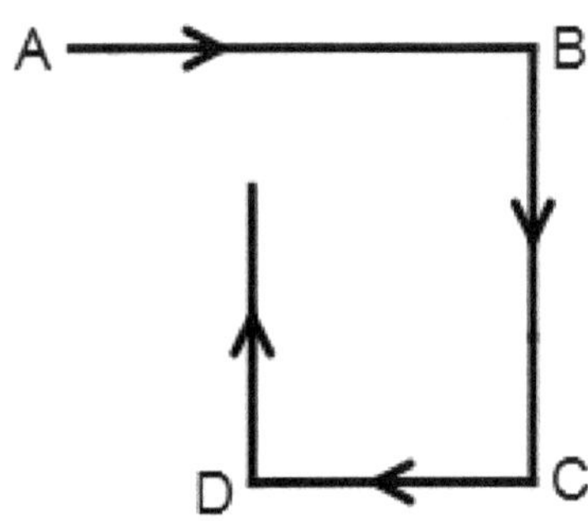

So, finally, Sujata will face towards North.
Hence, the correct option is (A).

31. The family tree is as follows:

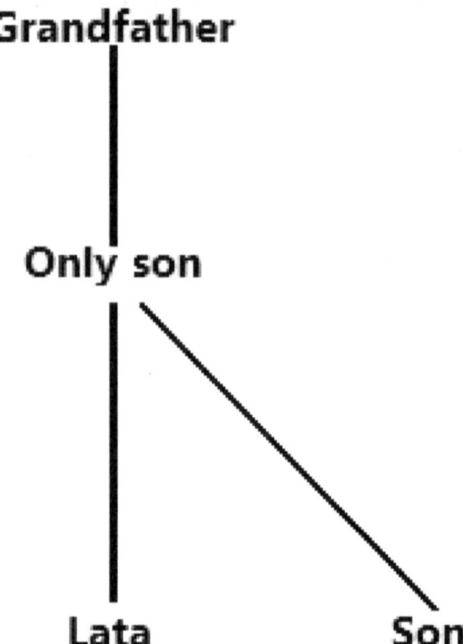

The man in the photograph is the son of the only son of Lata's grandfather i.e., the man is the son of Lata's father. So, the man is the brother of Lata.

Hence, the correct option is (A).

32.

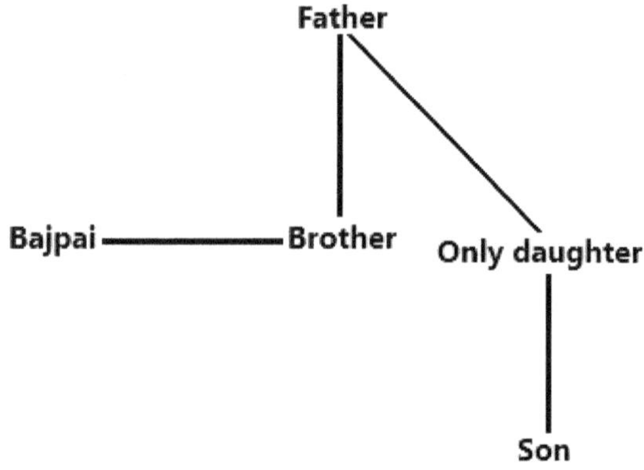

According to graph we can say that Bajpai is maternal uncle of the man in photograph.
Hence, the correct option is (D).

33.

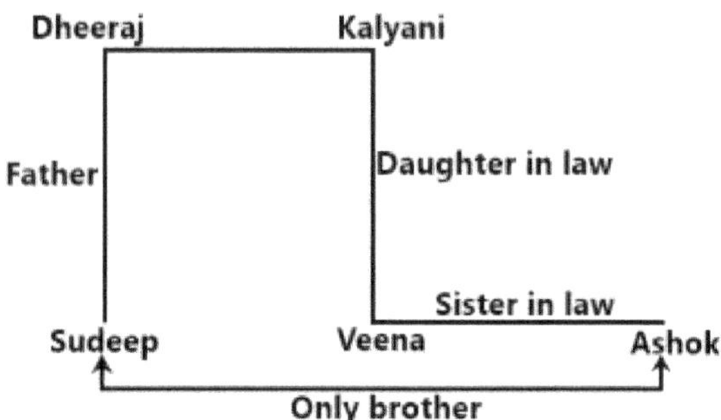

After looking the diagram we can say that Kalyani is the mother of Ashok.

Hence, the correct option is (D).

34. Safety is the opposite of Trouble and Slavery is the opposite of Freedom.
Hence, the correct option is (D).

35. Health is the opposite of Sickness in the same way Sorrow is the opposite of Happiness.
Hence, the correct option is (B).

36. Stone is Hard similarly Feather is Soft.
Hence, the correct option is (A).

37. The pattern here is:

T (+2) → V

H (-2) → F

E (+2) → G

N (-2) → L

So,

W (+2) → Y

O (-2) → M

R (+2) → T

D (-2) → B

Hence, the correct option is (B).

38.

D	E	L	H	I
-1	-2	-3	-4	-5
C	C	I	D	D

Same as,

B	O	M	B	A	Y
-1	-2	-3	-4	-5	-6
A	M	J	X	V	S

Hence, the correct option is (B).

39.

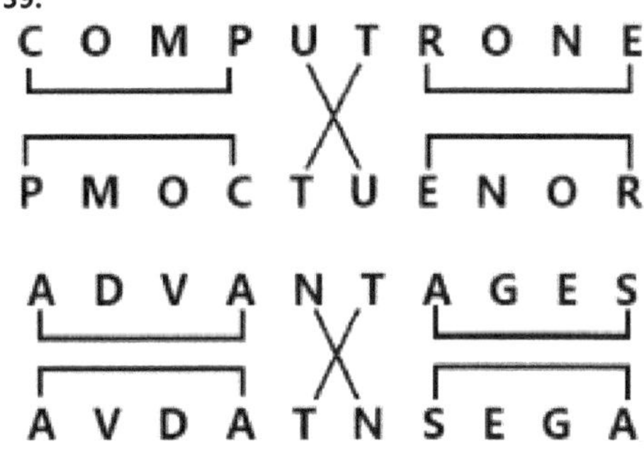

Hence, the correct option is (B).

40. Next term = $\dfrac{\text{Previous term}}{4}$

$$\frac{2816}{4} = 704$$

$$\frac{704}{4} = 176$$

$$\frac{176}{4} = 44$$

$$\frac{44}{4} = 11$$

Hence, the correct option is (A).

41. This is a simple alternating addition and subtraction series. In the first pattern, 3 is added; in the second, 2 is subtracted.
Hence, the correct option is (B).

42. S indicates those students who play all three games.
Hence, the correct option is (D).

43. Number of persons who can speak English and Hindi both only is 5.
Hence, the correct option is (A).

44. Number of persons can speak Marathi = 6

Number of persons can speak Telugu = 7

Persons can speak Marathi and Telugu both

= 6 + 7

= 13

Hence, the correct option is (C).

45. There is no such person who can speak all the languages.
Hence, the correct option is (D).

46.

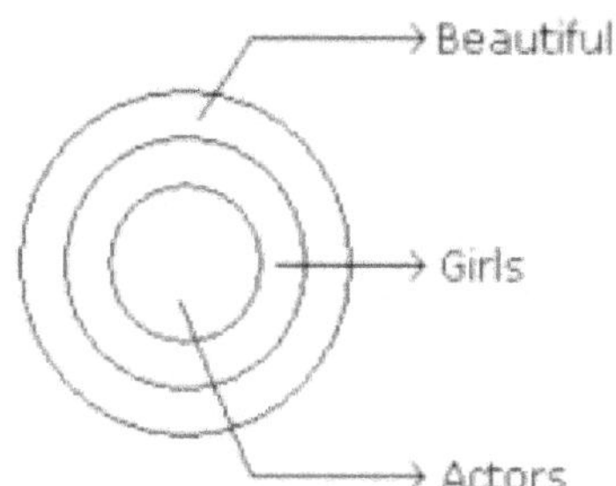

Both (I) and (II) follow.
Hence, the correct option is (D).

47.

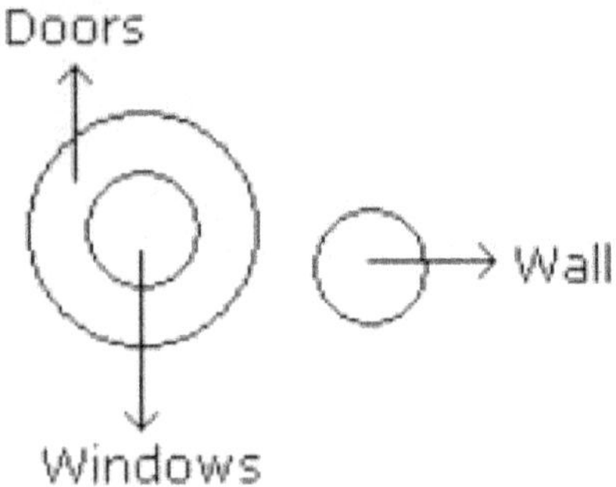

Only (II) follow.
Hence, the correct option is (B).

48. The increase in the fees of the private colleges and there is no increase in the same in Government colleges seem to be policy matters undertaken by the individual decisive boards at the two levels.
Hence, the correct option is (C).

49. Clearly, the withdrawal of funds by society members is bound to reduce the lending power of the society.
Hence, the correct option is (B).

50. The correct order of the given words are-

5. Advertisement

6. Application

2. Interview

3. Selection

4. Appointment

1. Probation

Hence, the correct option is (A).

51. Kanan will not be liable for killing the forest guard as he had no intention to kill him. He will be liable for trespassing the Forest Land, Attempt to poach etc. but not for killing the forest guard as both for homicide and Murder, intention needs to be proved.
Hence, the correct option is (B).

52. First of all the language of the facts make it clear that B and A's agreement is more of a social understanding rather than a legal agreement. Secondly, A waits on his own for 7 days which was not agreed to by B in his capacity as a neighbor. The court will dismiss the case.
Hence, the correct option is (C).

53. Supreme Court in a judgment struck down section 66A of the Information Technology Act, 2000 which provided provisions for the arrest of those who posted allegedly offensive content on the internet upholding freedom of expression. Section 66A defines the punishment for sending "offensive" messages through a computer or any other communication device like a mobile phone or tablet and a conviction of it can fetch a maximum of three years of jail and a fine.
Hence, the correct option is (A).

54. S. R. Bommai vs Union of India was a landmark judgment of the Supreme Court of India, where the Court discussed at length provisions of Article 356 of the Constitution of India and related issues. This case had a huge impact on Centre-State Relations. The judgment attempted to curb blatant misuse of Article 356 of the Constitution of India, which allowed the President's rule to be imposed over state governments.
Hence, the correct option is (A).

55. The Parliament was fully competent to enact Section 139AA of the Act and its authority to make this law was not diluted by the orders of this Court.

Court did not find any conflict between the provisions of the Aadhaar Act and Section 139AA of the Income Tax Act inasmuch as when interpreted harmoniously, they operate in distinct fields.

Section 139AA of the Act is not discriminatory nor does it offend equality
clause enshrined in Article 14 of the Constitution.
Hence, the correct option is (B).

56. The case of State of Uttar Pradesh vs Raj Narain was a 1975 case heard by the Allahabad High Court that found the Prime Minister of India Indira Gandhi guilty of electoral malpractices.
Hence, the correct option is (C).

57. The consent is not valid consent under all given statements.

Consent is not such a consent as it intended by any section of this Code if the consent is given by a person under fear of injury, or under a misconception of fact, and if the person doing the act knows, or has reason to believe, that the consent was given in consequence of such fear or misconception, or Consent of an insane person. if the consent is given by a person who, from unsoundness of mind, or intoxication, is unable to understand the nature and consequence of that to which he gives his consent; or Consent of a child, unless the contrary appears from the context if the consent is given by a person who is under twelve years of age.

Hence, the correct option is (D).

58. Section 406 in The Indian Penal Code- Punishment for criminal breach of trust. Whoever commits a criminal breach of trust shall be punished with imprisonment of either description for a term which may extend to three years, or with fine, or with both.
Hence, the correct option is (A).

59. Jus naturale is Latin for natural law, which is a philosophical system of legal and moral principles that are purported to be based on human nature and moralistic ideals of right and wrong rather than on legislation, judicial action, or statutes.
Hence, the correct option is (C).

60. JUS COGENS, meaning "compelling law" in Latin, are rules in international law that are peremptory or authoritative, and from which states cannot deviate. These norms cannot be offset by a separate treaty between parties intending to do so, since they hold fundamental values.
Hence, the correct option is (C).

61. International humanitarian law, or jus in bello, is the law that governs the way in which warfare is conducted. International

humanitarian law is purely humanitarian, seeking to limit the suffering caused. It is independent from questions about the justification or reasons for war, or its prevention, covered by jus ad bellum.
Hence, the correct option is (C).

62. Mare clausum (legal Latin meaning "closed sea") is a term used in international law to mention a sea, ocean or other navigable body of water under the jurisdiction of a state that is closed or not accessible to other states.
Hence, the correct option is (C).

63. When someone is non compos mentis, they are not sane or rational. When a person is declared by a judge to be non compos mentis, they can't legally speak for themselves. Non compos mentis literally means "not master of one's mind."
Hence, the correct option is (B).

64. The Supreme Court has ruled that narco analysis, brain mapping and polygraph tests cannot be conducted on any person without their consent. Such procedures "are illegal and a violation of personal liberty", ruled a three-judge bench headed by Chief Justice K.G. Balakrishnan. The order came in response to petitions questioning the validity of such tests that were filed by persons accused in various criminal cases.
Hence, the correct option is (B).

65. Certiorari means to be certified. The writ of certiorari can be issued by the Supreme Court or any High Court for quashing the order already passed by an inferior court, tribunal or quasi-judicial authority. There are several conditions necessary for the issue of writ of certiorari.
Hence, the correct option is (C).

66. Directive Principle of State Policy is conscience of Constitution which embody social philosophy of Constitution" was said by Granville Austin.

The Directive Principles of State Policy are referred to as the "Conscience of the Constitution". They aim to create a welfare state where the social and economic conditions are such that the citizens can lead a good life. They are the principles and guidelines to be kept in mind while framing the laws and policies for the nation.
Hence, the correct option is (A).

67. The Indian constitution is the world's longest. At its commencement, it had 395 articles in 22 parts and 8 schedules. It is made up of almost 80,000 words
Hence, the correct option is (A).

68. With its adoption, the Union of India officially became the modern and contemporary Republic of India and it replaced the Government of India Act 1935 as the country's fundamental governing document. The Constitution declares India to be a sovereign, socialist, secular, democratic republic, assuring its citizens of justice equality, and liberty, and endeavors to promote fraternity among them.
Hence, the correct option is (B).

69. According to Section 13, " two or more persons are said to be in consent when they agree upon the same thing in the same sense (Consensus-ad-idem). According to Section 14, Consent is said to be free when it is not caused by coercion or undue influence or fraud or misrepresentation or mistake.
Hence, the correct option is (C).

70. A contingent contract is an agreement that states which actions under certain conditions will result in specific outcomes. Contingent contracts usually occur when negotiating parties fail to reach an agreement. A contingent contract can also be viewed as protection against a future change of plans.
Hence, the correct option is (B).

71. Novation agreements are used to transfer the rights and obligations of one party under a contract to another party, whilst the other contracting party remains the same. The new party may be said to "step into the shoes" of the departing party.
Hence, the correct option is (C).

72. Under the Indian patent law, a patent can be obtained only for an invention which is new and useful. The invention must relate to the machine, article, or substance produced by a manufacturer, or the process of manufacture of an article.
Hence, the correct option is (A).

73. The Muhammadan Law defines the Hiba or gift as a transfer of a determinate (amount of) property without any exchange from one person to another and accepted by or on behalf of the latter. It is clear that under Muslim law, a gift is called Hiba. When a Muslim transfers his property through a gift, the transfer is called Hiba.

Hence, the correct option is (C).

74. The Child Marriage Restraint Act, 1929, passed on 28 September 1929, in the Imperial Legislative Council of India, fixed the age of marriage for girls at 14 years and boys at 18 years which was later amended to 18 for girls and 21 for boys. It is popularly known as the Sharda Act.
Hence, the correct option is (B).

75. On 13th December 1946, Jawaharlal Nehru moved the 'Objective Resolution', which later became the preamble to the Constitution of India.
Hence, the correct option is (D).

76. The stethoscope was invented in France in 1816 by Rene Laennec at the Necker-Enfants Malades Hospital in Paris. It consisted of a wooden tube and was monaural. Using this new instrument, he investigated the sounds made by the heart and lungs and determined that his diagnoses were supported by the observations made during autopsies.

Hence, the correct option is (A).

77. The term Log4Shell related to Cybersecurity.

A new vulnerability named Log4Shell is being touted as one of the worst cybersecurity flaws to have been discovered. The vulnerability is based on an open-source logging library used in most applications by enterprises and even government agencies.

Hence, the correct option is (A).

78. Sharavati is the name of the river that flows entirely in Karnataka. India's famous Jog falls is created by this river.
Hence, the correct option is (B).

79. Myanmar and India share a border of over 1,643 kilometers. Arunachal Pradesh, Nagaland, Manipur and Mizoram share borders with Myanmar. India shares a maritime boundary with Myanmar in Andaman Sea.
Hence, the correct option is (A).

80. Dr. M S Swami Nathan is known as the Father of the Green Revolution in India. Norman Borlaug is known as the Father of the Green Revolution Verghese Kurien is known as the Father of the white revolution in India.
Hence, the correct option is (B).

81. STRIVE (Skills Strengthening for Industrial Value Enhancement) is a World Bank-supported project for skill development in India. The aim of this project for skill development in India. The aim of this project is to improve access to quality and market-driven vocational training as well as apprenticeships.
Hence, the correct option is (C).

82. Article 63 of the Indian Constitution states that "There shall be a Vice President of India." The Vice President acts as President in the absence of the president due to death, resignation, impeachment, or other situations.
Hence, the correct option is (C).

83. The writ of habeas corpus facilitates the guarantee of personal freedom by allowing courts to determine whether legal authorities have legitimately detained individuals. Freedom from arbitrary arrest and detention is a central part of the personal freedoms recognized through this writ. Habeas corpus is a Latin phrase that translates to "that you have the body".
Hence, the correct option is (C).

84. Article 40 of the Directive Principles of State Policy directs the government to organize village panchayats and endow them with necessary powers and authority to enable them to function as units of self-government.
Hence, the correct option is (B).

85. The Reserve Bank of India (RBI) is conducting Open Market Operations (OMO) in the form of the purchase of Rs 10,000 crore worth of government securities.

Open market operations refer to central bank purchases or sales of government securities in order to expand or contract money in the banking system and influence interest rates.
Hence, the correct option is (B).

86. When the RBI reduces the cash reserve ratio, it lowers the amount of cash that banks are required to hold in reserves, allowing them to make more loans to consumers and businesses. This increases the nation's money supply and expands the economy.
Hence, the correct option is (C).

87. The Cocos Plate is bounded by several different plates. To the northeast it is bounded by the North American Plate and the Caribbean Plate. To the west it is bounded by the Pacific Plate and to the south by the Nazca Plate.
Hence, the correct option is (B).

88. The Great Victoria Desert is the largest desert in Australia. It consists of sand dunes, small sandhills, grassland plains, areas with closely packed pebbles and salt lakes. The area of the Great Victoria Desert is shared roughly equally by the states of South and Western Australia.
Hence, the correct option is (C).

89. Secularism, also called Secularity, is the idea of something being not religious or not connected to a church or other religious organization. An example of this is the government, which is independent of any religion in many states.

Secularism in India does not mean the separation of religion from state. Instead, secularism in India means a state that supports or participates in a neutral manner in the affairs of all religious groups.
Hence, the correct option is (A).

90. here are 3 methods used for calculating national income namely; Income method, expenditure method, and Product method. The diminishing cost method is not a method to calculate national income.
Hence, the correct option is (D).

91. Real national income is nominal or money national income (output) adjusted for inflation. It is also national income at 'at constant prices. The most frequently used measure of national income is Gross Domestic Product (GDP).
Hence, the correct option is (D).

92. The Laffer Curve is a theory developed by supply-side economist Arthur Laffer to show the relationship between tax rates and the amount of tax revenue collected by governments. The curve is used to illustrate Laffer's argument that sometimes cutting tax rates can increase total tax revenue.
Hence, the correct option is (B).

93. Tax expenditures are concessions and exemptions provided to the taxpayers by the government. These concessions are aimed to promote certain types of activities like R&D, public welfare, etc. So, though these are exemptions from paying taxes they are indirectly some sort of expenditure (to the tune of the tax concessions made to the taxpayer) made by the government to realize the given objective. These expenditures are described as tax preferences as well.

Tax expenditures are also termed revenue foregone.
Hence, the correct option is (B).

94. A bank rate is the interest rate at which a nation's central bank lends money to domestic banks, often in the form of very short-term loans. Managing the bank rate is a method by which central banks affect economic activity.
Hence, the correct option is (D).

95. The leading sugarcane-producing States are the leading sugar producers as well. They are Uttar Pradesh, Maharashtra, Andhra Pradesh, Tamil Nadu, Karnataka, Bihar and Jharkhand. There are more than 250 sugar mills in India.
Hence, the correct option is (C).

96. Army Chief General Manoj Pande was conferred with the Param Vishisht Seva Medal for his distinguished service of exceptional order at a defence investiture ceremony at Rashtrapati Bhawan on May 12th, 2022.

Hence, the correct option is (A).

97. 'Triangle of Sadness' directed by Ruben Ostlund has won the Palme d'Or at the 75th Cannes Film Festival for the second time.

Earlier, he had received the cinema's most prestigious prizes for his movie 'The Square' in 2017.

Indian filmmaker Shaunak Sen has won the 'L'Oeil d'Or' award for his documentary 'All That Breathes'.

Hence, the correct option is (D).

98. Dutch movie, "Turn Your Body to the Sun" has bagged the Golden Conch award at the 17th edition of the 2022 Mumbai International Film Festival (MIFF) for documentary, short fiction and animation films.

The award carries a golden conch, a certificate and cash prize of Rs 10 lakh.

This documentary was directed by Aliona Van der Horst.

Hence, the correct option is (A).

99. The 2015 film Bajrangi Bhaijaan fame actress Harshaali Malhotra has been awarded the 12th Bharat Ratna Dr Ambedkar Award 2022.

Hence, the correct option is (C).

100. Indian Representative Navdeep Kaur has claimed the Costume Round as she represented the country for her Kundalini Chakra dress at Mrs World 2022.

Hence, the correct option is (C).

English Language & Comprehension

Ques (1-5):Direction: Read the following passage and answer the question that follow.

No one can look back on his schooldays and say with truth that they were altogether unhappy. I have good memories of St Cyprian's, among a horde of bad ones. Sometimes on summer afternoons, there were wonderful expeditions across the Downs to a village called Birling Gap, or to Beachy Head, where one bathed dangerously among the boulders and came home covered with cuts. And there were still more wonderful mid-summer evenings when, as a special treat, we were not driven off to bed as usual but allowed to wander about the grounds in the long twilight, ending up with a plunge into the swimming bathe at about nine o'clock. There was the joy of waking early on summer mornings and getting in an hour's undisturbed reading (Ian Hay, Thackeray, Kipling, and H. G. Wells were the favourite authors of my boyhood) in the sunlit, sleeping dormitory. There was also cricket, which I was no good at but with which I conducted a sort of hopeless love affair up to the age of about eighteen. And there was the pleasure of keeping caterpillars — the silky green and purple puss-moth, the ghostly green poplar-hawk, the privet-hawk, large as one's third finger, specimens of which could be illicitly purchased for sixpence at a shop in the town and when one could escape long enough from the master who was 'taking the walk', there was the excitement of dredging the dew-ponds on the Downs for enormous newts with orange-coloured bellies. This business of being out for a walk, coming across something of fascinating interest, and then being dragged away from it by a yell from the master, as a dog jerked onwards by the leash, is an important feature of school life and helps to build up the conviction, so strong in many children, that the things you most want to do are always unattainable.

Q.1 We can infer that the writer was a-

A. Disobedient student   **B.** Lonely child
C. Mischievous boy   **D.** Studious boy

Q.2 Why does the writer call cricket a hopeless love affair?

[SSC Sub Inspector (CPO), 2019]

A. He was forced to give it up
B. He did not play it at all
C. He played it secretly
D. He tried hard to learn it

Q.3 "Where one bathed dangerously". Why does the writer call bathing dangerous?

A. They were punished later
B. There were snakes in the water
C. The boulders gave them bruises
D. The water was too deep

Q.4 What is the 'moral' the boy draws from his childhood experiences?

[SSC Sub Inspector (CPO), 2019]

A. Things you enjoy doing are always unreachable
B. Only do the things your masters tell you to
C. Do not walk alone in the grounds
D. Do not collect insects like caterpillars

Q.5 Which of the following did the boys not do on summer mornings?

[SSC Sub Inspector (CPO), 2019]

A. Read in bed   **B.** Sleep until late
C. Play cricket   **D.** Collect caterpillars

Ques (6-9):Direction: Select the most appropriate synonym of the given word.

Q.6 Fortify
A. Secure   **B.** Harm   **C.** Loosen   **D.** Neglect

Q.7 Enthral
A. Disgust   **B.** Free
C. Mesmerise   **D.** Repel

Q.8 Contempt
A. Respect   **B.** Approve   **C.** Permit   **D.** Hatred

Q.9 Solemn
A. Furious   **B.** Ordinary   **C.** Serious   **D.** Ignorant

Ques (10-12):Direction: Select the most appropriate antonym of the given word.

Q.10 Denounce
A. Criticise   **B.** Applaud   **C.** Vilify   **D.** Blame

Q.11 Slander
A. Appeal   **B.** Malign   **C.** Admire   **D.** Defame

Q.12 Hasty
A. Sudden   **B.** Cautious   **C.** Reckless   **D.** Urgent

Q.13 Direction: Select the most appropriate meaning of the given idiom.
Keep your shirt on
A. Leave   **B.** Stay calm
C. Be in your limits   **D.** Be confident

Q.14 Direction: Select the most appropriate meaning of the idiom/phrase given in bold in the sentence.
Don't **rundown** your friends in public.
A. Fight with   **B.** Follow
C. Make a mention of   **D.** Criticize

Q.15 Direction: Select the most appropriate option to fill in the blank.
You cannot learn music overnight. It is a _______ process.

A. intellectual   **B.** gradual
C. mellifluous   **D.** happening

Q.16 Direction: In the following question, a sentence is given with a blank to be filled in with an appropriate word. Select the correct alternative out of the four and indicate it by selecting the appropriate option.

We had to _______ the meeting as the electricity went off.

A. hold back   **B.** hold up
C. hold down   **D.** hold on

Q.17 Direction: Select the most appropriate option to fill in the blank.

I cannot believe they live ___ begging.

A. over   **B.** by   **C.** in   **D.** with

Q.18 Direction: Select the most appropriate option to substitute the underlined segment. If no substitution is required select 'No substitution'

The assignment <u>was so difficult</u> for Mohit to do on his own.

A. was too difficult
B. no substitution
C. was so much difficult
D. were so difficult

Q.19 Direction: Identify the best way to improve the underlined part of the given sentence. if there is no improvement required, select 'no improvement'-

My friend did not understand the story. She asked me <u>for explain it her</u>.

A. to explaining it for her
B. to explain it to her
C. can I explain that to her
D. no improvement

Q.20 Direction: Select the most appropriate option to substitute the underlined segment in the given sentence. If there is no need to substitute it, select No improvement.

His uncle advised Naveen **to keep away from** involving himself in the controversy.

A. for keep away from
B. No improvement
C. that he keeps away for
D. from keep away in

Ques (21-22):Direction: In the following question, a sentence has been given in Active Voice/Passive Voice, Out of the four alternatives suggested, select the one which best expresses the same sentence in Passive/ Active Voice.

Q.21 The burglar destroyed several items in the room. Even the carpet has been torn.

A. Several items destroyed in the room by the burglar. Even the carpet he has torn.
B. Several items in the room were destroyed by the burglar. Even the carpet was torn.
C. Including the carpet, several items in the room have been torn by the burglar.
D. The burglar, being destroyed several items in the room, also carpet has torn.

Q.22 We must respect the elders.

A. The elders deserve respect from us
B. The elders must be respected
C. The elders must respected
D. Respect the elders we must

Ques (23-24):Direction: The sentences given below are grammatically incorrect. Pick out the best suitable option to correct the sentence.

Q.23 A student was arrested for displaying an indecently art work in public.

A. indecent   **B.** unindecently
C. the indecently   **D.** any of indecently

Q.24 He did not like <u>me to smoking</u> in the presence of our teacher yesterday.

A. that I smoke   **B.** my smoking
C. me smoking   **D.** smoking by me

Q.25 Direction: Some parts of the sentence have errors and some are correct. Find out which part has an error and mark that part as your answer. If there are no errors, mark 'No error' as your answer.

The movie who came out last week was really good.

A. The movie who   **B.** Was really good
C. Came out last week   **D.** No error

Analytical Abilities

Q.26 Which of the following diagrams indicates the best relation between Profit, Dividend and Bonus?

A.    **B.** 

C.    **D.** 

Q.27 Which of the following diagrams indicates the best relation between Women, Mothers and Engineers?

A.    **B.** 

C. 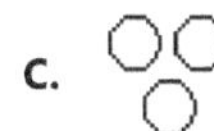   **D.** 

Ques (28-29):Direction: In the following question two statements (i) and (ii) are given. Which are followed by four conclusions (1), (2), (3) and (4). Choose the conclusions which logically follow from the given statements.

Q.28 Statement:
(i) No door is dog.
(ii) All the dogs are cats.
Conclusion:
(1) No door is cat.

(2) No cat is door.
(3) Some cats are dogs.
(4) All the cats are dogs.

A. Only (2) and (4)   **B.** Only (1) and (3)
C. Only (3) and (4)   **D.** Only (3)

Q.29 Statement:
(i) All green are blue.
(ii) All blue are white.

Conclusion:
(1) Some blue are green.
(2) Some white are green.
(3) Some green are not white.
(4) All white are blue.

A. Only (1) and (2)   **B.** Only (1) and (3)
C. Only (1) and (4)   **D.** Only (2) and (4)

Q.30 Grass in lawn grows equally thick and in a uniform rate. It takes 24 days for 70 cows and 60 days for 30 cows to eat the whole of the grass. How many cows are needed to eat the grass in 96 days?

A. 22 Cows   **B.** 20 Cows   **C.** 18 Cows   **D.** 16 Cows

Q.31 A Parking lot Contains 160 Vehicles. Each Vehicle is either a car or a truck, and each vehicle is either red or green. 70 vehicles are red, and 120 vehicles are cars. If there are 18 green trucks, how many red cars are there?

A. 54   **B.** 50   **C.** 48   **D.** 45

Ques (32-33):Direction: In the question are given two statements I and II. These statements may be either independent causes or may be effects of independent causes or a common cause. One of these statements may be the effect of the other statements. Read both the statements and decide which of the following answer choice correctly depicts the relationship between these two statements.

Q.32 Statement:
I. Standard of living among the middle class society is constantly going up since part of few years.
II. Indian Economy is observing remarkable growth.

A. Statement I is the cause and statement II is its effect.
B. Statement II is the cause and statement I is its effect.
C. Both the statements I and II are independent causes.
D. Both the statements I and II are effects of independent causes.

Q.33 Statement:
I. A huge truck overturned on the middle of the road last night.
II. The police had cordoned of entire area in the locality this morning for half of the day.

A. Statement I is the cause and statement II is its effect.
B. Statement II is the cause and statement I is its effect.
C. Both the statements I and II are independent causes.
D. Both the statements I and II are effects of independent causes.

Q.34 Direction: In the following question consists of one statement followed by two conclusions. You have to decide which one of them can be followed.

Statement:
Appointment of top bureaucrats as the head of top financial institutions was made by government. This is the reason of the downfall of those institutions.

Conclusions:
I. Government should appoint only those persons as the head, who have adequate expertise in the required field.
II. The appointed head should have the similar work experience as carried out by that financial institutions.

A. Only conclusion I is valid.
B. Only conclusion II is valid.
C. Either conclusion I or II is valid.
D. None of these

Q.35 Direction: In the following question consists of one statement followed by two conclusions. You have to decide which one of them can be followed.

Statement:
Destiny can be influenced by the choices made by the modern man unlike in the past.

Conclusions:
I. In the past, the number of options available to a man were less.
II. The desire to influence the past was also not present in the man during old times.

A. Only conclusion I is valid.
B. Only conclusion II is valid.
C. Either conclusion I or II is valid.
D. None of these

Ques (36-37):Direction: In the following question consists of one statement followed by two assumptions. You have to decide which one of them can be followed.

Q.36 Statement:
If you can solve H.C Verma's concepts of physics, you can excel in 12th standard.

Assumptions:
I. Physics is one of the important subjects and H.C Verma's concepts of physics clear the concepts regarding physics very well.
II. One must solve O.P Aggrawal's inorganic chemistry.

A. Only assumption I is practical.
B. Only assumption II is practical.
C. Either assumption I or II is practical.
D. Neither assumption I nor II is practical.

Q.37 Statement:
HSBC bank has announced to launch "Green Bonds" for raising funds for investments in environmental projects.

Assumptions:
I. By investing in environment, HSBC bank will become popular.
II. By investing in environment, HSBC bank will do its corporate social entrepreneurship.

A. Only assumption I is practical.
B. Only assumption II is practical.
C. Either assumption I or II is practical.

D. Both the assumptions are practical.

Ques (38-39):Direction: In the question given below consists of a statement, followed by two arguments numbered I and II. You have to decide which of the arguments is a 'strong' argument and which is a 'weak' argument. Give answer:

Q.38

Statement:

Should India encourage exports, when most things are insufficient for internal use itself?

Argument:

I. Yes. We have to earn foreign exchange to pay for our imports.

II. No. Even selective encouragement would lead to shortages.

A. Only argument I is strong

B. Only argument II is strong

C. Either I or II is strong

D. Neither I nor II is strong

Q.39 Statement:

Should India make efforts to harness solar energy to fulfil its energy requirements?

Argument:

I. Yes, Most of the energy sources used at present is exhaustible.

II. No. Harnessing solar energy requires a lot of capital, which India lacks in.

A. Only argument I is strong

B. Only argument II is strong

C. Either I or II is strong

D. Neither I nor II is strong

Q.40

If South-East becomes North, North-East becomes West and so on. What will West become?

A. North-East   **B.** North-West

C. South-East   **D.** South-West

Q.41 Rahul put his timepiece on the table in such a way that at 6 P.M. hour hand points to North. In which direction the minute hand will point at 9.15 P.M.?

A. South-East   **B.** South

C. North   **D.** West

Ques (42-43):Direction: In the following question find out the alternative which will replace the question mark.

Q.42 CUP : LIP :: BIRD : ?

A. BUSH   **B.** GRASS

C. FOREST   **D.** BEAK

Q.43

Flow : River :: Stagnant : ?

A. Rain   **B.** Stream   **C.** Pool   **D.** Canal

Q.44 Pointing to a photograph of a boy Suresh said, "He is the son of the only son of my mother". How is Suresh related to that boy?

A. Brother   **B.** Uncle   **C.** Cousin   **D.** Father

Q.45

A is son of C while C and Q are the sisters to one another. Z is the mother of Q. If P is the son of Z, Which one of the following statements is correct?

A. Q is the grandfather of A

B. P is the maternal uncle of A

C. P is the cousin of A

D. Z is the brother of C

Ques (46-47):Direction: Remember, you are looking for the word that does NOT belong in the same group as the others. Sometimes, all four words seem to fit in the same group. If so, look more closely to further narrow your classification.

Q.46

Which word does NOT belong with the others?

A. Core   **B.** Seeds   **C.** Pulp   **D.** Slice

Q.47 Which word does NOT belong with the others?

A. Fair   **B.** Just

C. Equitable   **D.** Favorable

Ques (48-49):Direction: In the question below is given a statement followed by two courses of action numbered I and II. You have to assume everything in the statement to be true and on the basis of the information given in the statement, decide which of the suggested courses of action logically follow(s) for pursuing. Give answer

Q.48 Statement:

The Secretary lamented that the electronic media was losing its credibility and that it should try to regain it by establishing better communications with the listeners and the viewers. He also emphasized the need for training to improve the functioning.

Courses of Action:

I. Efforts should be made to get organised feed back on the programme.

II. The critical areas in which the staff requires training should be identified.

A. Only I follows

B. Only II follows

C. Either I or II follows

D. Both I and II follow

Q.49 Statement:

Courts take too long in deciding important disputes of various departments.

Courses of Action:

I. Courts should be ordered to speed up matters.

II. Special powers should be granted to officers to settle disputes concerning their department.

A. Only I follows

B. Only II follows

C. Either I or II follows

D. Both I and II follow

Q.50 Direction: Find the statement that must be true according to the given information.

Vincent has a paper route. Each morning, he delivers 37 newspapers to customers in his neighborhood. It takes Vincent 50 minutes to deliver all the papers. If Vincent is sick or has other plans, his friend Thomas, who lives on the same street, will sometimes deliver the papers for him.

A. Vincent and Thomas live in the same neighborhood.

B. It takes Thomas more than 50 minutes to deliver the papers.

C. It is dark outside when Vincent begins his deliveries.

D. Thomas would like to have his own paper route.

Legal Awareness & Aptitude

Q.51 Which of the following recently became the 123rd State party to the International Criminal Court?

A. Israel **B.** Palestine

C. Jordan **D.** Bangladesh

Q.52 Which one of the following committee was constituted to review environmental law in the country?

A. Subramanian Committee

B. Kasturi Ranjan Committee

C. Madhav Nair Committee

D. Ullas Karanth Committee

Q.53 Who can remove the Judge of the Supreme Court?

A. Chief Justice of the Supreme Court

B. Only President

C. Only Parliament

D. Both Parliament and President

Q.54 Who among the following has the right to establish the bench of Supreme Court elsewhere in the country?

A. The Chief Justice of the Supreme Court

B. The President of India

C. The Parliament

D. Chief Justice of the Supreme Court has the right to allow to establish the bench of the Supreme Court elsewhere in the country with prior approval of the President.

Q.55 Which one of the following is NOT the main jurisdiction of the High Court of a State?

A. Supervisory Jurisdiction

B. Appellate Jurisdiction

C. Advisory Jurisdiction

D. Original Jurisdiction

Q.56 The chief justice of a High Court is appointed by:

A. Chief Justice of India

B. President on the advice of Governor of the state concerned and the chief Justice of India

C. President

D. Governor

Q.57 Which of the following state has a common High Court?

A. Gujarat-Odisha

B. Assam-Meghalaya

C. Maharashtra-Goa

D. Karnataka-Andhra Pradesh

Q.58 What is the meaning of the given words:

Pacta sunt servanda

A. Treaties are legally binding

B. Goods without an owner

C. Legal obligation

D. With the intention of making a will

Q.59 Which of the following is not an essential element of a valid contract?

A. Offer

B. Legality of object

C. Lawful consideration

D. Impossibility of performance

Q.60 Section 82 of IPC provides that nothing is an offence which is done by a child under:

A. Six years of age **B.** Seven years of age

C. Nine years of age **D.** Ten years of age

Q.61 Intoxication as defence is contained in:

A. Section 85 of IPC **B.** Section 86 of IPC

C. Section 87 of IPC **D.** Both (a) & (b)

Q.62 Which of the following is the closest in meaning to the legal maxim res communes?

A. Whence there is truth, there is light.

B. Things belonging to no body.

C. Things belonging to everybody.

D. Rest of the communities.

Q.63 En ventre sa mere is a person in being for the purpose of:

A. Punishment of abortion

B. Acquisition of property

C. Creation of partnership

D. Claiming compensation in torts

Q.64 Actionable Per se:

A. For the case or end at hand

B. The meetings of minds

C. In good faith

D. The very act is punishable, no proof of damage is required

Q.65 Which of the following committee suggested incorporating Fundamental Duties in the Indian Constitution?

A. Malhotra Committee

B. Raghavan Committee

C. Swaran Singh Committee

D. Narasimhan Committee

Q.66 Which of the following Article of the Indian Constitution guarantees 'Equality Before the Law and Equal Protection of Law within the Territory of India'?

A. Article 15 **B.** Article 14

C. Article 17 **D.** Article 18

Q.67 Which of the following Article of the Indian Constitution contains Fundamental Duties?

A. 45 A **B.** 51 A **C.** 42 **D.** 30B

Q.68 The Judges of the International Court of Justice are elected by the:
A. Security Council
B. General Assembly
C. General Assembly upon recommendation of the Security Council
D. General Assembly and the Security Council independently of one another

Q.69 The distinctive features of riot and unlawful assembly are an activity which is accompanied by________.
A. Causing alarm
B. Use of force and violence
C. Violence on a common purpose
D. All of the above

Q.70 The age of minority, in the case of kidnapping, has been defined as ___________ by the IPC.
A. 16 years
B. 18 years
C. 18 years for male and 21 for female
D. 16 years for male and 18 years for female

Q.71 Which of the following cases relates to the doctrine of basic structure?
A. Kesavananda Bharti v Union of India
B. Maneka Gandhi v Union of India
C. Sarla Mudgal v Union of India
D. Kesavananda Bharti v State of Kerala

Q.72 Which of the following statement is not true about India's Supreme Court?
A. The Supreme Court was inaugurated on January 28, 1950
B. At present, there are 35 judges in the Supreme Court
C. Judges of Supreme Court are appointed by the President of India
D. None of these

Q.73 The Bombay High Court does not have a bench at which one of the following places?
A. Nagpur
B. Panaji
C. Pune
D. Aurangabad

Q.74 Section 83 of IPC lays down:
A. A presumption of fact
B. An inconclusive or rebuttable presumption of law
C. Conclusive or irrebuttable presumption of law
D. Irrebuttable presumption of fact

Q.75 The maxim 'actus non facit rea nisi mens sit rea' means:
A. Crime has to be coupled with guilty mind
B. There can be no crime without a guilty mind
C. Crime is the result of guilty mind
D. Criminal mind leads to crime

General Knowledge

Q.76 Which of the following aircraft of the Indian Air Force participated in the 'Singapore Air Show-2022'?
A. Sukhoi 30 MKI
B. Rafale
C. Tejas MK-I
D. Brahmos

Q.77 Indian manned mission to space to be launched in 2023 is __________.
A. Mangalyaan-2
B. Vugolyaan
C. Gaganyaan
D. Antrix

Q.78 Recently seen in the news, DART mission is launched by ______.
A. CNSA
B. ISRO
C. NASA
D. ESA

Q.79 Which of the following states is not included in the sixth schedule of the Indian Constitution?
A. Meghalaya
B. Tripura
C. Mizoram
D. Manipur

Q.80 In which year, parliament passed the Citizenship Act?
A. 1950
B. 1955
C. 1960
D. 1965

Q.81 At which among the following places, the first summit of SAARC had taken place?
A. Islamabad
B. New Delhi
C. Dhaka
D. Katmandu

Q.82 Which among the following tides (as they are called) from the surf and winds?
A. Storm tides
B. Riptides
C. Neap tides
D. Tsunami

Q.83 Through open market operations, RBI plays a very important role in which of the following markets?
A. Gilt-edged market
B. Primary market
C. Secondary market
D. None of the above

Q.84 Which among the following publishes World Investment Report?
A. World Bank
B. IMF
C. OECD
D. United Nations Conference on Trade and Development

Q.85 What is the size of India's economy at present on a nominal GDP basis?
A. US$ 2.93 trillion
B. US$ 11.30 trillion
C. US$ 3.5 trillion
D. None of the above

Q.86 Which sector contributes the most income to India's economy?
A. Primary sector
B. Secondary sector
C. Tertiary sector
D. None of these

Q.87 In India, GST became effective from?
A. 1st April 2017
B. 1st January 2017
C. 1st July 2017
D. 1st March 2017

Q.88 In India GST came effective from July 1st, 2017 India has chosen ______ model of dual – GST.
A. USA
B. UK
C. Canadian
D. China

Q.89 When did India globally become the 7th largest vehicle manufacturer?

A. 2007   **B.** 2008   **C.** 2009   **D.** 2010

Q.90 When was the first modern paper mill of the country set up?

A. 1827   **B.** 1832   **C.** 1846   **D.** 1854

Q.91 Cooch Behar in West Bengal is famous for which among the following industries?
A. Cotton Cloth Industry
B. Silk Industry
C. Petroleum Industry
D. Glass Industry

Q.92 Investment is the ____________.
A. Net additions made to the nation's capital stocks
B. Person's commitment to buy a flat or house
C. Employment of funds on assets to earn returns
D. Employment of funds on goods and services that are used in production process

Q.93 Financial Management is mainly concerned with?
A. All aspects of acquiring and utilizing financial resources for firms activities
B. Arrangement of funds
C. Efficient Management of every business
D. Profit maximization

Q.94 The primary goal of financial management is?
A. To maximize the return
B. To minimize the risk
C. To maximize the wealth of owners
D. To maximize profit

Q.95 Which of the following Constitution Amendment Act provided for reservation of seats for scheduled tribes of Nagaland, Meghalaya, Mizoram, & Arunachal Pradesh state assemblies?
A. 52nd   **B.** 57th   **C.** 61st   **D.** 65th

Q.96 What is the number of items in the 12th schedule added by the 74th Amendment of the Constitution?
A. 11   **B.** 16   **C.** 18   **D.** 20

Q.97 If the contribution of the agricultural sector is decreasing in a country's economy, then what conclusion can be drawn?
A. The country is growing in the direction of being a developed nation
B. The country is moving towards becoming a developing nation
C. The country is moving towards becoming a less developed nation
D. The economic growth rate of the country has stopped

Q.98 Kalidas Samman award is presented by which state government?
A. Tamil Nadu   **B.** Karnataka
C. Andhra Pradesh   **D.** Madhya Pradesh

Q.99 In December 2021, who among the following has been named as the Badminton World Federation male Player of the Year 2021?

A. Viktor Axelsen   **B.** Lin Dan
C. Anderes Antonsen   **D.** Kento Momota

Q.100 Who has bagged a silver medal at Para World Taekwondo Championships?
A. Rakesh Kumar
B. Harvinder Singh
C. Chandeep Singh
D. Shyam Sundar Swami

// Smart Answer Sheet //

Correct Percentage of students who answered correctly. **Skipped** Percentage of students who skipped.

Q.	Ans.	Correct / Skipped	Q.	Ans.	Correct / Skipped	Q.	Ans.	Correct / Skipped	Q.	Ans.	Correct / Skipped	Q.	Ans.	Correct / Skipped
1	C	41.75 % / 42.33 %	17	B	64.32 % / 34.0 %	33	A	66.29 % / 31.91 %	49	D	78.0 % / 12.61 %	65	C	43.36 % / 43.82 %
2	D	61.56 % / 35.58 %	18	A	77.45 % / 19.0 %	34	C	54.03 % / 36.52 %	50	A	65.2 % / 30.54 %	66	B	68.94 % / 30.05 %
3	C	83.77 % / 14.91 %	19	B	46.26 % / 47.45 %	35	A	69.91 % / 30.02 %	51	B	62.93 % / 35.17 %	67	B	57.7 % / 39.75 %
4	A	66.15 % / 30.82 %	20	B	78.08 % / 11.72 %	36	A	52.28 % / 36.63 %	52	A	63.0 % / 32.27 %	68	D	76.1 % / 23.6 %
5	B	48.95 % / 46.64 %	21	B	49.3 % / 36.27 %	37	D	68.4 % / 31.52 %	53	D	49.01 % / 30.66 %	69	B	60.69 % / 33.45 %
6	A	78.84 % / 14.75 %	22	B	48.01 % / 49.47 %	38	A	68.31 % / 30.78 %	54	D	52.23 % / 35.31 %	70	D	84.86 % / 11.66 %
7	C	87.31 % / 10.59 %	23	A	55.15 % / 32.74 %	39	A	41.07 % / 53.39 %	55	C	40.01 % / 44.3 %	71	D	41.94 % / 34.18 %
8	D	81.12 % / 10.16 %	24	B	61.28 % / 30.07 %	40	C	52.44 % / 46.54 %	56	B	52.88 % / 37.75 %	72	B	59.82 % / 36.27 %
9	C	62.6 % / 37.19 %	25	A	59.0 % / 39.55 %	41	D	45.86 % / 45.11 %	57	C	52.63 % / 37.86 %	73	C	58.06 % / 35.62 %
10	B	57.93 % / 32.43 %	26	B	69.08 % / 30.41 %	42	D	68.97 % / 30.01 %	58	A	46.57 % / 45.04 %	74	B	49.72 % / 44.14 %
11	C	52.05 % / 43.41 %	27	A	50.8 % / 42.01 %	43	C	63.56 % / 30.97 %	59	D	44.96 % / 54.95 %	75	B	61.0 % / 38.27 %
12	B	77.37 % / 11.97 %	28	D	43.25 % / 37.23 %	44	D	50.81 % / 39.07 %	60	B	44.48 % / 52.97 %	76	C	89.21 % / 10.13 %
13	B	52.86 % / 33.95 %	29	A	87.0 % / 11.6 %	45	B	51.62 % / 46.37 %	61	D	59.67 % / 31.1 %	77	C	89.52 % / 10.28 %
14	D	81.51 % / 14.91 %	30	B	79.71 % / 14.3 %	46	D	52.37 % / 38.78 %	62	C	40.95 % / 58.57 %	78	C	82.49 % / 10.06 %
15	B	46.04 % / 50.69 %	31	C	57.97 % / 37.48 %	47	D	85.54 % / 11.79 %	63	B	58.57 % / 40.65 %	79	D	54.72 % / 35.89 %
16	B	63.46 % / 34.76 %	32	A	43.96 % / 53.9 %	48	D	56.83 % / 30.32 %	64	D	66.96 % / 30.32 %	80	B	43.15 % / 39.58 %

Q.	Ans.	Correct / Skipped
81	C	42.43 %
		51.37 %
82	B	49.14 %
		33.12 %
83	A	47.1 %
		37.78 %
84	D	49.93 %
		31.03 %

Q.	Ans.	Correct / Skipped
85	A	83.89 %
		12.89 %
86	C	55.49 %
		40.51 %
87	C	61.62 %
		31.16 %
88	C	63.41 %
		34.09 %

Q.	Ans.	Correct / Skipped
89	C	43.87 %
		31.31 %
90	B	62.77 %
		30.08 %
91	B	47.34 %
		31.05 %
92	C	57.05 %
		30.32 %

Q.	Ans.	Correct / Skipped
93	A	67.64 %
		31.77 %
94	C	53.78 %
		33.81 %
95	B	62.42 %
		30.03 %
96	C	69.68 %
		30.14 %

Q.	Ans.	Correct / Skipped
97	A	59.52 %
		32.6 %
98	D	31.32 %
		67.74 %
99	A	26.01 %
		70.15 %
100	C	16.34 %
		71.79 %

//Hints and Solutions//

1. After reading out the whole paragraph, one can conclude that the writer did too many naughty things in his childhood that tells about his playful nature. Thus we can say he was a mischievous boy.

Hence, the correct option is (C).

2. He called cricket a hopeless love affair as he was not good at it despite trying hard to learn it.

Hence, the correct option is (D).

3. The writer called the bathing process dangerous as it used to give them injuries in the form of bruises.

Hence, the correct option is (C).

4. As can be seen from the lines of the paragraph,' This business of being out for a walk, coming across something of fascinating interest and then being dragged away from it by a yell from the master, as a dog jerked onwards by the leash, is an important feature of school life,' the moral that the boy draws from his childhood experiences was that the things one want the most are always unattainable.

Hence, the correct option is (A).

5. The boys used to wake up early, read in the sunlit sleeping dormitory, play cricket and collect caterpillars. The only thing they did not do was sleeping until late.

Hence, the correct option is (B).

6. Fortify means to make strong or arm.

Secure means free from or not exposed to danger or harm.

Harm means injure.

Loosen means make less strict.

Neglect means the state of being uncared for.

Hence, the correct option is (A).

7. Enthral means to capture and hold one's attention; fascinate or mesmerise.

Mesmerise means to hold somebody's attention completely.

Disgust means a strong feeling of not liking or approving of something.

Free means costing nothing.

Repel means refuse to accept or reject.

Hence, the correct option is (C).

8. Contempt means a strong feeling of disliking and having no respect for somebody.

Hatred means an extremely strong feeling of dislike.

Respect means a feeling of honour for someone.

Approve means to like somebody/something.

Permit means officially allow someone to do something.

Hence, the correct option is (D).

9. Solemn means characterized by deep sincerity.

Serious means solemn or thoughtful in character or manner.

Furious means marked by the extreme and violent energy.

Ordinary means not exceptional in any way especially in quality, ability, size or degree.

Ignorant means uneducated in general; lacking knowledge or sophistication.

Hence, the correct option is (C).

10. The word Denounce (Verb) means to strongly criticize something/somebody. Hence, the words denounced and applaud are antonymous. Therefore, the words " applaud" which means to admire someone or something, would be the correct antonym of the given word.

Vilify means to speak or write about in an abusively disparaging manner.

Blame means feel or declare that (someone or something) is responsible for a fault or wrong.

Criticise means to find faults in something or someone.

Hence, the correct option is (B).

11. Slander means to say bad or untrue things in order to damage the reputation.

Admire means to respect or like somebody/something very much.

Appeal means to make a serious and urgent request.

Malign means to say unpleasant and untrue things about someone.

Defame means to say false or bad things about someone to damage his reputation.

Hence, the correct option is (C).

12. Hasty means done with excessive speed or urgency; hurried.

Cautious means careful to avoid potential problems or dangers.

Sudden means occurring or done quickly and unexpectedly or without warning.

Reckless means heedless of danger or the consequences of one's actions; rash or impetuous.

Urgent means requiring immediate action or attention.

Hence, the correct option is (B).

13. The idiom "keep your shirt" means not to lose your temper and to stay calm.

Hence, the correct option is (B).

14. The idiom "rundown" means to criticize or deride someone or something.

Hence, the correct option is (D).

15. Gradual means taking place or progressing slowly or by degrees.

Intellectual means relating to your ability to think and understand things, especially complicated ideas.

Mellifluous means (of a sound) pleasingly smooth and musical to hear.

Happening means an event or occurrence.

Hence, the correct option is (B).

16. Hold up means to delay something or someone.

Hold on means "wait" or "stop".

Hold down means physically holding something down.

Hold back means to restrain someone or something.

Hence, the correct option is (B).

17. By means to survive by (doing something).

Over means to reside in a house, apartment, etc., over someone or something.

In means to live in the place where you work.

With means to accept something unpleasant.

Hence, the correct option is (B).

18. Too is used to show a higher degree than is desirable, permissible, or possible and have a negative meaning. So the correct formation will be 'The assignment was too difficult for Mohit to do on his own'.

Hence, the correct option is (A).

19. The sentence carries prepositional error. Before the verb 'explain' we will use infinitive 'to.' The correct sentence will be: My friend did not understand the story. She asked me to explain it to her.

Hence, the correct option is (B).

20. The correct answer is 'No improvement'.

- The given sentence does not require any improvement.
- Because Keep away from is a Phrase.
- Keep away: stay away, or a situation in which someone tries to avoid answering questions or revealing information.

Hence, the correct option is (B).

21. Above it contains two sentences one is in Past Simple sentence (Active Voice) and Second sentence is in Present Perfect tense (Passive Voice). We change the first sentence according to voice rule and second sentence also be change according to same rule but tense of both sentence become same.

Hence, the correct option is (B).

22. The given sentence contains one of the model verb (Model Verb = will, shall, can, may, might, could, might, must, would). It is in active voice.

Hence, the correct option is (B).

23. 'Art work' is a noun phrase, before which an appropriate adjective should be used.

The underlined part 'indecently', which is an adverb, hence must be replaced with the adjective 'indecent' to make it a grammatically correct sentence.

Hence, the correct option is (A).

24. The underlined part 'me to smoking' must be replaced with 'my smoking' to make it a grammatically correct sentence.

As per the basic usage rules, 'like' is one of the verbs which are followed by a gerund e.g. swimming, dancing or travelling etc.

Since the gerund is a noun, it is logical to find it preceded by a possessive pronoun (his, her, your, my, our, etc) or a noun in the possessive form (Rohan's, Mr Sharma's, etc).

Hence, the correct option is (B).

25. The movie is not individual with an identity and hence should not be identified as a person. This means that the pronoun 'who' cannot be used to describe the movie. It is to be replaced by the correct pronoun 'which'. Thus the error is in the first part of the movie.

Hence, the correct option is (A).

26. Bonus and Dividend are different from each other. But both these are parts of profit.

Hence, the correct option is (B).

27. All mothers are women and some mothers and some women may be engineers.

Hence, the correct option is (A).

28.

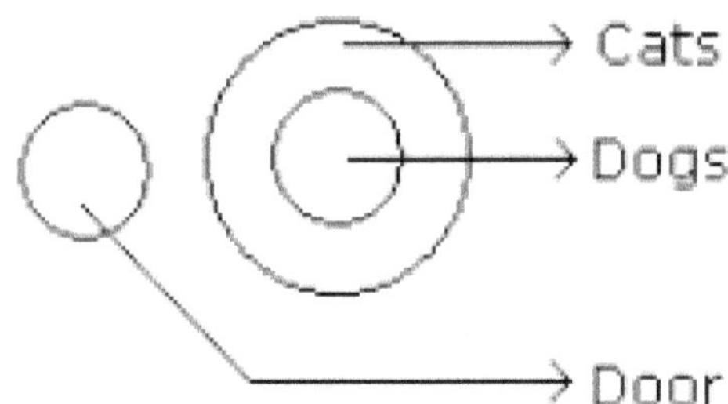

Hence, the correct option is (D).

29.

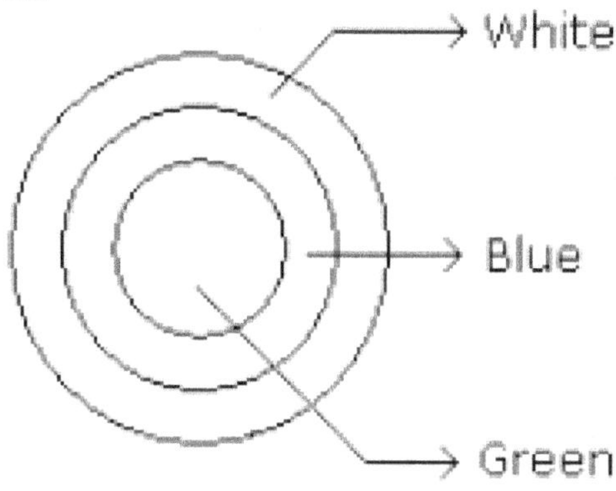

Hence, the correct option is (A).

30. Let n, g, r, and c be the no. of cows, grass initially, the rate at which grass grow/day, and grass eaten by cow/day respectively.

Now according to the question-

It takes 24 days for 70 cows to eat the whole of the grass.

$$g + 24r = 70 \times 24c = 1680c \rightarrow (i)$$

$$g + 60r = 60 \times 30c = 1800c$$

Again, given that it takes 60 days for 30 cows to eat the whole of the grass.

$$\therefore g = 1800c - 60r \rightarrow (ii)$$

From eq^n (i) & (ii), we have

$$c = \frac{3}{10}r \rightarrow (iii)$$

Now, to eat the grass in 96 days-

$$g + 96r = 96 \times nc$$

$$\Rightarrow 96 \times nc = 1800c - 60r + 96r$$

$$= 1800c + 36r = 1800c + 120c = 1920c$$

$$\Rightarrow n = 20$$

So, 20 cows are needed to eat the grass in 96 days.

Hence, the correct option is (B).

31. Total number of Vehicles = 160

There are 70 red vehicles thus rest 90 are green vehicles,

out of which 18 are green trucks then we get,

Green cars = 90 - 18 = 72

Given, Number of cars = 120

Then, number of red cars,

= 120 - 72

= 48 Red cars

Hence, the correct option is (C).

32. Since the standard of living among the middle class society is constantly going up so Indian Economy is observing remarkable growth.

Hence, the correct option is (A).

33. Since a huge truck overturned on the middle of the road last night, so, the police had cordoned off the entire area in the locality last morning for half of the day.

Hence, the correct option is (A).

34. It has been clearly mentioned in the statement that the appointment of the bureaucrats only spoiled the financial institutions. So the person having experience in the similar field and expertise should be appointed. Hence both conclusions are valid.

Hence, the correct option is (C).

35. From the given statement, it can be clearly understood that the first conclusion is valid whereas the second one does not have any link.

Hence, the correct option is (A).

36. Statement talk about Physics not about chemistry and HC Verma's book is recommended means definitely it is a good book.

Hence, the correct option is (A).

37. This is because by doing so, bank will get noticed by the public for a good cause and the bank will also complete its CSR stipulated by RBI.

Hence, the correct option is (D).

38. Clearly, India can export only the surplus and that which can be saved after fulfilling its own needs, to pay for its imports. Encouragement to export cannot lead to shortages as it shall provide the resources for imports. So, only argument I holds.

Hence, the correct option is (A).

39. Clearly, harnessing solar energy will be helpful as it is an inexhaustible resource unlike other resources. So, argument I holds. But argument II is vague as solar energy is the cheapest form of energy.

Hence, the correct option is (A).

40.

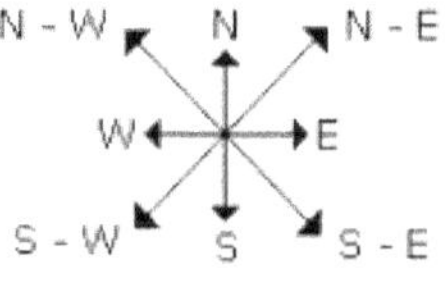

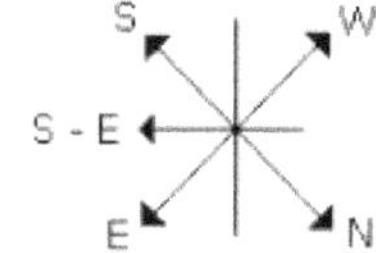

It is clear from the diagrams that new name of West will become South-East.

Hence, the correct option is (C).

41.

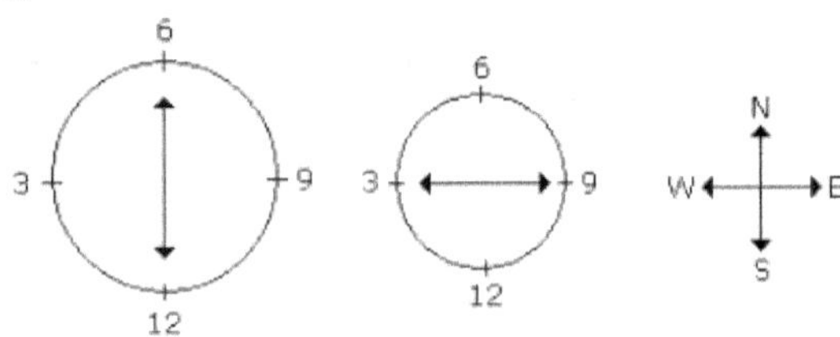

At 9.15 P.M., the minute hand will point towards West.

Hence, the correct option is (D).

42. Cup is used to drink something with the help of lips. Similarly birds collects grass with the help of beak to make her nest.

Hence, the correct option is (D).

43. As Water of a River flows similarly water of Pool is Stagnant.

Hence, the correct option is (C).

44. The boy in the photograph is the only son of the son of Suresh's mother i.e., the son of Suresh. Hence, Suresh is the father of boy.

Hence, the correct option is (D).

45. Since, C and Q are sisters to one another and A is the son of C. Hence, C is the mother of A, therefore, Z is maternal grandmother of A. As P is the son of Z. Hence, P is the maternal uncle of A.

Hence, the correct option is (B).

46. The core, seeds, and pulp are all parts of an apple. A slice would be a piece taken out of an apple.

Hence, the correct option is (D).

47. Fair, just, and equitable are all synonyms meaning impartial. Favorable means expressing approval.

Hence, the correct option is (D).

48. Clearly, both the courses directly follow from the pre-requisites mentioned in the statement.

Hence, the correct option is (D).

49. Clearly, either the work in the court needs to be speeded up or the system be reorganized so that more number of problems can be resolved at the lower levels itself, to provide speedy justice to the people. So, both the courses follow.

Hence, the correct option is (D).

50. The fact that Vincent and Thomas live on the same street indicates that they live in the same neighborhood. There is no support for any of the other choices.

Hence, the correct option is (A).

51. Palestine officially became a member of the International Criminal Court. Palestine is the 123rd state party to the International Criminal Court.

Hence, the correct option is (B).

52. T S R Subramanian Committee was constituted to review environmental laws in India. The committee has submitted its recommendations to the government recently.

Hence, the correct option is (A).

53. The proposal for the removal of the judge should be passed with a special majority in both the Houses of Parliament, while the decision to remove from the post is taken by the President.

Hence, the correct option is (D).

54. The Chief Justice of the Supreme Court has the right to seek the permission of the President before setting up the Supreme Court bench elsewhere in the country.

Hence, the correct option is (D).

55. Advisory Jurisdiction is when a lower court or any constitutional body seeks the advice of the higher Court in a matter of law. The practice of seeking advisory opinion of the judiciary has its beginning in England.

Hence, the correct option is (C).

56. The Chief Justice and Judges of the High Courts are to be appointed by the President under clause (1) of Article 217 of the Constitution.

Hence, the correct option is (B).

57. Maharashtra- Goa shares a common High court which is the Bombay (Mumbai) High Court. The Bombay High Court also includes the Union Territories of Dadra and Nagar Haveli and Daman and Diu along with the states of Maharashtra and Goa under its extent. Bombay (Mumbai) High Court has branches in Aurangabad, Nagpur, and Panaji (capital of Goa).

Hence, the correct option is (C).

58. Pacta sunt servanda means "Treaties are legally binding".

A Latin word for agreements is binding. It is a basic principle of civil law, international law, and canon law. The principle refers to private contracts, stressing that contained clauses are to be termed as law between the parties.

Pacta sunt servanda is directly referred to in many international agreements governing treaties, including the Vienna Convention on the Law of Treaties (1969), which concerns treaties between states, and the Vienna Convention on the Law of Treaties Between States and International Organizations or Between International Organizations (1986).

Hence, the correct option is (A).

59. A contract has six important elements so that it will be valid which is offer, acceptance, consideration, intention to create legal relation, certainty and capacity.

Hence, the correct option is (D).

60. Section 82: Act of a child under seven years of age.—Nothing is an offence which is done by a child under seven years of age.

Hence, the correct option is (B).

61. The defence of intoxication typically depends on whether the intoxication was voluntary or involuntary and what level of intent

is required by the criminal charge. Under the Indian Penal Code the criminal liability under intoxication is mentioned under section 85 and 86.

Hence, the correct option is (D).

62. Res communes is a Roman & civil law concept. It means things owned by no one and subject to use by all. Things (as light, air, the sea, running water) are incapable of entire exclusive appropriation and are considered as subject of Res communes.

Hence, the correct option is (C).

63. En ventre sa mere is a French legal phrase that is used for an unborn child who is inside his/her's mother's womb. This expression is used while referring to the child's rights i.e. that unborn child may be accepted to be a beneficiary for some purposes (like acquisition of property) provided that the child is subsequently born alive.

Hence, the correct option is (B).

64. Actions that do not require the allegation or proof of additional facts to constitute a cause of action. Such a tort is actionable simply because it happened.

Hence, the correct option is (D).

65. Fundamental Duties were incorporated in the Indian Constitution by the Constitution (Forty-Second Amendment) Act, 1976 upon the recommendations of the Swaran Singh Committee.

Hence, the correct option is (C).

66. Article 14 of the Indian Constitution guarantees equality before the law or the equal protection of the laws within the territory of India.

Hence, the correct option is (B).

67. The Fundamental Duties of citizens are mentioned in Article 51 A of the Indian Constitution.

To safeguard public property and to abjure violence; to strive towards excellence in all spheres of individual and collective activity so that the nation constantly rises to higher levels of endeavour and achievement.

Hence, the correct option is (B).

68. The International Court of Justice is composed of 15 judges elected to nine-year terms of office by the United Nations General Assembly and the Security Council.

Hence, the correct option is (D).

69. As provided under Section 146 of the Indian Penal Code, 1860, a riot is simply an unlawful assembly in a particular state of activity, that activity being accompanied by the use of force or violence. It is this use of force or violence that distinguishes rioting from an unlawful assembly.

Hence, the correct option is (B).

70. The age of minority, in the case of kidnapping, has been defined as 16 years for males and 18 years for female by the IPC.

Section 361 of the IPC explains kidnapping from lawful guardianship. According to this section, if a person takes away or entices a minor (i.e, a boy under the age of 16 years and a girl under the age of 18 years) or a person of unsound mind, away from his/her lawful guardian without the guardian's consent, then that person commits the offense of kidnapping from lawful guardianship.

However, it must be highlighted here that in Manipur, the age of 18 years of females in section 361 is replaced with 15 years. Hence if a female of 16 years is taken from her lawful guardians in Manipur, it would not result in kidnapping from lawful guardianship.

Hence, the correct option is (D).

71. Kesavananda Bharati case (1973).

This was a landmark case in defining the concept of the basic structure doctrine.

Hence, the correct option is (D).

72. The strength of Supreme Court judges increased from 31 to 34, including the Chief Justice of India in Sept.2019.

Hence, the correct option is (B).

73. The Bombay High Court, the chartered High Court is one of the oldest High Court in the country. It's jurisdiction covers the State of Maharashtra and Goa, and the Union Territories of Daman and Diu and Dadra and Nagar Haveli. In addition to the Principal seat at Bombay, it has benches at Aurangabad, Nagpur, Panaji (Goa).

Hence, the correct option is (C).

74. Act of a child above seven and under twelve of immature understanding. —Nothing is an offence which is done by a child above seven years of age and under twelve, who has not attained sufficient maturity of understanding to judge of the nature and consequences of his conduct on that occasion.

Hence, the correct option is (B).

75. The maxim that, generally, a person cannot be guilty of a crime unless two elements are present: the * actus reus("guilty act") and the * mens rea ("guilty mind").

Hence, the correct option is (B).

76. Tejas MK-I aircraft of the Indian Air Force participated in the 'Singapore Air Show-2022'.

A 44 member contingent of the Indian Air Force reached Changi International Airport in Singapore to participate in the 'Singapore Air Show-2022'.

Hence, the correct option is (C).

77. Indian manned mission to space to be launched in 2023 is Gaganyaan.

Gaganyaan is an orbital spacecraft that will have an Indian crew. It is being developed by ISRO and was decided to launch by 2022 when India completes 75 years of its independence. But in December 2021 the Union Minister of Atomic Energy and Space informed that the crewed Gaganyaan mission will finally be launched in 2023.

Hence, the correct option is (C).

78. DART mission is launched by NASA. The main aim of the mission is to test the newly developed technology that would allow a spacecraft to crash into an asteroid and change its course. DART is a low-cost spacecraft, weighing around 610 kg at launch and 550 kg at impact.

Hence, the correct option is (C).

79. The sixth Schedule of the Indian Constitution consists of provisions for administration of Tribal Area in Assam, Meghalaya, Tripura, and Mizoram & Arunachal Pradesh. District or the Regional Councils in these states may after its first constitution make rules with the approval of the Governor.

Hence, the correct option is (D).

80. The constitution of India did not codify permanent laws for citizenship and put this onus on parliament. Using the powers of article 10 and 11, the parliament enacted Citizenship Act 1955 which has been amended from time to time. This act mentions four ways in which a person may be an Indian citizen viz. by birth, by descent, by registration and by naturalization. Citizenship by birth and descent are called natural citizens.

Hence, the correct option is (B).

81. SAARC is a regional intergovernmental organization and geopolitical union in South Asia. It promotes the development of economical and regional integration. Member Countries: Bangladesh, Bhutan, India, Maldives, Nepal, Pakistan, Sri Lanka and Afghanistan (joined in 2007). The first SAARC summit was held in Dhaka (Bangladesh) in December 1985.

Hence, the correct option is (C).

82. Riptides are a strong channel of water flowing seaward from near the shore, typically through the surf line. They are again caused by the winds and not related to Tides.

Hence, the correct option is (B).

83. It's a market for Gilt-edged Securities. These are high-quality debt securities with very high creditworthiness issued by corporates or governments and hence they are named such. The probability of the organisation defaulting on interest and principal repayment is very low.

Hence, the correct option is (A).

84. The World Investment Report focuses is an official publication of the UNCTAD (United National Conference in Trade and Development). It reports the trends in foreign direct investment (FDI) worldwide, at the regional and country levels.

Hence, the correct option is (D).

85. India's economy is currently 2.93 trillion dollars on a nominal GDP basis. This figure is from the IMF 2019 report. Currently, India is the 5th largest economy in the world.

Hence, the correct option is (A).

86. The tertiary sector contributes the most to India's economy. There are many areas in this sector like the service sector, real estate, hotels and restaurants, telecommunications etc. Currently, the service sector contributes 53.66% to the Indian economy. The second place is occupied by the Secondary sector that is about 31% of GDP.

Hence, the correct option is (C).

87. The Goods and Service Tax Act was passed in Parliament on 29th March 2017. The Act came into effect on 1st July 2017. It is an Indirect Tax that has replaced many Indirect Taxes in India.

Hence, the correct option is (C).

88. India has chosen the Canadian model of dual GST. Only a handful of countries, such as India, Canada and Brazil, have a dual GST structure.

Hence, the correct option is (C).

89. The government claimed that India has become the seventh-largest vehicle producing nation in the world in 2009 which was six years ahead of the set target by auto mission plan.

Hence, the correct option is (C).

90. Paper and Paper Board is a forest-based industry. In 1832 the first modern paper mill of the country was set up at Serampore in West Bengal.

Hence, the correct option is (B).

91. Cooch Behar in West Bengal is famous for the Silk Industry. Silk in the Indian subcontinent is a luxury good.

Hence, the correct option is (B).

92. Investment is the employment of funds on assets to earn returns. An investment is a monetary asset purchased with the idea that the asset will provide income in the future or will later be sold at a higher price for a profit.

Hence, the correct option is (C).

93. Financial Management is mainly concerned with all aspects of acquiring and utilizing financial resources for firms activities. Financial Management is the application of general principles of management to the financial possessions of an enterprise.

Hence, the correct option is (A).

94. The primary goal of financial management is to maximize the wealth of owners. All businesses aim to maximize their profits, minimize their expenses and maximize their market share.

Hence, the correct option is (C).

95. 57th Amendment Act, 1987 had reserved seats for the STs in the legislative assemblies of the states of Arunachal Pradesh, Meghalaya, Mizoram and Nagaland.

Hence, the correct option is (B).

96. 74th amendment added the 12th schedule in the constitution comprising 18 items that fall under the purview of municipalities-

1. Urban planning including town planning.

2. Regulation of land use and construction of buildings.

3. Planning for economic and social development.

4. Roads and bridges

5. Water supply for domestic, industrial and commercial purposes.

6. Public health, sanitation, conservancy and solid waste management.

7. Fire services

8. Urban forestry, protection of the environment and promotion of ecological aspects.

9. Safeguarding the interests of weaker sections of society.

10. Slum improvement and upgradation.

11. Urban poverty alleviation.

12. Provision of urban amenities and facilities.

13. Promotion of cultural, educational and aesthetic aspects.

14. Burials and burial grounds, cremations and cremation grounds and electric crematoriums.

15. Cattle ponds, prevention of cruelty to animals.

16. Vital statistics including registration of births and deaths.

17. Public amenities including street lighting, parking lots, bus stops and public conveniences.

18. Regulation of slaughterhouses and tanneries.

Hence, the correct option is (C).

97. The country is growing in the direction of being a developed nation. The contribution of Agriculture in the GDP of developed nations decreases and the contribution of the service and manufacturing sector is very high.

Hence, the correct option is (A).

98. The Kalidas Samman is a prestigious arts award presented annually by the government of Madhya Pradesh in India. The award is named after Kalidasa, a renowned Classical Sanskrit writer of ancient India. The Kalidas Samman was first awarded in 1980.

Hence, the correct option is (D).

99. Denmark's Viktor Axelsen and Taiwan's Tai Tzu Ying have been named BWF (Badminton World Federation) Male and Female Player of the Year respectively.

- Kuala Lumpur, Malaysia-based Badminton World Federation (BWF) honoured all eight winners on 3 Dec 2021.
- Ou Zimo (China) was named Male Para-Badminton Player of the Year, and Leani Ratri Oktila (Indonesia) the Female Para-Badminton Player of the Year.

Hence, the correct option is (A).

100. Para-Athlete Chandeep Singh has bagged a silver medal at Para World Taekwondo Championships. He won the medal in the

Men's plus 80 kg event at the 9th Para World Taekwondo Championships held at Istanbul in Turkey from 9th to 12th December 2021. He became the first para-athlete from J&K to achieve the feat. This is India's first-ever medal in the history of Para-Taekwondo World Championship.

Hence, the correct option is (C).

English Language & Comprehension

Q.1 Direction: There is sentence with three parts labeled as (a), (b), and (c). Read the sentence to find out whether there is an error in any part and select your response i.e., (a) or (b) or (c). If you find no error, your response should be indicated as (d).

The driver took them (a)/ to a Spanish design home (b)/ few miles from the Hacienda. (c)/ No error (d)

A. (a) **B.** (b) **C.** (c) **D.** (d)

Q.2 Direction: There is s sentence with three parts labeled as (a), (b), and (c). Read the sentence to find out whether there is an error in any part and select your response i.e., (a) or (b) or (c). If you find no error, your response should be indicated as (d).

It was raining very hardly (a)/ and he had a very large umbrella (b)/ to keep off the rain-drops. (c)/ No error (d)

A. (a) **B.** (b) **C.** (c) **D.** (d)

Q.3 Direction: In this section, the following sentence has a blank space and four words are given below it. Select the word or group of words you consider most appropriate for the blank space.

His father asked him to have a back _____ plan regarding his career.

A. out **B.** up **C.** away **D.** on

Q.4 Direction: The following sentence has a blank space and four words are given below it. Select the word you consider most appropriate for the blank.

Anaita is on the _____ financial ruin.

A. side of **B.** periphery

C. boundary of **D.** brink of

Q.5 Direction: In the following question, out of the four alternatives, select the alternative which best expresses the meaning of the Idiom/Phrase.

To get scot-free

A. To walk like a native of Scotland

B. To get something free

C. To escape without punishment

D. To save tax

Ques (6-9):Direction: Read the following passage carefully and answer the question that follows.

The Madras High Court on Friday granted 30 days of ordinary leave to S. Nalini, 52, a life convict in the former Prime Minister Rajiv Gandhi's assassination case. The order was passed after she argued her case in person and made a fervent plea to the judges in a choked voice that she may be allowed to step out of prison for some days to make arrangements for the marriage of her daughter, who is residing in London.

Nalini had many years ago come out on short paroles of a day each to attend her brother Bhagyanathan's wedding and her father's last rites.

Justices M.M. Sundresh and M. Nirmal Kumar took judicial notice that the State Cabinet itself had on September 9 last year made a recommendation to the Governor to release all seven convicts in the Rajiv Gandhi assassination case. "If in the view of the government, the petitioner can be allowed to lead a normal life and she would not be a hindrance to the society, the request for leave can never be objected to," they said.

The judges also directed the State government to bear the expenses of providing escort to her during the period of leave since she expressed difficulty in paying the charges.

"There is no material to hold that she is a woman of means. Admittedly, she and her husband are in incarceration for decades. Asking the petitioner to pay the cost would in a way take away the very order passed by us when it is impossible of compliance," they said.

Q.6 Why was S. Nalini sentenced to lifetime imprisonment by the judiciary of the country?

A. She murdered a lot of people during her school days and that came out in the open later.

B. She murdered her family out of mercy though her husband had left her for another woman before that.

C. She did not do anything but the court was of the view that she could do something if left to fend for himself within the society.

D. She was involved in the assassination of the former Prime Minister of India.

Q.7 Which among the following is correct regarding the attitude of the State Government towards the sentence of life imprisonment given to S Nalini?

A. The state government has nothing to say about the whole issue since the case was dealt with by the central government.

B. The state government could not understand the fact that there was nothing wrong done by S Nalini many years ago.

C. The State government is of the opinion that the sentence given to S Nalini can be remitted at once.

D. The state government wants the convict to continue with the given sentence by the court for the crime committed by her.

Q.8 Which among the following is/ are NOT correct, as per the given passage?

I. This is the first time that S Nalini has been given permission to come out on parole.

II. S. Nalini has been granted the right to come out on parole to perform the last rites of her husband.

III. S Nalini has no child and that is why she is not at all happy with the sentence.

A. Both I and II **B.** Both II and III

C. Both I and III　　　　**D.** All I, II, and III

Q.9 Which among the following is/are correct regarding the observations of the Madras High Court regarding S Nalini?

I. S Nalini is a very rich woman and that is why no monetary support is required to be given to her.

II. S Nalini is a dreaded criminal and that is why she should be put behind the bars for life with no chance at any kind of reformation.

III. S Nalini has intentionally jeopardized her relationship with her husband and that is why she should be punished for that.

A. Both I and II　　　　**B.** Both II and III

C. Both I and III　　　　**D.** None of I, II and III

Q.10 Direction: In the following question, a part of the sentence is made bold. Below are given alternatives to the bold part which may improve the sentence. Choose the correct alternative.

Having leisure till outdoor activities such as taking a stroll down the park has become a rarity in this fast-paced life.

A. Having leisures till outdoor

B. Having laziness for outdoor

C. Having leisure in outdoor

D. Having leisure for outdoor

Q.11 Direction: In the following question, a part of the sentence is made bold. Below are given alternatives to the bold part which may improve the sentence. Choose the correct alternative.

India lent a helpful handshake to Nepal by giving them 2.1 billion Nepalese rupees for the reconstruction of houses flattened in the 2015 earthquake.

A. India lent a helping handshake

B. India lent a helpful hand

C. India lent a helping hand

D. India lending a helping hand

Q.12 Direction: The following question has two blanks. In blank, a preposition has been omitted. Choose the set of prepositions for each blank that best fits in the context of the sentence.

Pakistan Prime Minister Imran Khan's bluster ________ Kashmir and the implied threat of a nuclear war were irresponsible and ________ the top.

A. among, from　　　　**B.** on, over

C. at, above　　　　**D.** on, among

Q.13 Direction: The following question has two blanks. In blank a preposition has been omitted. Choose the set of prepositions for each blank that best fits in the context of the sentence.

The global financial institution has advocated ________ reforms that favour agribusiness and ignore peasants and indigenous peoples whose livelihoods depend ________ traditional land use.

A. for, about　　　　**B.** to, with

C. for, on　　　　**D.** despite, against

Q.14 Which of the following is opposite in meaning to the below given word.

Calamitous

A. Fortunate　　　　**B.** Haggard

C. Ambivalent　　　　**D.** Cantankerous

Q.15 Which of the following is opposite in meaning to the below given word.

Capricious

A. Caustic　　　　**B.** Predictable

C. Prescient　　　　**D.** Cogent

Q.16 Which of the following is the synonym in meaning to the below given word.

Stalemate

A. Degeneration　　　　**B.** Deadlock

C. Exhaustion　　　　**D.** Settlement

Q.17 Which of the following is the synonym in meaning to the below given word.

Squander

A. Expensive　　　　**B.** Waste

C. Litter　　　　**D.** Economical

Q.18 Direction: In this question, you need to replace the bold part of the sentence by the most suitable idiom/expression given as option.

Harish Salve is **an important and powerful** lawyer as he wins every court case he gets.

A. a jack of all trades　　　　**B.** a big shot

C. a big gun　　　　**D.** Both (B) and (C)

Q.19 Direction: In this question, you need to replace the bold part of the sentence by the most suitable idiom/expression given as option.

I have to **work late night** only then this task will be finished on time.

A. cut corners　　　　**B.** cut the mustard

C. burn midnight oil　　　　**D.** Both (B) and (C)

Q.20 Direction: In the following question, a sentence with four words printed in bold type is given. One of these four words printed in bold may be either wrongly spelled or inappropriate in context of the sentence. Find out the word which is wrongly spelled or inappropriate if any. The number of that word is your answer.

What makes the 2019 election **unprecedented** is not that **inappropriate** words were used and misinformation **spread**, but the fact that India **witnesses** an increasing tendency to normalise these.

A. Unprecedented　　　　**B.** Inappropriate

C. Spread　　　　**D.** Witnesses

Q.21 Direction: In the following question, a sentence with four words printed in bold type is given. One of these four words printed in bold may be either wrongly spelled or inappropriate in context of the sentence. Find out the word which is wrongly spelled or inappropriate if any. The number of that word is your answer.

On the one hand, **inform** discussions have **become** difficult, and on the other, social tensions have **risen**.

A. On   **B.** inform   **C.** become   **D.** risen

Q.22 Direction: In the following question, out of the four alternatives, select the alternative which is the best substitute for the given group of words.

The science of soil management and the production of field crops

A. Bibliography   **B.** Anthropology
C. Agronomy   **D.** Chronology

Q.23 Direction: In the following question, out of the four alternatives, select the alternative which is the best substitute for the given group of words.

Chemistry in ancient times

A. Anthropology   **B.** Bibliography
C. Astrology   **D.** Alchemy

Q.24 Direction: In the following question, out of the four alternatives, select the alternative that will be a noun.

Sharks and lampreys are not true fish because their skeletons are made of cartilage rather than bone.

A. True   **B.** Because   **C.** Their   **D.** Bone

Q.25 Direction: In the following question, out of the four alternatives, select the alternative that will be a noun.

Joe, have you met your new boss?

A. Have   **B.** Met   **C.** Your   **D.** Boss

Analytical Abilities

Q.26 Direction: In the following question, there is a certain relationship between two given words on one side of :: and one word is given on another side :: while another word is to be found from the given alternatives, having the same relation with this word as the words of the given pair bear. Choose the correct alternative.

RT : QU :: VX : ?

A. WY   **B.** TW   **C.** YW   **D.** UY

Q.27 Direction: In the following question, there is a certain relationship between two given words on one side of :: and one word is given on another side :: while another word is to be found from the given alternatives, having the same relation with this word as the words of the given pair bear. Choose the correct alternative.

123 : 4 :: 726 : ?

A. 23   **B.** 26   **C.** 14   **D.** 12

Q.28 Which of the following diagrams best depicts the relationship among Women, Mother and Doctor?

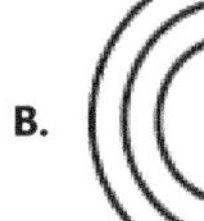

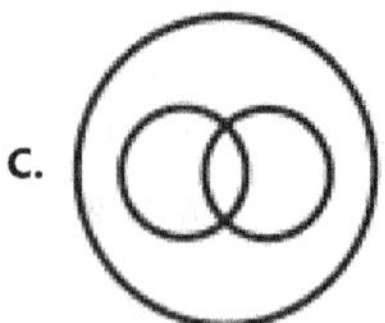
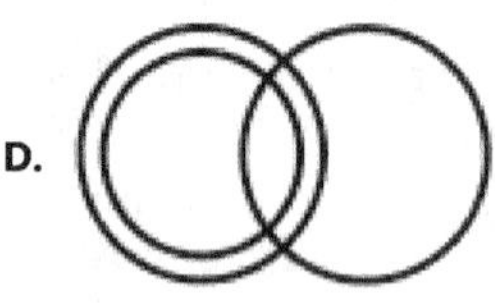

Q.29 Which of the following diagrams best depicts the relationship among Potato, Food and Vegetable?

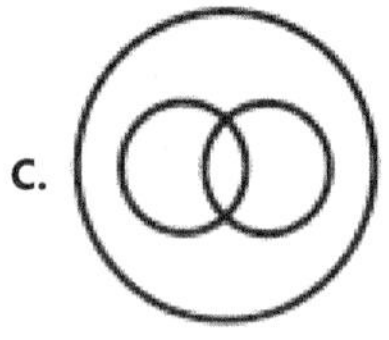
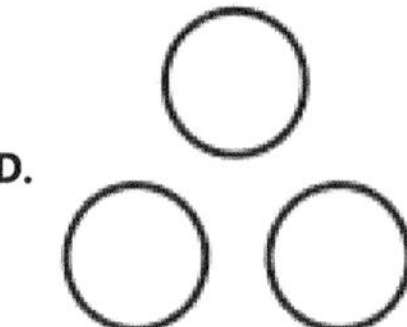

Q.30 Direction: In the question below there are given some statements followed by some conclusions. You have to take the given statements to be true even if they seem to be at variance with commonly known facts. Read all the conclusions and then decide which of the given conclusions logically follows/follow from the given statements, disregarding commonly known facts.

Statements:

No newspaper is magazine.

Not a single magazine is book.

Every book is story.

Conclusions:

I. Some stories which are books are newspapers as well.

II. No newspaper is a book.

III. Some stories are not magazines.

A. Only III follows
B. Either I or II follows
C. Only II and III follow
D. All follow

Q.31 Direction: In the question below there are given some statements followed by some conclusions. You have to take the given statements to be true even if they seem to be at variance with commonly known facts. Read all the conclusions and then decide which of the given conclusions logically follows/follow from the given statements, disregarding commonly known facts.

Statements:

Some hours are minutes.

All clocks are minutes.

No minute is second.

Conclusions:

I. Some hours are clocks.

II. All seconds being clocks is a possibility.

III. No hour is a clocks.

A. Only III follows

B. Either I or III follows

C. Only II and III follow

D. All follow

Ques (32-33):Direction: Read the following information carefully and answer the question given beside.

A, B, C and D are four males who are married to four females namely P, Q, R and S not necessarily in the same order. U, W, X, Y and Z are five children who belong to these four couples.

B is married to S, who does not have any child.

U is the only son of Q, who is not married to A.

W and X are siblings and are of different genders.

C is the father of two children.

Y is the daughter of R, who does not have any other child.

A has one daughter X.

Z is the sister of U.

Q.32 How many boys are there in the group of children?

A. 1   **B.** 2   **C.** 3   **D.** 4

Q.33 Who among the following is the father of Z?

A. A   **B.** B   **C.** C   **D.** D

Q.34 Direction: Study the following question carefully and choose the right answer.

Statement: Should teaching of 'Sanskrit' be made compulsory at school level in India?

Arguments:

I. No, where are the trained teachers to teach this language.

II. Yes, we should be proud of our ancient language.

A. Only I is strong

B. Only II is strong

C. Either I or II is strong

D. Neither I nor II is strong

Q.35 Direction: Study the following question carefully and choose the right answer.

Statement: Should all education be made free for girls and women of all ages of India?

Arguments:

I, No, this will weaken our present social structures.

II. Yes, this is the only way to bring back glory to Indian women hood.

A. Only I is strong

B. Only II is strong

C. Either I or II is strong

D. Neither I nor II is strong

Ques (36-37):Direction: Read the following information carefully and answer the question given beside.

In a certain code language,

Trip towards mountain hills is coded as "ju na mi po"

Rise hills towards river is coded as "gi mi ju ve"

River trip rafting mountain is coded as "po ve na fu"

Towards mountain slow rise is coded as "yb ju gi po"

Q.36 What is the code for "mountain"?

A. ve   **B.** po

C. na   **D.** Either na or ve

Q.37 Find the code for "slow rise"?

A. gi na   **B.** yb ve

C. yb gi   **D.** Can't be determined

Q.38 Direction: Study the following question carefully and choose the right answer.

Statement: "Do not lean out of the door of the bus." - a warning in a school bus.

Assumption:

I. Leaning out of a running bus is dangerous.

II. Children do not pay any heed to such warnings.

A. If only assumption I is implicit

B. If only assumption II is implicit

C. If either I or II is implicit

D. If neither I nor II is implicit

Q.39 Direction: Study the following question carefully and choose the right answer.

Statement: "If you are a mechanical engineer, we want you as our supervisor." - an advertisement by company X.

Assumption:

I. Mechanical engineers are expected to be better performers by company X.

II. The company X needs supervisors.

A. If only assumption I is implicit

B. If only assumption II is implicit

C. If either I or II is implicit

D. If neither I nor II is implicit

Q.40 Direction: Study the following question carefully and choose the right answer.

Statement: Be humble even after being victorious.

Assumption:

I. Many people are humble after being victorious.

II. Generally, people are not humble.

A. If only assumption I is implicit

B. If only assumption II is implicit

C. If either I or II is implicit

D. If neither I nor II is implicit

Q.41 Direction: Choose the correct alternative from the given ones that will complete the series.

AN, CP, ER, ?

A. VI   **B.** GT   **C.** AP   **D.** WJ

Q.42 Direction: Choose the correct alternative from the given ones that will complete the series.

CX, GT, JQ, LO, ?

A. NM   **B.** KP   **C.** MN   **D.** PK

Q.43 Direction: In the following question, there is a certain relationship between two given words on one side of :: and one word is given on another side :: while another word is to be found from the given alternatives, having the same relation with this word as the words of the given pair bear. Choose the correct alternative.

Ornithologist : Birds : : Anthropologist : ?

A. Plants   **B.** Animals

C. Mankind   **D.** Environment

Ques (44-45):Direction: Read the given information carefully and answer the question bwlow.

Point G is 30m to the east of point B, which is 20m to the north of point A. Point F is 16m to the west of point E. Point H is 12m to the south of point F. Point E is 10m to the south of point G. Point C is 13m to the east of point F.

Q.44 If point X is exactly between B and A then F is how far and in which direction from point X?

A. 15m, West   **B.** 14m, East

C. 12m, West   **D.** 13m, East

Q.45 If point Y is 6m south of point G then find the shortest distance between point C and point Y?

A. 6 m   **B.** 7 m   **C.** 5 m   **D.** 4 m

Q.46 Direction: Read the given information carefully and answer the question given beside.

Point A is 10m to the south of Point B, which is 8m to the west of Point C. Point D is 14m to the north of Point C. Point E is 4m to the east of Point F, which is 5m to the south of Point D. Point E is 8m to the west of Point G. Point H is 19m to the south of Point G. Point H is 12m to the east of Point I.

Find the shortest distance between Points D and G?

A. 10 m   **B.** 13 m   **C.** 12 m   **D.** 20 m

Q.47 Direction: Choose the correct alternative from the given ones that will complete the series.

66, 40, 67, 45, 69, ?

A. 50   **B.** 60   **C.** 75   **D.** 49

Q.48 Direction: Choose the correct alternative from the given ones that will complete the series.

50, 59, 75, 100, ?

A. 215   **B.** 121   **C.** 136   **D.** 125

Q.49 Shan is 55 years old, Sethian is 5 years junior to Shan and 6 years senior to Balan. The youngest brother of Balan is Devan and he is 7 years junior to him. So what is the age difference between Devan and Shan?

A. 15 years   **B.** 18 years   **C.** 13 years   **D.** 7 years

Q.50 Ramesh ranks 13th in the class of 33 students. There are 5 students below Suresh rankwise. How many student are there between Ramesh and Suresh?

A. 12   **B.** 14   **C.** 15   **D.** 16

Legal Awareness & Aptitude

Q.51 A person can directly file a writ petition before the Supreme Court of India for the enforcement of his fundamental right under Article ___________ of the Constitution of India.

A. 32   **B.** 226   **C.** 19   **D.** 368

Q.52 The writ of Habeas Corpus is issued for ___________.

A. Quashing wrongful appointment

B. Compel Public authority to perform duty

C. Quashing illegal quasi-judicial order

D. Against wrongful deprivation of personal body and produce person before Court

Q.53 Judge of the Supreme Court are appointed ___________.

A. President of India directly

B. President of India on the recommendation of the National judicial Appointment committee

C. President of India on the recommendation of Collegium of the Supreme Court

D. President of India on the recommendation of the Chief Justice of India

Q.54 The quorum to constitute a meeting of either House of the Parliament is ___________ .

A. 1/4th   **B.** 1/10th   **C.** 1/3rd   **D.** 100

Q.55 Every sitting of the Parliament starts with which of the following sessions?

A. Zero hour   **B.** Discussion hour

C. Question hour   **D.** None of the above

Q.56 Name the type of education which is not considered as a fundamental right ___________ .

A. Elementary education

B. Pre-primary education

C. Secondary education

D. Primary education

Q.57 The 86th amendment of the Indian Constitution makes education a fundamental right for all ___________ .

A. Children aged 6-14 years

B. Girls and women

C. Pre-primary infants and children

D. Working-class adults

Q.58 Bigamy laws are not applicable to ___________.

A. Hindus   **B.** Muslims   **C.** Sikhs   **D.** Jains

Q.59 The phrase 'locus standi' in legal terms means ___________.

A. An ambiguity in law

B. Place of offence

C. A right of appearance in a court

D. Cause of action

Q.60 Right to Information Act, 2005, secures access to information which is under the control of ___________.

A. An individual   **B.** A judge

C. Public authorities   **D.** Private bodies

Q.61 How many theories of punishment are there in the criminal justice system?

A. Two   **B.** Four   **C.** Five   **D.** Six

Q.62 Which of the following exercised the most profound influence in framing the Indian Constitution?

A. British Constitution

B. U.S. Constitution

C. Irish Constitution

D. Government of India Act, 1935

Q.63 Under Indian Penal Code, how many persons constitute an 'unlawful assembly'?

A. 4 or more persons   **B.** 5 or more persons

C. 2 or more persons   **D.** 3 or more persons

Q.64 The term 'Xenophobia' refers to _____________ .

A. Killing of a human race

B. Unreasonable hatred of foreigners

C. Discrimination on the basis of sex

D. Infliction of severe pain

Q.65 Who amongst the following is not appointed by the President of India?

A. Attorney General

B. Advocate General

C. Chief Justice of India

D. Chief Election Commission

Q.66 In which schedule of the constitution, the Anti-defection law is provided?

A. Seventh Schedule   **B.** Tenth Schedule

C. Ninth Schedule   **D.** Eighth Schedule

Q.67 How many fundamental duties are listed in the constitution?

A. 10   **B.** 11   **C.** 15   **D.** 12

Q.68 Which of the following became 123rd State party to the International Criminal Court?

A. Israel   **B.** Palestine

C. Jordan   **D.** Bangladesh

Q.69 Which body has launched the 'Group of Friends Against Terrorism'?

A. United Nations   **B.** European Union

C. ASEAN   **D.** SAARC

Q.70 In which Landmark case the Supreme Court held that Muslim women have the right to maintenance?

A. Indra Sawhney v. Union of India

B. Mohammed Ahmed Khan v. Shah Bano Begum

C. Hussainara Khatoon v. Home Secretary, State of Bihar

D. Sher Singh v. State of Haryana

Q.71 A and B agreed to commit the murder of C by poisoning and D was to procure poison, but he did not procure it. A and B are guilty of:

A. No offense

B. Criminal conspiracy to murder C

C. Abatement of murder by conspiracy

D. Attempt to murder with the aid of section 34 Indian Penal Code

Q.72 A by putting B in fear of grievous hurt dishonestly induces B to sign for affix his seal in black paper, and delivers it to A. B signs and delivers the paper to A. A has committed____.

A. Extortion   **B.** Robbery

C. Cheating   **D.** Dacoity

Q.73 Section 82 of IPC provides that nothing is an offense which is done by a child under:

A. Six years of age   **B.** Seven years of age

C. Nine years of age   **D.** Ten years of age

Q.74 A person is stated to be partially incapax under section 83, the Indian Penal Code if he is aged:

A. Above seven years and under twelve years

B. Above seven years and under ten years

C. Above seven years and under sixteen years

D. Above seven years and under eighteen years

Q.75 The maxim "actus non facit reum nisi mens sit rea" means:

A. Crime has to be coupled with a guilty mind

B. The act is not culpable unless the mind is guilty

C. Crime is the result of a guilty mind

D. Criminal mind leads to crime

General Knowledge

Q.76 In June 2021, which of the following institutes developed a new technique called "SWASTIIK" for disinfecting water by using natural oils?

A. Agharkar Research Institute

B. Tata Institute of Fundamental Research

C. National Chemical Laboratory

D. National Institute of Oceanography

Q.77 Long March 5B rocket was developed by which of the following organisations?

A. China Aerospace Science and Technology Corporation

B. Indian Space Research Organisation

C. NASA

D. None of the above

Q.78 Genetic screening is ________.

A. the analysis of DNA to check the presence of a particular gene in a person

B. analysis of gene in a population

C. pedigree analysis

D. screening of infertility in parents

Q.79 Who was the inventor of the railway engine?

A. Charles Babbage   **B.** Rudolf Diesel

C. James Watt   **D.** George Stephenson

Q.80 'Economics is what it ought to be' - This statement refers to:

A. Normative economics

B. Positive economics

C. Monetary economics

D. Fiscal economics

Q.81 The excess of price a person is to pay rather than forego the consumption of the commodity is called:

A. Price

B. Profit

C. Producers' surplus

D. Consumer's surplus

Q.82 The 'break-even' point is where:

A. Marginal revenue equals marginal cost

B. Average revenue equals average cost

C. Total revenue equals total cost

D. None of the above

Q.83 Relationship between price of related goods and quantity of a particular commodity is called as:

A. Income demand

B. Market demand

C. Cross demand

D. Price demand

Q.84 Total demand for goods and services at various levels of employment is called as:

A. Effective demand

B. National demand

C. Market demand

D. Employment demand

Q.85 'Zero Rating' is a recent term used in ___________.

A. Insurance

B. Credit Rating

C. Energy Efficiency

D. Net Neutrality

Q.86 Which Article of the Constitution of India was used to impose President Rule in Uttarakhand and placing the Assembly under suspended animation in March 2016?

A. Article 102

B. Article 143

C. Article 356

D. Article 365

Q.87 Union Budget is presented ___________.

A. Before Lok Sabha

B. Before Rajya Sabha

C. Before President of India

D. In the Joint Meeting of both houses of Parliament

Q.88 In which year, Indian Mountaineering Foundation was established?

A. 1957   **B.** 1958   **C.** 1959   **D.** 1960

Q.89 The Kachin Hills make a boundary between India and which of the following neighbours?

A. Bhutan

B. Myanmar

C. Nepal

D. China

Q.90 Which among the following is the largest river system among the Deccan system of rivers?

A. Godavari

B. Cauvery

C. Krishna

D. Periyar

Q.91 Bokaro Steel Plant was constructed with the collaboration of which of the following countries?

A. Russia

B. Germany

C. France

D. England

Q.92 According to study by the Reserve Bank of India, which state attracted the highest project investments in 2018-19?

A. Karnataka

B. Uttar Pradesh

C. Andhra Pradesh

D. Telangana

Q.93 India charges what fraction of the adjusted gross revenues (AGR) as license fee from telecom operators, due to which telecom operators claim that they are badly hit?

A. 5%   **B.** 8%   **C.** 10%   **D.** 12%

Q.94 Which Indian private sector bank has launched a self-service delivery facility called 'iBox'?

A. HDFC Bank

B. ICICI Bank

C. Kotak Mahindra Bank

D. Axis Bank

Q.95 The Supreme court has upheld that GST shall be imposed on which type of goods, referring as 'Actionable claims'?

A. Lottery

B. Medicine

C. Vaccine

D. Two-wheelers

Q.96 Which among the following is the highest credit risk rating that can be awarded to any company by CRISIL?

A. AAA   **B.** AAA+   **C.** AA+   **D.** A++

Q.97 Deposit Insurance and Credit Guarantee Corporation is a wholly-owned subsidiary of which of the following?

A. SBI   **B.** RBI   **C.** ICICI   **D.** SEBI

Q.98 With reference to astronomy, what is 'Osiris', that was seen in the news?

A. Meteor

B. Black Hole

C. Exo-Planet

D. Asteroid

Q.99 Who has become the first para-athlete to receive the Padma Bhushan award?

A. Mariyappan Thangavelu

B. Sumit Antil

C. Sundar Singh Gurjar

D. Devendra Jhajharia

Q.100 Who won the Filmfare Best Actor in a Leading Role (Male) award 2017?

[RRB/RRC Group D, 2018]

A. Shahrukh Khan

B. Ranveer Singh

C. Aamir Khan

D. Ranbir Kapoor

// Smart Answer Sheet //

Correct — Percentage of students who answered correctly.   **Skipped** — Percentage of students who skipped.

Q.	Ans.	Correct / Skipped	Q.	Ans.	Correct / Skipped	Q.	Ans.	Correct / Skipped	Q.	Ans.	Correct / Skipped	Q.	Ans.	Correct / Skipped
1	C	42.01 % / 30.38 %	17	B	40.22 % / 39.15 %	33	C	49.43 % / 37.05 %	49	B	45.74 % / 44.62 %	65	B	64.97 % / 32.45 %
2	A	59.79 % / 40.05 %	18	D	50.15 % / 46.19 %	34	D	64.42 % / 30.22 %	50	B	47.05 % / 34.21 %	66	B	22.12 % / 73.96 %
3	B	64.25 % / 33.19 %	19	C	60.8 % / 33.19 %	35	D	59.05 % / 35.98 %	51	A	51.33 % / 30.29 %	67	B	49.57 % / 43.36 %
4	D	46.17 % / 52.63 %	20	D	14.31 % / 83.57 %	36	B	58.43 % / 31.28 %	52	D	53.2 % / 46.18 %	68	B	87.35 % / 11.81 %
5	C	41.88 % / 45.4 %	21	B	41.79 % / 42.25 %	37	C	44.28 % / 41.99 %	53	C	64.08 % / 34.19 %	69	A	46.43 % / 30.81 %
6	D	17.91 % / 80.23 %	22	C	59.12 % / 39.72 %	38	A	54.3 % / 37.23 %	54	B	56.91 % / 36.48 %	70	B	40.66 % / 40.46 %
7	C	29.58 % / 69.56 %	23	D	52.68 % / 39.09 %	39	B	25.9 % / 67.74 %	55	C	44.45 % / 49.67 %	71	C	42.86 % / 54.53 %
8	D	23.38 % / 74.54 %	24	D	41.98 % / 33.01 %	40	D	65.44 % / 30.49 %	56	B	53.13 % / 45.3 %	72	A	21.69 % / 70.37 %
9	D	52.45 % / 32.75 %	25	D	79.2 % / 14.66 %	41	B	63.29 % / 32.15 %	57	A	51.02 % / 45.98 %	73	B	24.16 % / 73.87 %
10	D	49.02 % / 50.87 %	26	D	44.32 % / 53.38 %	42	C	47.92 % / 38.76 %	58	B	67.05 % / 30.08 %	74	A	63.67 % / 34.7 %
11	C	63.14 % / 32.37 %	27	D	52.15 % / 34.67 %	43	C	80.46 % / 13.98 %	59	C	79.15 % / 20.05 %	75	B	14.61 % / 76.92 %
12	B	65.64 % / 34.12 %	28	D	46.41 % / 41.99 %	44	B	63.71 % / 31.06 %	60	C	46.95 % / 48.66 %	76	C	32.59 % / 67.05 %
13	C	56.5 % / 34.83 %	29	A	61.4 % / 32.42 %	45	C	62.66 % / 34.89 %	61	B	86.12 % / 10.1 %	77	A	65.89 % / 31.25 %
14	A	56.06 % / 43.54 %	30	A	15.45 % / 70.1 %	46	B	58.84 % / 36.56 %	62	D	57.32 % / 31.47 %	78	B	60.88 % / 34.82 %
15	B	69.67 % / 30.12 %	31	B	58.81 % / 37.49 %	47	A	57.45 % / 39.83 %	63	B	59.85 % / 34.28 %	79	D	59.91 % / 36.12 %
16	B	40.24 % / 56.37 %	32	B	22.55 % / 70.4 %	48	C	44.71 % / 43.92 %	64	B	52.78 % / 32.87 %	80	A	67.08 % / 30.44 %

Q.	Ans.	Correct
		Skipped
81	C	59.07 %
		30.73 %
82	C	62.44 %
		31.32 %
83	A	21.32 %
		70.36 %
84	A	45.85 %
		53.8 %

Q.	Ans.	Correct
		Skipped
85	D	59.84 %
		31.94 %
86	C	67.19 %
		31.39 %
87	A	31.02 %
		67.14 %
88	A	45.33 %
		52.69 %

Q.	Ans.	Correct
		Skipped
89	B	48.31 %
		35.41 %
90	A	62.95 %
		32.54 %
91	A	65.74 %
		33.16 %
92	C	49.04 %
		30.06 %

Q.	Ans.	Correct
		Skipped
93	B	56.3 %
		39.9 %
94	B	25.69 %
		69.37 %
95	A	45.71 %
		39.06 %
96	A	42.65 %
		40.03 %

Q.	Ans.	Correct
		Skipped
97	B	56.93 %
		41.91 %
98	C	42.99 %
		37.05 %
99	D	49.87 %
		45.52 %
100	C	56.95 %
		32.53 %

//Hints and Solutions//

1. "Few", when used without a preceding 'a', means "very few" or "none at all". On the other hand, "a few" is used to indicate "not a large number". Here the context required a sense of "not much". So "a few" should be used instead of "few".

Then the correct sentence is, "The driver took them to a Spanish design home **a few** miles from the Hacienda."
Hence, the correct option is (C).

2. 'Hardly' means 'only just' or 'almost not' and is a synonym of 'barely' or 'scarcely'. The adverb 'hard' is used to modify a verb and means that the action is being done very "intensely". Here the context required a sense of "intensely". So "hard" should be used instead of "hardly".

Then the sentence is, "It was raining very **hard** and he had a very large umbrella to keep off the rain-drops."
Hence, the correct option is (A).

3. "Back up" is a phrasal verb that means something supportive. In this sentence, the father asks the son to have another plan in case the original plan does not work.

Then the sentence is, "His father asked him to have a back **up** plan regarding his career.
Hence, the correct option is (B).

4. 'On the side' is a phrase which means in addition to one's regular job.

'On the periphery of' means not a very important part of it.

'On the brink of' means about to happen.

By the meaning of words, the most appropriate is "on the brink of", it gives the proper sense to the sentence.

Then the sentence is, "Anaita is on the **brink of** financial ruin."

Hence, the correct option is (D).

5. The idiom 'to get scot-free' means to go unpunished; to be acquitted of a crime. Hence 'to escape without punishment' is the most suitable response.

For example, "Although the police caught him red-handed, the judge said there wasn't enough evidence and he **got off scot free**".

Hence, the correct option is (C).

6. Refer to, **"The Madras High Court on Friday granted 30 days of ordinary leave to S. Nalini, 52, a life convict in the former Prime Minister Rajiv Gandhi's assassination case."**

Among the given options, we can see that our answer is described in Option (D) whereas all the other options are incorrect as per the given information in the passage.

Hence, the correct option is (D).

7. Refer to, **"Justices M.M. Sundresh and M. Nirmal Kumar took judicial notice that the State Cabinet itself had on September 9 last year made a recommendation to the Governor to release all seven convicts in the Rajiv Gandhi assassination case."**

It is the case that the state government already moved a petition to free all the seven prisoners in the Rajiv Gandhi assassination case implying that they have no issue with the rest of the sentence getting remitted by the competent authority. Among the given options, we can see that Option (C) is our pick whereas others are not correct as per the given information given in the passage.

Hence, the correct option is (C).

8. Statement I is not correct for the fact that S Nalini has been given permission to come out on parole for the third time as she was given the permission twice before also. Refer to, **"Nalini had many years ago come out on short paroles of a day each to attend her brother Bhagyanathan's wedding and her father's last rites."**

Statement II is also not correct for the fact that S Nalini has been released on parole in order to attend her daughter's wedding and to make arrangements for the marriage. Her daughter is staying in London. Refer to, **"The order was passed after she argued her case in person and made a fervent plea to the judges in a choked voice that she may be allowed to step out of prison for some days to make arrangements for the marriage of her daughter, who is residing in London."**

Statement III is also not correct for the fact that it is already said that S Nalini has a daughter and that easily makes this particular statement incorrect.

Hence, the correct option is (D).

9. Statement I is not correct because the Madras HC has observed that S Nalini is a woman of no means since she does not have any regular source of income. That is why the court has asked the state to bear the expenses of her security during the parole. Refer to, "The judges also directed the State government to bear the expenses of providing escort to her during the period of leave since she expressed difficulty in paying the charges. "There is no material to hold that she is a woman of means" they said.

Statement II is not correct for the fact that the first part seems to be correct since S Nalini was sentenced to life imprisonment by the courts for the assassination of our former PM Rajiv Gandhi but it is nowhere referred to in the passage that she should not be given any chance to reform herself.

Statement III is also not correct because the court has held that there is no relation between S Nalini and her husband but there is no reference that she is the reason behind it.

Hence, the correct option is (D).

10. The word 'leisure' must be followed the preposition 'for' instead of 'till' in this context. The expression "leisure for" means 'free time for'.

Thus 'for' should be used in place of 'till' to make the sentence grammatically and contextually correct.

Among the given choices, only option (D) replaces the given bold part most appropriately.

The sentence after replacement becomes:

Having leisure for outdoor activities such as taking a stroll down the park has become a rarity in this fast-paced life.

Hence, the correct option is (D).

11. The correct idiomatic expression is 'a helping hand' and not 'a helpful handshake'.

Lend a helping hand (Idiom):

Meaning: To help or assist.

E.g.: Peter is always willing to lend a helping hand around the house.

Hence 'a helping hand' should be used in place of 'a helpful handshake' to make the sentence grammatically correct.

Among the given choices, only option (C) replaces the given bold part most appropriately.

The sentence after replacement becomes:

India lent a helping hand to Nepal by giving them 2.1 billion Nepalese rupees for the reconstruction of houses flattened in the 2015 earthquake.

Hence, the correct option is (C).

12. 'Bluster' means 'loudly boastful or threatening speech' and the only preposition that should follow it is 'on'. This eliminates options (A) and (C).

For the blank 2, the preposition 'over' is the most appropriate choice as the phrase 'over the top' must have been used here in the given context of the sentence.

Over the top (Adverbial phrase): To an excessive or exaggerated degree

The the sentence is, "Pakistan Prime Minister Imran Khan's bluster **on** Kashmir and the implied threat of a nuclear war were irresponsible and **over** the top."

Hence, the correct option is (B).

13. In the context of the sentence, the preposition following the verb 'advocated' must be 'for'.

Advocate (Verb): To speak in support of an idea or course of action

Example: The organization **advocates for** human rights.

Now, as we know that the verb 'depend' is followed by the preposition 'on', 'on' is the perfect choice for the blank 2.

Then the sentence is, "The global financial institution has advocated **for** reforms that favour agribusiness and ignore peasants and indigenous peoples whose livelihoods depend **on** traditional land use."

Hence, the correct option is (C).

14. Calamitous: Involving calamity

Fortunate: It was fortunate that he was at home when you phoned

Haggard: Looking tired or worried

Ambivalent: Having mixed feelings or contradictory ideas about something or someone

Cantankerous: Bad-tempered

Hence, the correct option is (A).

15. Capricious: Given to sudden and unaccountable changes of mood or behaviour

Predictable: Able to be known, seen, or declared in advance

Caustic: Sarcastic in a scathing and bitter way

Prescient: Having or showing knowledge of events before they take place

Cogent: Clear, logical, and convincing

Hence, the correct option is (B).

16. Stalemate: A position counting as a draw, in which a player is not in check but cannot move except into check

Deadlock: A situation in a game or match where the scores are level

Degeneration: The state or process of being or becoming degenerate; decline or deterioration

Exhaustion: A state of extreme physical or mental tiredness

Settlement: An official agreement intended to resolve a dispute or conflict

Hence, the correct option is (B).

17. Squander: Waste (something, especially money or time) in a reckless and foolish manner

Waste: Use or expend carelessly, extravagantly, or to no purpose

Expensive: costing a lot of money

Litter: An untidy collection of things lying about

Economical: Using no more of something than is necessary

Hence, the correct option is (B).

18. A jack of all trades (Idiom): A person who has dabbled in many skills

A bit shot (Idiom): An important or influential person

A big gun (Idiom): An important or influential person

Clearly, both options (B) and (C) are replacing the bold part appropriately.

Hence, the correct option is (D).

19. To work late night (Idiom): Burn Midnight oil

Cut Corners (Idiom): Do something to save money

Cut the mustard (Idiom): To come upto expectations

Hence, the correct option is (C).

20. The entire statement is in the past tense wherein events have already occurred. The word 'witnesses' is in the present continuous tense and is inappropriate in the current context.

Correct: What makes the 2019 election unprecedented is not that inappropriate words were used and misinformation spread, but the fact that India **witnessed** an increasing tendency to normalise these.

Hence, the correct option is (D).

21. Here, the correct word would be 'informed' and not 'inform'. Inform means to give (someone) facts or information while 'informed' means to do something based on an understanding of the facts of the situation. Thus, 'informed' is the correct adjective to be used ere.

Correct: On the one hand, **informed** discussions have become difficult, and on the other, social tensions have arisen.

Hence, the correct option is (B).

22. Agronomy - The science of soil management and crop production

Bibliography - A list of the books referred to in a scholarly work

Anthropology - The study of human societies and cultures and their development

Chronology - The arrangement of events or dates in the order of their occurrence

Hence, the correct option is (C).

23. Alchemy - The medieval forerunner of chemistry

Anthropology - The study of human societies and cultures and their development

Bibliography - A list of the books referred to in a scholarly work

Astrology - The study of the movements and relative positions of celestial bodies interpreted as having an influence on human affairs and the natural world

Hence, the correct option is (D).

24. Option (D) "bone" is a noun. Option (A) "true", is an adjective modifying the noun fish. Option (B) "because" is the conjunction. Option (C) "their" is a plural possessive third-person pronoun modifying the noun skeletons.

Hence, the correct option is (D).

25. Option (D) "boss" is a noun. Option (A) "have" is the auxiliary verb for the present perfect tense of the verb Option (B) "met". Option (C) "your" is a possessive second-person pronoun modifying the noun boss.

Hence, the correct option is (D).

26.

$$\begin{array}{cc} R & T \\ -1\downarrow & +1\downarrow \\ Q & U \end{array}$$

Similarly,

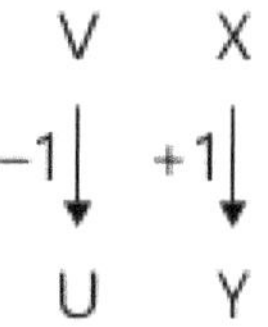

$$\begin{array}{cc} V & X \\ -1\downarrow & +1\downarrow \\ U & Y \end{array}$$

Hence, the correct option is (D).

27. $123 \Rightarrow \dfrac{12}{3} = 4$

Similarly,

$726 \Rightarrow \dfrac{72}{6} = 12$

In this question, first two digits of the given number are divided by the third one.
Hence, the correct option is (D).

28. We know that every mother is a woman but only some (and not all) mothers or women are doctors. Therefore, the following diagram represents the three given classes best.

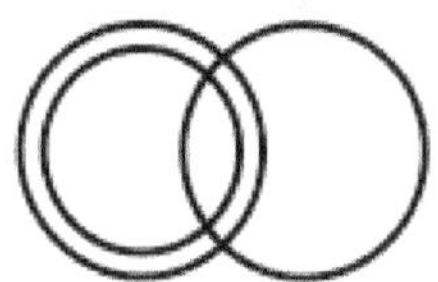

Hence, the correct option is (D).

29. Potato belongs to the class of Vegetables.Vegetables belong to the class of Food.

Hence, the correct option is (A).

30.

Hence, the correct option is (A).

31.

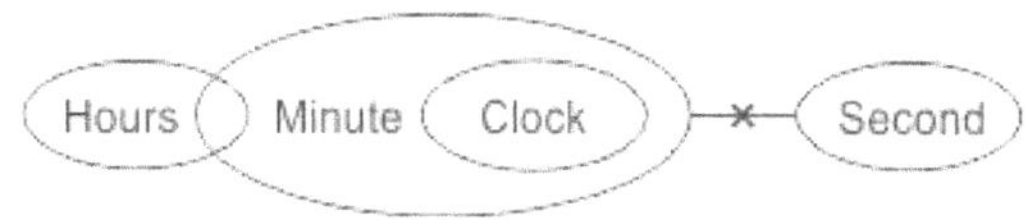

Hence, the correct option is (B).

32. There are only two boys in the group of children.

Husband	Wife	Son	Daughter
A	P	W	X

B	S	-	-
C	Q	U	Z
D	R	-	Y

Hence, the correct option is (B).

33. C is the father of Z.

Husband	Wife	Son	Daughter
A	P	W	X
B	S	-	-
C	Q	U	Z
D	R	-	Y

Hence, the correct option is (C).

34. Argument I may or may not follow in actual practice as it depends on one's individual perception. Thus argument I is not strong. It is true that we should be proud of our ancient language. But only for this reason, it is not desirable to make 'sanskrit' compulsory at school level.
Hence, the correct option is (D).

35. Neither argument I nor argument II is strong. There is no possibility of weakening of our present social structure is we give education to girls and women to India. argument I is also weak because it is not the only way to bring back glory to Indian women hood.
Hence, the correct option is (D).

36. Trip towards mountain hills is coded as "ju na mi po" --- (1)

Rise hills towards river is coded as "gi mi ju ve" --- (2)

River trip rafting mountain is coded as "po ve na fu" --- (3)

Towards mountain slow rise is coded as "yb ju gi po" --- (4)

From (1),(2) and (4), we get:

Towards – ju --- (5)

From (1),(2) and (5), we get:

Hills – mi --- (6)

From (2) and (3), we get:

River – ve --- (7)

From (1),(3),(4) and (5), we get:

Mountain – po --- (8)

From (1),(5),(6) and (8), we get:

Trip – na --- (9)

From (2), (5), (6) and (8), we get:

Rise – gi ---- (10)

From (3), (7), (8) and (9), we get:

Rafting – fu --- (11)

From (4), (5), (8) and (10), we get:

Slow – yb --- (12)
Hence, the correct option is (B).

37. Trip towards mountain hills is coded as "ju na mi po" --- (1)

Rise hills towards river is coded as "gi mi ju ve" --- (2)

River trip rafting mountain is coded as "po ve na fu" --- (3)

Towards mountain slow rise is coded as "yb ju gi po" --- (4)

From (1),(2) and (4), we get:

Towards – ju --- (5)

From (1),(2) and (5), we get:

Hills – mi --- (6)

From (2) and (3), we get:

River – ve --- (7)

From (1),(3),(4) and (5), we get:

Mountain – po --- (8)

From (1),(5),(6) and (8), we get:

Trip – na --- (9)

From (2), (5), (6) and (8), we get:

Rise – gi --- (10)

From (3), (7), (8) and (9), we get:

Rafting – fu --- (11)

From (4), (5), (8) and (10), we get:

Slow – yb --- (12)

From (12) and (10), we get

"Slow rise" - "yb gi"

Hence, the correct option is (C).

38. Leaning out of a running bus must be dangerous, otherwise the warning would not have been there. Therefore I is implicit. But II is not implicit. If the authorities would have assumed that children do not pay any heed to such warning, they would not have put it up there.
Hence, the correct option is (A).

39. I is not implicit. The company wants mechanical engineers. One reason could be that the company expects mechanical engineers to be good performers, as I suggests. But there could be another reason; for example, the company's supervisory job could be such that only a mechanical engineer could perform it. But one thing is certain. The advertisement was for supervisors; this means supervisors are needed. Thus II is implicit.
Hence, the correct option is (B).

40. The statement asks a man to be humble even after being victorious. This implies that people are usually not humble after victory. I is just the opposite of it. II is not implicit because it generalises the statement. Generally, people may be humble; the point is if they are humble or not after victory.
Hence, the correct option is (D).

41. A pattern of the series is:

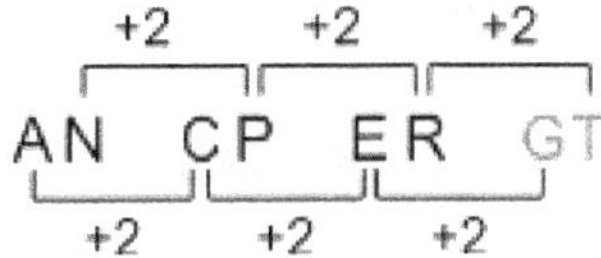

Hence, the correct option is (B).

42. From the below image we can say that MN is the missing term of series.

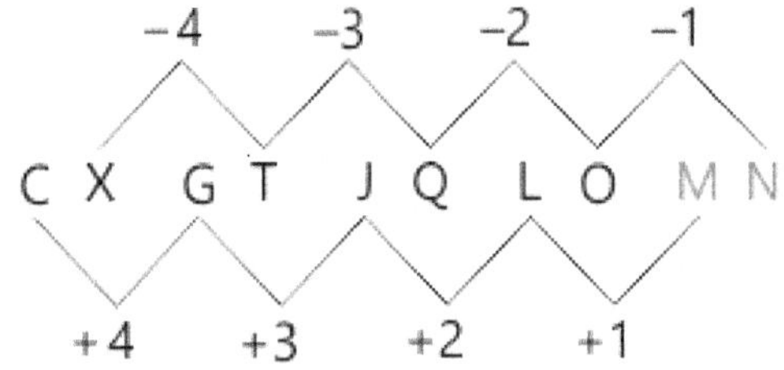

Hence, the correct option is (C).

43. Ornithologist specializes in the study of birds. Similarly, anthropologist specializes in the study of mankind.
Hence, the correct option is (C).

44. If point X is exactly between B and A then F is 14m to the east of point X.

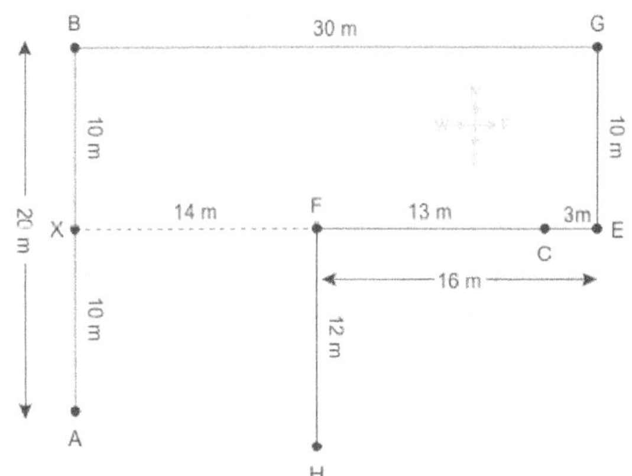

Hence, the correct option is (B).

45. If point Y is 6m south of point G then the shortest distance between point C and point Y is 5m.

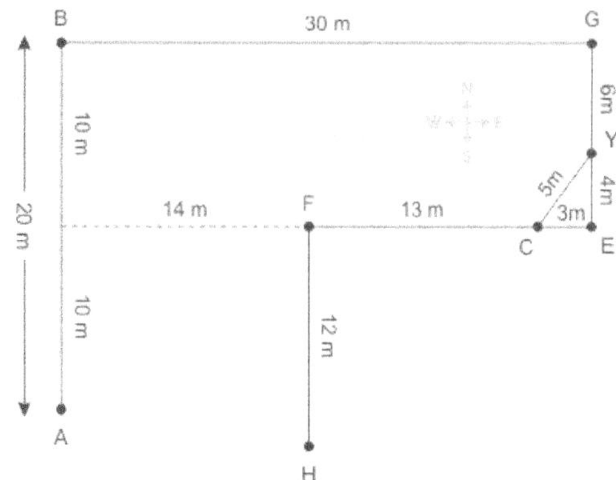

Hence, the correct option is (C).

46. The shortest distance between D and G is 13m.

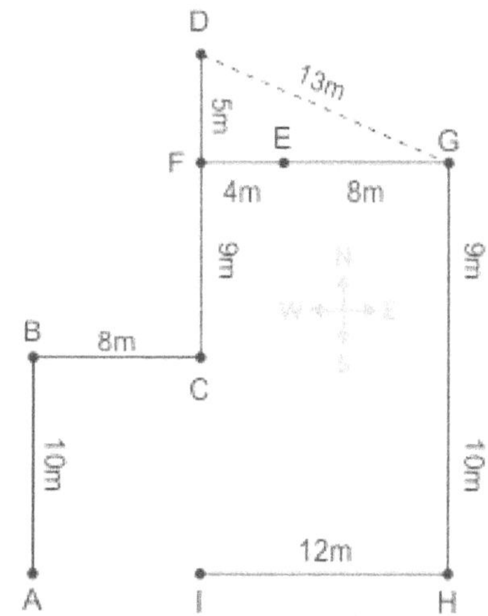

Hence, the correct option is (B).

47.

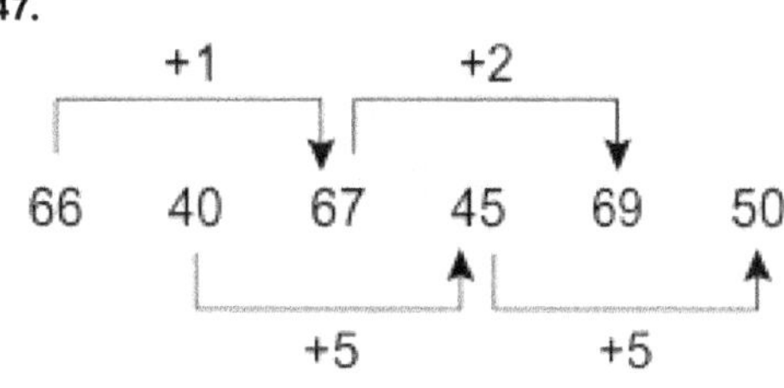

Hence, the correct option is (A).

48. $50 + 3^2 = 59,$

$59 + 4^2 = 75,$

$75 + 5^2 = 100,$

$100 + 6^2 = 136.$
Hence, the correct option is (C).

49. Age of Shan = 55 years

Age of Sethian = 55-5 = 50 years

Age of Balan = 50-6 = 44 years

Age of Deven = 44-7 = 37 years

Thus, difference between Devan and Shan,

= 55-37

= 18 years
Hence, the correct option is (B).

50.

1	2	3	4	5
6	7	8	9	10
11	12	Ramesh	14	...
...	...	...	...	...
...	...	...	...	Suresh
5	4	3	2	1

Total Number of Student = 33
Number of student in between Ramesh and Suresh is,
= 33 - (13+6)
= 14.
Hence, the correct option is (B).

51. Under Article 32, a writ petition can be filed in the Supreme Court. The High Court may grant a writ for the enforcement of fundamental rights or for any other purpose such as violation of any statutory duties by a statutory authority.
Hence, the correct option is (A).

52. A writ of habeas corpus is used to bring a prisoner or other detainee (e.g. institutionalized mental patient) before the court to determine if the person's imprisonment or detention is lawful. A habeas petition proceeds as a civil action against the State agent (usually a warden) who holds the defendant in custody.
Hence, the correct option is (D).

53. Every Judge of the Supreme Court shall be appointed by the President by warrant under his/her hand and seal after consultation with such of the Judges of the Supreme Court and of the High Court in the States as President may deem necessary for the purpose and shall hold office until he attains the age of 65 years.
Hence, the correct option is (C).

54. Under article 100 of the Constitution, the quorum to constitute a meeting of either House of Parliament is one-tenth of the total number of members of the House.
Hence, the correct option is (B).

55. Every sitting of the Parliament starts with a question hour. Question Hour is the first hour of a parliamentary sitting. Asking questions in Parliament is the free and unfettered right of members, and during Question Hour they may ask questions of ministers on different aspects of administration and government policy in the national and international spheres.

Hence, the correct option is (B).

56. Education is a fundamental right but the education of children below six years i.e. before primary school is not. The Union Ministry of Human Resource Development (HRD) is responsible for elementary education but the Ministry of Women

and Child Development (WCD) looks at pre-primary education.
Hence, the correct option is (B).

57. The 86th amendment to the constitution of India in 2002, provided Right to Education as a fundamental right in part-III of the Constitution. The same amendment inserted Article 21A which made Right to Education a fundamental right for children between 6-14 years.
Hence, the correct option is (A).

58. In India, bigamy is an offense against marriage and it is also a criminal offense under Indian Penal laws. The bigamy law applicable to Hindus, Jains, Buddhists, Sikhs, Parsis, Christians [except Muslims]. Bigamy is one of the grounds to seek divorce under the Hindu Marriage Act 1955.
Hence, the correct option is (B).

59. 'Locus standi' means a right to appear in a court or before anybody on a given question: "A right to be heard". In legal terms, Locus Standi essentially applies to a plaintiff's attempt to show to the court that there is ample relation or correlation or cause of action to the plaintiff from the suit.
Hence, the correct option is (C).

60. Implementation of 'The Right to Information Act, 2005' in the Universities/Colleges. This Act provides for the right to information for citizens to secure access to information under the control of public authorities in order to promote transparency and accountability in the working of every public authority.
Hence, the correct option is (C).

61. There are majorly four theories of punishment. These theories are the deterrent theory, retributive theory, preventive theory, and reformative theory.
Hence, the correct option is (B).

62. The Government of India Act,1935, exercised the most profound influence in framing the Indian Constitution. This act of 1935 was extremely important for a number of reasons. It governed India as this was the last major legislation that the British passed before Independence was granted. One of the reasons was for which it was important was that some provincial autonomy was granted.
Hence, the correct option is (D).

63. The term 'Unlawful Assembly' has been defined under section 141 of the Indian Penal Code, 1860 as an assembly of five or more persons having a common object to perform an omission or offence.
Hence, the correct option is (B).

64. Xenophobia, or fear of strangers, is a broad term that may be applied to any fear of someone who is different from us. Hostility towards outsiders is often a reaction to fear. It typically involves the belief that there is a conflict between an individual's ingroup and an outgroup.

Hence, the correct option is (B).

65. The President appoints the Prime Minister, Chief Justice of India and other judges of SC and HCs, CAG, Chief Election Commissioner and other Election Commissioners, The Attorney General, etc. The authority and function of Advocate General is also specified in the Constitution of India under Article 165 and 177. The Governor of each State shall appoint a person who is

qualified to be appointed as a Judge of a High Court to be Advocate General for the State.
Hence, the correct option is (B).

66. The anti-defection law in India, technically the Tenth Schedule to the Indian Constitution, was enacted to address the perceived problem of instability caused by democratically elected legislators in India's Parliamentary System of Government shifting allegiance from the parties they supported at the time of election or disobeying their parties' decisions at critical times such as during voting on an important resolution.
Hence, the correct option is (B).

67. Originally ten in number, the fundamental duties were increased to eleven by the 86th Amendment in 2002, which added a duty on every parent or guardian to ensure that their child or ward was provided opportunities for education between the ages of six and fourteen years.
Hence, the correct option is (B).

68. The Palestine officially became a member of the International Criminal Court. Palestine is the 123rd state party to the International Criminal Court.
Hence, the correct option is (B).

69. The UN Office of Counter-Terrorism (UNOCT) is pleased to be an observer member of the Group of Friends of Victims of Terrorism (the Group), which was launched by the Secretary-General, H.E. Mr. António Guterres on 25 June 2019 at the UN Headquarters in New York.
Hence, the correct option is (A).

70. In M. Ahmed Khan v. Shah Bano Begum, the Supreme Court held that Muslim Women have the right to claim maintenance under Section 125 of Cr.P.C. the Remedy under Section 125 is available to the wife (including a divorced wife), irrespective of the religion to which she belongs.
Hence, the correct option is (B).

71. A and B are guilty of Abatement of murder by conspiracy. Criminal conspiracy has a wider jurisdiction than abetment by a conspiracy. An individual is guilty of conspiracy with the mere agreement between a group of people to commit an offense.
Hence, the correct option is (C).

72. A by putting B in fear of grievous hurt dishonestly induces B to sign for affix his seal in black paper, and delivers it to A. B signs and delivers the paper to A. A has committed Extortion. Whoever, in order to the committing of extortion, puts any person in fear or attempts Central Government Act Cites 0 - Cited by 2112.
Hence, the correct option is (A).

73. Section 82 of IPC provides that nothing is an offense that is done by a child under seven years of age. Section 82 and 83 of the Indian Penal Code deals with criminal liability under infancy. Article 82 is based on the assumption that a child under the age of 7 cannot commit a crime and therefore cannot be held liable for a crime. A child under the age of seven is doli incapax and therefore receives absolute immunity.
Hence, the correct option is (B).

74. According to Section 83 of the Indian Penal Code, nothing is a crime, which is committed by an infant above the age of seven years and below the age of twelve years, whose understanding

has not matured enough to reveal the nature of his conduct on that occasion and Decide the results.
Hence, the correct option is (A).

75. "Mens rea" means to have "a guilty mind." The rationale behind the rule is that it is wrong for society to punish those who innocently cause harm. "Actus reus" literally means "guilty act," and generally refers to an overt act in furtherance of a crime. The standard common law test of criminal liability is expressed in the Latin phrase "actus reus non facit reum nisi mens sit rea", i.e. "the act is not culpable unless the mind is guilty".
Hence, the correct option is (B).

76. The CSIR-National Chemical Laboratory (CSIR-NCL) at Pune has developed the novel hybrid technology called SWASTIIK for disinfecting water by using natural oils.

Disinfection of water is essential for removing pathogenic microorganisms that are responsible for causing a number of water-borne diseases. The technology was developed by CSIR-NCL with support from the Water Technology Initiative of the department of science and technology (DST).

Hence, the correct option is (C).

77. The Long March 5B rocket, carrying a module for a Chinese space station, lifts off from southern China's Hainan Province on April 29.

China's space agency said a core segment of its biggest rocket reentered Earth's atmosphere above the Maldives in the Indian Ocean and that most of it burned up early. Debris from a Chinese rocket made an uncontrolled re-entry into the Earth's atmosphere and disintegrated over the Indian Ocean, with remnants falling at a location to the west of Maldives.

Hence, the correct option is (A).

78. Genetic screening is analysis of gene in a population.

It is a process to analyze blood or skin for the systematic search for persons with a particular genotype in a defined population. It also serves as an important tool of modern preventive medicine.

Hence, the correct option is (B).

79. George Stephenson was the inventor of the railway engine.

George Stephenson was a British civil engineer and mechanical engineer. Renowned as the "Father of the Railway", Stephenson was regarded by Victorian individuals as a great example of diligent application and thirst for reform. Stephenson designed his first locomotive in 1814, a traveling engine designed to haul coal.

Hence, the correct option is (D).

80. 'Economics is what it ought to be' - This statement refers to Normative economics.

Normative economics is a part of economics that expresses value or establishing judgments about economic fairness or what the outcome of the economy or goals of public policy ought to be.

Economists commonly prefer to distinguish normative economics 'what ought to be' from positive economics 'what is'.
Hence, the correct option is (A).

81. In terms of Producers' surplus is the amount that producers benefit by selling at a market price that is higher than the least that they would be willing to sell for. Similarly, Consumers' surplus is the monetary gain obtained by consumers because they are able to purchase a product for a price that is less than the highest price that they would be willing to pay.
Hence, the correct option is (C).

82. Break-even is the point of balance between making either a profit or a loss. The term originates in finance, but the concept has been applied widely since.

In economics & business, specifically, cost accounting, the break-even point is the point at which cost or expenses and revenue are equal.

Hence, the correct option is (C).

83. The demand for a commodity is affected by the changes in prices of the related goods also. The effect of changes in prices of a commodity on the amount demanded of related commodities is called Cross Demand. The measure is calculated by taking the percentage change in the quantity demanded of one good, divided by the percentage change in the price of the substitute good.

There are three types of Demand:

1. Price Demand

2. Income Demand

3. Cross Demand

Hence, the correct option is (A).

84. The famous economist Keynes applied the term effective demand to denote the total demand for goods and services at various levels of employment. Each level of employment represents a different level of aggregate demand.
Hence, the correct option is (A).

85. Zero Rating is presented as a solution to expensive basic internet subscriptions and data limits on mobile plans and used as a way to enable customers to visit unlimited sites that they might use frequently. Largely in developing countries, Facebook is one example of a zero rating website.
Hence, the correct option is (D).

86. Under Article 356 of the Constitution of India, in the event that a state government is unable to function according to Constitutional provisions, the Union government can take direct control of the state machinery.
Hence, the correct option is (C).

87. The budget, which is presented by means of the Finance Bill and the Appropriation bill has to be passed by Lok Sabha before it can come into effect, the start of India's financial year. The Union Budget of India, referred to as the Annual Financial Statement in Article 112 of the Constitution of India, is the annual budget of the Republic of India, presented each year on the very first day of February by the Finance Minister of India in Parliament.
Hence, the correct option is (A).

88. Indian Mountaineering Foundation (IMF) is an apex national body for mountaineering, skiing, rock climbing, and trekking at high altitudes in India and established in 1957. The main objectives are to organize, support and provide a base for expeditions for mountaineering, rock climbing, trekking at high altitudes and to promote, encourage, support and execute schemes for related adventure activities and environmental protection work in the Himalaya.
Hence, the correct option is (A).

89. The Kachin Hills are located at the extreme northeastern area of the Kachin State of Myanmar and they make a boundary between India and Myanmar. They range north-south and are bordered on the northwest by the Arunachal Pradesh state of India, on the north by the Tibet autonomous region of China, and on the east by Yunnan province of China.
Hence, the correct option is (B).

90. With a length of 1465 Kilometers, Godavari is India's second-largest river that runs within the country and also the longest river in South India. It originates near Trimbak in the Nashik District of Maharashtra state and flows east across the Deccan Plateau into the Bay of Bengal near Narasapuram in the West Godavari district of Andhra Pradesh.

The river is also known as Dakshin Ganga and Gautami. The Manjra and Indravati rivers are their major tributaries.
Hence, the correct option is (A).

91. Bokaro Steel Plant was constructed with the collaboration of Russia. Bokaro Steel Plant (BSP) is located in the Bokaro district of Jharkhand. It is the fourth integrated public sector steel plant in India built with Soviet help. It was incorporated as a limited company in 1965. It was later merged with the state-owned Steel Authority of India Limited (SAIL).
Hence, the correct option is (A).

92. By the Reserve Bank of India (RBI), Andhra Pradesh topped the list of states which attracted the highest project investments in 2018-19.

Maharashtra, which was the topper of last year, missed its top spot in 2018-19, but was ranked first in terms of investments over a five-year period between 2014-15 and 2018-19. In 2018-19, Andhra Pradesh has the highest share (11.8 percent) in total cost of projects sanctioned in 2018-19 followed by Tamil Nadu and Maharashtra.

Hence, the correct option is (C).

93. India levies license fees of 8% of adjusted gross revenues (AGR) from every telecom license holder. The SC on October 24 defined AGR as all revenues of a license holder, and not just revenues from telecom services. Apart from dealing a body blow to telcos, the order also made non-telecom companies holding licenses for internal communications and signaling liable to pay license fees on their entire revenue, even when they do not offer any telecom services.
Hence, the correct option is (B).

94. Leading Private lender of India, ICICI Bank launched a unique self-service delivery facility called 'iBox'. Using this facility, the customers of the bank can avail various banking services including- collecting their debit card, credit card, a cheque from a nearby branch.

The 'iBox' terminals are to be placed outside the premises of the branches, which can be accessed even after office hours. The customer will get an SMS about the status of the package through a completely automated process. These products can be collected by the customers at the time of their choice, on all days including holidays.

Hence, the correct option is (B).

95. The Bench also highlighted that the GST Act, 2017 defines the goods to include 'actionable claims' and included only three categories of such claims namely lottery, betting and gambling, to levy GST. Actionable claim is the claim for a debt related to any benefit from unpossessed movable property and for which relief can be claimed in civil court. The Supreme court upheld that the Goods and Service Tax (GST) shall be imposed on the sale of lotteries, betting and gambling.
Hence, the correct option is (A).

96. CRISIL was the first credit rating agency in India, formed in the year 1988. In 2005, it became a subsidiary of American company S & P Global. The highest credit risk rating awarded to any company is 'AAA' and the lowest is 'D'.
Hence, the correct option is (A).

97. Deposit Insurance and Credit Guarantee Corporation is a wholly-owned subsidiary of the Reserve Bank of India (RBI). It was established on 15 July 1978 under the Deposit Insurance and Credit Guarantee Corporation Act, 1961 for the purpose of providing insurance of deposits and guaranteeing of credit facilities.
Hence, the correct option is (B).

98. 'Osiris', which is officially called HD 209458 b, is the first-ever planet the astronomers have spotted beyond the Earth's solar system.

As per a new study published in Nature, it has been found that six chemicals are present in the atmosphere of Osiris. The composition of the chemicals confirm that the exoplanet is over 100 times farther than its current position, when it came into existence.

Hence, the correct option is (C).

99. Devendra Jhajharia became the first para-athlete to receive the Padma Bhushan, the country's third-highest civilian award. Jhajharia has won many Paralympic medals, including his first gold at the 2004 Paralympics in Athens, his second gold at the 2016 Rio Games, and a silver medal at the 2020 Tokyo Olympics.

Hence, the correct option is (D).

100. Aamir Khan won the best actor award at the 2017 Filmfare awards for playing the character of Mahavir Singh Phogat in the movie Dangal.

- The 1st Filmfare Awards were held on March 21, 1954, which honoured the best in Hindi cinema in 1953.

- That year they were known as Clare Awards, after Clare Mendonca, a film critic of The Times of India who had

died in the same year. The award for best actor was won by Dilip Kumar for his movie Daag.

Hence, the correct option is (C).

Ques (1-2):Direction: A series is given with one term missing. Select the correct alternative from the given ones that will complete the series.

Q.1 OTE, PUF, QVG, RWH, ?

A. SYJ   **B.** TCI   **C.** SXI   **D.** WKL

Q.2 UPI, SHJ, ODP, MBQ, ?

A. EVA   **B.** IAW   **C.** SIJ   **D.** THK

Q.3 In a certain code language '481' means 'sky is blue', '246' means 'sea is deep' and '698' means 'sea looks blue'. What number is the code for 'blue'?

A. 8   **B.** 6   **C.** 1   **D.** 9

Q.4 In a certain code language '289' means 'read from paper', '276' means 'tea from field' and '85' means 'wall paper'. Which of the following is the code for 'paper'?

A. 9   **B.** 2

C. 8   **D.** Cannot say

Q.5 Identify the diagram that best represents the relationship among the given classes.

Humans, Male, Teachers

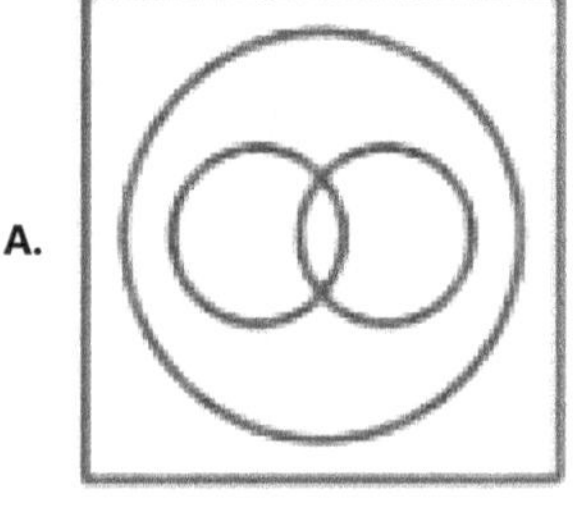  

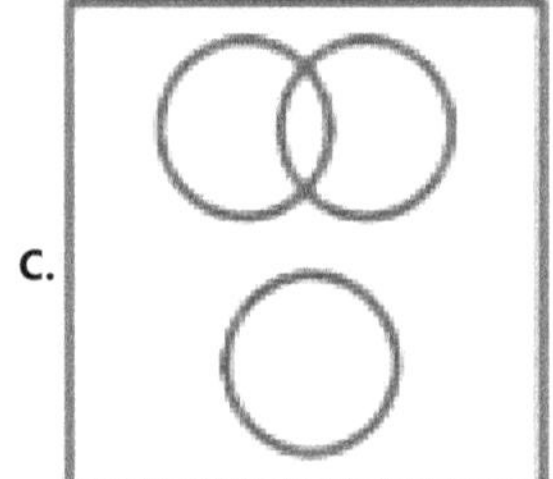 

Q.6 Identify the diagram that best represents the relationship among the given classes.

Mother, Grandmother, Females

 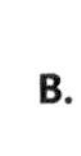 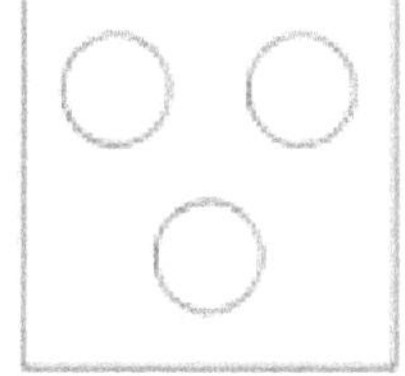

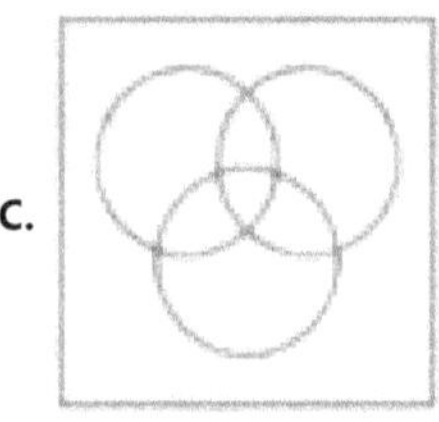

C.

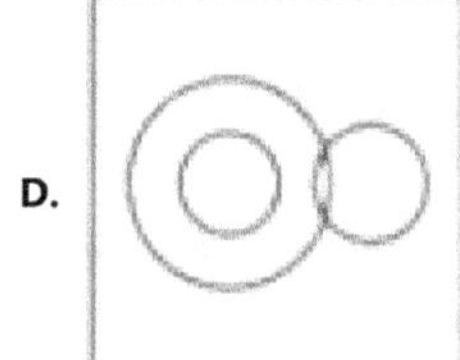

D.

Ques (7-8):Direction: In the following question statements are given and these statements are followed by conclusions. You have to take the given statements to be true even if they seem to be at variance from commonly known facts. Read the conclusions and then decide which of the given conclusions logically follows from the given statements, disregarding commonly known facts.

Q.7 Statements:

All the pencils are pens.

All the pens are inks.

Conclusions:

I. All the pencils are inks.

II. Some inks are pencils.

A. Only (I) conclusion follows

B. Only (II) conclusion follows

C. Either (I) or (II) follows

D. Both (I) and (II) follow

Q.8 Statements:

All the trucks are flies.

Some scooters are flies.

Conclusions:

I. All the trucks are scooters.

II. Some scooters are trucks.

A. Only (I) conclusion follows

B. Only (II) conclusion follows

C. Either (I) or (II) follows

D. Neither (I) nor (II) follows

Q.9 Some equations are solved on the basis of a certain system on the same basis, find out the correct answer for the unsolved equation.

If 8 − 7 = 6, 4 − 7 = 2, 13 − 6 = 12, then what should 18 − 9 be?

A. 9   **B.** 13   **C.** 14   **D.** 12

Q.10 Amit is taller than Brian who is shorter than Chirag. Dylan is shorter than Amit but taller than Chirag. Two other men are taller than Amit. Who is the shortest?

A. Brian   **B.** Chirag   **C.** Amit   **D.** Dylan

Ques (11-12):Direction: In the question are given two statements I and II. These statements may be either independent causes or may be effects of independent causes or a common cause. One of these statements may be the effect of the other statements. Read both the statements and decide which of the following answer choice correctly depicts the relationship between these two statements.

Q.11 Statements:

I. A huge truck overturned on the middle of the road last night.

II. The police had cordoned of entire area in the locality this morning for half of the day.

A. Statement I is the cause and statement II is its effect

B. Statement II is the cause and statement I is its effect

C. Both the statements I and II are independent causes

D. Both the statements I and II are effects of independent causes

Q.12

Statements:

I. Importance of Yoga and exercise is being realized by all sections of society.

II. There is an increasing awareness about health in society particularly among middle ages groups of people.

A. Statement I is the cause and statement II is its effect

B. Statement II is the cause and statement I is its effect

C. Both the statements I and II are independent causes

D. Both the statements I and II are effects of independent causes

Q.13 Direction: Read the statement and select a conclusion from the given alternatives:

Statement:

Steel Authority Of India Limited Company has moved India from a position of shortage to self-sufficiency in the metal.

Conclusions:

I. Previously India had to import steel.

II. In this regard, it can soon become a foreign exchange earner.

A. Only conclusion I follows

B. Only conclusion II follows

C. Either I or II follows

D. Neither I nor II follows

Q.14 Direction: In the question below is given a statement followed by two conclusions numbered I and II. You have to assume everything in the statement to be true, then consider the two conclusions together and decide which of them logically followed and decide which of them logically followed beyond a reasonable doubt from the information given in the statement.

Statement: If you are a good orator, then we definitely have a job for you.

Conclusions:

I. Good orator is never jobless

II. We are in need of a good orator.

A. Only conclusion I follows

B. Only conclusion II follows

C. Both I and II follow

D. Neither I nor II follows

Ques (15-16):Direction: In the question below is a statement followed by two assumptions numbered I and II. You have to consider the statement and the following assumptions and decide which of the assumptions is implicit in the statement.

Q.15 Statement: The government is proposing to impose an extra tax on vehicles coming to a hill station for its conservation and maintenance.

Assumptions:

I. Vehicles are the cause of pollution in the hill station.

II. The facilities available at the hill station are not sufficient for visitors.

A. If only assumption I is implicit

B. If only assumption II is implicit

C. If both I or II are implicit

D. If neither I nor II is implicit

Q.16 Statement: The problem of food poisoning due to consumption of fish has increased in the coastal areas.

Assumption:

I. Many people consume fish in coastal areas.

II. Fish in coastal areas consume contaminated material as their food.

A. If only assumption I is implicit

B. If only assumption II is implicit

C. If neither I nor II is implicit

D. If both I and II are implicit

Ques (17-18):Direction: The question given below is followed by two arguments numbered I and II. You have to decide which of the argument is a strong argument and which is a weak argument.

Q.17 Statement: Should India sign the Comprehensive Test Ban Treaty (CTBT)?

Arguments:

I. No. India will not be able to protect its border if it does so.

II. Yes. This is the only way to reduce tension in the Asian sub-continent.

A. Only I is strong

B. Only II is strong

C. Either I or II is strong

D. Both I and II are strong

Q.18 Statement: Should Chinese products be banned in India?

Arguments:

I. Yes. Nowadays we are totally dependent on Chinese products and it affects the market of Indian handmade products.

II. No, Chinese products are cheaper and the middle-class and the poor people can afford them.

A. Only I is strong

B. Only II is strong

C. Either I or II is strong

D. Both I and II are strong

Q.19 Ananya is the mother of Satya and Stephen is the son of Bhima. Ernest is the brother of Ananya. If Satya is the sister of Stephen. How is Bhima related to Ernest?

A. Son   **B.** Mother

C. Cousin   **D.** Brother in law

Q.20 Sumit's grandfather's brother is the father of Hemant's father. How is Sumit related to Hemant?

A. Brother   **B.** Cousin   **C.** Father   **D.** Uncle

Q.21 A man is facing north–west. He turns 90° in the clockwise direction and then 135° in the anticlockwise direction. Which direction is he facing now?

A. East   **B.** West   **C.** North   **D.** South

Q.22 One morning Meena started walking towards the sun, after walking a while she turned towards her left. After walking a while, she turned left. In which direction is she facing now?

A. East   **B.** West   **C.** South   **D.** North

Q.23 Direction: Based on the relationship between the first two words, find out the missing word.

INDIA : RUPEE :: SOUTH AFRICA : _______

A. RIEL
B. RAND
C. SOUTH AFRICAN DOLLAR
D. RUBLE

Q.24 Direction: In the following question, select the related word from the given alternatives.

Ornithologist: Bird :: Archaeologist:?

A. Artifact   **B.** History   **C.** Arbiter   **D.** Aquatic

Q.25 In the following question, select the one which is different from the other three responses.

A. 25, 36   **B.** 144, 169   **C.** 100, 121   **D.** 9, 64

// Smart Answer Sheet //

Correct Percentage of students who answered correctly. **Skipped** Percentage of students who skipped.

Q.	Ans.	Correct	Skipped
1	C	63.88 %	5.25 %
2	B	49.73 %	5.9 %
3	A	66.24 %	2.78 %
4	C	59.7 %	8.15 %
5	A	54.02 %	5.89 %

Q.	Ans.	Correct	Skipped
6	A	49.41 %	11.25 %
7	D	30.33 %	11.15 %
8	D	32.37 %	11.68 %
9	C	31.4 %	7.94 %
10	A	59.49 %	10.71 %

Q.	Ans.	Correct	Skipped
11	A	48.87 %	9.54 %
12	B	30.23 %	9.0 %
13	A	34.62 %	11.58 %
14	B	56.7 %	8.79 %
15	A	46.3 %	7.83 %

Q.	Ans.	Correct	Skipped
16	B	24.87 %	7.5 %
17	A	26.05 %	9.96 %
18	D	32.48 %	10.39 %
19	D	68.38 %	4.82 %
20	B	54.23 %	10.72 %

Q.	Ans.	Correct	Skipped
21	B	46.3 %	7.61 %
22	B	61.95 %	6.54 %
23	B	32.48 %	12.43 %
24	B	56.27 %	10.61 %
25	D	64.2 %	3.32 %

//Hints and Solutions//

1. The first letters of the terms are in alphabetical order and so are the second and third letters.

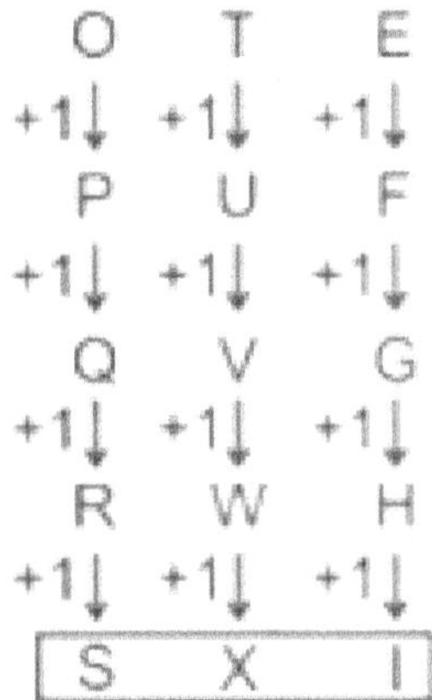

Hence, the correct option is (C).

2. The pattern is as follows,

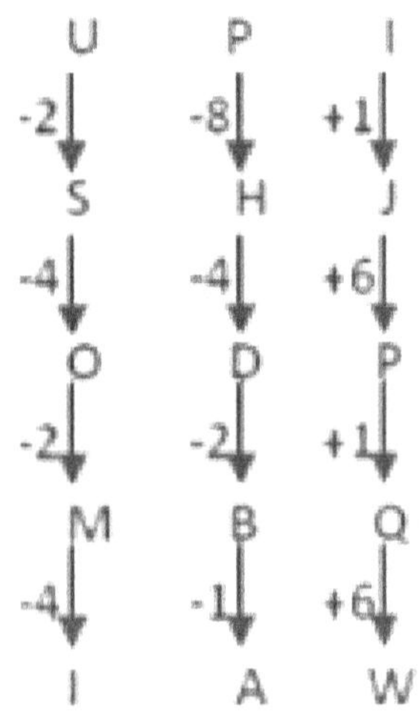

Hence, the correct option is (B).

3.

Hence, the correct option is (A).

4. Here the information can be represented as,

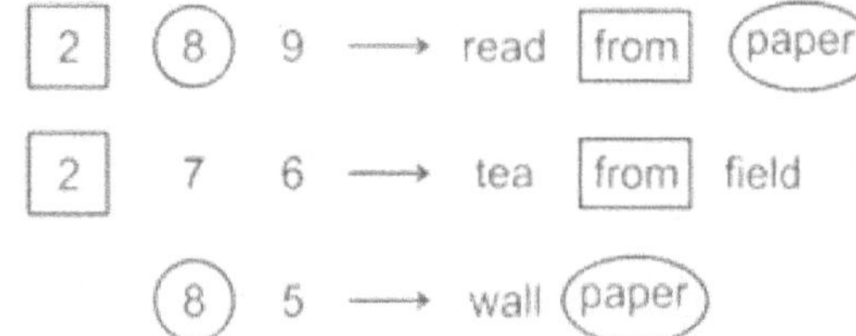

Hence, the correct option is (C).

5. Some teachers may be male, and all teachers and male are human.

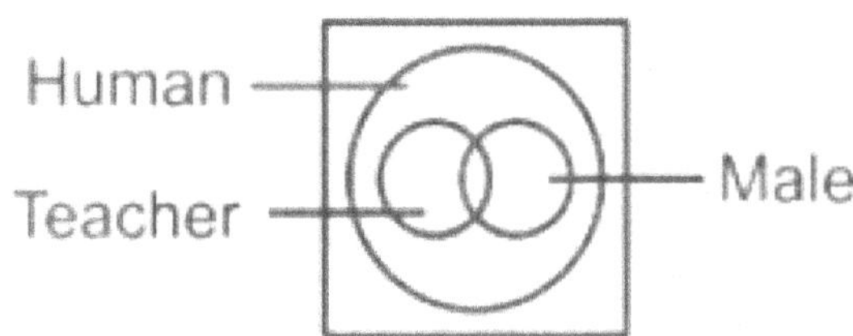

Hence, the correct option is (A).

6. As, all grandmothers are mothers and both mother and grandmother are female.

Therefore, it can be best shown as

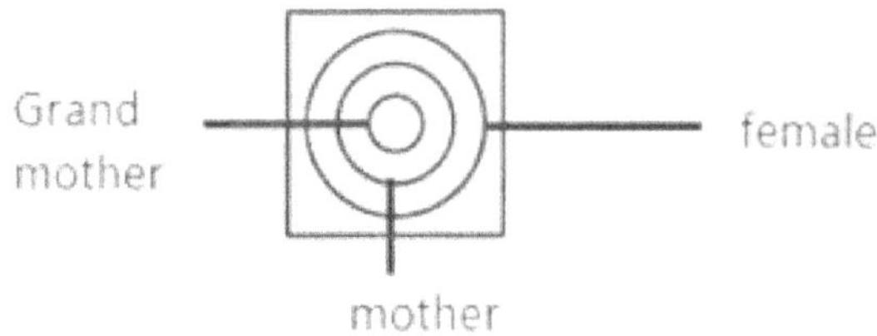

Hence, the correct option is (A).

7.

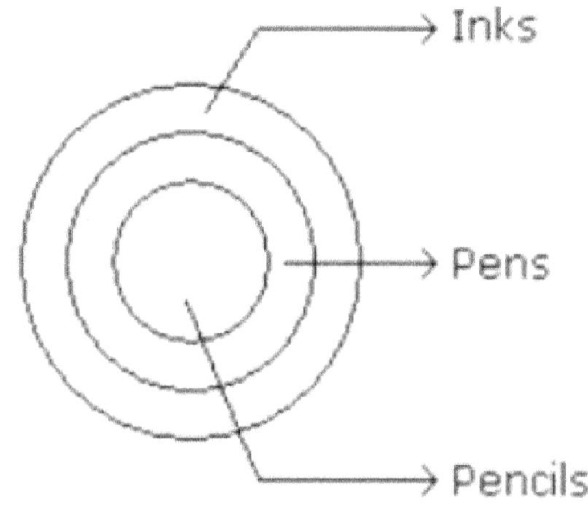

Hence, the correct option is (D).

8. The Venn diagram is as follows:

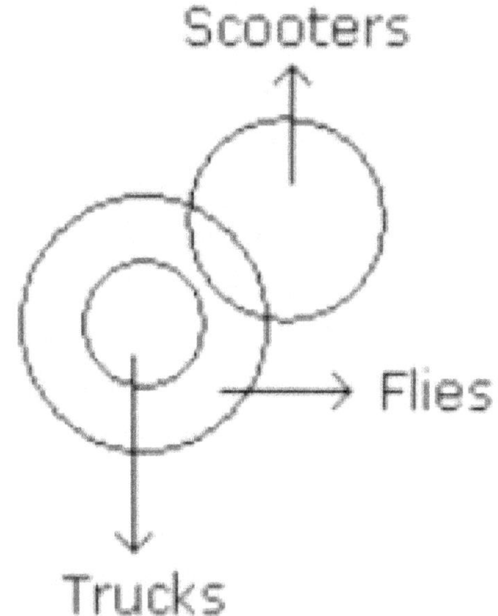

Conclusions:

I. All the trucks are scooters - False (It is true in possibility but not in definite case)

II. Some scooters are trucks - False (It is true in possibility but not in definite case)

Hence, the correct option is (D).

9. The relation between the numbers are:

$8 - 7 = 1$

$\Rightarrow 1 + 5 = 6$

$4 - 7 = -3$

$\Rightarrow -3 + 5 = 2$

$13 - 6 = 7$

$\Rightarrow 7 + 5 = 12$

Thus,

$18 - 9 = 9$

$\Rightarrow 9 + 5 = 14$

Hence, the correct option is (C).

10. We rewrite the conditions using inequalities and try to find a relationship between the people

1. Amit > Brian

2. Brian < Chirag

3. Dylan < Amit

4. Dylan > Chirag

Rewriting them, we get,

Amit > Dylan > Chirag > Brian

Thus, from the above inequalities, we get that Brian is the shortest.

Hence, the correct option is (A).

11. Since a huge truck overturned on the middle of the road last night, so, the police had cordoned off the entire area in the locality last morning for half of the day.

Hence, the correct option is (A).

12. As the awareness about health in the society is increasing particularly among middle-aged group of people, the importance of Yoga and exercise is being realized by all sections of the society.

Hence, the correct option is (B).

13. As statement is given: "Steel Authority Of India Limited Company has moved India from a position of shortage to self-sufficiency in the metal."

Hence, we can conclude that previously India had shortage of steel, and previously India had to import steel.

But nothing in the statement gives us the knowledge that in future India might become a foreign exchange earner, hence, conclusion II does not follow.

Hence, the correct option is (A).

14. The given statement tells about the requirement of good orators which does not exclusively say that good orators are jobless or not. Therefore conclusion I is not logical.

Conclusion II follows the statement because in the statement it is given that if you are a good orator then we definitely have job for you. From this it is clear that we are in need of a good orator.

Hence, the correct option is (B).

15. If an extra tax is imposed on the vehicles arriving at the hill station then the number of vehicles will decrease causing a reduction in the pollution level. Hence assumption I is implicit. But there is no information provided in the statement regarding the lack of facilities for tourists in the hill station. Hence, assumption II is not implicit.

Hence, the correct option is (A).

16. The statement talks of the number of cases of food poisoning due to consumption of fish and not of the number of people consuming fish So, I is not implicit. Food poisoning is a direct result of consuming contaminated material which in this case is fish so fish is contaminated either due to bad storage or due to pollutants consumed by fish. Hence, assumption II is implicit.

Hence, the correct option is (B).

17. India will be in danger of invasion by neighboring countries who possess atom bombs, long-range missiles, etc., if it signs the Comprehensive Test Ban Treaty (CTBT). There is no tension in the Asian sub-continent due to CTBT.

Hence, the correct option is (A).

18. Argument I says that we are totally dependent on Chinese product and it affects the market of Indian handmade products. But the prices of Chinese product are cheaper as compared to

Indian products, so poor people and middle-class people can easily afford them. A total ban is not the solution and we should try to increase the production and market of Indian products.

Hence, the correct option is (D).

19. Below table shows symbols and their description,

Symbol in Diagram	Meaning
◯	Female
▢	Male
═══	Married Couple
───	Siblings
│	Difference of A Generation

1) Ananya is the mother of Satya and Stephen is the son of Bhima.

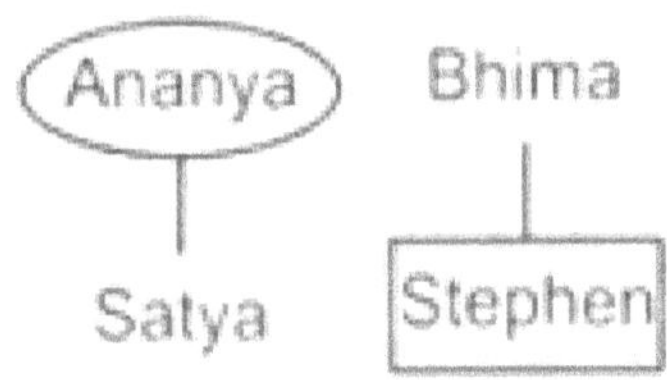

2) Ernest is the brother of Ananya.

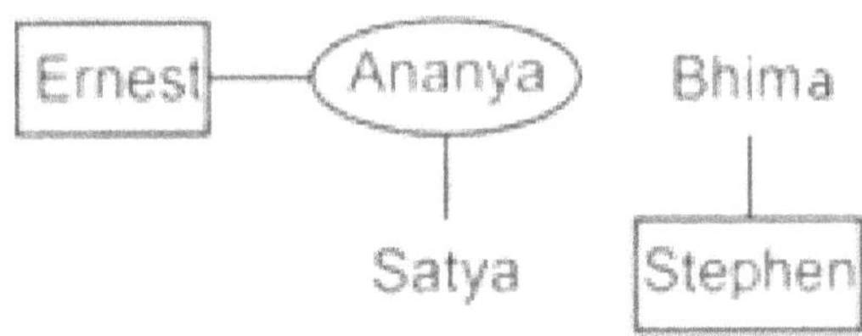

3) If Satya is the sister of Stephen, Ananya is the spouse of Bhima.

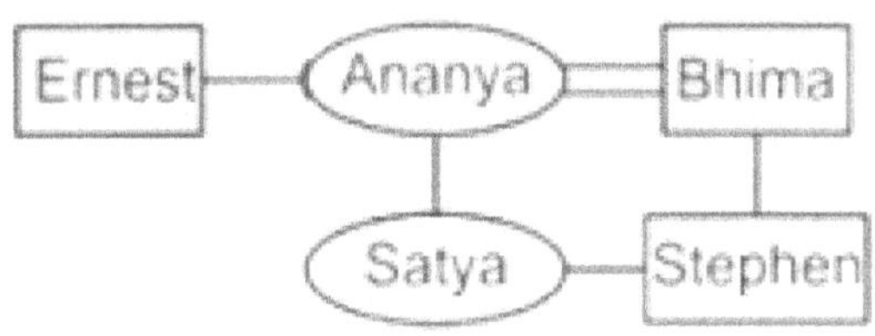

Thus, Bhima is Ernest's brother in law.

Hence, the correct option is (D).

20. Table is drawn describing symbols and their meanings:

Symbol in Diagram	Meaning
◯	Female
▢	Male
═══	Married Couple
───	Siblings
│	Difference of A Generation

Sumit's grandfather's brother is the father of Hemant's father.

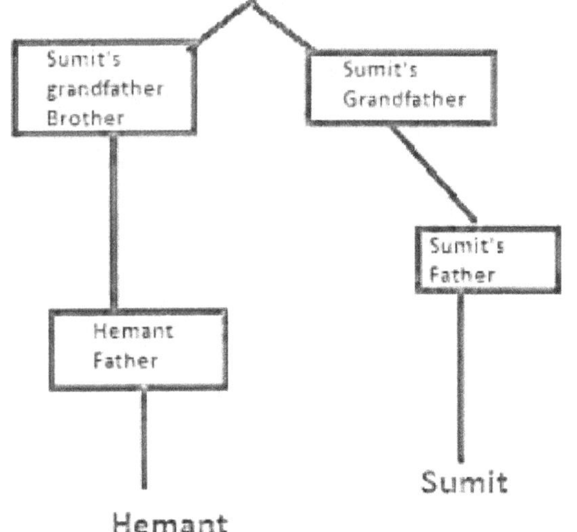

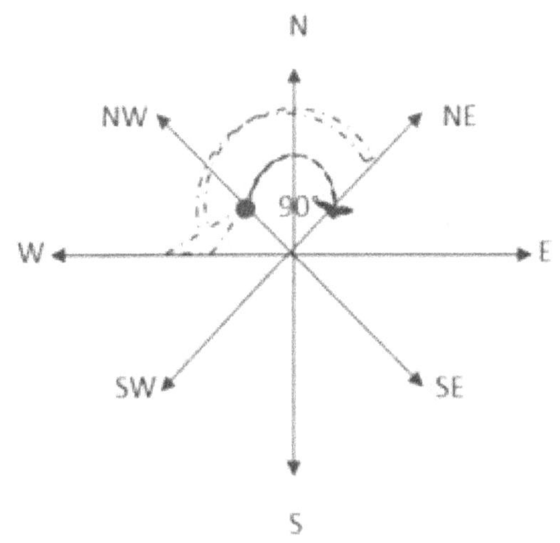

Thus, Sumit is Cousin of Hemant.

Hence, the correct option is (B).

21. There is 90° angle between NW and NE and 135° angle between NE and W. So final direction will be West.

Hence, the correct option is (B).

22.

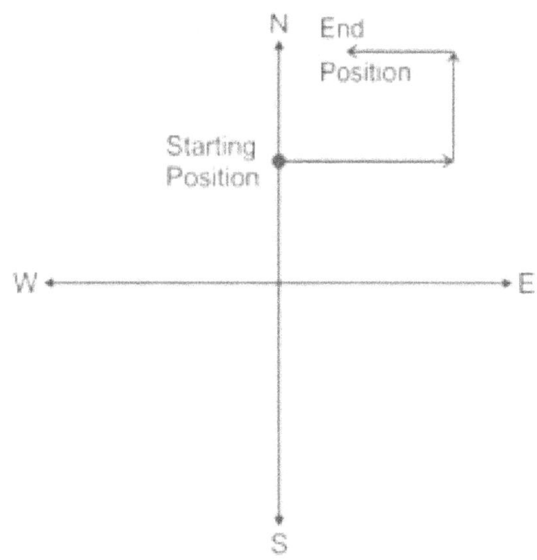

Hence, the correct option is (B).

23. Rupee is currency of India.

Similarly, Rand is currency of South Africa.

Hence, the correct option is (B).

24. As Ornithologist is a specialist of Birds, similarly Archeologist is the specialist of History.

Hence, the correct option is (B).

25. The pattern followed is:

Pair of numbers are square of consecutive numbers.

$5^2 = 25$ and $6^2 = 36$

$12^2 = 144$ and $13^2 = 169$

$10^2 = 100$ and $11^2 = 121$

But in option 9, 64

$3^2 = 9$ and $8^2 = 64$ which is different from others.

Hence, the correct option is (D).

Q.1 In the following question, choose the correct code form.

If, in a language, 'one' is called 'two', 'two' is called 'three', 'three' is called 'four', 'four' is called 'five', and 'five' is called 'six'.

Then what is the square of number 2?

A. Three   **B.** Four   **C.** Five   **D.** Six

Q.2 If 'dog' is called 'lion', 'lion' is called 'bison', 'bison' is called 'snake', 'snake' is called 'mongoose', 'mongoose' is called 'crocodile', then which one is reared as pet?

A. Lion   **B.** Bison

C. Snake   **D.** Mongoose

Q.3 Direction: Read the following information to answer the given question.

- Five brothers are standing in a row facing North.

- Tony is not adjacent to Bony or Mony. Sony is not adjacent to Bony. Tony is adjacent to Dony. Dony is at the middle in the row.

Then, which pair is at the extreme ends?

A. Tony, Dony   **B.** Dony, Bony

C. Sony, Mony   **D.** Mony, Tony

Q.4 Direction: In the following question below some statements are given followed by some conclusions. Taking the given statements to be true even if they seem to be at variance from commonly known facts, read all the conclusions and then decide which of the given conclusions logically follows the given statements.

Statement: Some ants are parrots. All the parrots are apples.

Conclusion:

1. All the apples are parrots.

2. Some ants are apples.

A. Only (1) conclusion follows

B. Only (2) conclusion follows

C. Either (1) or (2) follows

D. Neither (1) nor (2) follows

Q.5 Direction: In the following question below some statements are given followed by some conclusions. Taking the given statements to be true even if they seem to be at variance from commonly known facts, read all the conclusions and then decide which of the given conclusions logically follows the given statements.

Statement: All the windows are doors. No door is a wall.

Conclusion:

1. Some windows are walls.

2. No wall is a door.

A. Only (1) conclusion follows

B. Only (2) conclusion follows

C. Either (1) or (2) follows

D. Neither (1) nor (2) follows

Q.6 Direction: In the following question below some statements are given followed by some conclusions. Taking the given statements to be true even if they seem to be at variance from commonly known facts, read all the conclusions and then decide which of the given conclusions logically follows the given statements.

Statement: Some cows are crows. Some crows are elephants.

Conclusion:

1. Some cows are elephants.

2. All crows are elephants.

A. Only (1) conclusion follows

B. Only (2) conclusion follows

C. Either (1) or (2) follows

D. Neither (1) nor (2) follows

Q.7 Which one of the following venn diagrams correctly illustrates the relationship among the classes: Carrot, Food, Vegetable?

A.
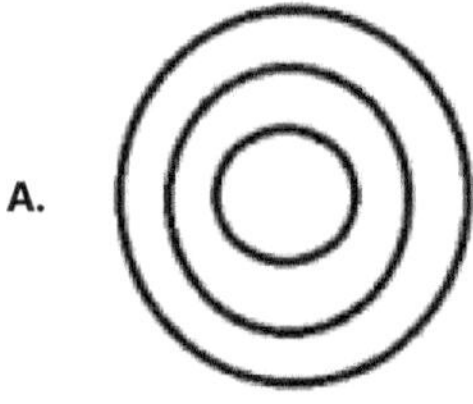

B.

C.

D.
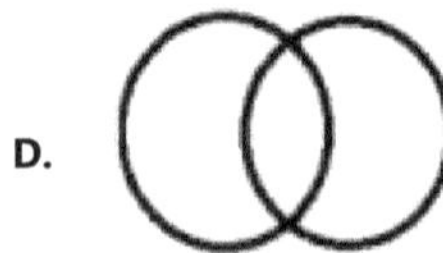

Q.8 Direction: Based upon the items given, logically draw the venn diagrams according to the relation between them.

Men, Authors, Teachers:

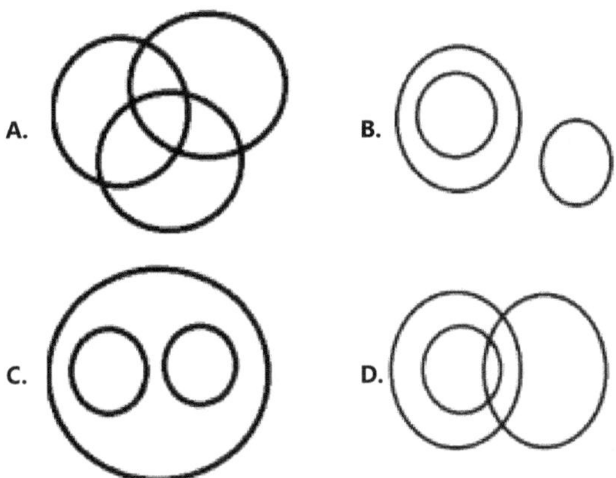

Q.9 Direction: Based upon the items given, logically draw the venn diagrams according to the relation between them.

Sparrows, Birds, Mice:

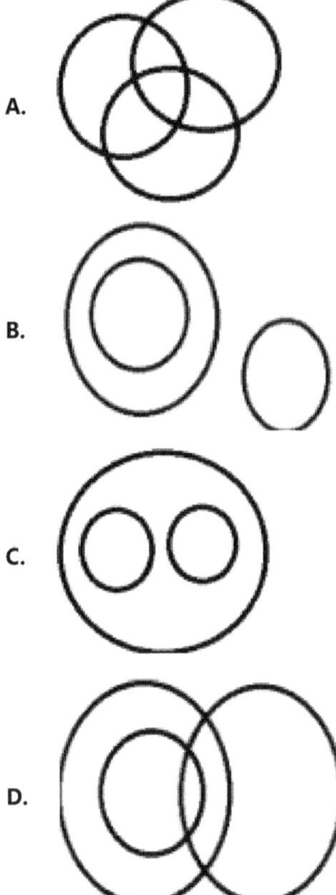

A.

B.

C.

D.

Q.10 Direction: Read the given information carefully and answer the related question.

8 friends, Anu, Beni, Carrie, Dolly, Isha, Freight, Gibran, and Harry went together to see the film and sitting facing north, sitting in an eight-seat line (not necessarily in this order).

i) Gibran who is at the left end is seated on the sixth seat from the left of Freight.

ii) Carrie and Anu sit beside each other but they were not neighbors of Gibran and freight. Two people are sitting between Anu and Freight.

iii) Carrie is sitting on the immediate right side of Isha.

iv) Harry sitting next to Dolly and sitting on the second seat from the right side of Anu.

Who sits between Gibran and Carrie?

A. Anu   **B.** Dolly   **C.** Isha   **D.** Harry

Q.11 John, Rohit, Pranish, Siva, Vinith and Naren are sitting in row but not necessarily in the same order. Rohit and John are sitting at the extreme ends. Pranish sits next to Siva. There are two persons in between Siva and John. Vinith sits immediate left of John and Pranish sits third to the left of Vinith. If the arrangement is reversed who sits second to the right of Siva?

A. Naren   **B.** Vinith   **C.** Pranish   **D.** Rohit

Q.12 Six persons Saif, Alia, Ileana, Varun, Kareena and Ranveer are sitting around the circular table(not necessarily in same order). Saif sits second to the right of Ranveer. Kareena sits opposite to Alia but not adjacent to Saif. Varun is not adjacent to Saif. Who sits second to the left of Varun?

A. Kareena   **B.** Saif   **C.** Ilean   **D.** Ranveer

Q.13 Direction: Complete the following series by filling in the question mark?

7, 9, 8, 6, 10, 9, 5, 11, 10, ? ,12-

A. 4   **B.** 11   **C.** 56   **D.** 5

Q.14 Direction: Complete the following series by filling in the question mark?

1, 3, 2, 6, 3, 11, 4, 18, 5, ?-

A. 27   **B.** 25   **C.** 23   **D.** 29

Q.15 Direction: Complete the following series by filling in the question mark?

17, 16, 14, 12, 11, 8, 8, ?-

A. 4   **B.** 7   **C.** 3   **D.** 2

Q.16 If A is the brother of B; B is the sister of C; and C is the father of D, how D is related to A?

A. Brother
B. Sister
C. Nephew
D. Cannot be determined

Q.17 A is son of C while C and Q are the sisters to one another. Z is the mother of Q. If P is the son of Z, Which one of the following statements is correct?

A. Q is the grandfather of A
B. P is the maternal uncle of A
C. P is the cousin of A
D. Z is the brother of C

Q.18 Direction: Answer the question mark according to the analogy given:

Float : Sink :: Boat : ?

A. Ship   **B.** War
C. Submarine   **D.** Missile

Q.19 Direction: Answer the question mark according to the analogy given:

Interest : Moneylender :: Salary: ?

A. Employees   **B.** Zamindar

C. Workers   **D.** Prisoners

Q.20 Direction: Two statements I and II are given. These statement may be either independent causes or may be effects of independent causes or a common cause. One of these statements may be the effect of the other statements. Read both the statements and decide which of the following answer choice correctly depicts the relationship between these two statements.

Mark answer:

I. The Central Government has recently declared to finish the rebate on farming.

II. The Central Government faced financial loss on account of giving rebate on farming for the last few years.

A. If statement I is the cause and statement II is its effect.

B. If statement II is the cause and statement I is its effect.

C. If both the statements I and II are independent causes.

D. If both the statements I and II are effects of independent causes.

Q.21 Direction: Two statements I and II are given. These statement may be either independent causes or may be effects of independent causes or a common cause. One of these statements may be the effect of the other statements. Read both the statements and decide which of the following answer choice correctly depicts the relationship between these two statements.

Mark answer:

I. Many people visited the religious place during weekend.

II. Few people visited the religious place during the week days.

A. If statement I is the cause and statement II is its effect.

B. If statement II is the cause and statement I is its effect.

C. If both the statements I and II are effects of independent causes.

D. If both the statement I and II are effects of some common cause.

Q.22 Direction: In the following question statement is given followed by argument. Answer according to arguments given in options.

Statement: Should all the drugs patented and manufactured in Western countries be first tried out on sample basis before giving licence for sale to general public in India?

Argument:

I. Yes. Many such drugs require different doses and duration for Indian population and hence it is necessary.

II. No. This is just not feasible and hence cannot be implemented.

A. Only argument I is strong

B. Only argument II is strong

C. Either I or II is strong

D. Neither I nor II is strong

Q.23 Direction: In the following question statement is given followed by an argument. The answer according to arguments given in options.

Statement: Should there be students union in college/university?

Argument:

I. No. This will create a political atmosphere in the campus.

II. Yes, it is very necessary Students are future political leaders.

A. Only argument I is strong

B. Only argument II is strong

C. Either I or II is strong

D. Both I and II are strong

Q.24 Direction: In each question below is given one/more statements that followed by two assumptions numbered I and II. Consider the statement and decide which of the given assumptions is implicit.

Statement:

a) Sunita to Sahil, "Don't you have a presentation to make".

b) Sahil to Sunita, "Why hurry? I will do it tomorrow".

c) Sunita to Sahil," You have been saying the same thing for past five days".

Assumption:

I. Sahil is a procrastinator.

II. Sahil has been very busy in the last few days.

A. Only assumption I is implicit.

B. Only assumption II is implicit.

C. If either assumption I or II is implicit.

D. If neither I nor II is implicit.

Q.25 Direction: A statement is given followed by two inferences I and II. You have to consider the statement to be true even if it seems to be at variance from commonly known facts. You have to decide which of the given inferences, if any, follow from the given statement.

Statement: My mother always cooks her special curry when guests visit us.

Assumption:

I: Her curry is very impressive.

II: She is a hospitable woman

A. Only assumption I is implicit

B. Only assumption II is implicit

C. Both assumption I and II are implicit

D. None of the assumptions are implicit

// Smart Answer Sheet //

Correct Percentage of students who answered correctly. **Skipped** Percentage of students who skipped.

Q.	Ans.	Correct / Skipped
1	C	53.12 % / 1.57 %
2	A	65.62 % / 10.94 %
3	C	61.72 % / 8.59 %
4	B	57.03 % / 10.94 %
5	B	57.81 % / 15.63 %

Q.	Ans.	Correct / Skipped
6	D	46.88 % / 10.93 %
7	A	63.28 % / 10.94 %
8	A	46.09 % / 10.16 %
9	B	73.44 % / 12.5 %
10	C	51.56 % / 10.94 %

Q.	Ans.	Correct / Skipped
11	D	45.31 % / 10.16 %
12	C	46.88 % / 10.15 %
13	A	48.44 % / 7.03 %
14	A	53.91 % / 10.93 %
15	A	39.84 % / 11.72 %

Q.	Ans.	Correct / Skipped
16	D	27.34 % / 7.82 %
17	B	63.28 % / 14.84 %
18	C	67.19 % / 10.93 %
19	A	82.81 % / 8.6 %
20	B	58.59 % / 7.82 %

Q.	Ans.	Correct / Skipped
21	D	34.38 % / 10.15 %
22	A	55.47 % / 10.94 %
23	D	22.66 % / 8.59 %
24	A	46.88 % / 10.93 %
25	C	43.75 % / 14.06 %

//Hints and Solutions//

1. The square of 2 is 4 or four.

But four is called five in the statement given in the question, therefore the answer is Five.

Hence, the correct option is (C).

2. Generally, the dog is reared as a pet.

But the dog is called a lion in the statement, so 'lion' is reared as pet.

Hence, the correct option is (A).

3. If a person is facing North, then "Your left and right" will be the same as the "Person facing North"

Dony is the middle i.e. ____, ____, Dony, ____, ____

Tony is adjacent to Dony i.e. ____, Tony, Dony ___, _____.

Tony is not adjacent to Bony or Mony i.e.

____, Tony, Dony, Bony, Mony.

So, the sequence becomes - Sony, Tony, Dony, Bony, Mony.

Hence, the correct option is (C).

4. We logically, draw the following Venn diagrams,

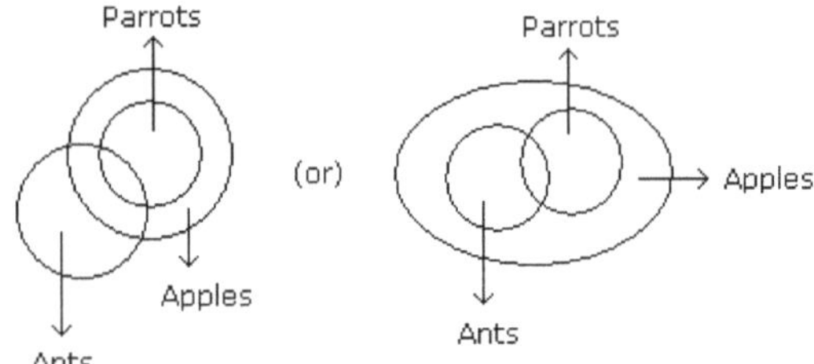

From above, we conclude only (2) follows.

Hence, the correct option is (B).

5. We logically draw the following diagrams,

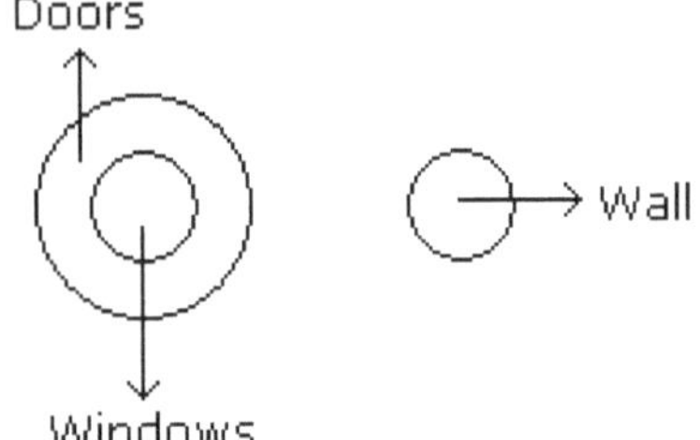

From, above we conclude only (2) follows.

Hence, the correct option is (B).

6. We logically draw the following diagrams,

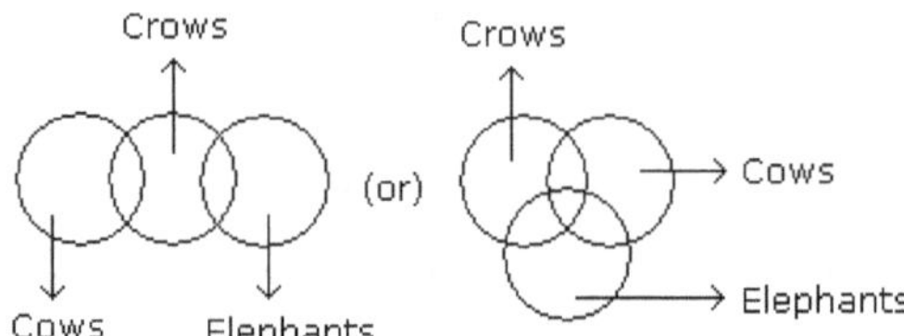

From, above we conclude, neither (1) nor (2) follows.

Hence, the correct option is (D).

7. All carrots are vegetables. All vegetables are foods.

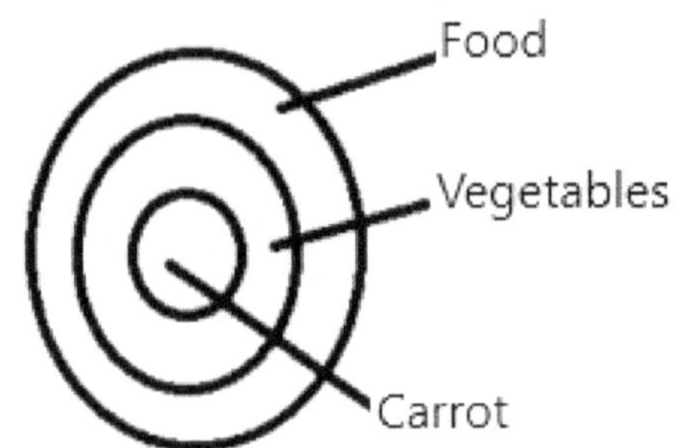

Hence, the correct option is (A).

8. Some authors can be teachers. Some teachers can be men. Some authors can be men. So, the given items are partly related to each other.

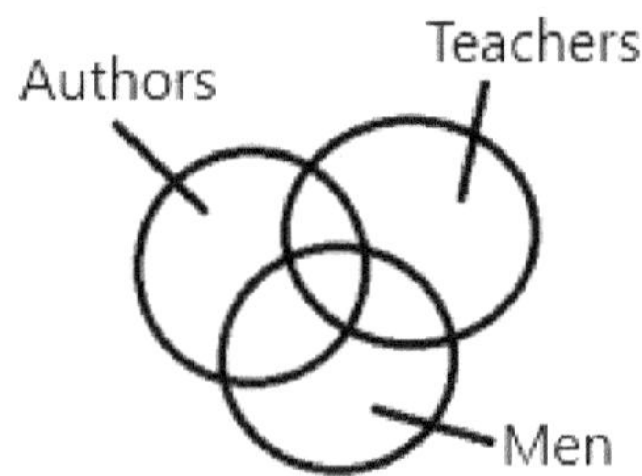

Hence, the correct option is (A).

9. All sparrows are birds. But, mice is entirely different.

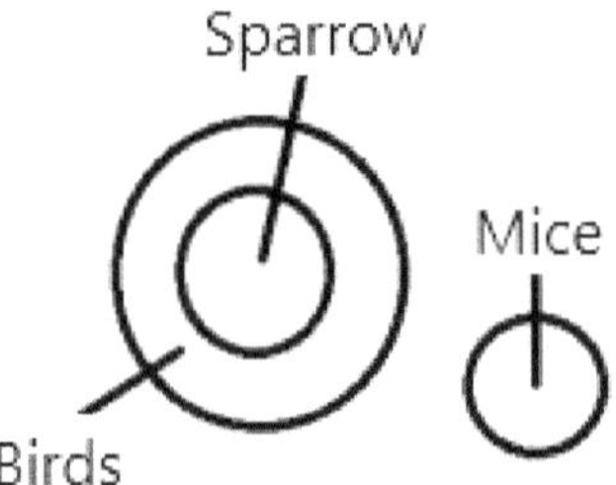

Hence, the correct option is (B).

10. The arrangement will be as shown below:

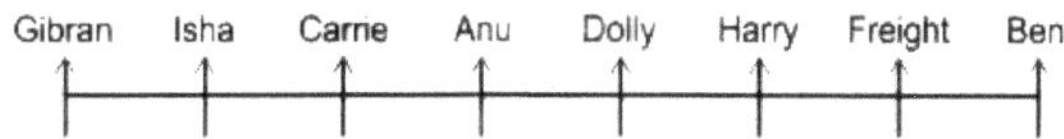

Thus, 'Isha' sits between Gibran and Carrie.

Hence, the correct option is (C).

11. 1) Six persons: John, Rohit, Pranish, Siva, Vinith and Naren

2) Rohit and John are sitting at the extreme ends.

3) There are two persons in between Siva and John.

Diagram

4) Vinith sits immediate left of John and pranish sits third to the left of Vinith.

5) Pranish sits next to Siva.

6) Therefore, the final arrangement is as follows:

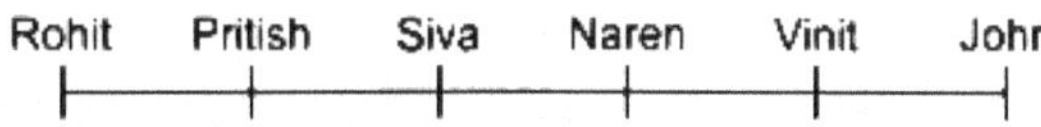

7) If the arrangement is reversed:

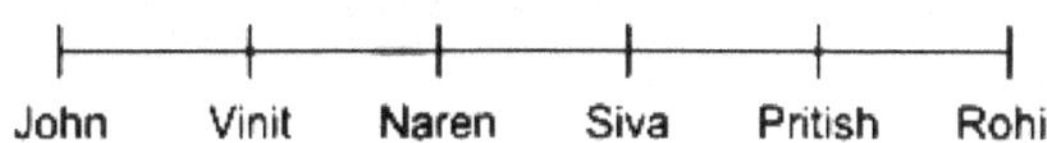

Hence, the correct option is (D).

12. Persons: Saif, Alia, Ileana, Varun, Kareena and Ranveer.

1. Saif sits second to the right of Ranveer. (as nothing is mention about direction then we can assume they are facing inside)

2. Kareena sits opposite to Alia but not adjacent to Saif.

3. Varun is not adjacent to Saif

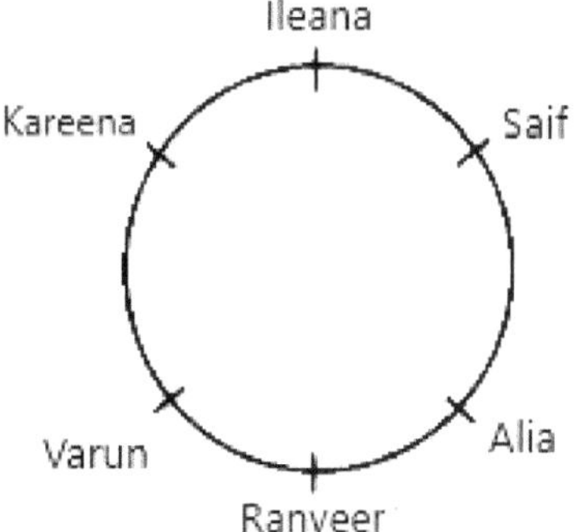

Therefore, Ileana sits second to the left of Varun.

Hence, the correct option is (C).

13. There are three parallel series going on in this question. The 1st, 4th, 7th terms are using logic of -1, 2nd, 5th and 8th terms are using logic of +1 and 3rd, 6th and 9th terms are using logic of +1 again. Answer will be 4, which belongs to 1st, 4th and 7th term.

Hence, the correct option is (A).

14. By following the figure we get,

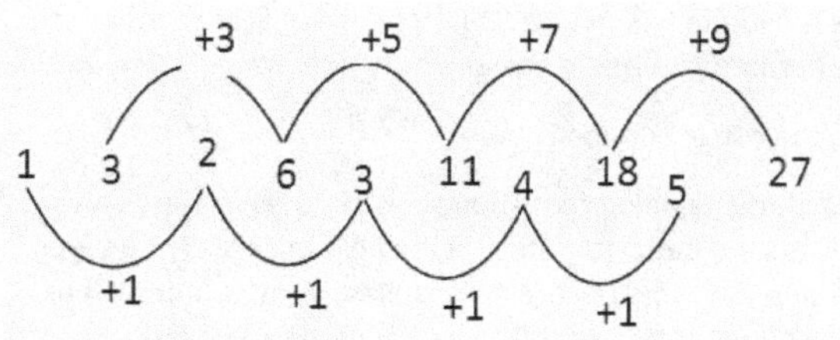

Hence, the correct option is (A).

15. There are two series:

Ist : 17 14 11 8 and 2nd: 16 12 8 ?

In first series, -3 , -3 ,-3..... and in 2nd series , -4 , -4 ,-4....

Therefore, next term will be 8 – 4 = 4.

Hence, the correct option is (A).

16. If D is Male, the answer is Nephew.

If D is Female, the answer is Niece.

As the sex of D is not known, hence, the relation between D and A cannot be determined.

Note: Niece - A daughter of one's brother or sister, or of one's brother-in-law or sister-in-law. Nephew - A son of one's brother or sister, or of one's brother-in-law or sister-in-law.

Hence, the correct option is (D).

17. Since, C and Q are sisters to one another and A is the son of C. Hence, C is the mother of A, therefore, Z is maternal grandmother of A. As P is the son of Z. Therefore, P is the maternal uncle of A.

Hence, the correct option is (B).

18. Float means above water and sink means under water. In same way, Boat floats on water and submarine moves under water.

Hence, the correct option is (C).

19. Interest is given to money lender and salary is given to employees.

Mind it wages are given to Workers.

Hence, the correct option is (A).

20. As the Central Government faced financial loss on accounts of giving rebate on farming for the last few years, therefore, they declared to finish the rebate on farming. Therefore, II is the cause while I is the effect.

Hence, the correct option is (B).

21. Clearly, lesser number of people is visiting a place during the week days and more people are visiting during the weekend, both imply events that go together, and must have happened due to a common cause such as, it being a holiday during the weekend.

Hence, the correct option is (D).

22. Clearly, health of the citizens is an issue of major concern for the Government. So, a product like drugs, must be first studied

and tested in the Indian context before giving licence for its sale. So, only argument I holds strong.

Hence, the correct option is (A).

23. The students union formation shall be a step towards giving to students the basic education in the field of politics. However, it shall create the same political atmosphere in the campus. Thus, both the arguments hold strong.

Hence, the correct option is (D).

24. Since Sahil has been stalling his work, this makes him a procrastinator. It is not possible to assume from statement that Sahil was busy or not in the past few days. Therefore, only assumption I is implicit is correct.

Hence, the correct option is (A).

25. The curry is special, according to the statement. So the curry must be very good or impressive. Also, it is cooked when guests visit. This means that the mother is a very hospitable woman. Therefore both the assumptions are implicit and the most suitable option is (C).

Hence, the correct option is (C).

Q.1 Direction: In the following question, choose the correct alternative from the given ones that will complete the series.

27, 64, 125, 216, ?, 512

A. 289   **B.** 343   **C.** 390   **D.** 400

Q.2 Direction: In the following question, choose the correct alternative from the given ones that will complete the series.

8, 18, 32, 50, 72, ?

A. 98   **B.** 80   **C.** 70   **D.** 76

Q.3 If in a certain code, 'bir le nac' means 'green and tasty';

'pic nac hor' means 'tomato is green' and

'coc bir hor' means 'food is tasty'.

Which of the following means 'tomato is tasty' in that code?

A. bir le hor   **B.** pic hor nac

C. hor bir pic   **D.** None of these

Q.4 If the alphabets A to Z represent each other in the reverse order i.e A = Z, B = Y, C = X etc., then how TOUR would be written?

A. GLIF   **B.** GLFI

C. GILF   **D.** None of these

Q.5 Direction: Identify the diagram that best represents the relationship among the classes given below:

Liquid, Milk, River's Water

A.

B.

C.

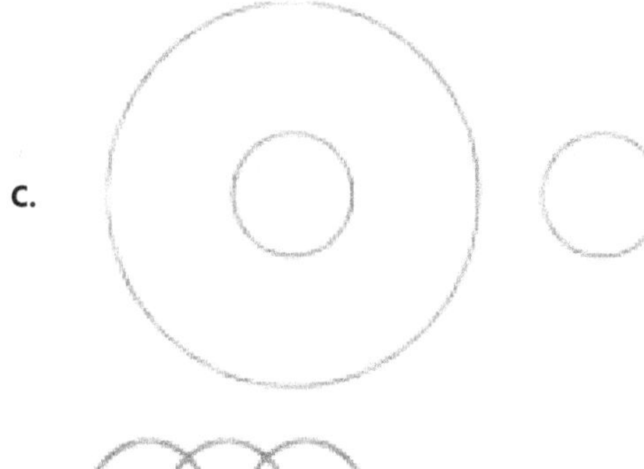

D.

Q.6 The following diagram represents people who speak different languages.

(i) Kannada

(ii) English

(iii) Hindi

(iv) Marathi

What does the shaded area include?

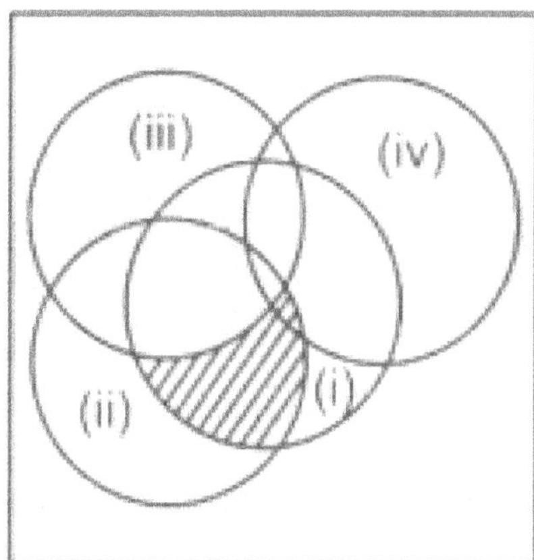

A. People who speak Kannada and English

B. People who speak English and Hindi

C. People who speak Kannada, English and Hindi

D. People who speak Kannada, English and Marathi

Ques (7-8):Direction: In the following question statements are given and these statements are followed by conclusions. You have to take the given statements to be true even if they seem to be at variance from commonly known facts. Read the conclusions and then decide which of the given conclusions logically follows from the given statements, disregarding commonly known facts.

Q.7 Statement:

I. No key is door.

II. All doors are pens.

III. Some pens are houses.

Conclusion:

I. No key is house.

II. Some pens are doors.

A. Only I follows

B. Only II follows

C. Either I or II follows

D. Only I and II follows

Q.8 Statement:

I. All fruits are lions.

II. All lions are foxes.

III. Some foxes are beggars.

Conclusion:

I. All fruits are foxes.

II. Some fruits are beggars.

A. Only I follows

B. Only II follows

C. Either I or II follows

D. Both I and II follow

Q.9 If 14 % 32 = 46, 52 % 20 = 72 then what is the value of 35 % 14?

A. 39 **B.** 29 **C.** 19 **D.** 49

Q.10 B is twice as old as A but twice younger than F. C is half the age of A but is twice older than D. Who is the second oldest?

A. B **B.** F **C.** C **D.** D

Ques (11-12):Direction: In the question are given two statements I and II. These statements may be either independent causes or may be effects of independent causes or a common cause. One of these statements may be the effect of the other statements. Read both the statements and decide which of the following answer choice correctly depicts the relationship between these two statements.

Q.11 Statements:

I. There was a huge rush of people to the temple last Sunday the 15th of the month.

II. The temple authority had decided to close down the temple for repairs from 17th of the month.

A. Statement I is the cause and statement II is its effect

B. Statement II is the cause and statement I is its effect

C. Both the statements I and II are independent causes

D. Both the statements I and II are effects of independent causes

Q.12 Statements:

I. The Reserve Bank of India has recently put restrictions on few small banks in the country.

II. The small banks in the private and co-operative sector in India are not in a position to withstand the competition of the bigger banks in the public sector.

A. Statement I is the cause and statement II is its effect

B. Statement II is the cause and statement I is its effect

C. Both the statements I and II are independent causes

D. Both the statements I and II are effects of independent causes

Ques (13-14):Direction: In the question below is a statement followed by two conclusions numbered I and II. You have to assume everything in the statement to be true, then consider the two conclusions together and decide which of them logically follows beyond a reasonable doubt from the information given in the statement.

Q.13 Statement:

Only science students are permitted to attend the conference, other than science students no one is permitted.

Conclusions:

I. All students present at the conference are science students.

II. Those who do not have a science background are not allowed in the conference.

A. If only conclusion I follows

B. If only conclusion II follows

C. If neither I nor II follows

D. If both I and II follow

Q.14 Statements:

1. Depleting natural resources is a major concern in our country.

2. Unless we go for renewable energy sources in a big way, increase in population being a heavy burden on the energy resources, will reduce the quality of life.

Conclusions:

I. Depleting resources impacts quality of life.

II. Use of renewable energy sources is a solution to counter increase in population.

A. Only conclusion I follows

B. Only conclusion II follows

C. Both I and II follow

D. Neither I nor II follows

Q.15 Direction: In the question below is given a statement followed by two assumptions numbered I and II. You have to consider the statement and the following assumptions and decide which of the assumptions is implicit in the statement.

Statement:

A's advice to B - 'If you want to study accounts, join Institute Y'.

Assumptions:

I. A believes that institute Y provides a good accounts education.

II. B will listen to A's advice.

A. Only assumption I is implicit

B. Only assumption II is implicit

C. Neither I nor II is implicit

D. Both I and II are implicit

Q.16 Which of the following assumptions follow?

Statement:

Is 'Maruti Car' twice as fuel efficient as an ordinary car?

Assumption:

I: A large number of people use 'Maruti Car'.

II: The sale of 'Maruti Car' has increased.

A. Only assumption I follow

B. Only assumption II follow

C. Both assumption I and II follow

D. Both assumption I and II don't follow

Ques (17-18):Directions: The question given below is followed by two arguments numbered I and II. You have to decide which of the argument is a strong argument and which is a weak argument.

Q.17 Statement:

Should the retirement age for the employees be reduced to 56 years?

Arguments:

I. Yes. It will provide employment opportunities for many unemployed people.

II. Yes. It will provide good output because the average age of an employee is reduced.

A. Only I is strong

B. Only II is strong

C. Either I or II is strong

D. Both I and II are strong

Q.18 Statement:

Should a total ban be put on trapping wild animals?

Arguments:

I. Yes, trappers are making a lot of money.

II. No, bans on hunting and trapping are not effective.

A. Only I is strong

B. Only II is strong

C. Neither I nor II is strong

D. Both I and II are strong

Q.19 Deepak has a brother Anil. Deepak Is the son of Prem. Vimal is Prem's father. How is Anil related to Vimal?

A. Son

B. Grandson

C. Brother

D. Grandfather

Q.20 Karan has a brother 'Prem' and a sister 'Neesha'. Karan's wife is 'Naj' and has a daughter 'Naksha'. Naksha got married with Neesha's son Akbar and has a baby girl 'Riya'. What is relation between 'Naksha' and 'Neesha'?

A. Sisters

B. Niece and Aunt

C. Mother and grand daughter

D. Mother and daughter

Q.21 One morning Sita started to walk towards the Sun. After covering some distance she turned to right then again to the right and after covering some distance she again turns to the right. Now in which direction is she facing?

A. North

B. East

C. North-East

D. South-East

Q.22 B is South-West of A, C is to the East of B and South-East of A and D is to the North of C in line with B and A. In which direction of A is D located?

A. North

B. East

C. South-West

D. North-East

Q.23 Directions: In the question below select the related number from the given alternative.

$$\frac{1}{9} : \frac{1}{81} :: \frac{1}{13} : ?$$

A. $\frac{1}{169}$

B. $\frac{1}{125}$

C. $\frac{1}{120}$

D. $\frac{1}{127}$

Q.24 Direction: Select the related word from the given alternatives.

Shell : Coconut : : Envelope : ?

A. Letter-box

B. Letter

C. E- Mail

D. Stamp

Q.25 Four of the following form are alike and form a group. Which is the one that does not belong to the group?

A. Banana

B. Mango

C. Apple

D. Rose

// Smart Answer Sheet //

Correct Percentage of students who answered correctly.   **Skipped** Percentage of students who skipped.

Q.	Ans.	Correct / Skipped
1	B	62.5 % / 3.41 %
2	A	70.45 % / 9.1 %
3	C	39.77 % / 10.23 %
4	B	77.27 % / 10.23 %
5	B	54.55 % / 13.63 %

Q.	Ans.	Correct / Skipped
6	D	55.68 % / 14.77 %
7	B	38.64 % / 10.22 %
8	A	44.32 % / 10.23 %
9	D	59.09 % / 12.5 %
10	A	50.0 % / 11.36 %

Q.	Ans.	Correct / Skipped
11	B	31.82 % / 14.77 %
12	B	30.68 % / 13.64 %
13	D	54.55 % / 11.36 %
14	A	30.68 % / 11.37 %
15	A	63.64 % / 10.22 %

Q.	Ans.	Correct / Skipped
16	D	35.23 % / 12.5 %
17	A	47.73 % / 10.22 %
18	C	47.73 % / 10.22 %
19	B	67.05 % / 12.5 %
20	B	70.45 % / 10.23 %

Q.	Ans.	Correct / Skipped
21	A	70.45 % / 10.23 %
22	D	38.64 % / 15.91 %
23	A	72.73 % / 13.63 %
24	B	71.59 % / 10.23 %
25	D	86.36 % / 10.23 %

//Hints and Solutions//

1. Here every number is a perfect cube of consecutive numbers starting from 3.

27 = 3 × 3 × 3

64 = 4 × 4 × 4

125 = 5 × 5 × 5

216 = 6 × 6 × 6

343 = 7 × 7 × 7

512 = 8 × 8 × 8

So, 343 is the missing number.

Hence, the correct option is (B).

2. 8 + **10**

⇒ 18

18 + (10 + 4)

⇒ 18 + **14**

⇒ 32

32 + (10 + 8)

⇒ 32 + **18**

⇒ 50

50 + (10 + 12)

⇒ 50 + **22**

⇒ 72

72 + (10 + 16)

⇒ 72 + **26**

⇒ 98

Hence, the correct option is (A).

3.

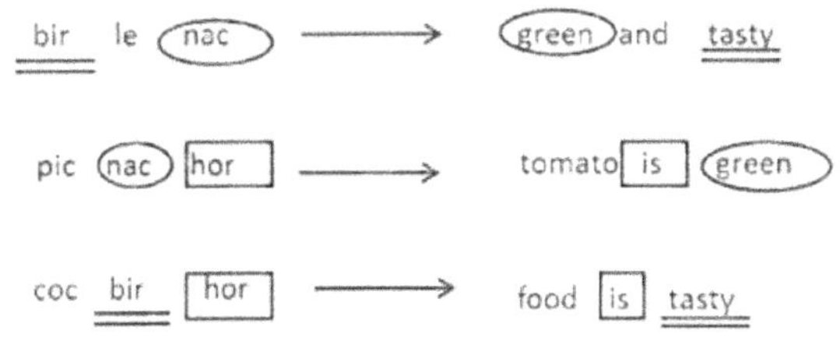

The code for "tomato" is "pic".

The code for "is" is "hor".

The code for "tasty" is "bir".

Hence, "tomato is tasty" can be coded as "hor bir pic".

Hence, the correct option is (C).

4.

Dictionary Order:

A B C D E F G H I J K L M N O P Q R S T U V W X Y Z

Z Y X W V U T S R Q P O N M L K J I H G F E D C B A

Reverse Dictonary Order

By this logic, T will be equal to G, O will give L, U will give F and R will give I.

So, 'TOUR' will be written as "GLFI".

Hence, the correct option is (B).

5. Both milk and Rivers Water are liquids.

So, the liquid should contain two items milk and river water which do not have anything common, so are separated by a distance.

Hence, the correct option is (B).

6.

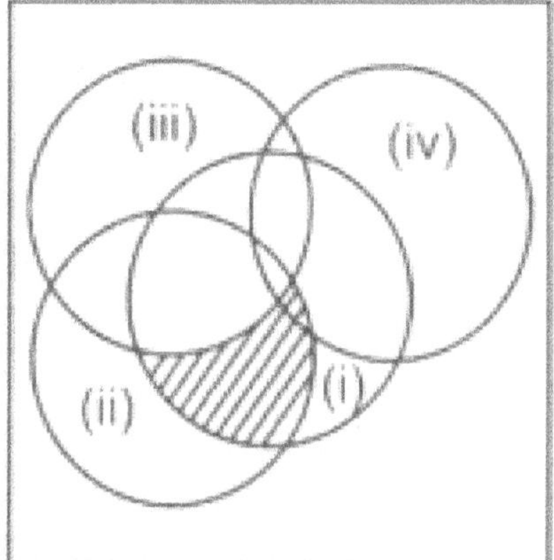

The shaded region includes some of the parts of (i), (ii) and (iv) but not (iii). So, this includes the people who speak Kannada, English and Marathi but not Hindi.

Hence, the correct option is (D).

7.

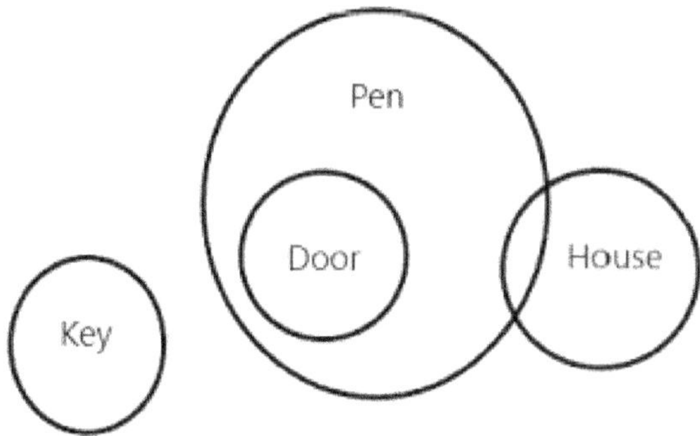

Hence, the correct option is (B).

8.

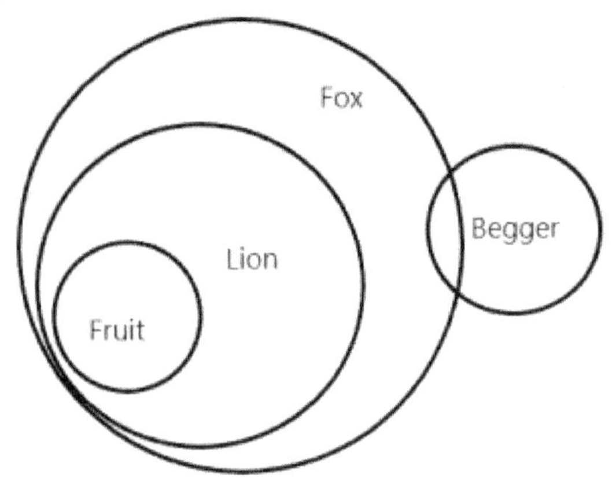

Hence, the correct option is (A).

9. The pattern is as follows:

Here the % sign represents the + sign

14 + 32 = 46,

52 + 20 = 72

Similarly,

35 + 14 = 49

Hence, the correct option is (D).

10. Let, A = x

Then, B = $2x$

and, F = $4x$

C = $\dfrac{x}{2}$

and D = $\dfrac{x}{4}$

So, by the given expression, it is clear that B is the second oldest.

Hence, the correct option is (A).

11. Since the temple authority had decided to close down the temple for repairs from 17th of the month, hence, there was a huge rush of people to the temple last Sunday the 15th of the month.

Hence, the correct option is (B).

12. As, the small banks in the private and co-operation sector in India are not in a position to withstand the competitions of the bigger banks in the public sector, therefore, the Reserve Bank of India has recently put restrictions on few small banks in the country.

Hence, the correct option is (B).

13. From the statement we can see that only science students are permitted to attend the conference. So, obviously, all the students present are of science background and also students who are not from science will not be permitted. Therefore, both conclusions I and II follow.

Hence, the correct option is (D).

14. 1. Depleting natural resources is a major concern in our country.

2. Unless we go for renewable energy sources in a big way, increase in population being a heavy burden on the energy resources, will reduce the quality of life.

The usage of renewable resources does not have any effect on the increasing population.

Hence, the correct option is (A).

15. It goes with reason to believe that A is giving the advice is because according to A the institute must be providing good tuition in accounts. Thus, assumption I is implicit.

There is no information provided in the statement that suggests that person A will listen to his friend's advice. Hence, assumption II is not implicit.

Hence, the correct option is (A).

16. Statement: Is 'Maruti Car' twice as fuel efficient as an ordinary car?

⇒ Here, a question is being asked which seeks to compare the fuel efficiency of 'Maruti Car' vis-à-vis an ordinary car. This question also asks if the fuel efficiency is double in a 'Maruti Car'.

Assumption I: A large number of people use 'Maruti Car'.

⇒ This assumption is not implicit as the number of people buying the 'Maruti Car' does not speak to its fuel efficiency, just to its popularity.

Assumption II: The sale of 'Maruti Car' has increased

⇒ This assumption is not implicit because the recent sales could be because of anything. There's data regarding sales of 'Maruti Car' not fuel efficiency of 'Maruti Car'. This is not enough to answer the question in the statement.

Hence, the correct option is (D).

17. Clearly, if the retirement age for the employee is reduced then it will create employment opportunity for many unemployed people. Argument II is not strong as the relationship between 'good output' and the 'average age of an employee' is not clear.

Hence, the correct option is (A).

18. The ban should be imposed not for the reason that trappers are making money, but for protecting our natural environment. Argument II is not strong as there is no information provided in favor of it. We cannot say that bans are not effective.

Hence, the correct option is (C).

19. 1) Deepak has a brother Anil.

2) Deepak is the son of Prem.

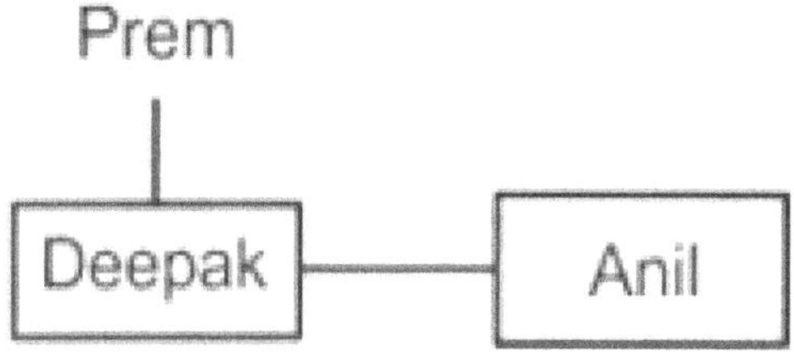

3) Vimal is Prem's father.

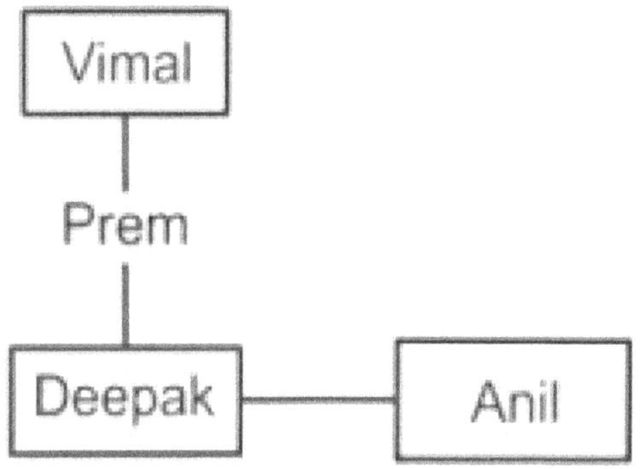

Anil is the grandson of Vimal.

Hence, the correct option is (B).

20. From given information above we can make family tree as shown below:

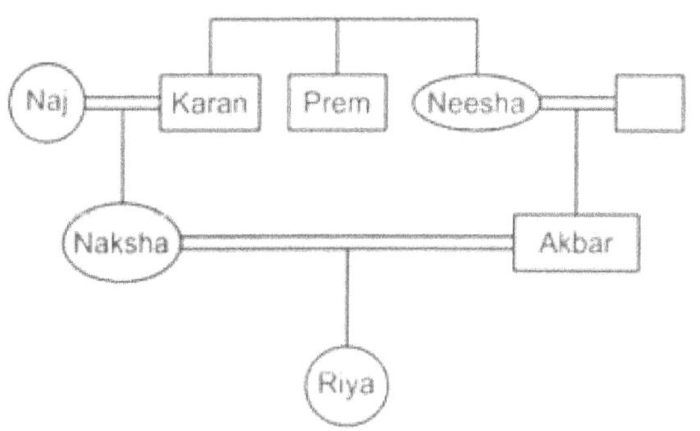

As we can see in above family diagram Neesha is Aunt of Naksha.

Thus, Niece and Aunt is relationship between Naksha and Neesha.

Hence, the correct option is (B).

21. At morning Sun is towards east.

The path followed by Sita is traced as followed,

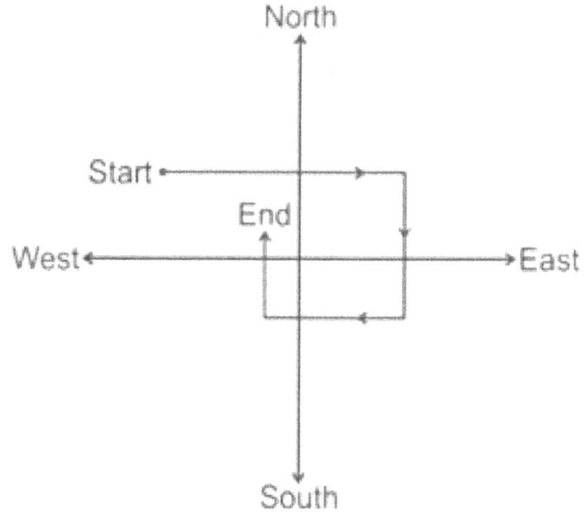

Clearly, Sita is facing towards the North.

Hence, the correct option is (A).

22.

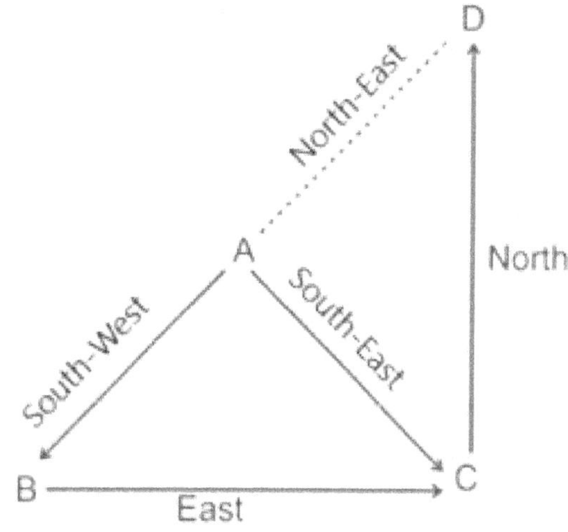

Clearly D is located towards North East of A.

Hence, the correct option is (D).

23. Consider the following relation:

$$\frac{1}{9} : \frac{1}{9 \times 9}$$

$$\Rightarrow \frac{1}{9} : \frac{1}{81}$$

Then following the same relation:

$$\frac{1}{13} : \frac{1}{13 \times 13}$$

$$\Rightarrow \frac{1}{13} : \frac{1}{169}$$

Hence, the correct option is (A).

24. First encloses the second one, the Envelope contains a letter, as a Shell contains a coconut.

Hence, the correct option is (B).

25. Banana, Mango, Apple are fruits. But Rose is not a fruit, it is a flower. So, Rose is the odd one out.

Hence, the correct option is (D).

Q.1 Crescograph was invented by:

A. S.N. Bose **B.** P.C. Roy

C. J.C. Bose **D.** P.C. Mahalanobis

Q.2 Satellite Mission - TRISHNA is for:

A. Eco-system stress and water use monitoring

B. Pesticide monitoring

C. Ecological balance monitoring

D. None of the above

Q.3 Niyamgiri hill is located in:

A. Odisha **B.** West Bengal

C. Punjab **D.** Kerala

Q.4 India is the largest producer and exporter of:

A. Cotton **B.** Copper **C.** Tea **D.** Mica

Q.5 The atomic power station in Rajasthan is situated at:

A. Pokhran **B.** Suratgarh

C. Rawatbhata **D.** Chittorgarh

Q.6 What is the prime target of the first five-year plan of India?

A. Development of the industries

B. Development of agriculture

C. Development of infrastructure

D. Development of ports

Q.7 The word 'Secular' was added in the Preamble to the Constitution of India by:

A. First Amendment Act

B. Seventh Amendment Act

C. Forty-Second Amendment Act

D. Forty-Fourth Amendment Act

Q.8 A Judge of the Supreme Court can be removed from his office on the grounds of:

A. Proved misbehavior or incapacity

B. Violation of the Constitution

C. Both (A) and (B)

D. None of the above

Q.9 The power of the President of India to issue an ordinance is a:

A. Legislative power

B. Executive power

C. Quasi-judicial power

D. Judicial power

Q.10 First Bank to introduce ATM in India is:

A. ICICI Bank **B.** HSBC Bank

C. HDFC Bank **D.** YES Bank

Q.11 When is the Golden Jubilee of Bank Nationalisation in India?

A. July 19, 2019 **B.** July 20, 2019

C. Aug 19, 2019 **D.** Aug 20, 2019

Q.12 In India, the first bank of limited liabilities managed by Indians and founded in 1881 was:

A. Hindustan Commercial Bank

B. Oudh Commercial Bank

C. Punjab National Bank

D. Punjab and Sind Bank

Q.13 How many banks were first nationalized?

A. 10 **B.** 12 **C.** 14 **D.** 16

Q.14 National Income of the country is also known as:

A. Gross National Product (GNP)

B. Gross Domestic Product (GDP)

C. Net National Product (NNP)

D. Net Domestic Product (NDP)

Q.15 Which statement is correct for nominal GDP?

i. Nominal GDP is calculated based on current prices.

ii. Nominal GDP is calculated based on the base prices.

iii. Data on Nominal GDP shows an accurate picture of the economy as compared to real GDP.

A. Only ii, iii **B.** Only ii

C. Only i **D.** Only i, iii

Q.16 The value of which work is added in the calculation of GDP?

A. Housewives' works

B. A teacher teaching his own child

C. The value of resale of old shares

D. Construction of new house by an artisan

Q.17 Which is called as the heavy engineering industry?

A. Heavy Electricals **B.** Heavy Machinery

C. Glass **D.** Iron and steel

Q.18 When was the first modern paper mill of the country set up?

A. 1827 **B.** 1832 **C.** 1846 **D.** 1854

Q.19 Which among the following does not belong to the list of leading sugarcane-producing States?

A. Uttar Pradesh **B.** Andhra Pradesh

C. Madhya Pradesh **D.** Maharashtra

Q.20 Open market operation is a part of:

A. Credit Policy **B.** Debit Policy

C. Deposit Policy **D.** None of these

Q.21 Income tax in India was introduced by:

A. William Jones **B.** James Wilson

C. Nicholas Kaldor **D.** Mahavir Tyagi

Q.22 At present, the number of nationalized banks are:

A. 19 **B.** 17 **C.** 15 **D.** 12

Q.23 Largest fresh water lake in India is _______.

A. Lonar lake **B.** Dal lake
C. Wular lake **D.** Tilyar lake

Q.24 During which five Year plan was phase of heavy industrialization initiated?

A. Second five year plan
B. First five year plan
C. Third five year plan
D. Fourth five year plan

Q.25 Income tax is the most important source of revenue in India. Income tax is:

A. Direct and proportional
B. Indirect and proportional
C. Direct and progressive
D. Indirect and progressive

// Smart Answer Sheet //

Correct Percentage of students who answered correctly.   **Skipped** Percentage of students who skipped.

Q.	Ans.	Correct / Skipped
1	C	49.94 % / 44.02 %
2	A	42.84 % / 52.3 %
3	A	68.97 % / 30.69 %
4	D	80.44 % / 19.17 %
5	C	58.72 % / 30.34 %

Q.	Ans.	Correct / Skipped
6	B	45.25 % / 48.69 %
7	C	57.21 % / 36.83 %
8	A	58.21 % / 36.23 %
9	A	69.11 % / 30.14 %
10	B	21.94 % / 72.42 %

Q.	Ans.	Correct / Skipped
11	A	42.16 % / 50.63 %
12	B	42.75 % / 42.15 %
13	C	45.33 % / 36.39 %
14	C	76.99 % / 13.4 %
15	C	58.37 % / 39.93 %

Q.	Ans.	Correct / Skipped
16	D	13.67 % / 67.04 %
17	B	59.22 % / 39.98 %
18	B	67.87 % / 30.77 %
19	C	45.36 % / 33.39 %
20	A	87.82 % / 10.3 %

Q.	Ans.	Correct / Skipped
21	B	50.34 % / 44.46 %
22	D	54.61 % / 42.24 %
23	C	30.16 % / 67.71 %
24	A	54.79 % / 31.88 %
25	C	61.12 % / 34.46 %

//Hints and Solutions//

1. A Crescograph is a device for measuring the growth in plants. It was invented in the early 20th century by Sir Jagadish Chandra Bose.

Hence, the correct option is (C).

2. Satellite Mission - TRISHNA is for Eco-system stress and water use monitoring. It stands for Thermal infraRed Imaging Satellite for High-resolution Natural resource Assessment. ISRO and CNES have completed the feasibility study to realize the earth observation satellite mission with a thermal infrared imager.

Hence, the correct option is (A).

3. The Niyamgiri is a hill range situated in the districts of Kalahandi and Rayagada in Odisha. These hills are home to Dongria Kondh indigenous people. In recent times these hills are in media discussions due to the conflict of inhabitant tribals and the Bauxite Mining Project by Vedanta Aluminium Company.

Hence, the correct option is (A).

4. India is not only the largest producer but also the largest exporter of mica in the world. Andhra Pradesh is the largest producer of mica. It is the second-largest producer and exporter of tea after China in the world.

Hence, the correct option is (D).

5. The Rajasthan Atomic Power Station (RAPS) is located at Rawatbhata in the Chittorgarh district of the state. Commissioned on 16 December 1973, it is operated by the Nuclear Power Corporation of India. Currently, (RAPS) has six Pressurized Heavy Water Reactor (PHWR) units operating with a total installed capacity of 1,180MW.

Hence, the correct option is (C).

6. The main focus of the first five-year plan was the agricultural development of the country. Agriculture is still the backbone of the Indian economy in terms of employment generation.

Hence, the correct option is (B).

7. The Forty-Second Amendment also amended Preamble and changed the description of India from a "sovereign democratic republic" to a "sovereign, socialist, secular, democratic, republic", and also changed the words "unity of the nation" to "unity and integrity of the nation".

Hence, the correct option is (C).

8. A Judge of the Supreme Court cannot be removed from office except by an order of the President passed after an address in each House of Parliament supported by a majority of the total membership of that House and by a majority of not less than two-thirds of members present and voting, and presented to the President in. "Proved misbehavior or incapacity" is mentioned in Article 124(4) of the Constitution. It is the ground for the impeachment of a Supreme Court judge.

Hence, the correct option is (A).

9. Article 123 of the Constitution empowers the president to issue/promulgate ordinances during the recess of the Parliament.

The ordinance-making power of the President is not a parallel power of the legislation. It is held to be the legislative power of the President by the Supreme court of India.

Hence, the correct option is (A).

10. HSBC (Hongkong and Shanghai Banking Corporation) is the first bank to introduce the ATM concept in India in the year 1987 in Mumbai.

Hence, the correct option is (B).

11. On July 19, 2019, India completed the 50th anniversary of the bank nationalization program undertaken in 1969.

Hence, the correct option is (A).

12. Oudh Commercial Bank or Awadh Commercial Bank was an Indian bank established in 1881 in Faizabad and operated until 1958 when it failed. It was the first commercial bank in India having limited liability and an entirely Indian board of directors.

Hence, the correct option is (B).

13. The Government of India issued the Banking Companies (Acquisition and Transfer of Undertakings) Ordinance, 1969 and nationalized the 14 largest commercial banks with effect from the midnight of 19 July 1969. These banks contained 85 percent of bank deposits in the country.

The following banks were nationalized in 1969:

- Allahabad Bank (now Indian Bank)
- Bank of Baroda
- Bank of India
- Bank of Maharashtra
- Central Bank of India
- Canara Bank
- Dena Bank (now Bank of Baroda)
- Indian Bank
- Indian Overseas Bank
- Punjab National Bank
- Syndicate Bank (now Canara Bank)
- UCO Bank
- Union Bank of India
- United Bank of India (now Punjab National Bank)

Hence, the correct option is (C).

14. Net National Product (NNP) can be calculated in two ways:

(i) At market prices of goods and services.

(ii) At factor cost.

When NNP is obtained at factor cost it is known as National Income.

Hence, the correct option is (C).

15. Nominal GDP is calculated on the basis of current prices. While real GDP is calculated on the base year prices and its data are more reliable or accurate as compared to Nominal GDP.

Hence, the correct option is (C).

16. Gross domestic product (GDP) is the total monetary or market value of all the finished goods and services produced within a country's borders in a specific time period.

The value of the construction of a new house is added in the calculation of the GDP because it is a new production work in the economy.

Hence, the correct option is (D).

17. Heavy Machinery is also called the heavy engineering industry. The major plants are located at Ranchi, Visakhapatnam and Durgapur.

Hence, the correct option is (B).

18. Paper and Paper Board is a forest-based industry. In 1832 the first modern paper mill of the country was set up at Serampore in West Bengal.

Hence, the correct option is (B).

19. The leading sugarcane-producing States are the leading sugar producers as well. They are Uttar Pradesh, Maharashtra, Andhra Pradesh, Tamil Nadu, Karnataka, Bihar and Jharkhand. There are more than 250 sugar mills in India, with the largest number located in Uttar Pradesh including Uttarakhand followed by Maharashtra.

Hence, the correct option is (C).

20. Open Market Operations refer to the purchase and sale of the Government securities (G-Secs) by RBI from / to market. The objective of Open Market Operations is to adjust the rupee liquidity conditions in the economy on a durable basis. When RBI sells government security in the markets, the banks purchase them. When the banks purchase Government securities, they have a reduced ability to lend to the industrial houses or other commercial sectors. This reduced surplus cash, contracts the rupee liquidity and consequently credit creation / credit supply. When RBI purchases the securities, the commercial banks find them with more surplus cash and this would create more credit in the system. Thus, in the case of excess liquidity, RBI resorts to sale of G-secs to suck out rupee from system. Similarly, when there is a liquidity crunch in the economy, RBI buys securities from the market, thereby releasing liquidity.

Hence, the correct option is (A).

21. The 19th century saw the establishment of British rule in India. Following the Mutiny of 1857, the British government faced an acute financial crisis. To fill up the treasury, the first Income-tax Act was introduced in February 1860 by James Wilson, who became British-India's first Finance Minister.

Hence, the correct option is (B).

22. At present, the number of nationalized banks are 12.

1. Bank of Baroda

2. Bank of India

3. Bank of Maharashtra

4. Canara Bank

5. Central Bank of India

6. Indian Bank

7. Indian Overseas bank

8. Punjab and Sind Bank

9. Punjab National Bank

10. State Bank of India

11. UCO Bank

12. Union Bank of India

Hence, the correct option is (D).

23. Wular lake is considered the largest freshwater lake in India. It is located in the Bandipora district of Jammu and Kashmir.

Hence, the correct option is (C).

24. The Second Five-Year plan accorded highest priority to Industrialisation. The plan was based on famous Mahalanobis Model. Mahalanobis model set out the task of establishing basic and capital goods industries on a large scale to create a strong base for the industrial development.

Hence, the correct option is (A).

25. Income tax is a type of tax that the central government charges on the income earned during a financial year by the individuals and businesses. Taxes are sources of revenue for the government. Government utilizes this revenue for developing infrastructure, providing healthcare, education, subsidy to the farmer/ agriculture sector and in other government welfare schemes. Taxes are mainly of two types, direct taxes and indirect form of taxes. Tax levied directly on the income earned is called as direct tax, for example Income tax is a direct tax. The tax calculation is based on the income slab rates applicable during that financial year.

Hence, the correct option is (C).

Q.1 Indian Mission Aditya -L1 is related to which of the following?

A. Sun   **B.** Moon   **C.** Mars   **D.** Jupiter

Q.2 Which of the following is India's first 3D printed humanoid robot?

A. KEMPA   **B.** MANAV   **C.** INDRO   **D.** DAKSH

Q.3 Who is competent to prescribe conditions as for acquiring Indian Citizenship?

A. State Legislatures   **B.** Parliament
C. President   **D.** Attorney General

Q.4 Currently there are how many fundamental rights are recognized by the Indian constitution?

A. Five   **B.** Four   **C.** Nine   **D.** Six

Q.5 The elected representatives in India are part of ___.

A. Judiciary   **B.** Legislature
C. Executive   **D.** Cabinet

Q.6 Which among the following states produces 60% Salt of India?

A. Rajasthan   **B.** Odisha
C. Gujarat   **D.** Maharashtra

Q.7 Which among the following is the major source of water for the industries in India?

A. Surface water   **B.** Ground Water
C. Municipal water   **D.** Marine resources

Q.8 Tropical rainforests in India are found in the:

1. Andaman and Nicobar Islands
2. North-East India
3. Western Ghats

Select the correct option from codes given below:

A. 1 & 2 Only   **B.** 1 & 3 Only
C. 2 & 3 Only   **D.** 1, 2 & 3

Q.9 In context with the banking business, which among the following is a correct definition of liquidity risk?

A. Risk arising from funding of long term assets by short term liabilities or funding of short term assets by long term liabilities

B. Risk arising from adverse movement of interest rates during a liquidity crunch in the markets

C. Risk arising from the adverse movement of the value of the assets /investments etc.

D. Risk arising from a party becoming defaulter

Q.10 Which among the following is used for a situation of "Too much money chasing too few goods"?

A. Demand Pull Inflation

B. Cost pull inflation

C. Stagflation

D. Hyperinflation

Q.11 Consider the following:

1. Rhizobium
2. Azotobacter
3. Blue Green Algae

Which of the above are used as bio fertilizers?

A. 1 & 2 Only   **B.** 2 & 3 Only
C. 1 & 3 Only   **D.** 1, 2 & 3

Q.12 GDP at factor cost is?

A. GDP Minus indirect taxes plus subsidies
B. GNP minus depreciation allowance
C. NNP plus depreciation allowance
D. GDP Minus subsidies plus indirect taxes

Q.13 Per Capita Income is obtained by dividing National Income by?

A. Total population of the country
B. Total working population
C. Area of the country
D. Volume of the capital used

Q.14 Net National Product (NNP) of a country is?

A. GDP minus depreciation allowances
B. GDP plus net income from abroad
C. GNP minus net income from abroad
D. GNP minus depreciation allowances

Q.15 India's GST structure are based on how many structures?

A. 6   **B.** 4   **C.** 3   **D.** 5

Q.16 The maximum rate for SGST/UTGST is?

A. 28   **B.** 14   **C.** 20   **D.** 30

Q.17 Which code is used to classify goods and services under GST?

A. HSN Code   **B.** SAC/HSN Code
C. GST Code   **D.** SAC Code

Q.18 Capital adequacy norm helps the banks

(i) For strengthening capital base of banks

(ii) For sanctioning more loan

A. Both (i) and (ii) are correct
B. Both (i) and (ii) are incorrect
C. (i) is correct but (ii) is incorrect
D. (ii) is correct but (i) is incorrect

Q.19 The statement of Banking Definition is given by:

A. T.G. Hart   **B.** White Head
C. Kinley   **D.** All of these

Q.20 Match the following:

List-I (Name of the Merging Entity)	List-II (Name of the Merged Entity)
(a) 20th century Finance Company	(i) ICICI Bank
(b) Bareilly Corporation Bank	(ii) Centurian Bank
(c) Sikkim Bank	(iii) HDFC Bank
(d) Times Bank	(iv) Bank of Baroda
(e) Bank of Madurai	(v) Union Bank of India

A. (a)-(ii), (b)-(iv), (c)-(v), (d)-(iii), (e)-(i)
B. (a)-(iii), (b)-(iv), (c)-(i), (d)-(iii), (e)-(v)
C. (a)-(v), (b)-(iv), (c)-(iii), (d)-(ii), (e)-(i)
D. (a)-(v), (b)-(ii), (c)-(i), (d)-(iii), (e)-(iv)

Q.21 Which is the most important company in machine tools?

A. HMT Machine Tools
B. PMT Machine Tools
C. Guindy Machine Tools
D. Praga Tools

Q.22 When was the "Package for Promotion of Micro and Small Enterprises" announced?

A. August 2005 **B.** February 2007
C. March 2009 **D.** November 2010

Q.23 In February 2021, which of the following has received the Asia Environmental Enforcement Award-2020 awarded by the United Nations Environment Programme (UNEP)?

A. Central Zoo Authority
B. National Tiger Conservation
C. PETA India
D. Wildlife Crime Control Bureau

Q.24 Who got Chameli Devi Jain Award?

A. Journalist Aarefa Johari
B. Ramnath Goenka
C. Alka Dhupkar
D. None of the above

Q.25 Who won Golden Peacock award 2021?

A. JSW Steel Limited
B. SAIL
C. Rashtriya Ispat Nigam Limited
D. GAIL

// Smart Answer Sheet //

Correct — Percentage of students who answered correctly.   **Skipped** — Percentage of students who skipped.

Q.	Ans.	Correct / Skipped
1	A	76.79 % / 18.21 %
2	B	80.82 % / 15.74 %
3	B	40.38 % / 45.22 %
4	D	52.21 % / 35.95 %
5	B	45.34 % / 53.0 %
6	C	46.22 % / 53.11 %
7	A	44.38 % / 49.39 %
8	D	51.25 % / 44.5 %
9	A	64.35 % / 31.46 %
10	A	68.09 % / 31.09 %
11	D	65.59 % / 33.18 %
12	A	62.11 % / 35.48 %
13	A	47.87 % / 40.5 %
14	D	56.79 % / 36.22 %
15	B	65.56 % / 33.67 %
16	C	54.87 % / 41.05 %
17	B	69.28 % / 30.34 %
18	C	48.3 % / 39.23 %
19	D	68.03 % / 30.18 %
20	A	50.91 % / 33.8 %
21	A	46.32 % / 42.56 %
22	B	58.23 % / 34.94 %
23	D	68.21 % / 30.89 %
24	A	45.4 % / 30.06 %
25	B	49.62 % / 36.9 %

//Hints and Solutions//

1. Aditya or Aditya-L1 is a spacecraft mission to study the Sun.

The Aditya-L1 mission was conceived as a 400kg class satellite carrying one payload, the Visible Emission Line Coronagraph (VELC) and was planned to launch in an 800 km low earth orbit.

Hence, the correct option is (A).

2. MANAV is India's first 3D printed humanoid robot.

Manav, which means man in Sanskrit, is two feet tall humanoid robot. It has in-built vision and sound processing capability. It is built with 21 sensors, two cameras in its eye sockets and two mikes on either side of its head.

Hence, the correct option is (B).

3. The Parliament is the competent body to prescribe conditions for acquisition of citizenship. The Parliament of India can prescribe conditions as for acquiring Indian citizenship.

Parliament is the supreme legislative body of India. The Indian Parliament comprises of the President and the two Houses - Rajya Sabha (Council of States) and Lok Sabha (House of the People).

Hence, the correct option is (B).

4. There are six fundamental rights-

1) Right to equality.

2) Right to freedom.

3) Right against exploitation.

4) Right to freedom of religion.

5) Cultural and educational rights.

6) Right to constitutional remedies.

Hence, the correct option is (D).

5. A Member of the Legislative Assembly (MLA) is a representative elected by the voters of an electoral district (constituency) to the legislature of State government in the Indian system of government. From each constituency, the people elect one representative who then becomes a member of the Legislative Assembly (MLA).

Hence, the correct option is (B).

6. India is the world's third-largest producer of salt, after the US and China. The country produces about 27 million tonnes of the product that is synonymous with loyalty, inspiring many Hindi film dialogues and advertisement campaigns. The major salt-producing states in India are Gujarat, Rajasthan, Tamil Nadu, Maharashtra, Andhra Pradesh and Odisha. Gujarat produces about 60 percent of the total salt, followed by Tamil Nadu and Andhra pradesh. With around 160 Lakh tons of production, India is the third-largest salt-producing country in the world. Gujarat, Rajasthan, Andhra Pradesh and Tamilnadu are 4 largest salt-producing states in India.

Hence, the correct option is (C).

7. Surface water is the major source of water for the industries (41%) followed by groundwater (35%) and municipal water (24%). The use of municipal water is limited to industries located in urban/ peri-urban areas. A vast majority of industries use surface and groundwater in conjunction with groundwater being relied as a source when surface water availability is on a decline or is impacted by water pollution bound to have an impact on the industrial process.

Hence, the correct option is (A).

8. Tropical rainforests in India are found in western ghats, Andaman and Nicobar Islands & North-East India. These forests contain several tree species of great commercial significance. Tropical rainforests receive 175 to 300 inches precipitation annually. Mean monthly temperatures exceed 18 °C during all months of the year, due to location near to equator.

Hence, the correct option is (D).

9. Risk arising from funding of long term assets by short term liabilities or funding of short term assets by long term liabilities.

Liquidity risk occurs when an individual investor, business, or financial institution cannot meet its short-term debt obligations. The investor or entity might be unable to convert an asset into cash without giving up capital and income due to a lack of buyers or an inefficient market.

Hence, the correct option is (A).

10. Demand-pull inflation refers to the inflation from rapid growth in aggregate demand and when excess demand causes "too much money chasing too few goods". This generally happens when an economy is growing at a faster rate.

Hence, the correct option is (A).

11. Bio fertilizers are substances, which contain microorganisms, which when added to plants add nutrients through natural process of nitrogen fixation and solubilising phosphorus thus stimulating plant growth. Some important bio fertilizers are: Rhizobium, Azotobacter, Azospirilium and blue green algae (BGA).

Hence, the correct option is (D).

12. GDP and GVA are the tools that are used for measuring the economic growth of a nation. GDP stands for Gross Domestic Product and is the measure of the value of the end-products produced in a country. GVA stands for Gross Value Added, and it quantifies the value of the total production of goods and commodities in a nation.

GDP at Factor Cost = Sum of all GVA at factor cost= GDP Minus indirect taxes plus subsidies.

Hence, the correct option is (A).

13. Per capita income (PCI) or average income measures the average income earned per person in a given area (city, region, country, etc.) in a specified year. It is calculated by dividing the area's total income by its total population.

Per capita income is national income divided by population size.

Hence, the correct option is (A).

14. Net national product (NNP) is gross national product (GNP), the total value of finished goods and services produced by a country's citizens overseas and domestically, minus depreciation. NNP is often examined on an annual basis as a way to measure a nation's success in continuing minimum production standards.

Hence, the correct option is (D).

15. The GST was carefully crafted to keep both the burden of the common man and inflation rates in mind. The 4 tier tax structure contains four separate rates: a zero rate, a lower rate, a standard rate, and a higher rate. This article is aimed at providing a brief overview of each GST rate.

Hence, the correct option is (B).

16. As per UTGST Act, 2017, Union Territory Goods and Services Tax refers to a tax that is levied on intra-state supply of goods and services together with tax charged under CGST Act, 2017. These goods and services do not include supply of alcoholic liquor for human consumption.

Furthermore, it is charged at a rate not exceeding 20% which is notified by the Central Government as per the suggestions given by the GST Council.

Hence, the correct option is (C).

17. HSN stands for Harmonized System of Nomenclature and is used to classify goods in a systematic manner. It was developed by the World Customs Organization (WCO) and is considered the global standard when it comes to naming goods.

This 6-digit uniform code can be used to classify more than 5,000 products, and are also used for classification for tax purposes.

Hence, the correct option is (B).

18. The capital adequacy ratios ensure the efficiency and stability of a nation's financial system by lowering the risk of banks becoming insolvent. Generally, a bank with a high capital adequacy ratio is considered safe and likely to meet its financial obligations.

Hence, the correct option is (C).

19. A bank statement is an official summary of financial transactions occurring within a given period for each bank account held by a person or business with a financial institution. The bank statement shows the cumulative balance of cash in the account, net of all the preceding transactions, as of the end of each day in the reporting period. Some banks still print these statements along with an accompanying set of images of all cleared checks. These all statements reflect the definition given by T.G. Hart, White Head and Kinley.

Hence, the correct option is (D).

20.

List-I (Name of the Merging Entity)	List-II (Name of the Merged Entity)
(a) 20th century Finance Company	(ii) Centurian Bank
(b) Bareilly Corporation Bank	(iv) Bank of Baroda
(c) Sikkim Bank	(v) Union Bank of India
(d) Times Bank	(iii) HDFC Bank
(e) Bank of Madurai	(i) ICICI Bank

Hence, the correct option is (A).

21. HMT Limited, formerly Hindustan Machine Tools Limited, is a state-owned holding company under the Ministry of Heavy Industries and Public Enterprises in India. The company's wholly-owned subsidiaries include HMT Machine Tools Limited and HMT International Limited. HMT also holds a majority stake in Praga Tools Limited (51%).

Hence, the correct option is (A).

22. In February 2007, a "Package for Promotion of Micro and Small Enterprises" was announced. This includes measures addressing concerns of credit, fiscal support, cluster-based development, infrastructure, technology, and marketing. Capacity building of MSME Associations and support to women entrepreneurs are the other important attributes of this package.

Hence, the correct option is (B).

23. The Wildlife Crime Control Bureau (WCCB) has received the Asia Environmental Enforcement Award-2020 awarded by the United Nations Environment Programme (UNEP).

United Nations Environment Programme has given this award. The WCCB received this award in the 'Innovation category', in a virtual ceremony held on 17th Feb 2021.

This is the second time WCCB has bagged Asia Environmental Enforcement Award. Earlier it had received this award in 2018 in the same category.

Hence, the correct option is (D).

24. Journalist Aarefa Johari got Chameli Devi Jain Award. The jury praised Johari's work saying it shone through with its combination of meticulous reportage, humanism and empathy, all reflecting a high order of journalistic excellence.

A journalist from Mumbai, Aarefa Johari was awarded the Chameli Devi Jain Award for an Outstanding Woman Media person 2021. It was announced by the Media Foundation. Aarefa Johari works for 'Scroll. in' in Mumbai, Maharashtra

Hence, the correct option is (A).

25. Steel Authority of India Ltd. (SAIL), under the Ministry of Steel, has been awarded with the prestigious Golden Peacock Environment Management Award 2021 for successive three years.

SAIL has been the winner of this award for successive three years. The company's environmental protections measures are focused on adopting various environmental measures including upgrading pollution control facilities.

Hence, the correct option is (B).

Q.1 Chandrayan - 1, India's first mission to Moon was launched successfully on _______ from, Sriharikota.
A. 22 October, 2008   **B.** 13 December, 2009
C. 30 March, 2010   **D.** 7 July, 2011

Q.2 GSLV stands for:
A. Global Stationary Launching Vehicle
B. Geosynchronous Satellite Launching Vehicle
C. Global Satellite Launch Vehicle
D. Geosynchronous Satellite Launch Vehicle

Q.3 Which of the following products launched by most of the banks help farmers in getting instant credit for various agricultural purposes?
A. Kisan Credit Card   **B.** Personal Loan
C. Business Loan   **D.** ATM Card

Q.4 RBI was nationalized on:
A. 1 July 1949   **B.** 26 January 1951
C. 1 January 1949   **D.** 1 July 1955

Q.5 Who decides the Base Rate of commercial banks?
A. SBI
B. RBI
C. NABARD
D. Commercial Bank itself

Q.6 Which of the following is called "paper gold"?
A. Yuan   **B.** Euro   **C.** SDR   **D.** Dollar

Q.7 When a bank returns a cheque unpaid, it is called:
A. Cancelling of the cheque
B. Drawing of the cheque
C. Drawing of the cheque
D. Dishonor of the cheque

Q.8 Which among the following is the oldest steel plant in India?
A. TISCO   **B.** IISCO   **C.** HSL   **D.** BSL

Q.9 Which is the only industry in India which is self-reliant?
A. Textile industry   **B.** Iron and Steel
C. Electrical   **D.** Sugar

Q.10 Which of the following is not a Maha-Ratna industry?
A. Gas Authority of India Limited
B. Coal India Limited
C. Steel Authority of India Limited
D. Airports Authority of India

Q.11 Make in India programme is mainly for the promotion of:
A. Construction   **B.** Manufacturing
C. Service   **D.** Agricultur

Q.12 The income tax in India is:

A. Indirect and progressive
B. Direct and proportional
C. Direct and progressive
D. Indirect and proportional

Q.13 General Sales Tax (GST) is charged on:
A. Selling Price   **B.** Retail Price
C. Manufacturing Cost   **D.** None of these

Q.14 Who is the current chief of the World Bank Group?
A. Donald Tusk   **B.** David Malpass
C. Christine Lagarde   **D.** Jim Yong Kim

Q.15 Which of the following is the direct tax in India?
A. Sales Tax
B. VAT
C. Wealth tax
D. Goods and services Tax

Q.16 The net value of GDP after deducting depreciation from GDP is:
A. Net National Product
B. Net Domestic Product
C. Gross National Product
D. Disposable Income

Q.17 The correct chronological order of the formation of Haryana, Sikkim, Arunanchal Pradesh, and Nagaland as full states of Indian Union is:
A. Haryana-Sikkim-Arunachal Pardesh-Nagaland
B. Nagaland-Arunachal Pradesh Haryana Sikkim
C. Nagaland-Haryana-Arunachal Pradesh-Sikkim
D. Nagaland-Haryana-Sikkim-Arunachal Pradesh

Q.18 The speaker of the Lok Sabha can ask a member of the house to stop speaking and let another member speak. This phenomenon is known as:
A. Crossing the floor
B. Yielding the floor
C. Point of Order
D. Calling Attention Motion

Q.19 By which Constitutional Amendment Act was the number of Lok sabha seats increased from 525 to 545?
A. The Twentieth Amendment Act, 1966
B. The Forty-second Amendment Act, 1976
C. The Forty-fourth Amendment Act, 1978
D. Thirty-first Constitutional Amendment Act, 1973

Q.20 How much geographical area of India is forest land?
A. 22%   **B.** 23%   **C.** 26%   **D.** 28%

Q.21 Apatanis are the tribes found in:
A. Himanchal Pradesh   **B.** Nagaland
C. Sikkim   **D.** Arunachal Pradesh

Q.22 Through which one of the following Indian states the Tropic of Cancer does not pass?

A. Manipur

B. Tripura

C. Gujarat

D. Rajasthan

Q.23 Revenue of the state governments are raised from the following sources, except:

A. Entertainment tax

B. Expenditure tax

C. Agricultural income tax

D. Land revenue

Q.24

In the last one decade, which one among the following sectors has attracted the highest foreign direct investment inflows into India?

A. Chemicals other than fertilizers

B. Services sector

C. Food processing

D. Telecommunication

Q.25 The value of national income adjusted for inflation is called:

A. Per capita income

B. Disposable income

C. Inflation rate

D. Real national income

// Smart Answer Sheet //

Correct — Percentage of students who answered correctly. **Skipped** — Percentage of students who skipped.

Q.	Ans.	Correct / Skipped	Q.	Ans.	Correct / Skipped	Q.	Ans.	Correct / Skipped	Q.	Ans.	Correct / Skipped	Q.	Ans.	Correct / Skipped
1	A	65.59 % / 33.83 %	6	C	56.15 % / 33.69 %	11	B	45.25 % / 41.63 %	16	B	63.52 % / 35.75 %	21	D	44.62 % / 36.14 %
2	D	67.83 % / 30.34 %	7	D	41.39 % / 31.23 %	12	C	51.1 % / 39.99 %	17	D	60.81 % / 38.55 %	22	A	48.31 % / 49.81 %
3	A	58.86 % / 33.87 %	8	A	51.18 % / 39.89 %	13	B	61.96 % / 32.31 %	18	B	29.29 % / 70.1 %	23	C	66.32 % / 32.95 %
4	C	46.7 % / 50.27 %	9	A	55.44 % / 43.33 %	14	B	67.43 % / 30.35 %	19	D	21.58 % / 71.45 %	24	D	63.87 % / 34.26 %
5	B	58.67 % / 37.15 %	10	D	54.35 % / 38.45 %	15	C	68.32 % / 31.09 %	20	A	44.51 % / 37.16 %	25	D	67.07 % / 30.6 %

//Hints and Solutions//

1. Chandrayan - 1, India's first mission to Moon was launched successfully on 22 October 2008 from, Sriharikota.

Chandrayan - 1 is India's first lunar probe developed by the Indian Space Research Organization (ISRO). The Chandrayan - 1 mission performed high-resolution remote sensing of the Moon in the visible, near-infrared (NIR), low-energy X-ray and high-energy X-ray regions.

Hence, the correct option is (A).

2. GSLV stands for Geosynchronous Satellite Launch Vehicle.

Geosynchronous Satellite Launch Vehicle is an expendable launch system operated by the Indian Space Research Organization.

- The first stage comprises a solid booster with a propellant and four liquid strap-on motors.
- The second stage is a liquid engine carrying liquid propellant.
- The third stage is the indigenously built Cryogenic Upper Stage.

Hence, the correct option is (D).

3. The Government of India intends to reach out to 1 crore farmers in 100 days through the Kisan Credit Card Scheme. The KCC loan offers farmers a source of formal credit so as someone in the agriculture sector, farmers can avoid stepping into a debt trap associated with informal borrowing. Instead, farmers can avail of low-interest funding by obtaining a Kisan Credit Card.

Hence, the correct option is (A).

4. The Reserve Bank (RBI) of India was nationalized with effect from 1 January, 1949 on the basis of the Reserve Bank of India (Transfer to Public Ownership) Act, 1948. All shares in the capital of the Bank were deemed transferred to the Central Government on payment of a suitable compensation.

Hence, the correct option is (C).

5. Base rate is the minimum rate set by the Reserve Bank of India (RBI) below which banks are not allowed to lend to its customers. Base rate is decided in order to enhance transparency in the credit market and ensure that banks pass on the lower cost of fund to their customers.

Hence, the correct option is (B).

6. The SDR unit of valuation is known as paper gold. SDR represents Special Drawing Rights. It is an accounting entry and measures a nation's reserve assets with IMF.

Hence, the correct option is (C).

7. In other words, dishonor of cheque is a condition in which the bank refuses to pay the amount of cheque to the payee. Whenever the cheque is dishonoured, the drawee bank instantly issues a 'Cheque Return Memo' to the payee banker specifying the reasons for dishonour.

Hence, the correct option is (D).

8. Tata Iron and Steel Company (TISCO) is one of the largest manufacturing plants in Asia. It is situated in Jamshedpur. It is the oldest steel plant of India. It was established by Jamshedji Tata in 1907.

Hence, the correct option is (A).

9. India is self-sufficient in textile industry. India is first in global jute production and constitutes 63% of global textile and garment market. India is 2nd in global textile manufacturing and also 2nd in silk and cotton production.

Hence, the correct option is (A).

10. The list of Maharatna Companies (As of January 2020)

1. National Thermal Power Corporation (NTPC)
2. Oil and Natural Gas Corporation (ONGC)
3. Steel Authority of India Limited (SAIL)
4. Bharat Heavy Electricals Limited (BHEL)
5. Indian Oil Corporation Limited (IOCL)
6. Hindustan Petroleum Corporation Limited (HPCL)
7. Coal India Limited (CIL)
8. Gas Authority of India Limited (GAIL)
9. Bharat Petroleum Corporation Limited (BPCL)
10. Power Grid Corporation of India (POWERGRID)

Hence, the correct option is (D).

11. Make in India is a major national programme of the Government of India designed to facilitate investment, foster innovation, enhance skill development, protect intellectual property and build best in class manufacturing infrastructure in the country.

Hence, the correct option is (B).

12. Progressive taxation is a system where the tax outgo of the people is disproportionately higher as their income rises. Direct taxes increase as income increases, which makes them progressive. India follows a progressive tax regime. A progressive tax system means that high-income earners are taxed more than low-income ones.

Hence, the correct option is (C).

13. Retail prices are the prices that the customers buying goods at retail outlets pay. Consumers respond to a lower retail price by switching their purchases of the manufacturer's product to the lower-priced retailer.

General Sales Tax (GST) is charged on Retail Price

Hence, the correct option is (B).

14. The President of the World Bank Group is the head of World Bank Group. 'David Malpass' is the Incumbent President of the World Bank Group. He is on the post since April 9, 2019. David has replaced Jim Yong Kim.

Hence, the correct option is (B).

15. Wealth tax is the direct tax which is imposed on the assets (House, rented buildings etc.) of the Individual. Other direct taxes are corporation tax, income tax and wealth tax.

Hence, the correct option is (C).

16. After deducting the depreciation charges of plant and machinery from GDP, we get the net value of GDP which is called NDP (Net Domestic Product).

Net domestic product (NDP) is an annual measure of the economic output of a nation that is adjusted to account for depreciation. It is calculated by subtracting depreciation from the Gross Domestic Product (GDP).

NDP = GDP - Depreciation charges

Hence, the correct option is (B).

17. Nagaland on 1st December 1963.

Haryana on 1st November 1966.

Sikkim on 16th May 1975.

Arunachal Pradesh on 20th Feb 1987.

Hence, the correct option is (D).

18. Yielding the floor: The speaker of the Lok sabha can ask a member of the house to stop speaking and let another member speak.

Crossing the floor: Passing between the member addressing the House and the Chair which is considered breach of Parliamentary etiquette.

Point of Order: A Member of Parliament may raise a point of order if he feels that the proceedings of' the House do not follow the normal rules. The presiding officer decides whether the point of order raised by the member should be allowed.

Calling Attention Motion: With the prior permission of the Speaker, any member of the Parliament may call the attention of a Minister to a matter of urgent public importance. The Minister may make a brief statement about the matter or he may ask for time to make a statement later.

Hence, the correct option is (B).

19. Thirty-first Constitutional Amendment Act, 1973- By this amendment, the seats of Lok Sabha were increased from 525 to 545 but reduced the representation of UT's (Union Territory) in Lok Sabha from 25 to 20.

Hence, the correct option is (D).

20. Forest cover is the total geographical area declared as forest by the government. As of 2019, the total forest cover in India is almost 712,249 Sq km (71.22 million hectares), which is 21.67 (almost 22%) percent of the total geographical area.

Hence, the correct option is (A).

21. The Apatanis, or Tanw, also known by Apa and Apa Tani, are a tribal group of people living in the Ziro valley in the Lower Subansiri district of Arunachal Pradesh in India.

Hence, the correct option is (D).

22. Tropic of cancer does not pass through Manipur. The tropic of cancer passes through 8 Indian states. They are Gujarat, Rajasthan, Madhya Pradesh, Chhattisgarh, West Bengal, Jharkhand, Tripura, and Mizoram.

Hence, the correct option is (A).

23. In India, agriculture is not considered as commercial activity, it is considered as activity of subsistence from hundreds of years. Other areas such as entertainment, expenditure, and land revenue can be seen as business activities for purpose of profit making. This is the main reason for being exclusion of agricultural revenue out side taxation.

Hence, the correct option is (C).

24. Telecommunication is communication at a distance using electrical signals or electromagnetic waves. Examples of telecommunications systems are the telephone network, the radio broadcasting system, computer networks and the Internet.

India is currently the world's second-largest telecommunications market and has registered strong growth in the past decade and half. The Indian mobile economy is growing rapidly and is expected to contribute substantially to India's Gross Domestic Product (GDP).

India is currently the world's 2nd largest telecommunications market with a subscriber base of 1.2 billion and has registered strong growth in the past decade and half. The industry has witnessed exponential growth over the last few years primarily driven by affordable tariffs, wider availability, roll out of Mobile Number Portability (MNP), expanding 3G and 4G coverage, evolving consumption patterns of subscribers and a conducive regulatory environment.

Hence, the correct option is (D).

25. The value of national income adjusted for inflation is called Real national income. This is adjusted for inflation which is calculated from a reference year which is also called a base year.

Real national income is nominal or money national income (output) adjusted for inflation. It is also national income at constant prices. The most frequently used measure of national income is Gross Domestic Product (GDP).

Hence, the correct option is (D).

Q.1 Whether a Bill is a Money Bill or not is certified by the ______________ and his decision is conclusive.

A. President

B. Chairman of Rajya Sabha

C. Speaker of Lok Sabha

D. Chairman of Public Accounts Committee

Q.2 In which Landmark case Fundamental Rights were considered as Inviolable part of the Indian Constitution?

A. Golak Nath vs the State of Punjab

B. Keshavnanada Bharti vs Union of India

C. S.R Bommai vs Union of India

D. Prem Singh vs State of Haryana

Q.3 In which landmark case the Supreme Court of India held that the power of judicial review vested in the High court under Article 226 and right to move the Supreme Court under Article 32 is an integral and essential feature of the Constitution?

A. Chandra Kumar vs Union of India

B. Sajjan Singh vs State of Rajasthan

C. Keshavnanada Bharti vs Union of India

D. Sheela barse vs Union of India

Q.4 Which of the following means that the prosecution has to prove the charge against the accused in criminal cases?

A. Judicial review

B. The margin of appreciation

C. Burden of proof

D. Devolution

Q.5 Age of minority, in the case of kidnapping, has been defined as ______________ by the IPC.

A. 16 years

B. 18 years

C. 18 years for male and 21 for female

D. 16 years for male and 18 years for female

Q.6 Principle: Nothing is an offence which is done by a child above seven years of age and under twelve, who has not attained sufficient maturity of understanding to judge of the nature and consequences of his conduct on that occasion.

Facts: A is a nine-year-old boy who is jealous of his friend B's many toys. One day while playing at B's house, he steals one of B's smaller toys. Has he committed theft?

A. Yes

B. No

C. Only if B really attached to the toy

D. Cannot be determined

Q.7 A voluntary burns a valuable security belonging to B intending to cause wrongful loss to B.

A. A is guilty of cheating

B. A is guilty of breach of contract

C. A is guilty of mischief

D. None of them

Q.8 A, enters a house with the intention of committing theft. But moved by the poverty of the householder he drops a rupee note and left the place. In this case

A. A will be liable for criminal trespass

B. A will not be liable for criminal trespass

C. No offence

D. None of the above

Q.9 No one can be convicted twice for the same offence. This doctrine is called:

A. Burden of proof   **B.** Double conviction

C. Double jeopardy   **D.** Corpus delicti

Q.10 A participant in commission of crime is popularly known as:

A. Respondent   **B.** Under-trial

C. Defendant   **D.** Accomplice

Q.11 Which of the following is not payable to Central Government?

A. Land revenue   **B.** Customs duty

C. Income tax   **D.** Wealth tax

Q.12 Article-173 of the Indian Constitution "Qualification for membership of the State Legislature" deals with:

A. The Directive Principles of State Policy

B. The State Government

C. The Union Government

D. The fundamental rights of the Indian Citizen

Q.13 Which Article of the Indian Constitution empowers the Parliament to regulate right of citizenship?

A. Article 8   **B.** Article 9

C. Article 10   **D.** Article 11

Q.14 Which of the following article describes India also as Bharat?

A. Article 1   **B.** Article 2   **C.** Article 3   **D.** Article 4

Q.15 The motive under section 81 of IPC should be:

A. Prevention of harm to person

B. Prevention of harm to property

C. Both (A) and (B)

D. Either (A) or (B)

Q.16 'Infancy' as an exception has been provided under:

A. Section 80   **B.** Section 81

C. Section 82   **D.** Section 84

Q.17 When the offence punishable under I.P.C. is tried by summary procedure, its punishment shall not exceed?

A. One Year   **B.** Three months

C. Six months   **D.** Two years

Q.18 A person is stated to be partially incapax under section 83, IPC if he is aged:

A. Above seven years and under twelve years

B. Above seven years and under ten years

C. Above seven years and under sixteen years

D. Above seven years and under eighteen years

Q.19 Section 84 of IPC provides for:

A. Medical insanity

B. Legal insanity

C. Moral insanity

D. Unsoundness of mind of any kind

Q.20 When any law is said to be intra vires:

A. It means it is within the powers of legislature and it does not go beyond the supreme and fundamental law of the land

B. It means it is not within the powers of legislature and it goes beyond the supreme and fundamental law of the land

C. Neither (A) nor (B)

D. It is in the powers of the Legislature but outside the power of being Delegated Legislation.

Q.21 Noscitur a Sociis means:

A. It is fixed that no one is bound to perform impossibilities

B. No man can be compelled to incriminate himself

C. The meaning of an unclear word or phrase should be determined by the words immediately surrounding it

D. None of the above

Q.22 Which of the following is not an essential of a valid contract?

A. Agreement

B. Adequate consideration

C. Lawful Object

D. Not barred by law

Q.23 A contract will still be a valid contract if it is:

A. Opposed to public policy

B. In restraint of marriage

C. In restraint of Trade

D. Without adequate consideration

Q.24 A void contract is a contract which:

A. Is not enforceable by law

B. Does not have reasonable terms

C. Declared void by the Indian contract act

D. Both (A) and (C)

Q.25 What do you understand by the legal term habeas corpus?

A. That the body required for response

B. Easement rights to move freely

C. The same cause of Damage

D. A claim on legal grounds

// Smart Answer Sheet //

Correct Percentage of students who answered correctly.   **Skipped** Percentage of students who skipped.

Q.	Ans.	Correct / Skipped	Q.	Ans.	Correct / Skipped	Q.	Ans.	Correct / Skipped	Q.	Ans.	Correct / Skipped	Q.	Ans.	Correct / Skipped
1	C	67.09 % / 1.02 %	6	B	72.64 % / 2.77 %	11	A	67.57 % / 2.7 %	16	C	39.8 % / 2.43 %	21	C	33.38 % / 1.96 %
2	A	53.72 % / 2.83 %	7	C	75.27 % / 2.84 %	12	B	70.81 % / 3.11 %	17	C	38.04 % / 3.31 %	22	B	48.78 % / 3.11 %
3	A	33.18 % / 2.23 %	8	A	75.54 % / 3.04 %	13	D	57.91 % / 1.68 %	18	A	76.55 % / 3.04 %	23	D	57.16 % / 1.29 %
4	C	77.77 % / 3.18 %	9	C	83.45 % / 3.04 %	14	A	90.0 % / 2.97 %	19	B	30.81 % / 2.16 %	24	D	69.8 % / 2.97 %
5	D	54.05 % / 2.91 %	10	D	68.45 % / 2.97 %	15	D	21.01 % / 2.57 %	20	A	60.0 % / 1.89 %	25	A	76.69 % / 3.24 %

//Hints and Solutions//

1. Whether a Bill is a Money Bill or not is certified by the Speaker of Lok Sabha and his decision is conclusive.

To make sure that Rajya Sabha doesn't amend the bill by adding some non-money matters (known as Financial Bill), the Speaker of the Lok Sabha certifies the bill as a money bill before sending it to the upper house, and the decision of the Speaker is binding on both the Houses.

Hence, the correct option is (C).

2. In 1967, in Golak Nath vs the State of Punjab, a bench of eleven judges (such a large bench constituted for the first time) of the Supreme Court deliberated as to whether any part of the Fundamental Rights provisions of the constitution could be revoked or limited by amendment of the constitution. Secondly, declared that the Fundamental Rights were transcendental and inviolable and the Parliament of India had no power to take away or abridge any of the Fundamental Rights guaranteed by the Constitution by way of the Constitutional amendments. Their lordship felt that the liberty of the Individual in the Indian Constitution is subject to various "reasonable restrictions" which are expressly mentioned in the Constitution and that no further limitations should be imposed on it at any time.

Hence, the correct option is (A).

3. The Supreme Court in this case held the exclusion of right to appeal under Article 226 and 32 is unconstitutional. These provisions in Article 323-A and 323-B are unconstitutional because they deny judicial review which is the basic feature of the Constitution.

Hence, the correct option is (A).

4. The burden of proof is the obligation of a party in a trial to produce the evidence that will prove the claims they have made against the other party. In a legal dispute, one party is initially presumed to be correct and gets the benefit of the doubt, while the other side bears the burden of proof.

Hence, the correct option is (C).

5. Section 361 of the IPC explains kidnapping from lawful guardianship. According to this section, if a person takes away or entices a minor (i.e, a boy under the age of 16 years and a girl under the age of 18 years) or a person of unsound mind, away from his/her lawful guardian without the guardian's consent, then that person commits the offense of kidnapping from lawful guardianship.

However, it must be highlighted here that in Manipur, the age of 18 years of females in section 361 is replaced with 15 years. Hence if a female of 16 years is taken from her lawful guardians in Manipur, it would not result in kidnapping from lawful guardianship.

Hence, the correct option is (D).

6. A has not committed theft as while stealing he was not mature to understand the nature and consequences of the act. He has stolen toys just out of jealousy, he was unaware of the nature of the act.

Hence, the correct option is (B).

7. Offense defined- A person is guilty of criminal mischief if he:

1. damages tangible property of another intentionally, recklessly, or by negligence in the employment of fire, explosives, or other dangerous means listed in section 3302(a) of this title (relating to causing or risking catastrophe).

2. intentionally or recklessly tampers with tangible property of another so as to endanger person or property.

3. intentionally or recklessly causes another to suffer pecuniary loss by deception or threat.

4. intentionally defaces or otherwise damages tangible public property or tangible property of another with graffiti by use of any aerosol spray-paint can, broad-tipped indelible marker or similar marking device.

5. intentionally damages real or personal property of another.

Hence, the correct option is (C).

8. A actually entered the house without the permission of the owner and also had a 'mens rea' or an intention of committing theft, hence he is liable for criminal trespass irrespective of whether he left after leaving money.

Hence, the correct option is (A).

9. Double jeopardy, "non bis in idem or ne bis in idem" is a procedural defence that prevents an accused person from being tried again on the same (or similar) charges following a valid acquittal or conviction.

Hence, the correct option is (C).

10. A person who knowingly, voluntarily or intentionally gives assistance to another in the commission of crime. An accomplice is criminally liable to the same extent as the principal.

Hence, the correct option is (D).

11. Land is a matter on which only State Governments can govern, thus the Stamp duties on transfer of immovable properties are levied by State Governments.

Hence, the correct option is (A).

12. Article-173 under Part-VI of constitution deals with subject matters of state government or machinery. It mentions qualification required for membership of State Legislature. Any person who is citizen of India and has completed the age of 25 years in case of Legislative Assembly and 30 years in case of Legislative Council is qualified to be member of State Legislature.

Hence, the correct option is (B).

13. Artical 11, under Part-II of constitution authorizes Paliamemnt to make any provision with respect to acquisition and termination of citizenship and all other matters related to it. Based on this, parliament passed Citizenship (acquisition and termination) act. 1955.

Hence, the correct option is (D).

14. Article 1 in the Constitution states that India, that is Bharat, shall be a Union of States. The territory of India shall consist of:

The territories of the states, The Union territories, and Any territory that may be acquired in the future.

Hence, the correct option is (A).

15. Section 81 of IPC - Act likely to cause harm, but done without criminal intent, and to prevent other harm.—Nothing is an offence merely by reason of its being done with the knowledge that it is likely to cause harm, if it be done without any criminal intention to cause harm, and in good faith for the purpose of preventing or avoiding other harm to person or property. Explanation.—It is question of fact in such a case whether the harm to be prevented or avoided was of such a nature and so imminent as to justify or excuse the risk of doing the act with the knowledge that it was likely to cause harm.

Hence, the correct option is (D).

16. Infancy under Chapter IV:

The defence of 'infancy' is provided under sections 82 and 83 of the Indian Penal Code section 82 provides for all acts to not be an offence which is done by a child of under seven of age while section 83 specifically talks about acts which are not an offence and done by a child above seven years of age but below twelve years of age who is of immature understanding or has not yet attained sufficient maturity.

Hence, the correct option is (C).

17. The offense should be punishable either solely with a fine or with imprisonment for not more than six months with/without a fine. The scope extends to any abatement or attempts to commit any such abovementioned offense.

Hence, the correct option is (C).

18. Section 83 of IPC

Act of a child above seven and under twelve of immature understanding—Nothing is an offence which is done by a child above seven years of age and under twelve, who has not attained sufficient maturity of understanding to judge of the nature and consequences of his conduct on that occasion.

Hence, the correct option is (A).

19. Section 84 of IPC:

Act of a person of unsound mind—Nothing is an offense which is done by a person who, at the time of doing it, by reason of unsoundness of mind, is incapable of knowing the nature of the act, or that he is doing what is either wrong or contrary to law.

legal insanity means, at the time of the commission of the act, the person should be suffering from mental illness and also have a loss of reasoning power. This issue is clearly depicted in Section 84 IPC as that person incapable of knowing the nature of the act

Hence, the correct option is (B).

20. If an act requires legal authority and it is done with such authority, it is characterised in law as intra vires ("within the powers"). If it is done without such authority, it is ultra vires. Acts that are intra vires may equivalently be termed "valid" and those that are ultra vires "invalid".

Hence, the correct option is (A).

21. Noscitur a Sociis means that the meaning of an unclear word or phrase should be determined by the words immediately surrounding it.

The principle of Noscitur a Sociis is a rule of construction. It is one of the rules of the language used by courts to interpret legislation. In other words, the meaning of a word is to be judged by the company it keeps.

Hence, the correct option is (C).

22. Indian Contract Act, 1872 administer law about the contract. Section 2(h) of the Contract Act defines a contract as those agreements which are enforceable by law. Section 2(e) of the Act specifies agreement as every promise or set of promises, forming the consideration for each other. The proposal is said to be accepted when the person to whom such proposal is made gives his consent, then the proposal is said to be accepted and becomes a promise.

An agreement is an accepted promise, and a contract is an agreement enforceable by law. Two parties are involved in the law of contract promisor (a person who promise to do something in return of consideration) and promisee (a person who pay such consideration). Section 10 of the Act states that if parties have given their consent which is free from coercion or undue influence with lawful consideration and lawful object, then all agreements are considered to be contract and such contracts would not be declared void. All contracts are considered to be agreements but all agreements are not contracts.

Hence, the correct option is (B).

23. If a person renders voluntary services without any request or promise from another and the person receiving the services makes a promise to pay for the services, then such a promise is enforceable in India under Section 25(2) of the Indian Contract Act, 1872 which states: "An agreement made without consideration is void unless it's a promise to compensate, wholly or in part, a person who has already voluntarily done something for the promisor, or something which the promisor was legally compellable to do; or unless."

Hence, the correct option is (D).

24. Void agreements are those agreements which are not enforced by law courts. Section 2(g) of the Indian Contract Act defines a void agreement as, "an agreement not enforceable by law". Thus the parties to the contract do not get any legal redress in the case of void agreements.

Hence, the correct option is (D).

25. A writ requiring a person under arrest to be brought before a judge or into court, especially to secure the person's release unless lawful grounds are shown for their detention. Habeas corpus is a law that states that a person cannot be kept in prison unless they have first been brought before a court of law, which decides whether it is legal for them to be kept in prison.

Hence, the correct option is (A).

Q.1 What is meant by Affidavit?

A. Evidentiary Document

B. Document

C. Letter of oath

D. A request made to the court

Q.2 In pretended bidding, the sale is-

A. Voidable at the option of the seller.

B. Valid

C. Voidable at the option of the buyer.

D. Illegal

Q.3 The term 'common law' has three different meanings. Which of the following is not a meaning of the term 'common law'?

A. The body of law as made by judges through the determination of cases.

B. A legal system that is based on that of England.

C. Laws created by Parliament.

D. The system of law emerged following the Norman Conquest in 1066.

Q.4 The Judges of the International Court of Justice are elected by the-

A. Security Council

B. General Assembly

C. General Assembly upon recommendation of the Security Council

D. General Assembly and the Security Council independently of one another

Q.5 The distinctive features of riot and unlawful assembly are an activity which is accompanied by __________.

A. Causing alarm

B. Use of force and violence

C. Violence on a common purpose

D. All of the above

Q.6 Right to Privacy is a _______?

A. Fundamental right

B. Legal Right

C. Statutory Right

D. Legislative Right

Q.7 Section 82 of IPC provides that nothing is an offence which is done by a child under:

A. Six years of age

B. Seven years of age

C. Nine years of age

D. Ten years of age.

Q.8 'Infancy' as an exception has been provided under:

A. Section 80

B. Section 81

C. Section 82 & 83

D. Section 84

Q.9 A hangman who hangs the prisoners pursuant to the order of the court is exempt from criminal liability by virtue of:

A. Section 77 of IPC

B. Section 78 of IPC

C. Section 79 of IPC

D. Section 76 of IPC.

Q.10 What is the ordinary geographical scope of jurisdiction?

A. Jurisdiction is ordinarily extra-territorial

B. Jurisdiction is ordinarily on the high seas

C. Jurisdiction is ordinarily territorial

D. Jurisdiction is determined by the location of the offender.

Q.11 What is passive personality jurisdiction?

A. It is jurisdiction based on the nationality of the offender

B. It is jurisdiction based on where the offense was committed

C. It is jurisdiction based on the nationality of the victims

D. It is jurisdiction based on the country where the legal person was Registered

Q.12 What is the protective principle of jurisdiction?

A. It is jurisdiction based on the harm to national interests by conduct committed abroad

B. It is jurisdiction in order to protect one's nationals abroad

C. It is jurisdiction in order to protect international human rights

D. It is jurisdiction based on the nationality of the offender

Q.13 In which landmark case the Supreme Court held that the Second marriage of Hindu man is invalid even if he converts to Islam before marriage?

A. Daniel latiffi vs. Union Of India

B. Sarla Mudgal vs. Union Of India

C. Roopa Hurrah vs. Ashok Hurrah.

D. Ramchandra Saraswati vs. Neena Bajpai

Q.14 T Sareetha v Venkatasubbaiah is a case relating to-

A. Inheritance

B. Conjugal rights

C. Partition of Property

D. None of these

Q.15 Shankari Prasad case is related to which article?

A. Article 366

B. Article 245

C. Article 368

D. Article 338

Q.16 Mother of a Hindu Child, was declared by the Apex Court, to be the natural guardian, during the life time of his/her father, in

A. Madhegowda v Ankegowda

B. Githa Hariharan v Reserve Bank of India

C. Pannilal v Rajinder Singh

D. None of the above

Q.17 On whose authority, prisoners are admitted to open-air jail:

A. Police

B. Judiciary

C. Jail Authorities

D. None of the above

Q.18 Human trafficking is a form of:

A. Hate crime

B. Organised crime

C. Violent crime

D. Property crime

Q.19 In agreements of a purely domestic nature, the intention of the parties to create a legal relationship is-

A.   To be proved to the satisfaction of the court

B.   Presumed to exist

C.   Required to the extent of consideration

D.   Not relevant at all

Q.20 A promises to deliver his watch to B and, in return, B Promise to pay a sum of 2,000. There is said to be a/ an

A. Agreement

B. Proposal

C. Acceptance

D. Offer

Q.21 What is meant by the Legal Maxim/word "mare liberum"?

A.   Liberty of the mind

B.   Intention of the mind

C.   High seas

D.   Liberty in International law to ships

Q.22 What is meant by the Legal Maxim/word "curator"?

A.   Agent

B.   Commissioner of the property

C.   Pitch maker

D.   Guardian

Q.23 When the proclamation of emergency is made, the citizen's right to move to the Supreme Court for the enforcement of his rights under Part 3 of the Constitution of India are suspended by the:-

A.   Prime Minister of India

B.   President of India

C.   Speaker of Lok Sabha

D.   Cheif Justice of Supreme Court

Q.24 Right to Safety, Right to information, Right to Choose, Right to be heard & Right to Seek Redressal are the essential components of which among the following?

A.   Fundamental Rights in the Constitution of India

B.   The Consumer Protection Act

C.   The Essential Commodities Act

D.   Prevention of Corruption Act

Q.25 The Panchayats (Extension to Scheduled Areas) Act (PESA) does not authorize the States to give the Gram Sabhas power to regulate and restrict which of the following?

A.   Sale/consumption of liquor

B.   Minor Forest Produce

C.   Identify the beneficiary of the schemes

D.   Manage mineral resources

// Smart Answer Sheet //

Correct Percentage of students who answered correctly. **Skipped** Percentage of students who skipped.

Q.	Ans.	Correct / Skipped
1	C	56.34 % / 1.88 %
2	C	38.5 % / 5.87 %
3	C	29.81 % / 5.64 %
4	D	35.45 % / 5.86 %
5	B	28.64 % / 4.93 %
6	A	77.23 % / 5.63 %
7	B	88.5 % / 6.1 %
8	C	67.14 % / 5.86 %
9	B	38.5 % / 5.4 %
10	C	42.02 % / 5.63 %
11	C	18.78 % / 5.87 %
12	A	24.65 % / 6.1 %
13	B	63.62 % / 5.16 %
14	D	14.55 % / 5.87 %
15	C	59.39 % / 6.1 %
16	B	28.64 % / 5.87 %
17	C	51.41 % / 5.63 %
18	B	59.62 % / 5.64 %
19	A	36.62 % / 4.69 %
20	A	79.58 % / 5.4 %
21	C	25.82 % / 4.93 %
22	D	41.55 % / 5.63 %
23	B	86.38 % / 4.0 %
24	B	50.0 % / 5.87 %
25	D	33.33 % / 6.11 %

//Hints and Solutions//

1. A written statement confirmed by oath or affirmation, for use as evidence in court. An affidavit is a voluntary statement or written compilation of the facts of a case under oath. The affidavit relates specifically to the issue to be decided and should be the person's own account of events.

Hence, the correct option is (C).

2. In an Auction sale, if the seller makes use of pretended bidding to raise the price, the sale is voidable at the option of the buyer (he may avoid it). Sometimes, a group of persons may form a combination to prevent competition among themselves in an auction.

Hence, the correct option is (C).

3. Parliament creates laws in the form of statutes and such laws stand in contrast to judge-made law. Accordingly, the statute is not referred to as 'common law.' Common law is a body of unwritten laws based on legal precedents established by the courts. Common law influences the decision-making process in unusual cases where the outcome cannot be determined based on existing statutes or written rules of law.

Hence, the correct option is (C).

4. The International Court of Justice is composed of 15 judges elected to nine-year terms of office by the United Nations General Assembly and the Security Council. The Court may not include more than one national of the same State. Moreover, the Court as a whole must represent the main forms of civilization and the principal legal systems of the world. These organs vote simultaneously but separately. In order to be elected, a candidate must receive an absolute majority of the votes in both bodies independtly. This sometimes makes it necessary for a number of rounds of voting to be carried out. In order to ensure a measure of continuity, one-third of the Court is elected every three years. Judges are eligible for re-election. Should a judge die or resign during his or her term of office, a special election is held as soon as possible to choose a judge to fill the unexpired part of the term.

Hence, the correct option is (D).

5. The discretion remains with the Court whether to order a separate or a joint trial depending upon which of the two would better serve the purpose of justice in riot cases. Generally, every person is entitled to insist that his case be tried separately. Therefore the result is force and violence.

Hence, the correct option is (B).

6. It was held in the Justice K. S. Puttaswamy (Retd.) and Anr. vs Union Of India that the right to privacy is protected as an intrinsic part of the right to life and personal liberty under Article 21 and as a part of the freedoms guaranteed by Part III of the Constitution. The right to privacy in India has developed through a series of decisions over the past 60 years.

Hence, the correct option is (C).

7. Section 82 and section 83 of the Indian Penal Code confer immunity from criminal liability to children up to 12 years.

Children below 7 years get a complete defense from criminal liability whereas, for children from 7 to 12 years, the immunity conferred depends on their maturity of understanding during the commission of the crime.

Section 82: Act of a child under seven years of age.—Nothing is an offence which is done by a child under seven years of age

Section 83: Act of a child above seven and under twelve of immature understanding.—Nothing is an offence which is done by a child above seven years of age and under twelve, who has not attained sufficient maturity of understanding to judge of the nature and consequences of his conduct on that occasion.

Hence, the correct option is (B).

8. The defence of infancy is provided under sections 82 and 83 of the Indian Penal Code. Section 82 provides for all acts to not be an offence which are done by a child of under seven of age while Section 83 specifically talk about acts that are not an offence and done by a child above seven years or age but below twelve years of age who is of immature understanding or has not yet attained sufficient maturity.

Hence, the correct option is (C).

9. Section 78: Nothing which is done in pursuance of, or which is warranted by the judgment or order of, a Court of Justice, if done whilst such judgment or order remains in force, is an offense, notwithstanding the Court may have had no jurisdiction to pass such judgment or order, provided the person doing the act in good faith believes that the Court had such jurisdiction. Therefore person gets exempted from criminal viability.

Hence, the correct option is (B).

10. An ordinary jurisdiction has a general competence to settle all types of disputes in all matters, except when specific competence is expressly attributed to another jurisdiction. At first instance, the civil ordinary jurisdiction is the court of the first instance. Territorial jurisdiction is the court's power to bind the parties to the action. This law determines the scope of federal and state court power.

Hence, the correct option is (C).

11. Personal jurisdiction based on the fact that a State has the right to extend the application of its laws to its nationals even with respect to events occurring entirely abroad. The passive personality principle allows states, in limited cases, to claim jurisdiction to try a foreign national for offenses committed abroad that affect its own citizens.

Hence, the correct option is (C).

12. It is extraterritorial jurisdiction based on the harm to national interests in respect of conduct committed abroad. The protective principle recognizes that a sovereign can adopt a statute that criminalizes conduct that occurs outside of its borders when that conduct affects the sovereign itself. Under that principle, a nation can adopt laws that make it a crime to engage in an act that obstructs the function of government or threatens its security as a state without regard to where or by whom the act is committed.

Hence, the correct option is (A).

13. Sarla Mudgal vs. Union of India:- The case is related to the offence of Bigamy, the conflict between the personal laws and a strong need for a uniform civil code in the country. The court held that the second marriage of a Hindu man after being converted to Islam will be invalid if the first marriage has not been dissolved.

Hence, the correct option is (B).

14. T Sareetha v VenkataSubbaiah when it held that "the right to privacy belongs to an individual and is not lost by marital association". The court observed that the enforcement of section 9 against an individual compelled her to have sexual relations with her spouse, thus depriving her of control over her body.

Hence, the correct option is (D).

15. This case dealt with the amenability of Fundamental Rights (the First Amendment's validity was challenged). The SC contended that the Parliament's power to amend under Article 368 also includes the power to amend the Fundamental Rights guaranteed in Part III of the Constitution.

Hence, the correct option is (C).

16. Mother of a Hindu Child was declared by the Apex Court, to be the natural guardian, during the lifetime of his/her father, in the case of Githa Hariharan v Reserve Bank of India. Ms Githa Hariharan was married to Dr Mohan Ram and they had a son named Rishab. She applied to the Reserve Bank of India (RBI) for bonds to be held in the name of their minor son Rishab and had signed off as his guardian. The RBI sent back the application to her advising her to either produce the application signed by the father of Rishab or produce a certificate of guardianship from a competent authority in her favour. RBI was of the opinion that Dr Mohan was the natural guardian of Rishab on the basis of Section 6(a) of the Hindu Minority and Guardianship Act, 1956 (HMGA). That provision stated that the father is the natural guardian of a Hindu minor child and the mother is the guardian "after" the father. Ms Hariharan challenged the constitutional validity of this provision in the Supreme Court on grounds that it violated the right to equality guaranteed under Articles 14 and 15 of the Indian Constitution.

Hence, the correct option is (B).

17. Every state law defines the eligibility criteria of inmates who can be in an open prison. The principal rule is that an inmate eligible for open-air prison has to be a convict. Good conduct in prison and at least five years spent in a controlled jail are the rules followed by the Rajasthan open prisons.

Hence, the correct option is (C).

18. Human trafficking, also known as trafficking in persons (TIP), is a modern-day form of slavery. It is a crime under federal and international law; it is also a crime in every state in the United States. It is a type of organised crime. According to the report, the most common form of human trafficking (79%) is sexual exploitation. The victims of sexual exploitation are predominantly women and girls. Surprisingly, in 30% of the countries which provided information on the gender of traffickers, women make up the largest proportion of traffickers.

Hence, the correct option is (B).

19. In agreements of a purely domestic nature, the intention of the parties to create a legal relationship is to be proved to the satisfaction of the court. Intention to create legal relations is defined as an intention to enter a legally binding agreement or contract. Intention to create legal relations is one of the necessary elements in the formation of a contract.

Hence, the correct option is (A).

20. According to Section 2(e);" Every promise and every set of promises forming the consideration for each other is an agreement." In an agreement there is a promise from both sides, For example, A promises to deliver his watch to B and in return B promises to pay a sum of Rs.2000 to A, there is said to be an agreement between A and B.

Hence, the correct option is (A).

21. A body of water open to all. Typically a synonym for International Waters, or in other legal parlance, the "High Seas".

Hence, the correct option is (C).

22. Guardian under a curatorship (cura). Types are:

Curator ad litem - guardian ad litem

Curator bonis - guardian of the property

Curator personae - guardian of the person.

Hence, the correct option is (D).

23. A Proclamation of Emergency declaring that the security of India or any part of the territory thereof is threatened by war or by external aggression or by armed rebellion may be made before the actual occurrence of war or of any such aggression or rebellion, if the President is satisfied that there is imminent danger thereof then emergency occurs.

Hence, the correct option is (B)

24. The Consumer Rights under Consumer Protection Act include several rights such as the Right to safety, Right to choose, Right to be informed, Right to consumer education, Right to be heard, Right to Seek redressal etc.

Hence, the correct option is (B).

25. Panchayats (Extension to Scheduled Areas) Act (PESA) authorizes the States to give the Gram Sabhas power to regulate and restrict sale/consumption of liquor; ownership of minor forest produce; power to prevent alienation of land and restore alienated land; power to manage village markets, control money lending to STs and power to manage village markets, control money lending to STs and Mandatory executive functions to approve plans of the Village Panchayats, identify beneficiaries for schemes, issue certificates of the utilization of funds.

Hence, the correct option is (D).

Q.1 Which of the following punishment cannot be awarded under the Indian Penal Code?

A. Forfeiture of property
B. Rigorous imprisonment
C. Transportation for life
D. Death

Q.2 Nothing is an offence which is done by a child below the age of:

A. Eight years
B. Ten years
C. Seven years
D. Twelve year

Q.3 Delhi court has recently granted bail to climate activist Disha Ravi, arrested in connection with allegedly being involved in sharing a "toolkit" on social media related to the farmers' protest, terming evidence produced by police as scanty and sketchy. The Freedom of Press (in India) is not absolute in nature and it is subject to certain restrictions under :

A. Article 19(1) of the Constitution
B. Article 19(1)(a) of the Constitution
C. Article 21 of the Constitution
D. Article 19(2) of the Constitution

Q.4 A' instigates 'B' to instigate 'C' to murder 'Z'. 'B' accordingly instigate 'C' to murder 'Z' and 'C' commits that offence in consequence of 'B's instigation. 'A' is:

A. Not guilty of any offence
B. Not guilty of abetting murder
C. Guilty of abetment by conspiracy
D. Guilty of abetting murder

Q.5 What will be effect of mistake of the law in force in India on the agreement?

A. Not voidable
B. Voidable
C. Void
D. Not void

Q.6 "A" promises for no consideration to give to 'B' Rs. 1000 agreement is:

A. Voidable
B. Void
C. Enforceable
D. Not enforceable on being in writing

Q.7 Where no application is made and no time is specified for performance of promise, there the agreement be performed within:

A. Three years
B. Two years
C. One years
D. Reasonable time

Q.8 A proposal when accepted:

A. Becomes a promise
B. Becomes an agreement
C. Becomes a contract
D. Becomes a consideration

Q.9 Legal representative under Section 2(11) of Cr.P.C means a person who is a:

A. Relative of parties to the suit
B. Co-sharer of the benefits assuming to the parties to the suit
C. Who in law represents the estate of the deceased
D. None of the above

Q.10 Lodging of caveat under Section 148 - A of C.P.C.

A. Entitles the caveator to receive notice of the application
B. Makes the caveat or a party to the suit
C. Both (A) and (B)
D. None of the above

Q.11 Provisions of Section 10 of C.P.C. are:

A. Directory
B. Mandatory
C. Discretionary
D. None of the above

Q.12 Parties by their consent/agreement:

A. Can confer jurisdiction on a Court, where there is none in law
B. Can oust the jurisdiction of the Court where there is one in law
C. Can oust the jurisdiction of one of the Courts when there are two simultaneously having jurisdiction in law
D. None of the above

Q.13 Which one among the following statements regarding the Government of India Act, 1935 is not correct?

A. Provincial autonomy came into existence
B. Bicameral legislatures were provided in six provinces
C. The principles of communal electorates and weightages were further extended
D. The states were compelled to enter the federation

Q.14 The Indian Constitution has borrowed the Ideas of Preamble from the:

A. Italian Constitution
B. Canadian Constitution
C. French Constitution
D. Constitution of USA

Q.15 Act of State can be questioned and challanged in:

A. Privy Council
B. Queens Court
C. High Court
D. Supreme Court

Q.16 The writ of Habeas corpus means:

A. To produce the Body of a person illegally detained before a Court
B. Respect the Human Rights of a person
C. Stop the violation of a right of a man
D. None of the above

Q.17 Which of the following is the closest in meaning to the legal maxim res communes?

A. Whence there is truth, there is light
B. Things belonging to no body
C. Things belonging to everybody
D. Rest of the communities

Q.18 Lex tallienis denotes:
A. The law of the place
B. The law of the strong
C. Oral law
D. The law of Retributive Justice

Q.19 Comments made at the beginning of a trial by the attorneys to the jury summarizing the factual and legal issues of the case:

A. Closing Arguments
B. Opening Statements
C. Miranda Rights
D. Briefs

Q.20 If the removal motion is admitted then the Speaker/Chairman constitutes a three-member committee to investigate the allegations charged against the judge. The three-member committee comprises of

1. The Chief Justice of Session Court

2. Senior most judge of Supreme Court

3. Chief justice of the High Court

Choose from the following options.

A. 1 and 2 Only
B. 2 and 3 Only
C. 1 and 3 Only
D. All of them

Q.21 Consider the following statements.

1. The Constitution declares Delhi as the seat of the Supreme Court.

2. It also authorises the CJI to appoint other place or places as the seat of the Supreme Court.

3. He can make a decision in this regard only with the approval of the Parliament.

Which of these statements are correct?

A. 1 and 2 Only
B. 2 and 3 Only
C. 1 and 3 Only
D. All of them

Q.22 Which Landmark constitutional case is known as the Mandal Case?
A. Indra Sawhney vs union of India
B. Ahmed Khan vs Shah Bano Begum
C. Hussainara khatoon vs Home Secretary, State of Bihar
D. Mithu vs State of Punjab

Q.23 Which Landmark case of the Supreme Court talked about Speedy Trial?
A. Nandini Satpathi vs P.L. Dani
B. Hussainara khatoon vs Home Secretary, State of Bihar
C. Ahmed Khan vs Shah Bano Begum
D. Rajagopal vs State of Tamilnadu

Q.24 The charge of having commited a crime, based on the judgment of a grand jury:
A. Arrest
B. Fraud
C. Indictment
D. Injunction

Q.25 Contracts that are implied from the action and conduct of the parties rather than stated in oral or written words:
A. Implied-in-fact Contract
B. Agreement
C. Illegal Contract
D. Breach of Contract

// Smart Answer Sheet //

Correct — Percentage of students who answered correctly. **Skipped** — Percentage of students who skipped.

Q.	Ans.	Correct / Skipped	Q.	Ans.	Correct / Skipped	Q.	Ans.	Correct / Skipped	Q.	Ans.	Correct / Skipped	Q.	Ans.	Correct / Skipped
1	C	64.88 % / 1.68 %	6	B	56.86 % / 4.68 %	11	B	28.09 % / 5.02 %	16	A	90.3 % / 4.35 %	21	A	39.46 % / 4.69 %
2	C	86.96 % / 4.68 %	7	D	63.88 % / 5.02 %	12	C	32.44 % / 5.35 %	17	C	39.8 % / 5.02 %	22	A	80.6 % / 4.68 %
3	D	31.77 % / 4.02 %	8	A	48.83 % / 4.68 %	13	D	39.13 % / 4.35 %	18	D	32.44 % / 4.68 %	23	B	66.22 % / 4.01 %
4	D	49.5 % / 4.68 %	9	C	33.44 % / 5.02 %	14	D	74.92 % / 4.68 %	19	B	50.84 % / 3.68 %	24	C	38.8 % / 5.01 %
5	A	17.73 % / 4.01 %	10	A	15.38 % / 5.02 %	15	D	53.51 % / 4.68 %	20	B	47.49 % / 4.35 %	25	A	58.19 % / 5.36 %

//Hints and Solutions//

1. Forfeiture of Property

Section 126 – Committing depradation on territories of power at peace with the Govt of India.

Section 127 – Receiving property taken by war or depredation mentioned in Section 125 and 126 of I.P.C. Section 169 – Public servant unlawfully buying or bidding for a property.

Rigorous imprisonment

Indian Penal Code provides for imprisonment that may be rigorous or simple. Rigorous imprisonment for a specified duration is awarded in offences of serious nature such as house trespass (Section 449) or giving or fabricating false evidence with intent to procure conviction of capital offence (Section 194).

Death

The Indian Penal Code, 1860 awards death sentence as a punishment for various offenses. Some of these capital offences under the IPC are punishment for criminal conspiracy (Section 120B), murder (Section 302), waging or attempting to wage war against the Government of India (Section 121), abetment of mutiny (Section 132), dacoity with murder (Section 396) and others. Apart from this, there are provisions for the death penalty in various legislations like the NDPS Act, anti-terrorism laws etc.

Hence, the correct option is (C).

2. Nothing is an offence which is done by a child above seven years of age and under twelve, who has not attained sufficient maturity of understanding to judge of the nature and consequences of his conduct on that occasion.

Hence, the correct option is (C).

3. The Freedom of Press (in India) is not absolute in nature and it is subject to certain restrictions under Article $19(2)$ of the Constitution.

- The Freedom of the Press comes within the ambit of Freedom of Speech & Expression. In a democracy, freedom of the press is highly essential as it acts as a watchdog on the three organs of a democracy viz. the legislature, the executive & the judiciary.

- But, the freedom of the press is not absolute in nature. It is subject to certain restrictions which are mentioned in Article 19(2) of the Constitution. The following are the grounds of restrictions laid down in Article 19(2) :

1. Sovereignty & Integrity of India
2. Security of the State
3. Friendly relations with the Foreign States
4. Public Order Decency or Morality and Contempt of Court

Hence, the correct option is (D).

4. Section 108 in The Indian Penal Code

Abettor.—A person abets an offence, who abets either the commission of an offence, or the commission of an act which would be an offence, if committed by a person capable by law of committing an offence with the same intention or knowledge as that of the abettor.

The abetment of an offence being an offence, the abetment of such an abetment is also as offence.

A instigates B to instigate C to murder Z. B accordingly instigates C to murder Z, and C commits that offence in consequence of B's instigation. B is liable to be punished for his offence with the punishment for murder; and, as A instigated B to commit the offence, A is also liable to the same punishment.

Hence, the correct option is (D).

5. Section 21 - Effect of mistakes as to law

A contract is not voidable because it was caused by a mistake as to any law in force in India; but a mistake as to a law not in force in India has the same effect as a mistake of fact.

For example, A and B make a contract grounded on the erroneous belief that a particular debt is barred by the Indian Law of Limitation; the contract is not voidable.

Hence, the correct option is (A).

6. Section 25 in The Indian Contract Act, 1872

Agreement without consideration, void, unless it is in writing and registered or is a promise to compensate for something done or is a promise to pay a debt barred by limitation law.—An agreement made without consideration is void, unless— An agreement made without consideration is void, unless"

(1) It is expressed in writing and registered under the law for the time being in force for the registration of 1[documents], and is made on account of natural love and affection between parties standing in a near relation to each other; or unless

(2) It is a promise to compensate, wholly or in part, a person who has already voluntarily done something for the promisor, or something which the promisor was legally compellable to do; or unless.

(3) It is a promise, made in writing and signed by the person to be charged therewith, or by his agent generally or specially authorized in that behalf, to pay wholly or in part a debt of which the creditor might have enforced payment but for the law for the limitation of suits. In any of these cases, such an agreement is a contract.

For example, A promises, for no consideration, to give to B Rs. 1,000. This is a void agreement. (a) A promise, for no consideration, to give to B Rs. 1,000. This is a void agreement."

Hence, the correct option is (B).

7. Section 46 in The Indian Contract Act, 1872

Time for performance of promise, where no application is to be made and no time is specified.—Where, by the contract, a promisor is to perform his promise without application by the promisee, and no time for performance is specified, the engagement must be performed within a reasonable time. — Where, by the contract, a promisor is to perform his promise without application by the promisee, and no time for performance is specified, the engagement must be performed within a reasonable time." Explanation.—The question "what is a reasonable time" is, in each particular case, a question of fact.

Hence, the correct option is (D).

8. Promise 2(b): A Proposal when accepted becomes a promise. In simple words, when an offer is accepted it becomes a promise.

When the person to whom the proposal is made signifies his assent thereto, the proposal is said to be accepted. A proposal, when accepted, becomes a promise.

Hence, the correct option is (A).

9. "Legal representative" as defined in Civil Procedures Code, under Section 2(11), means a person who in law represents the estate of a deceased person and includes any person who intermeddles with The estate of the deceased and where the party sues or is prosecuted in a representative manner by the person to whom the estate is transferred upon the death of the party so suing or sued.

Hence, the correct option is (C).

10. 148 A Right to lodge a caveat-

(1) Where an application is expected to be made, or has been made, in a suit or proceeding instituted, or about to be instituted, in a Court , any person claiming a right to appear before the Court on the hearing of such application may lodge a caveat in respect thereof.

(2) Where a caveat has been lodged under sub-section (1), the person by whom the caveat has been lodged (hereinafter referred to as the caveator) shall serve a notice of the caveat by registered post, acknowledgement due, on the person by whom the application has been, or is expected to be, made, under sub-section (1).

(3) Where, after a caveat has been lodged under sub-section (1), any application is filed in any suit or proceeding, the Court, shall serve a notice of the application on the caveator.

(4) Where a notice of any caveat has been served on the applicant, he shall forthwith furnish the caveator at the caveators expense, with a copy of the application made by him and also with copies of any paper or document which has been, or may be, filed by him in support of the application.

(5) Where a caveat has been lodged under sub-section (1), such caveat shall not remain in force after the expiry of ninety days from the date on which it was lodged unless the application referred to in sub-section (1) has been made before the expiry of the said period.

Hence, the correct option is (A).

11. The use of negative expression in Section 10, i.e. "no court shall proceed with the trial of any suit" makes the provision mandatory and the Court in which the subsequent suit has been filed is prohibited from proceeding with the trial of that suit if the conditions laid down in Section 10 of the Code are satisfied.

Hence, the correct option is (B).

12. Parties to a contract are barred from agreeing to absolutely oust the jurisdiction of all the Courts which would otherwise have the jurisdiction to decide a dispute in relation to a contract between them. Such agreements are considered as unlawful and void by Section 28 of the Indian Contract Act, 1872.

Hence, the correct option is (C).

13. The Government of India Act, 1935 provided for the establishment of an All-India Federation consisting of provinces and princely states as units. It abolished dyarchy in the provinces and introduced 'provincial autonomy' in its place. It introduced bicameralism in six out of eleven provinces. The extension of the principle of communal representation by providing separate electorates for Sikhs, Indian Christians, Anglo-Indians, and Europeans were introduced by the Government of India Act, 1919.

Hence, the correct option is (D).

14. The Indian Constitution has borrowed the ideas of Preamble from the Constitution of the USA. Indian Constitution has borrowed the following features from the Constitution of the USA:

1. Impeachment of the president

2. Fundamental Rights

3. Judicial review

Hence, the correct option is (D).

15. State governments cannot complain of fundamental rights being violated. Therefore, the Constitution provides that whenever a State feels that its legal rights are under threat or have been violated, it can take the "dispute" to the Supreme Court.

Hence, the correct option is (D).

16. A writ of habeas corpus is in the nature of an order upon the person who has detained another to produce the latter before the court, in order to let the court know on what ground he has been confined and set him free if there is no legal justification for the imprisonment.

Hence, the correct option is (A).

17. Res communes is a Roman & civil law concept. It means things owned by no one and subject to use by all. Things (as light, air, the sea, running water) are incapable of entire exclusive appropriation and are considered as subject of Res communes.

Hence, the correct option is (C).

18. Lex tallienis is the principle or law of retaliation that a punishment inflicted should correspond in degree and kind to the offense of the wrongdoer, as an eye for an eye, a tooth for a tooth; retributive justice.

Retributive justice is a theory of punishment that when an offender breaks the law, justice requires that they suffer in return and that the response to a crime is proportional to the offense.

Hence, the correct option is (D).

19. The opening statement is the time during which the attorney may speak to the jury and describe the case. The opening statement is not an argument, however; in fact, legal arguments are prohibited during the opening statement. It is during the opening statement that attorneys will tell the story of the case and what they hope to prove using the evidence that will be presented.

Hence, the correct option is (B).

20. The three-member committee comprises

(1) The Chief Justice or senior-most judge of the Supreme Court

(2) Chief justice of the High Court and

(3) A prominent jurist

Hence, the correct option is (B).

21. The seat of Supreme Court The Constitution declares Delhi as the seat of the Supreme Court. It also authorises the CJI to appoint other place or places as the seat of the Supreme Court. He can take a decision in this regard only with the approval of the President. This provision is only optional and not compulsory. This means that no court can give any direction either to the President or to the Chief Justice to appoint any other place as the seat of the Supreme Court.

Hence, the correct option is (A).

22. Indra Sawhney vs union of India is also known as Mandal Commission Case. The court has held that barring any extraordinary situations reservation should not exceed 50 per cent.

Hence, the correct option is (A).

23. Speedy Trial: means that the defendant is tried for the alleged crimes within a reasonable time after being arrested. In the most extreme situations, when a court determines that the delay between arrest and trial was unreasonable and prejudicial to the defendant, the court dismisses the case altogether.

In the Hussainara khatoon case, the Supreme Court talked about the right to Speedy Trial. The Court recognized the right to a speedy trial and the right to legal aid services as basic and essential rights.

Hence, the correct option is (B).

24. Indictment - The formal charge issued by a grand jury stating that there is enough evidence that the defendant committed the crime to justify having a trial; it is used primarily for felonies.

Hence, the correct option is (C).

25. An implied-in-fact contract is a form of an implied contract formed by non-verbal conduct, rather than by explicit words. The United States Supreme Court has defined it as "an agreement 'implied in fact'" as "founded upon a meeting of minds, which, although not embodied in an express contract, is inferred, as a fact, from conduct of the parties showing, in the light of the surrounding circumstances, their tacit understanding.

Although the parties may not have exchanged words of agreement, their conduct may indicate that an agreement existed.

Hence, the correct option is (A).

Q.1 Notorious

A. Infamous   **B.** Anonymous

C. Scandalous   **D.** famed

Q.2 Direction: In the following question, out of the four alternatives, choose the word which best expresses the meaning of the given word.

Embrace

A. Accept   **B.** Reject   **C.** Disturb   **D.** Exclude

Ques (3-4):Direction: In the following question, some part of the sentence is underlined. Which of the options given below the sentence should replace the part underlined to make the sentence grammatically correct?

Q.3 I was **eagerly about** joining the piano classes.

A. Eager in   **B.** Eager about

C. Eagerly in   **D.** No improvement

Q.4 The **herd of cattles** belonged to the man who lives in the house next to mine.

A. Herd cattles   **B.** Cattles

C. Herd of cattle   **D.** No Correction

Ques (5-6):Direction: Choose the correct alternative which can be substituted for the below given word/ sentence.

Q.5 To remove an objectionable part from a book.

A. Exterminate   **B.** Expurgate

C. Extirpate   **D.** Eradicate

Q.6 Showing an inclination to disagree

A. Fallacy   **B.** Contentious

C. Bickering   **D.** Conduit

Ques (7-8):Direction: Fill in the blank with an appropriate preposition.

Q.7 He is jealous ____ her success.

A. about   **B.** of   **C.** in   **D.** on

Q.8 Unfortunately, we had to cancel it owing ____ the bad weather.

A. about   **B.** to   **C.** of   **D.** in

Ques (9-10):Direction: In the following question, the sentence given with a blank is to be filled in with an appropriate word. Select the correct alternative out of the four and indicate it by selecting the appropriate option.

Q.9 He actually lacked the ______ to go alone and talk to the Principal.

A. Sense   **B.** Wisdom

C. Confidence   **D.** Action

Q.10 They have started a charitable ______ in their city.

A. Story   **B.** Foundation

C. Incentive   **D.** Company

Ques (11-15):Direction: Read the passage carefully and answer the question that follows by choosing the correct alternative out of the given four options.

In the earliest Vedic literature are found not only hymns in praise of the accepted Gods, but also doubts in regard to the worth of these Gods, the beginnings of a new religion incorporated into the earliest records of the old. And later, when, Megasthenes was in India, the descendants of those first theosophists were still discussing the questions that lay at the root of all religions. And in many things they held the same opinions with the Greeks, saying that the universe was begotten and will be destroyed, and the world is a sphere, that there are different beginnings of all things, but water is the beginning of world-making.

India's literature was pre-eminently priestly and religious. Religion forms either the subject-matter of the most important works, or, as in the case of the epics, the basis of **didactic excursions** and sectarian interpolations, which impart to worldly themes a tone peculiarly theological. History and oratory are unknown in Indian literature. The early poetry consists of hymns and religious poems; the early prose, of liturgies, linguistics, law, theology, sacred legends and other works, all of which are intended to supplement the knowledge of the Vedas, to explain ceremonies, or to inculcate religious principles. At a later date, formal grammar systems of philosophy, fables, and commentaries are added to the prose; epics, secular lyric drama, the Puranas and such writings to the poetry. But in all this great mass, till after the Hindus came into close contract with foreign nations, notably the Greek, from which has been borrowed, perhaps, the classical Hindu drama, there is no real literature that was not religious originally, or, at least, so apt for priestly use as to become chiefly moral and theosophical; while the most popular works of modern times are sectarian tracts, Puranas, Tantras and remodelled worldly poetry. The sources from which knowledge of Hindu religions is to be drawn are the best possible- the original texts. The information furnished by foreigners, from the times of Ktesias and Megasthenes to that of Mandelslo, is considerable, but one is warranted in assuming that what little in it is novel is inaccurate, since otherwise the information would have been furnished by the Hindus themselves; and that, conversely, an outsider's statements often may give an inexact impression through lack of completeness. To take an example- Ktesias tells half the truth in regard to ordeals. His account is true, but he gives no notion of the number or elaborate character of these interesting ceremonies.

The sources to which we shall refer will be the two most important collections of Vedic hymns- the Rig Veda and the Atharva Veda; the Brahmanic literature, with the supplementary Upanishads, and the Sutras or mnemonic abridgements of religious and ceremonial rules; the legal texts, and the religious and theological portions of the epic; and the later sectarian writings, called the Puranas. The great heresies again have their own special writings. Thus, far we shall draw on the native literature. Only for some of the wild modern sects, and for the religious of the wild tribes which have no literature, shall we have to depend on the accounts of European writers.

Q.11 The author would recommend which of the following for the authentic knowledge of Hindu religion?

A. The accounts of foreigners like Megathenes.

B. The accounts of the Greek scholars.

C. The original religious texts of the Hindus.

D. The later books and commentaries on Hinduism.

Q.12 What contradictory feature of early Vedic literature is mentioned by the author in the passage?

A. Vedic literature was pre-eminently priestly and religious.

B. They are the best sources of Hindu religion.

C. They assimilated writings of foreigners also.

D. They contained both hymns in praise of Gods and doubts in regard to the worth of the Gods.

Q.13 What does "Didactic excursion" as mentioned in the passage mean?

A. Intended to teach moral lessons.

B. Used as guides in religious trips.

C. Intended to delay religious examinations.

D. Intended to aid understanding of the other worldly.

Q.14 Literature in India was:

A. Mostly classical drama

B. Mostly Religious

C. Mostly Dialectic

D. Mostly superstitious

Q.15 Which of the following is true in relation to the European writings about India?

A. They are not accurate about religious and ceremonial rules.

B. They can be used for religions and sects who have no literature.

C. They are only useful for legal interpretations of texts.

D. They are the modern versions of epics and mythologies.

Q.16 Direction: In the following question, an idiomatic expression or a proverb is highlighted. Select the alternative which best describes its use in the sentence.

He's always been the **black sheep** of the family.

A. Main person

B. Most talented person

C. The one who brings fame

D. Odd one out

Q.17 Direction: In the following question, out of the four alternatives, select the alternative which best expresses the meaning of the Idiom/Phrase.

To have an axe to grind

A. To fail to arouse interest

B. To have a selfish reason for doing something

C. To have no result

D. To work for both sides

Q.18 In the question four words are given out of which only one word is correctly spelt. Find the correctly spelt word.

A. Honourarium

B. Honorarium

C. Honourerium

D. Honourrarium

Q.19 In the following question, a group of four words is given. In the group, one word is correctly spelt. Find the correctly spelt word.

A. Circuiteous

B. Clairvoyant

C. Chivel

D. Cavelcade

Ques (20-21):Direction: In the question, a sentence has been given in active/passive voice. Out of the given four alternatives, suggest the one which best expresses the given sentence in passive/active voice.

Q.20 The accountant took the money from the customer.

A. The money is taken from the customer by the accountant.

B. The money was taken from the customer by the accountant.

C. The customer was taken the money by the accountant.

D. The money had been taken from the customer by the accountant.

Q.21 They made him a king.

A. A king has been made by him.

B. He was made a king by them.

C. They have been made king by him.

D. He has been made a king by them.

Q.22 Subjective pronoun in sentences "We cannot go to movie, until my mom gives permission to go." is:

A. my   B. we   C. until   D. can

Q.23 Relative pronoun in sentence "success is only for those who believe in hard working." is:

A. is   B. for   C. who   D. in

Q.24 What type of noun does the underlined portion of the following sentence represent?

Officer Tarun should get an award for his bravery.

A. Collective

B. Proper

C. Common

D. Abstract

Q.25 Select the answer choice that identifies the noun in the sentence.

Sparta and Athens were enemies during the Peloponnesian War.

A. And   B. Were   C. During   D. War

// Smart Answer Sheet //

Correct Percentage of students who answered correctly.   **Skipped** Percentage of students who skipped.

Q.	Ans.	Correct / Skipped
1	B	26.47 % / 4.66 %
2	A	67.89 % / 3.92 %
3	B	62.99 % / 8.33 %
4	C	51.72 % / 8.57 %
5	B	22.79 % / 5.64 %
6	B	28.19 % / 6.37 %
7	B	67.16 % / 10.05 %
8	B	62.25 % / 10.05 %
9	C	80.88 % / 8.34 %
10	B	76.47 % / 8.82 %
11	C	54.17 % / 8.82 %
12	D	47.79 % / 9.07 %
13	A	28.92 % / 9.07 %
14	B	73.77 % / 7.36 %
15	B	28.68 % / 8.82 %
16	D	61.03 % / 8.33 %
17	B	46.81 % / 9.07 %
18	B	31.86 % / 9.32 %
19	B	21.57 % / 9.31 %
20	B	53.68 % / 7.35 %
21	B	50.25 % / 7.59 %
22	B	45.59 % / 3.67 %
23	C	63.97 % / 9.07 %
24	D	61.03 % / 8.09 %
25	D	58.58 % / 6.37 %

//Hints and Solutions//

1. 'Anonymous' is the correct antonym of the word 'Notorious'.

- 'Notorious' means famous or well known, typically for some bad quality or deed.

- 'Anonymous' means having no outstanding, individual, or unusual features.

Hence, the correct option is (B).

2. 'Embrace' means to accept (a belief, theory, or change) willingly and enthusiastically.

'Accept' is a better fit synonym for the given word as it means regard favourably or with approval.

Hence, the correct option is (A).

3. The usage of the adverb 'eagerly' is incorrect. It should be replaced with the adjective **'eager'**

The preposition **'about'** does not need any change.

Hence, the correct option is (B).

4. 'Cattle' is never used with the 's' joined to its end. The word **'herd'** is needed before the word **'cattle'** to give a plural meaning.

Hence, the correct option is (C).

5. 'Exterminate' means to kill.

'Extirpate' means to destroy.

'Eradicate' is similar in meaning to 'exterminate'.

'Expurgate' means to purge or clean up.

Hence, the correct option is (B).

6. Contentious - Not agreeing easily

Fallacy - A mistaken belief, especially one based on unsound arguments.

Bickering - Quarrelsome

Conduit - Passage through which electrical wires pass

Hence, the correct option is (B).

7. He is jealous **of** her success.

Of expresses the relationship of a part of something to its whole. It is the most used preposition in English.

For example:

He is a boy of 15.

Some parts of his body were injured.

Hence, the correct option is (B).

8. Unfortunately, we had to cancel it owing **to** the bad weather.

Use the preposition 'to' when indicating that there is movement from one place to another. In other words, the preposition 'to' with verbs such as drive, walk, go, hike, fly, sail, etc. We're flying to San Francisco on Thursday for a meeting.

Hence, the correct option is (B).

9. The correct word here is 'confidence' which means 'the feeling or belief that one can have faith in or rely on someone or something.

Hence, the correct option is (C).

10. The blank must contain a noun, as the word before it is an adjective, 'charitable'. The only word that can fit with the verb 'started' and the adjective 'charitable' is 'foundation', as the others cannot form a meaningful sentence.

Hence, the correct option is (B).

11. In the second paragraph, the author says the best sources to know Hindu religion are the originals texts; the information furnished by foreign writers is considerable but inaccurate: 'The sources from which knowledge of Hindu religions is to be drawn are the best possible- the original text, an outsider's statements often may give an inexact impression through lack of completeness'.

Option (A), (B), and (D) are incorrect as they are not supported by the author.

Hence, the correct option is (C).

12. Refer to the first few lines of the passage where the author says, 'In the earliest Vedic literature are found not only hymns in praise of the accepted Gods, but also doubts in regard to the worth of these Gods'.

Hence, the correct option is (D).

13. In the second paragraph the author says that religion forms the basis of didactic excursions. Didactic means 'intending to teach, particularly in having moral instruction as an ulterior motive.' In the context of the passage, it means that religion carries a purpose of teaching morals.

Hence, the correct option is (A).

14. Refer to the second paragraph where the author says, 'India's literature was pre-eminently priestly, there is no real literature that was not religious originally'. India's literature was pre-eminently priestly and religious.

Hence, the correct option is (B).

15. Refer to the last part of the second paragraph which says 'only for some of the modern sects, and for the religions of the wild tribes which have no literature, shall we have to depend on the accounts of European writers.

Hence, the correct option is (B).

16. 'Black sheep' means 'an undesirable member of a group, odd one out, a disliked person, somebody who causes shame or embarrassment due to deviation.'

Hence, the correct option is (D).

17. The meaning of "To have an axe to grind" is: "To have a selfish interest".

Synonyms for the given phrase: motive, Hidden agenda, Score to settle.

Hence, the correct option is (B).

18. The correct spelling is 'Honorarium' which means 'stipend'.

Stipendan- amount of money that is paid regularly to somebody as wages or an allowance usually for some specific purpose

All others are wrong.

Hence, the correct option is (B).

19. "Clairvoyant" is the only word with correct spelling which means a person who claims to have a supernatural ability to perceive events in the future or beyond normal sensory contact.

The correct spellings of the other words:

Circuitous: (of a route or journey) longer than the most direct way

Chive: a small Eurasian plant related to the onion

Cavalcade: a formal procession of people walking, on horseback, or riding in vehicles.

Hence, the correct option is (B).

20. The money was taken from the customer by the accountant.

Given sentence is in Past simple tense and it is in active voice, we need to change it into passive voice.

Rule:

Subject + (was / were) + V3 + Objects

Hence, the correct option is (B).

21. He was made a king by them.

Given that sentence is in Past simple tense and in active voice, we need to change it into passive voice.

Rule:

Subject + (was / were) + V^3 + Optional

Hence, the correct option is (B).

22. In the sentence "We" is the subjective pronoun.

Subjective pronouns tell us who or what the sentence is about. Objective pronouns receive the action in the sentence. There are some pronouns that are always subjective and others that are always objective.

For example: I, you, he, she, it, we, you, they

Hence, the correct option is (B).

23. A relative pronoun is a pronoun that heads an adjective clause.

Most common relative pronouns being: who, whom, which, whoever, whomever, whichever, and that. So, here "who" is the relative pronoun.

Hence, the correct option is (C).

24. An abstract noun is a noun that refers to an intangible concept such as an emotion, a feeling, a quality, or an idea. In other words, an abstract noun does not refer to a physical object.

It is sometimes helpful to think of an abstract noun as a word that names something that you cannot see, hear, touch, smell, or taste (i.e., something you cannot perceive with one of your five senses). For example: consideration, parenthood, belief, anger, bravery.

Hence, the correct option is (D).

25. "War" is a proper noun here.

"And" is conjunction.

"Were" is a verb.

"During" is a preposition.

Normally, "war" is just a noun, but in this case, it's used as a name for a specific war, so it's a proper noun.

Hence, the correct option is (D).

Ques (1-5):Direction: Read the following passage and answer the following question:

In terms of labour, for decades the relatively low cost and high quality of Japanese workers conferred considerable competitive advantage across numerous durable goods and consumer electronics industries (eg. Machinery, automobiles, televisions, radios). Then labour-based advantages shifted to South Korea, then to Malaysia, Mexico and other nations. Today, China appears to be capitalizing best on the basis of labour. Japanese firms still remain competitive in markets for such durable goods, electronics and other products, but the labour force is no longer sufficient for competitive advantage over manufacturers in other industrializing nations. Such shifting of labour-based advantage is clearly not limited to manufacturing industries. Today, a huge number of IT and service jobs are moving from Europe and North America to India, Singapore, and like countries with relatively well-educated, low-cost workforces possessing technical skills. However, as educational levels and technical skills continue to rise in other countries, India, Singapore, and like nations enjoying labour-based competitive advantage today are likely to find such advantage cannot be sustained through the emergence of new competitors.

In terms of capital, for centuries the days of gold coins and later even paper money restricted financial flows. Subsequently, regional concentrations were formed where large banks, industries and markets coalesced. But today capital flows internationally at rapid speed. Globa commerce no longer requires regional interactions among business players. Regional capital concentrations in places such as New York, London and Tokyo still persist, of course, but the capital concentrated there is no longer sufficient for competitive advantage over other capitalists distributed worldwide. Only if an organization is able to combine, integrate and apply its resources (eg. Land, labour, capital, IT in an effective manner that is not readily imitable by competitors can such an organization enjoy competitive advantage sustainable overtime.

In a knowledge-based theory of the firm, this idea is extended to view organizational knowledge as a resource with at least the same level of power and importance as the traditional economic inputs. An organization with superior knowledge can achieve a competitive advantage in markets that appreciate the application of such knowledge. Semiconductors, genetic engineering, pharmaceuticals, software, military warfare, and like knowledge-intensive competitive arenas provide both time-proven and current examples. Consider semiconductors (e.g. computer chips), which are made principally of sand and common metals. These ubiquitous and powerful electronic devices are designed within common office buildings, using commercially available tools, and fabricated within factories in many industrialized nations. Hence, the land is not the key competitive resource in the semiconductor industry.

Q.1 Which country enjoyed competitive advantages in automobile industry for decades?

A. South Korea **B.** Japan

C. Mexico **D.** Malaysia

Q.2 Why labour-based competitive advantages of India and Singapore cannot be sustained in IT and service sectors?

A. Due to diminishing levels of skill

B. Due to capital-intensive technology making inroads

C. Because of new competitors

D. Because of shifting of labour-based advantage in manufacturing industries

Q.3 How can an organization enjoy a competitive advantage sustainable overtime?

A. Through regional capital flows.

B. Through regional interactions among business players.

C. By making large banks, industries and markets coalesced.

D. By effective use of various instrumentalities.

Q.4 What is required to ensure competitive advantages in specific markets?

A. Access to capital

B. Common office buildings

C. Superior knowledge

D. Common metals

Q.5 The passage also mentions the trend of:

A. Global financial flow

B. Absence of competition in manufacturing industry

C. Regionalisation of capitalists

D. Organizational incompatibility

Q.6 Direction: Choose the synonym of the given word.

Gradual

A. Continuous **B.** Hasty

C. Uneven **D.** Abrupt

Q.7 Direction: Choose the synonym of the given word.

Foundation

A. Structure **B.** Base **C.** Building **D.** Top

Q.8 Direction: Choose the synonym of the given word.

Annoy

A. Please **B.** Satisfy **C.** Irritate **D.** Gratify

Q.9 Pick out the appropriate words from the options given below the sentence to complete it meaningfully.

I was late _______ the cab was not on time.

A. because **B.** though

C. if **D.** in order to

Q.10 Select the most appropriate word to fill in the blank.

_______ had she stepped out of her house when the rain started.

| A. Scarce | B. When |
| C. No sooner | D. Hardly |

Q.11 Select the most appropriate word to fill in the blank.

The volcanic eruption __________ destroyed the whole village.

| A. near | B. nearest | C. nearly | D. nearer |

Q.12 In the following sentence, one phrase has been printed in bold. Below the sentence, three meanings are given. Select the correct meaning of the phrase from the options given below.

I thought that Jake really loved me, but in the end, I was just a **cat's-paw** so he could stir up jealousy in his ex-girlfriend.

A. A special person

B. A person who is lazy

C. A person used by another as a dupe or tool

| A. Only A | B. Only B |
| C. Only C | D. Both B and C |

Q.13 In the following sentence, one phrase has been printed in bold. Below the sentence, three meanings are given. Select the correct meaning of the phrase from the options given below.

John got a **swelled head** after he won the prize and this annoyed everyone.

A. Get a headache

B. To be very happy and joyful

C. To be conceited, arrogant, or self-aggrandizing

| A. Only A | B. Only B |
| C. Only C | D. Both B and C |

Q.14 In the following question, an idiom is given. It is then followed by three sentences which may or may not accurately represent the meaning of the idiom. Choose the best set of alternatives from the five options given below of the sentences which embody the meaning of the given idiom perfectly.

Good Samaritan

A. We should always avoid all the selfish and the mean persons.

B. The rich industrialist will be ruined someday because of his son's bad habits.

C. He is a person who even helps strangers because he always comes to the help of the old and the children in difficulties.

| A. Only A | B. Only B |
| C. Only C | D. Both A and B |

Q.15 In the following question, out of the four alternatives, select the alternative which is the best substitute of the phrase.

A person who lives by himself

| A. Colleague | B. Assassin |
| C. Linguist | D. Recluse |

Q.16 In the following question, out of the four alternatives, select the alternative which is the best substitute of the phrase.

An official pardon for people who have been convicted of political offenses

| A. Draw | B. Amnesty |
| C. Octagon | D. Bureaucracy |

Q.17 In the following question, out of the four alternatives, select the alternative which is the best substitute of the phrase.

A thing that is kept as a reminder of a person, place or event.

| A. Souvenir | B. Honorarium |
| C. Barricade | D. Trapeze |

Q.18 Four words are given, out of which one word is spelt correctly. Choose the correctly spelt word and click the button corresponding to it.

| A. Enterpreneur | B. Entreperneur |
| C. Entreprenuer | D. Entrepreneur |

Q.19 Four words are given, out of which only one word is spelt correctly. Choose the correctly spelt word and click the button corresponding to it.

| A. Connoisseur | B. Connisseur |
| C. Conniosseur | D. Connoiseur |

Q.20 Choose the word which is correctly spelled.

| A. Commited | B. Committed |
| C. Comitteed | D. Committeed |

Q.21 Direction: A sentence has been given in Active/Passive Voice. Out of the four alternatives suggested, select the one which best expresses the same sentence in Passive/Active voice.

The driver parked the car safely.

A. The car had been parked safely by the driver.

B. The car was parked safely by the driver.

C. The car has been parked safely by the driver.

D. The car was to be parked safely by the driver.

Q.22 Choose the appropriate noun form to complete the sentence.

My __________ who lives in Bombay has come to stay with us.

| A. brothers-in-law | B. brother-in-laws |
| C. brother-in-law | D. brother's-in-law |

Q.23 Choose the appropriate form of the adjective to complete the given sentence.

Bodyweight exercises are __________ exercise with weight for the students who prepare for CPO.

| A. most preferable | B. the preferable |
| C. preferable | D. preferable to |

Q.24 Direction: Choose the appropriate preposition for the given sentence:

Barring strong headwinds, the plane will arrive ____ schedule.

| A. during | B. for | C. by | D. on |

Q.25 Which one of the following words is an adjective?

| A. Use | B. Useful |
| C. Using | D. Usefulness |

// Smart Answer Sheet //

Correct Percentage of students who answered correctly.　　**Skipped** Percentage of students who skipped.

Q.	Ans.	Correct / Skipped
1	B	70.0 % / 4.55 %
2	C	51.82 % / 10.0 %
3	D	47.27 % / 10.91 %
4	C	59.09 % / 10.91 %
5	A	37.27 % / 10.91 %
6	A	71.82 % / 10.91 %
7	B	78.18 % / 10.91 %
8	C	80.0 % / 10.91 %
9	A	84.55 % / 7.27 %
10	D	50.91 % / 10.91 %
11	C	80.91 % / 10.91 %
12	C	73.64 % / 10.91 %
13	C	63.64 % / 10.91 %
14	C	59.09 % / 10.91 %
15	D	52.73 % / 10.91 %
16	B	70.91 % / 10.91 %
17	A	52.73 % / 10.91 %
18	D	59.09 % / 10.91 %
19	A	45.45 % / 10.91 %
20	B	70.91 % / 10.91 %
21	B	61.82 % / 10.91 %
22	C	76.36 % / 10.91 %
23	D	27.27 % / 10.91 %
24	D	76.36 % / 10.91 %
25	B	58.18 % / 10.91 %

//Hints and Solutions//

1. "In terms of labour, for decades the relatively low cost and high quality of Japanese workers conferred considerable competitive advantage across numerous durable goods and consumer electronics industries (eg. Machinery, automobiles, televisions, radios)."

Upon the perusal of the given extract, it is obvious that Japan enjoyed competitive advantages in the automobile industry for decades.

Hence, the correct option is (B).

2. "However, as educational levels and technical skills continue to rise in other countries, India, Singapore, and like nations enjoying labor-based competitive advantage today are likely to find such advantage cannot be sustained through the emergence of new competitors."

Upon the perusal of the given extract, it is obvious that labor-based competitive advantages of India and Singapore cannot be sustained in the IT and service sectors because of the new competitors.

Hence, the correct option is (C).

3. "Only if an organization is able to combine, integrate and apply its resources (eg. Land, labour, capital, IT) in an effective manner that is not readily imitable by competitors can such an organization enjoy competitive advantage sustainable overtime."

Upon the perusal of the given extract, it is obvious that an organization can enjoy a competitive advantage sustainable overtime through the effective use of various instrumentalities.

Hence, the correct option is (D).

4. "An organization with superior knowledge can achieve a competitive advantage in markets that appreciate the application of such knowledge."

Upon the perusal of the given extract, it is obvious that superior knowledge is required to ensure competitive advantages in specific markets.

Hence, the correct option is (C).

5. "Today, a huge number of IT and service jobs are moving from Europe and North America to India, Singapore, and like countries with relatively well-educated, low-cost workforces possessing technical skills."

Upon the perusal of the given extract, it is obvious that the passage also mentions the trend of global financial flow.

Hence, the correct option is (A).

6. The word 'Gradual' means taking place or progressing slowly or by degrees.

The synonyms of the word 'Gradual' are "continuous, progressive, stepped".

From the synonym of the given word, we can say that the word 'continuous' is the same in meaning.

The word 'continuous' means forming an unbroken whole; without interruption.

Hence, the correct option is (A).

7. The word 'Foundation' means an immaterial thing upon which something else rests.

The synonyms of the word 'Foundation' are "base, bedrock, bottom".

From the synonym of the given word, we can say that the word 'base' is the same in meaning.

The word 'base' means an immaterial thing upon which something else rests.

Hence, the correct option is (B).

8. The synonym of the given word 'Annoy' is 'Irritate'.

Annoy - to make someone angry ⇒ Tina really annoyed me in the meeting this morning.

Irritate - to make someone angry or annoyed ⇒ After a while, her behavior really began to irritate me.

Hence, the correct option is (C).

9. The sentence presents a situation and the reason for the situation.

The subordinating conjunction 'because' is used to give reasons.

Thus, 'because' is the correct answer.

The sentence should be 'I was late because the cab was not on time.'

Hence, the correct option is (A).

10. 'When' is a conjunction and 'hardly' means 'scarcely; barely'.

'Hardly' is always used with 'when' whereas 'No sooner' is used with 'than'.

So, 'Hardly' is the correct answer. Other options are rejected because:

'Scarce' is an adjective that means 'hard to find, not often found'.

When' and 'as soon as' are grammatically incorrect for the sentence.

Hence, the correct option is (D).

11. 'nearly' is the correct solution because it means almost and is the adverb form of near. 'near' is noun form of near. 'nearest' is it superlative form and 'nearer' is its comparative form which are wrong because they are used for comparison.

So, the correct solution is, The volcanic eruption nearly destroyed the whole village.

Hence, the correct option is (C).

12. The phrase 'cat's paw' means a person who is used by another to carry out an unpleasant or dangerous task. Here, the speaker was used by Jake just to make his ex-girlfiend jealous. Only option (C) which is A person used by another as a dupe or

tool which is in accordance with the meaning of the phrase 'cat's paw'.

Hence, the correct option is (C).

13. The phrase "annoyed everyone" suggests that whatever behavioural changes occurred in John after winning the prize were not positive ones. The phrase 'swelled head' means to be conceited i.e. develop undue pride in oneself. If someone has a swollen head, that person thinks they are more intelligent and more important than they really are. Only option (C) which is To be conceited, arrogant, or self-aggrandizing is in accordance with the meaning of the phrase 'swelled head'.

Hence, the correct option is (C).

14. The meaning of the given idiom 'Good samaritan' means 'One who helps strangers'. Out of the given sentences, only sentence C fits the context of the idiom and other sentences are not relevant to the given idiom.

Hence, the correct option is (C).

15. Colleague - A person who is working in the same institution.

Assassin - A murderer, especially one who kills a politically prominent person for fanatical or monetary reasons.

Linguist - A person who studies languages.

Recluse - A person who lives by himself.

Hence, the correct option is (D).

16. Draw - A game in which no one wins.

Amnesty - An official pardon for people who have been convicted of political offenses.

Octagon - A geometrical figure with eight sides.

Bureaucracy - A system of government in which most of the important decisions are taken by state officials rather than by elected representatives.

Hence, the correct option is (B).

17. Souvenir - A thing that is kept as a reminder of a person, place or event.

Honorarium - A fee paid for a nominally free service.

Barricade - A barrier set up by police to stop traffic on a street or road in order to catch a fugitive or inspect traffic, etc.

Trapeze - A swing used by circus acrobats.

Hence, the correct option is (A).

18. The correctly spelt word is Entrepreneur.

Entrepreneur-A person who sets up a business or businesses, taking on financial risks in the hope of profit.

Example:

He was one of the entrepreneurs of the 80s who made their money in property.

Hence, the correct option is (D).

19. Connoisseur-A person who knows a lot about and enjoys one of the arts, or food, drink, etc., and can judge quality and skill in that subject.

Example:

The mushrooms had the chewy, savory flavor preferred by connoisseurs.

Hence, the correct option is (A).

20. Commited is wrongly spelt as one 't' is missing and thus, doesn't have any existence.

Committed is correctly spelt and it means pledged or bound to a certain course or policy; dedicated.

Comiteed is wrongly spelt as one 'm' is missing, one 'e' is extra and thus, doesn't have any existence.

Committeed is wrongly spelt as one 'e' is extra and thus, doesn't have any existence.

Hence, the correct option is (B).

21. The given sentence is in the Active voice form, thus we need to convert it into Passive voice form.

In the given sentence the subject is 'The driver' and the object is 'the car' so for making the passive form of this sentence we need to exchange their places of object and subject.

We need to follow these instructions while changing the active voice into passive voice.

The preposition 'by' will commence the sentence.

The objective case 'the car' will use as a subject and it will take a singular verb.

The subjective case 'the driver' will use as an object.

If in the given question which is in a form of 'past indefinite' we follow this structure.

Active form: Sub + V$_2$ + obj

Passive form: obj + was/were + V$_3$ + by + sub

let's see the example:

Active: Reema cleaned the floor.

Passive: The floor was cleaned by Reema.

So following these steps we finally get.

Hence, the correct option is (B).

22. The most appropriate noun form to complete the sentence is 'brother-in-law'. The given sentence is an example of a compound noun. Some hyphenated terms are made up of a noun and some other part of speech.

For example, the passer by is made up of a noun (passer) and a preposition (by).

Hence, the correct option is (C).

23. The most appropriate form of the adjective to complete the given sentence is 'preferable to'.

The following comparative adjectives are followed by the preposition 'to':

Senior, Junior, Prior, Anterior, Posterior, Superior, Inferior, Preferable, Elder, etc.

Hence, the correct option is (D).

24. The preposition 'during' means throughout the course or duration of a period of time.

The preposition 'for' is used for saying the particular time or date that something is planned to happen.

The preposition 'by' is used for indicating a deadline or the end of a particular time period.

The preposition 'on' means at the time of.

Hence, the correct option is (D).

25. An adjective is a part of speech that qualifies nouns. Generally, it is written before nouns but there are cases when it is used after 'be' forms of verbs as well.

For example- A book is useful when read properly. It answers the question 'how' a thing is. If we ask 'How is the book?', we will get the answer that the book is useful'.

While 'use' is a verb, 'using' is a gerund and 'usefulness' is a noun.

Hence, the correct option is (B).

Q.1 Direction: In the following question, out of the four alternatives, choose the word which is the best express in meaning to the given word.

Worsening

A. Improve **B.** Ameliorate

C. Recover **D.** Aggravate

Q.2 Direction: In the following question, out of the four alternatives, choose the word which is opposite in meaning to the given word.

Abate

A. Moderate **B.** Complement

C. Aggravate **D.** Decrease

Ques (3-4):Direction: In the following question, some part of the sentence is underlined. Which of the options given below the sentence should replace the part underlined to make the sentence grammatically correct?

Q.3 A student was arrested for displaying an **indecently** art work in public.

A. indecent **B.** unindecently

C. the indecently **D.** any of indecently

Q.4 The scenery around the hill station of Himachal Pradesh is **quite picturesque and enjoyed**.

A. quite picturesque and enjoyable

B. quite picturesque and enjoyed

C. quietly picturesque and enjoyed

D. quietly picturesque and enjoyable

Ques (5-6):Direction: Choose the correct alternative which can be substituted for the below given word/ sentence.

Q.5 The use of many words where only a few are necessary

A. Circumlocution **B.** Circumspection

C. Circumscription **D.** Circumvention

Q.6 Familiar with and at ease in many different countries and cultures.

A. Bohemian **B.** Cosmopolitan

C. Philanthropist **D.** Internationalist

Ques (7-8):Direction: Fill in the blank with an appropriate preposition.

Q.7 He beat him _____ a stick.

A. for **B.** with **C.** by **D.** to

Q.8 We are engaged _______ our work.

A. into **B.** in **C.** at **D.** on

Ques (9-10):Direction: Fill in the blank with the most appropriate word out of the four alternatives suggested below the question.

Q.9 Studying the current global, political conditions some predict that world war III is _______.

A. Eminent **B.** Imminent

C. Immanent **D.** Nascent

Q.10 Ashwin is a _______ reader and has read more than fifteen books this month.

A. Avid **B.** Voracious

C. Keen **D.** Demur

Ques (11-15):Direction: Read the following passage carefully and answer the questions that follow.

India's admittance into the Wassenaar Arrangement, a multilateral export control regime, as its 42nd participating member is a big step forward in its quest for formal acceptance as a responsible nuclear power. This has come a year after India made the request for membership. As a non-signatory to the Nuclear Non-Proliferation Treaty (NPT), New Delhi has been at pains to convey to the international community that it adheres to, and is invested in, a rules-based order. The Wassenaar Arrangement was founded in 1996, and is clubbed with mechanisms such as the Nuclear Suppliers Group (NSG), the Missile Technology Control Regime (MTCR) and the Australia Group. Its stated aim is "to contribute to regional and international security and stability, by promoting transparency and greater responsibility in transfers of conventional arms and dual-use goods and technologies, thus preventing destabilizing accumulations." India's Wassenaar success at the Vienna plenary meeting last week presumes a broad acceptance among its members of the country's credentials as a **fastidious** adherent to export controls. It comes on the heels of membership last year of the MTCR. Ever since India signed the 123 Agreement in 2005, the underlying assumption was that the United States would help chaperone New Delhi into global nuclear acceptability after it separated its civil and military nuclear programmes and plugged the loopholes to prevent diffusion of nuclear materials and technology in a way that is demonstrably in line with best practices followed by the members of the NSG.

However, over the past couple of years it has become evident that Delhi has to do most of the heavy lifting to gain a seat at various global high tables. The Wassenaar Arrangement membership is also a lesson on the need for quiet diplomacy in sensitive nuclear issues, compared to the botched attempt to gain entry to the NSG last year. While India's efforts at the NSG were stopped by China, which is not a member of the Wassenaar Arrangement, raising the pitch publicly at the time came with costs. It made the task of forging a consensus on membership to the NSG more difficult. And when that attempt failed, it gave the setback the appearance of being significantly more insurmountable. Nonetheless, now that more and more countries are signing on to India's steadily strengthening credentials in the nuclear area, there is hope that a fresh momentum will be imparted to a future bid for the NSG. It will not be easy. The Australia Group, which focuses on biological and chemical weapons, may be easier to crack given that China is not a member. But meanwhile, the Wassenaar Arrangement will embed India deeper in the global non-proliferation architecture and enable access to critical technologies in the defence and space sectors.

Q.11 Which among the following is the significance of the acceptance of the membership of our country into the Wassenaar Agreement?

A. India can now get everything from countries which have not signed nuclear agreements with the country.

B. India and Pakistan can now become friends regarding the expansion of nuclear weapons development in their respective countries.

C. The India-Pakistan relationship is based on the necessity to understand the importance of diplomacy within the confines of the neighborhood.

D. India has been recognized as a country that is committed towards responsible development and use of nuke energy in the world.

Q.12 Consider the following statements regarding the Wassenaar Group.

I. This group was formed in the 21st century by the nuclear-enabled countries in order to ensure the development of nuclear energy in a responsible manner.

II. All the members of the Nuclear Suppliers' Group are not members of the Wassenaar Group also.

III. The Wassenaar Agreement works in tandem with Missile Technology Control Regime, Australia Group, and NSG in order to prevent the nuclear technology from disturbing the global order

Which among the above statements is/are correct with reference to the information given in the passage?

A. Both I and II

B. Both II and III

C. Only III

D. Only I

Q.13 Which among the following is a lesson that should be learnt from the diplomacy surrounding the acceptance of membership of India into the Wassenaar Agreement?

A. It is easier to sneak into any group where other Asian countries are not there and common interests are not taken into account.

B. The government should understand the way in which partnership can be forged rather than shouting too much on the public forum.

C. India should have good spokespersons so that the stand taken by the country can be explained at any international summits without any confusion.

D. The government should keep China out of any deal that it gets from other countries regarding nuclear power development in the country

Q.14 Which among the following is correct regarding the assumption of Indian government regarding the reaction of the USA towards the development of nuclear energy in India?

A. USA is happy that its ally is going to develop nuclear energy in its arena and it is going to assist the country in understanding the Asian geography.

B. The US government is convinced that India will not be able to develop nuclear energy and that is why it is just giving financial support to our country.

C. The US Government is convinced about the intention of the Government of India in case of development of nuclear energy and therefore it is supporting India's cause.

D. India is not getting enough support from its allies regarding the membership into the important nuclear groups of the world.

Q.15 Which among the following is/are not correct regarding the Australian Group associated with the development of nuclear energy in the world?

A. Australian Group is mainly concerned about chemical and biological weapons and that is why it is not considered as an important organization.

B. India is a member of the Australia Group and China also supported our membership bid in that group.

C. China is yet to give due importance to the Australia Group as the USA has not been inducted into this group till date.

D. All (A), (B) and (C)

Ques (16-17):Direction: In the following question, out of the four alternatives, choose the alternative which best expresses the meaning of the idiom/phrase.

Q.16 to play fast and loose

A. To talk aloud

B. Complete and safe

C. To work hard

D. To act unreliably

Q.17 Barking up the wrong tree

A. Said when someone is displaying traits or behaving in the same way as their relatives (especially parents)

B. Looking in the wrong place or accusing the wrong person

C. Allowing many details of a situation to obscure the situation as a whole

D. The highest position or level in an organization, field, etc.

Q.18 Four words are given in each question, out of which only one word is correctly spelt. Find the correctly spelt word.

A. Prediliction

B. Predalection

C. Pridilection

D. Predilection

Q.19 In the question four words are given out of which only one word is correctly spelt. Find the correctly spelt word.

A. Narsicissism

B. Narcicicism

C. Narcissism

D. Narcisism

Ques (20-21):Direction: In the following question, a sentence has been given in Active/Passive Voice. Out of the four alternatives suggested, select the one which best expresses the same sentence in Passive/Active Voice.

Q.20 It is impossible to do this.

A. Doing this is impossible

B. This is impossible to be done

C. This must not be done

D. This can't be done

Q.21 We must take care of all living species on earth.

A. All living species on earth must be taken care of by us.

B. All living species on earth must taken care of by us.

C. All living species on Earth had been taken care of by us.

D. All living species on earth will be taken care of by us.

Q.22 Reciprocal pronoun in sentence "Ali and Imran are helping to each other in completing their projects." is:

A. in   **B.** each other
C. their   **D.** to

Q.23 Relative pronoun in sentence "That was boy whom I saw in party last night." is:

A. that   **B.** I   **C.** whom   **D.** them

Q.24 Select the answer choice that identifies the noun in the sentence.

To seize a foreign embassy and its inhabitants is flagrant disregard for diplomatic neutrality.

A. Seize   **B.** Its
C. Flagrant   **D.** Neutrality

Q.25 Select the answer choice that identifies the noun in the sentence.

It will take all of your energy and will to be able to walk again.

A. Take   **B.** All   **C.** Your   **D.** Energy

// Smart Answer Sheet //

Correct Percentage of students who answered correctly.   **Skipped** Percentage of students who skipped.

Q.	Ans.	Correct / Skipped
1	D	55.56 % / 0.0 %
2	C	36.11 % / 8.33 %
3	A	76.39 % / 8.33 %
4	A	76.39 % / 8.33 %
5	A	43.06 % / 8.33 %
6	B	41.67 % / 8.33 %
7	B	81.94 % / 6.95 %
8	B	61.11 % / 6.95 %
9	B	36.11 % / 6.95 %
10	B	26.39 % / 8.33 %
11	D	44.44 % / 5.56 %
12	B	33.33 % / 6.95 %
13	B	18.06 % / 6.94 %
14	C	33.33 % / 4.17 %
15	D	40.28 % / 5.55 %
16	D	63.89 % / 6.94 %
17	B	72.22 % / 6.95 %
18	D	37.5 % / 6.94 %
19	C	50.0 % / 8.33 %
20	B	51.39 % / 8.33 %
21	A	76.39 % / 8.33 %
22	B	55.56 % / 6.94 %
23	C	70.83 % / 4.17 %
24	D	36.11 % / 8.33 %
25	D	68.06 % / 6.94 %

//Hints and Solutions//

1. 'Worsening' means to make or become worse.

'Aggravatet' means to make something worse or more serious.

'Improve' means to become or to make something better.

'Ameliorat' means to make something better.

Hence, the correct option is (D).

2. Abate: means 'making something less intense'; 'reduce or remove'.

Aggravate: To intensify or make something more serious or intense.

Moderate: Average in amount, intensity, quality, or degree.

Complement: A thing that contributes extra features to something.

Decrease: To lessen in quantity.

Hence, the correct option is (C).

3. 'Art work' is a noun phrase, before which an appropriate adjective should be used.

The underlined part 'indecently', which is an adverb, hence must be replaced with the adjective 'indecent' to make it a grammatically correct sentence.

Hence, the correct option is (A).

4. The word 'enjoyed' must be replaced with the adjective 'enjoyable' to make it a grammatically correct sentence.

Hence, the correct option is (A).

5. Circumlocution: The usage of many words where a few words would also do.

Circumspection: Not willing to take risks

Circumscription: A boundary

Circumvention: Avoiding something unpleasant by tactful action

Hence, the correct option is (A).

6. Cosmopolitan: A person who is familiar with and at ease in many different countries and cultures

Bohemian: One who practices an unconventional style of living

Philanthropist: A person who seeks to promote the welfare of others, especially by the generous donation of money to good causes

Internationalist: A political principle of fostering co-operation between countries and people

Hence, the correct option is (B).

7. He beat him **with** a stick.

You can use 'with' when you're talking about people, or things being together. So if you're with someone, then you're probably in the same place as them. I was with Jane yesterday when the accident happened. This means I was physically in the same place as Jane yesterday while the accident was happening.

Hence, the correct option is (B).

8. We are engaged **in** our work.

To refer to a place, use the prepositions "in" (the point itself), "at" (the general vicinity), "on" (the surface), and "inside" (something contained). They will meet in the lunchroom. She was waiting at the corner. He left his phone on the bed.

Hence, the correct option is (B).

9. The meanings of the words given in the options are as follows:

Imminent: Very near or about to happen.

Eminent: Distinguished and highly respected person.

Immanent: An inherent quality.

Nascent: Beginning to exist or develop; to be newly born or understood.

Thus, since the sentence suggests that the World War III is possible, 'imminent' is the correct answer.

Hence, the correct option is (B).

10. Voracious: engaging in an activity with great eagerness or enthusiasm.

Avid: having or showing a keen interest in or enthusiasm for something.

Keen: having or showing eagerness or enthusiasm.

Demur: raise objections or show reluctance.

When we refer to 'reading books' voracious is the right word. Avid and Keen are not appropriate in the context.

Hence, the correct option is (B).

11. Refer to, "India's admittance into the Wassenaar Arrangement, a multilateral export control regime, as its 42nd participating member Is a big step forward in its quest for formal acceptance as a responsible nuclear power. This has come a year after India made the request for membership."

From the above lines it is clear that India is now considered as a responsible nuclear power of the world and that is why despite not being a member of NPT, the member countries of the Wassenaar Agreement have accepted the membership of the country into this club.

Among the given options, Option (A), (B), and (C) are completely out of context since none of these statements follows from the information given in the passage. Only Option (D) implies the meaning of the acceptance of the membership request of India by the Wassenaar Agreement group.

Hence, the correct option is (D).

12. Statement I is incorrect since the Wassenaar Group is dedicated towards making the use and development of nuclear energy responsible and beneficial to the world rather than disturbing the global peace but it is not correct regarding the year of formation of Wassenaar Group. Refer to, "The Wassenaar

Arrangement was founded in 1996, and is clubbed with mechanisms such as the Nuclear Suppliers Group (NSG), the Missile Technology Control Regime (MTCR) and the Australia Group. Its stated aim is "to contribute to regional and international security and stability, by promoting transparency and greater responsibility in transfers of conventional arms and dual-use goods and technologies, thus preventing destabilizing accumulations." The Wassenaar Group was formed in 1996 i.e. in the 20th century and not in the 21st century as given in the statement.

Statement II is correct since it is mentioned in the passage that China is not a member of the Wassenaar Group whereas it is a member of the NSG and it blocked the application from our country at the NSG Meeting last year. Refer to, "While India's efforts at the NSG were stopped by China, which is not a member of the Wassenaar Arrangement, raising the pitch publicly at the time came with costs."

Statement III is also correct since the Wassenaar Agreement functions in tandem with the other agreement such as the NSG, Australia Group etc. to develop a world with better nuclear energy. Refer to, "The Wassenaar Arrangement was founded in 1996, and is clubbed with mechanisms such as the Nuclear Suppliers Group (NSG), the Missile Technology Control Regime (MTCR) and the Australia Group. Its stated aim is "to contribute to regional and international security and stability, by promoting transparency and greater responsibility in transfers of conventional arms and dual-use goods and technologies, thus preventing destabilizing accumulations."

Hence, the correct option is (B).

13. Refer to, "The Wassenaar Arrangement membership is also a lesson on the need for quiet diplomacy in sensitive nuclear issues, compared to the botched attempt to gain entry to the NSG last year."

From the above lines, it is clear that India needs to understand the importance of quiet diplomacy at the international level so that it can get the most out of such moves rather than just making its point at the public forums where there are other countries that may stall moves by the government.

Among the given options, option (A) is not correct since it is irrelevant in the context of the passage whereas option (C) is not correct since this point is nowhere referred to in the passage. The same can be said about option (D) which can be eliminated since they do not imply the actual lesson that should be learnt by India in the whole episode. Only (B) implies the actual answer.

Hence, the correct option is (B).

14. Refer to, "Ever since India signed the 123 Agreement in 2005, the underlying assumption was that the United States would help chaperone New Delhi into global nuclear acceptability after it separated its civil and military nuclear programmes and plugged the loopholes to prevent diffusion of nuclear materials and technology in a way that is demonstrably in line with best practices followed by the members of the NSG."

It is clear that USA is supporting India's cause in the global stage regarding the nuclear acceptability as India is now following the best practices of the NSG group. There is no reason to believe

that India will do something irresponsible with nuclear weapons developed in the country.

Among the given options, option (A) is not correct since it is giving the right idea regarding the assumption but the stated reason is not correct whereas option (B) is not correct since there is no reference in the passage regarding monetary support by USA to India in the area of nuclear program in the country. Option (D) can be eliminated since they also do not convey the actual assumption of the Indian government regarding the reaction of USA towards the development of nuclear weapons in the country. Option (C) is the correct choice as it correctly explains that USA is favoring India and it is also supporting our country in the global platforms.

Hence, the correct option is (C).

15. Refer to, "The Australia Group, which focuses on biological and chemical weapons, may be easier to crack given that China is not a member."

Option (A) cannot be considered as correct since there is no reference in the passage regarding the importance of the Australia Group though the first part regarding the functional area of the group is correct.

Option (B) cannot be considered as correct since it is clear that India is not a member of the Australia Group and it is said that entry to this group will be easier for India since China is not a member of this group.

Option (C) is not correct since the sentence is not relevant to the passage and that is why it can be eliminated easily as an inference that follows from the given passage.

Hence, the correct option is (D).

16. The meaning of the given idiom is; to be recklessly irresponsible, unreliable, or deceitful.

Hence, the correct option is (D).

17. The given expression means to be pursuing a mistaken or misguided line of thought or course of action.

Trying to do something in a way that will not work.

Hence, the correct option is (B).

18. 'Predilection' is the correct spelling of the given word that means 'a liking or a soft spot for something'.

Some common synonyms of predilection are bias, prejudice, and prepossession.

Hence, the correct option is (D).

19. 'Narcissism' is the correct spelling of the given word that means 'self-obsession and pride.'

Hence, the correct option is (C).

20. This is impossible to be done.

In the given sentence,

Verb = (am /is /are/ was /were) +to + verb[1]

Rule:

Subject + (am /is /are/ was /were) +to + Be + verb[3]

Hence, the correct option is (B).

21. All living species on earth must be taken care of.

The given sentence contains one of Model verb (Model Verb = will, shall, can, may, might, could, might, must, would). It is in active voice.

Rule:

Subject + Model verb + be + V^3 + Optional Objects.

Hence, the correct option is (A).

22. A reciprocal pronoun is a pronoun used to identify an action or feeling that is reciprocated. For this reason, it always refers to more than one person.

For example,

Anne is waving to Sean and Sean is waving to Anne.

So we say:

Anne and Sean are waving to each other.

Hence, the correct option is (B).

23. A relative pronoun is a pronoun that heads an adjective clause. The relative pronouns are "that," "which," "who," "whom," and "whose."

Hence, the correct option is (C).

24. "Neutrality" is a noun.

"Seize" is a verb.

"Its" is a possessive pronoun modifying the noun inhabitants.

"Flagrant" is an adjective modifying the noun disregard.

A noun is a word that names something, such as a person, place, thing, or idea.

Hence, the correct option is (D).

25. "Energy" is a noun, as is will here.

"Take" is a verb.

"All" is an adverb modifying take.

"Your" is an adjective modifying energy and will.

A noun is a word that names something, such as a person, place, thing, or idea.

Hence, the correct option is (D).

Ques (1-5):Direction: Read the passage and answer the following question.

What I have tried to do is to discern and articulate the natural laws of a particular kind of human undertaking, which I have described as "the enterprise of subjecting human conduct to the governance of rules". These natural laws have nothing to do with any "brooding omnipresence in the skies." Nor have they the slightest affinity with any such proposition as that the practice of contraception is a violation of God's law. They remain entirely terrestrial in origin and application. They are not "higher" laws; if any metaphor of elevation is appropriate they should be called "lower" laws. They are like the natural laws of carpentry, or at least those laws respected by a carpenter who wants the house he builds to remain standing and serve the purpose of those who live in it. Though these natural laws touch one of the most vital of human activities they obviously do not exhaust the whole of man's moral life. They have nothing to say on topics as polygamy, the study of Marx, the worship of God, the progressive income tax, or the subjugation of women. If the question be raised whether any of these subjects, or others like them, should be taken as objects of legislation, that question relates to what I have called the external morality of law. As a convenient (though not wholly satisfactory) way of describing the distinction being taken we may speak of a procedural, as distinguished from a substantive natural law. What I have called the internal morality of law is in this sense a procedural version of natural law, though to avoid misunderstanding the word 'procedural' should be assigned a special and expanded sense so that it would include, for example, a substantive accord between official action and enacted law. The term 'procedural' is, however, broadly appropriate as indicating that we are concerned, not with the substantive aims of legal rules, but with the ways in which a system of rules for governing human conduct must be constructed and administered if it is to be efficacious and at the same time remain what it purports to be.

Q.1 The passage is an explanation of:

1. Legal Morality
2. The Worship of God
3. Natural Law
4. God's Law

Choose the correct option from below.

A. 1,2,3 & 4   **B.** 1 and 3 only
C. 2 and 3 only   **D.** 3 only

Q.2 The procedural version of natural law relates to:

A. Internal morality
B. External morality
C. Objects of legislation
D. Human activities

Q.3 Natural laws, according to this passage, are:

1. The ones, having brooding omnipresence in the skies

2. Terrestrial in origin and application
3. Higher laws
4. Lower laws

Choose the correct option from below:

A. 1 and 3 both   **B.** 1,2 and 3 only
C. 2 and 3 both   **D.** 2 and 4 both

Q.4 The term 'procedural' means and includes:

1. A substantive accord between official action and enacted law
2. Administration of a system of rules for governing human conduct
3. Construction of a system of rules for governing human conduct
4. External morality

Choose the correct option from below:

A. 1,2,3 & 4   **B.** 1,2 and 3 only
C. 2 and 3 only   **D.** 4 only

Q.5 The enterprise of subjecting human conduct to the governance of rules relates to:

1. Natural laws
2. God's Laws
3. Objects of legislation
4. Higher laws

Choose the correct option from below:

A. 1,2,3 & 4   **B.** 1 only
C. 2 and 3 both   **D.** 4 only

Q.6 According to the World Bank's 'Ease of Doing Business rankings', benchmarked to May 2019, India is ranked at:

A. 89   **B.** 75   **C.** 63   **D.** 91

Q.7 The difference between total revenue and total expenditure of a government is termed as:

A. Fiscal deficit   **B.** Revenue deficit
C. Primary deficit   **D.** Monetised deficit

Q.8 In 2019, the Sveriges Riksbank Prize in Economic Sciences in memory of Alfred Nobel was awarded to:

A. Richard H. Thaler
B. William D. Nordhaus
C. Paul M. Romer
D. Michael Kremer

Q.9 As per law, the monetary policy framework in India shall be operated by:

A. NITI Aayog
B. Reserve Bank of India
C. Department of Economic
D. Department of Revenue

Q.10 The head office of the Securities and Exchange Board of India is located at:

A. Delhi   **B.** Kolkata   **C.** Mumbai   **D.** Chennai

Q.11 Who among the following was not a recipient of a Nobel Prize?

A. Madam Marie Curie   **B.** Abhijeet Banerjee

C. Mahatma Gandhi   **D.** Mother Teresa

Q.12 Which of the following represents the correct order of organizing Tennis Grand Slams in an year (from January to December)?

A. Australian Open, French Open, Wimbledon, US Open

B. US Open, Wimbledon, Australian Open, French Open

C. Australian Open, Wimbledon, French Open, US Open

D. Wimbledon, French Open, US Open, Australian Open

Q.13 Who among the following was not in the list of Bharat Ratna awardees in 2019?

A. Pranab Mukherjee

B. Bhupen Hazarika

C. Nanaji Deshmukh

D. Deen Dayal Upadhyay

Q.14 Who won the Dadasaheb Phalke Award, 2019?

A. Rajinikanth   **B.** Amitabh Bachhan

C. Bhupen Hazarika   **D.** None of these

Q.15 Who among the following are the recipients of the Rajiv Gandhi Khel Ratna Award, 2019?

A. Virat Kohli and Cheteswar Pujara

B. Deepa Malik and Bajrang Punia

C. Fouaad Mirza and Gaurav Singh Gill

D. Pooja Dhanda and Gurmeet Singh Sandhu

Q.16 Who among the following was the recipient of Raman Magsaysay Award, 2019?

A. Ravish Kumar

B. Arnab Goswami

C. Sandip Pandey

D. Punya Prasun Bajpai

Q.17 Which country won the FIFA World Cup Final 2018?

A. Croatia   **B.** France

C. Brazil   **D.** Germany

Q.18 Where was the ICC Women's T20 World Cup 2020 organized?

A. England   **B.** South Africa

C. Australia   **D.** West Indies

Q.19 Who among the following have won the best actress and best actor awards for 66th National Film Awards 2019?

A. Keerthy Suresh, Ayushmann Khurana, Vicky Kaushal

B. Deepika Padukon, Ayushmann Khurana, Akshay Kumar

C. Kangana Ranaut, Vicky Kaushal, Swanand Kirkere

D. Keerthy Suresh, Akshay Kumar, Swanand Kirkere

Q.20 Which of the following city was granted cleanest capital city award as per the Swachh Survekshan Awards 2019?

A. Lucknow   **B.** Mumbai

C. Panaji   **D.** Bhopal

Q.21 Who won the Ranji Trophy 2019-20?

A. Saurashtra   **B.** Vidarbha

C. Delhi   **D.** Karnataka

Q.22 'Vyom Mitra' is ________.

A. An unmanned aerial vehicle to observe air quality

B. A nanosatellite developed by India in association with Japan

C. A humanoid which will be sent by ISRO in space

D. An indigenously designed aircraft to rescue people from natural disasters

Q.23 Which of the following reports is/are released by the World Bank?

A. Women, Business and the Law

B. The World's Women

C. Economic Freedom Index

Choose the correct answer from the options given below:

A. A only   **B.** C only

C. A and C only   **D.** A and B only

Q.24 Consider the following statements regarding Bharat Interface for Money (BHIM) and answer the following question.

1. It is a payment interface developed by Reserve Bank of India (RBI) to allow real-time fund transfer.

2. It allows for the linking of multiple bank accounts and the option of applying in Initial Public Offer (IPO).

Which of the statements given above is/are correct?

A. 1 only   **B.** 2 only

C. Both 1 and 2   **D.** Neither 1 nor 2

Q.25 Which among the following releases the Human Capital Index?

A. World Bank

B. International Monetary Fund

C. United Nation Development Program

D. World Economic Forum

Q.26 'Mohiniyattam', a classical solo dance, originated in:

A. Odisha   **B.** Kerala

C. Tamil Nadu   **D.** None of these

Q.27 Which among the following stands for USB in relation to laptops and computers?

A. Unique Storage Bus

B. Universal Series Bus

C. Universal Serial Bus

D. Unique Series Bus

Q.28 Which one of these is not a specialized agency of the United Nations?

A. International Civil Aviation Organization

B. International Labour Organization

C. Food and Agricultural Organization

D. World Trade Organization

Q.29 Which Indian Judge was a member of the International Criminal Tribunal for the Far East (Tokyo Tribunal)?

A. Judge Radha Binod Paul

B. Judge Nagendra Singh
C. Judge Dalveer Bhandari
D. Judge Hiralal J. Kania

Q.30 Which one of the following is a tripartite UN agency?
A. International Civil Aviation Organization
B. International Maritime Organization
C. International Labour Organization
D. International Criminal Court

Q.31 Which one of the following was established by the Rome Statute?
A. International Criminal Court
B. International Criminal Tribunal for Rwanda
C. International Crimes Tribunal, Bangladesh
D. Special court for Sierra Leone

Q.32 Which one of the following is not a principal organ of the United Nations?
A. Trusteeship Council
B. General Assembly
C. Human Rights Council
D. Security Council

Q.33 In India, the writ of prohibition may be issued, when there is _______.
A. Both an absence of jurisdiction or excess of jurisdiction & violation of principles of natural justice
B. Violation of principles of natural justice
C. An absence of jurisdiction or excess of jurisdiction
D. A request to produce the body of the person

Q.34 Which Schedule of the Constitution of India, 1950 prescribes the forms of oaths or affirmations for constitutional functionaries?
A. Sixth Schedule **B.** Second Schedule
C. Fifth Schedule **D.** Third Schedule

Q.35 Who declared a state of emergency in India under Article 352 of the Constitution of India in the year 1975?
A. Indira Gandhi
B. Giani Zail Singh
C. Fakhruddin Ali Ahmed
D. Sanjay Gandhi

Q.36 Who among the following has a casting vote over a bill in a joint parliamentary session?
A. Chairman of Rajya Sabha
B. Speaker of Lok Sabha
C. Deputy Speaker of Rajya Sabha
D. President of India

Q.37 Exchange of Enclaves between India and Bangladesh was executed through:
A. 100th Constitutional Amendment Act
B. 101th Constitutional Amendment Act
C. 102th Constitutional Amendment Act
D. 99th Constitutional Amendment Act

Q.38 Article 44 of the Constitution of India is related to:

A. Uniform Civil Code for citizens
B. Provision of early childhood care and education to children below the age of 6 years
C. The duty of the state to raise the level of nutrition
D. Organization of agriculture and animal husbandry

Q.39 Supreme Court of India's judgement in Justice K.S. Puttaswamy (Retd.) and Anr. v Union of India and Ors is related to:
A. Right to Privacy **B.** 2G Spectrum
C. Coal gate Scam **D.** Section 377 of IPC

Q.40 Indian legal system confers citizenship in the following manner:
Choose the correct option:
A. By Birth
B. By Descent
C. By Naturalization
D. By Registration
A. A and B only **B.** B and C only
C. A, B and C only **D.** All of these

Q.41 The Citizenship (Amendment) Act, 2019 provides for special provisions for citizenship for migrants from the following countries:
A. Myanmar
B. Afghanistan
C. Bangladesh
D. Pakistan
A. A, C and D only **B.** B, C and D only
C. A, B and C only **D.** All of these

Q.42 According to the Constitution of India, which of the following fundamental rights cannot be suspended during national emergency?
A. Article 19 and 21 **B.** Article 14 and 21
C. Article 14 and 19 **D.** Article 20 and 21

Q.43 The pardoning power of the Governor of a state includes:
A. Power to pardon a sentence of life imprisonment
B. Power to grant pardon where the punishment or sentence is by Court Martial
C. Power to remit a sentence.
Choose the correct answer from the options given below:
A. A and C only **B.** B and C only
C. A only **D.** All of these

Q.44 Which among the following recommended the inclusion of Fundamental Duties in the Constitution of India?
A. Swaran Singh Committee
B. Nehru Committee
C. Gadgill Committee
D. Mandal Commission

Q.45 Which of the following option(s) are available for a party aggrieved by a decision of the Supreme Court of India?
Choose the correct answer from the options given below:
A. Curative Petition

B. Review Petition

C. Writ Petition

D. Public Interest Litigation

A. A and B only   **B.** B, C and D only

C. B and C only   **D.** All of these

Q.46 Under Article 25 of the Constitution of India, the right to profess, practice and propagate religion is subject to the following restrictions:

A. Public Interest

B. Morality

C. Health

D. Other Provisions of Part III (Fundamental Rights) of the Constitution of India

Choose the correct answer from the options given below:

A. A and B only   **B.** B, C and D only

C. B and C only   **D.** All of these

Q.47 The provision relating to ex post facto law is embodied in:

A. Article 20 (1)   **B.** Article 20 (2)

C. Article 20 (3)   **D.** Article 13 (2)

Q.48 Which of the following terms was inserted in the Preamble of the Constitution of India through the 42 Constitutional Amendment Act?

A. Sovereign   **B.** Democratic

C. Secular   **D.** Unity

Q.49 Which of the following grounds can be invoked to restrict freedom of speech and expression according to the Constitution of India?

Choose the correct answer from the options given below:

A Sovereignty and Integrity of India

B. Friendly relations with foreign States

C. Security of the State

D. Contempt of court

A. A, B and D only   **B.** B, C and D only

C. A, B and C only   **D.** All of these

Q.50 Which is not true with regard to "common intention" under the Indian Penal Code?

A. Acts done by several persons

B. Pre-arranged plan

C. Prior meeting of minds

D. Membership of an unlawful assembly

Q.51 Which of the following is an offence under the Indian Penal Code?

A. Marital rape

B. Adultery

C. Stalking

D. Both, Marital rape and Stalking

Q.52 Which chapter of the Indian Penal Code deals with general exceptions?

A. Chapter III   **B.** Chapter IV

C. Chapter V   **D.** Chapter VI

Q.53 When a man inserts, to any extent, any object or a part of the body, not being his penis, into the vagina, the urethra or anus of a woman or makes her to do so with him or any other person, he commits:

A. Rape   **B.** Sexual Harassment

C. Sexual Assault   **D.** None of these

Q.54 The Doctrine of Rarest of Rare was established in:

A. Bachan Singh vs. State of Punjab

B. Mithu vs. State of Punjab

C. Shatrughan Singh Chauhan vs. Union of India

D. None of these

Q.55 Mens rea is not a necessary condition for:

A. Kidnapping   **B.** Murder

C. Theft   **D.** Wrongful Restraint

Q.56 The Maxim 'ignorantia facti excusat, ignorantia juris non excusat' means:

A. Ignorance of fact excuses, ignorance of law does not excuse

B. Ignorance of law excuses, ignorance of fact does not excuse

C. Ignorance due to which mistake occurs is excused if done in good faith

D. Ignorance due to which a vital mistake occurs, is not excused even if done in good faith

Q.57 Under the Indian Penal Code, nothing is considered to be an offence if it is done by a child under_____ years of age.

A. Six   **B.** Seven   **C.** Eight   **D.** Nine

Q.58 The right of private defence under the Indian Penal Code is available for the protection of:

A. Other humans only

B. Only self

C. Self and other humans

D. Only property

Q.59 X threatens to publish a defamatory libel concerning Y unless Y gives you money. He thus induces Y to give him money. Here X has committed the offense of:

A. Defamation

B. Mischief

C. Criminal Intimidation

D. Extortion

Q.60 In Navtej Singh Johar case, dealing with transgenders' issues, the Supreme Court of India asked the Center to include them in:

A. Other Backward Classes

B. Scheduled Castes/Tribes

C. Economically Backward Classes

D. None of these

Q.61 'A' in his madness, attempts to kill 'B'. 'B' hits 'A' with an iron rod seriously injuring him. Choose the correct option from below.

A. 'B' has no right of private defence since 'A' is mad

B. 'B' has right of private defence though 'A' is mad

C. 'B' is guilty of inflicting grievous injury on 'A'

D. None of these

Q.62 The Fundamental Duties towards environment were imposed on the citizens in the year:

A. 1978   **B.** 1974   **C.** 1976   **D.** 1992

Q.63 Bharat Stage Emission Standards (BSES) are set by the:

A. Central Pollution Control Board

B. Ministry of Environment, Forest and Climate Change

C. Ministry of Transport and Highways

D. Supreme Court of India

Q.64 The Blue Flag, a certification that a beach, marina, or sustainable boating tourism operator meets its stringent standards, is awarded by:

A. Ministry of Environment, Forest and Climate Change

B. Foundation for Environmental Education (FEE)

C. United Nations

D. International Seabed Authority

Q.65 The United Nations Conference on Environment and Development (UNCED) is also known as the:

A. Earth Summit   **B.** Paris Convention

C. Kyoto Protocol   **D.** Montreal Protocol

Q.66 Which among the following is an international treaty related to the protection of the ozone layer?

A. Kyoto Protocol   **B.** Paris Agreement

C. Montreal Protocol   **D.** Aarhus Convention

Q.67 The United Nations Programme on Reducing Emissions from Deforestation and Forest Degradation (or UN-REDD Programme) is a collaborative programme of the:

A. Food and Agriculture Organization of the United Nations (FAO)

B. United Nations Development Programme (UNDP)

C.United Nations Environment Programme (UNEP)

Choose the correct answer from the options given below:

A. A and C only   **B.** B and C only

C. None   **D.** All of these

Q.68 Which of the following is a legal effect of adoption?

A. An adopted child shall be deemed to be the child of his or her adoptive father or mother.

B. All the ties of the child in the family of his or her birth shall be deemed to be severed.

C. Both (A) and (B)

D. None of these

Q.69 Under Muslim law, a legal guardian may:

A. Sell the movable property in the interest of the child

B. Exercise right of pre-emption on behalf of the child

C. Acknowledge a debt on behalf of the child

D. All of these

Q.70 Which among the following is not a ground for divorce under the Special Marriage Act, 1954?

A. Adultery

B. Desertion

C. Mental disorder

D. Irretrievable breakdown of marriage

Q.71 Degrees of prohibited relationships is applicable between two persons if they are related by:

A. Full blood

B. Half or uterine blood

C. Adoption

D. All of these

Q.72 Which of the following is provided in section 7 of the Hindu Marriage Act, 1955?

A. Registration

B. Ceremonies for solemnizing a Hindu marriage

C. Adoption of child

D. All of these

Q.73 The manager of Waqf is known as:

A. Mujwar   **B.** Mutawalli

C. Khadim   **D.** Sajjada Nashin

Q.74 Which Amendment of the Constitution of India reduced the voting age from 21 years to 18 years?

A. 73rd Constitutional Amendment

B. 69th Constitutional Amendment

C. 61st Constitutional Amendment

D. 83rd Constitutional Amendment

Q.75 The Election Commission of India does not have the power to:

A. Register a political party

B. Re-register a political party

C. Conduct election to State Legislatures

D. None of these

Q.76 Who elects the representatives of the states in Rajya Sabha?

A. Elected members of State Legislative Assemblies

B. All registered voters in India

C. Elected Members of Parliament

D. Elected members of State Legislative Assemblies and Parliament

Q.77 Which practices among the following constitute 'corrupt practice' in the Parliamentary election?

A. Bribery

B. Procuring assistance of the government servants

C. Promoting the feeling of hatred and enmity between different classes of citizens on ground of religion, caste etc

D. All of these

Q.78 What can be the maximum number of representatives of States and Union Territories in the Council of States?

A. 238   **B.** 240   **C.** 245   **D.** 250

Q.79 An agreement consists of reciprocal promises between at least:

A. Four parties   **B.** Six parties

C. Three parties   **D.** Two parties

Q.80 Who among the following does not have the capacity to enter into a contract?

A. Corporation

B. Minor

C. A person convicted of an offence

D. All of these

Q.81 The age of majority for entering into a contract under the Indian Contract Act, 1872 is:

A. 18 years   **B.** 21 years   **C.** 16 years   **D.** 25 years

Q.82 A contract of insurance is an example of:

A. Quasi Contract   **B.** Contingent Contract

C. Both   **D.** None of these

Q.83 Agreement of social nature is unenforceable because it lacks:

A. Intention to create moral relationship

B. Intention to create social relationship

C. Intention to create legal relationship

D. Intention to create an agreement

Q.84 Doctrine of privity of contract implies:

A. Only those persons who are party to a contract can enforce the same

B. Only those persons who are not party to a contract can enforce the same

C. Only those persons who are known to the promisor can enforce the contract

D. Only those persons who are known to the promisee can enforce the contract

Q.85 In India, provisions of the Indian Contract Act, 1872 apply to:

A. Citizens   **B.** Persons

C. Companies   **D.** All of these

Q.86 Product patent in India was introduced in:

A. 2004   **B.** 2005   **C.** 2003   **D.** 2006

Q.87 Industrial design specifically refers to:

A. Form of expression

B. Functionality

C. Form of expression with aesthetic appeal

D. Invention

Q.88 Which among the following combinations is not mentioned under the TRIPS?

A. Patents, Trademarks and Copyright

B. Patents, Trademarks and Industrial Designs

C. Patents, Copyright and Data Exclusivity

D. Patents, Copyright and Undisclosed Information

Q.89 Intellectual property rights are _______ in their enforcement.

A. Territorial   **B.** Regional

C. International   **D.** All of these

Q.90 The trade-related intellectual property disputes are settled by:

A. WIPO

B. WTO

C. ICJ

D. World Economic Forum

Q.91 The formula of making Coca Cola is protected under:

A. Copyright   **B.** Trademarks

C. Trade Secrets   **D.** None of these

Q.92 Direction: In the following question, choose the correct alternative which can replace the question mark.

Ignominous: Honourable:: Cajole: ?

A. Notorious   **B.** Coax

C. Bully   **D.** Filch

Q.93 Direction: In the following question, choose the correct alternative which can replace the question mark.

Condign: Deserved :: Veracity : ?

A. Mercy   **B.** Boring

C. Obloquy   **D.** Accuracy

Q.94 Complete the series.

RESTITUTION, ESTITUTIO, TITUTIO, ITUTI, _______?

A. UTI   **B.** TUT   **C.** ITU   **D.** TI

Q.95 If A x B means A is to the north of B; A + B means A is to the south of B; A % B means A is to the west of B; A - B means A is to the east of B; then in P % Q + R - S, S is in which direction with respect to Q?

A. South-West   **B.** South-East

C. North-East   **D.** North-West

Ques (96-97):Direction: Read the passage and answer the following question.

Nine diplomats R, S, T, U, V, W, X, Y and Z are sitting around a table facing the center. Z sits 5th to the right of X. T is not an immediate neighbour of either X or Z. S sits between Y and V. T sits 4th to the left of V. U sits 2nd to the right of W. Y is not an immediate neighbour of Z.

Q.96 Which of the following is U's position with respect to S in the anti-clock wise direction starting from S?

A. 3rd to the Left   **B.** 4th to the Left

C. 5th to the Right   **D.** 7th to the Right

Q.97 Three of the following pairs are alike based on their seating positions in the above arrangement and so form a group. Find the odd one out.

A. TR   **B.** ZS   **C.** YW   **D.** UV

Q.98 Direction: Read the passage and answer the following one question.

A wildlife sanctuary contains animals of at least two of the following six kinds--nilgai, chinkara, black buck, wild boar, leopards, jackals. No other kinds of animals are in the sanctuary. The following conditions must hold:

1. Jackals are not in the sanctuary if Chinkaras are

2. Black bucks are not in the sanctuary if Wild boars are

3. Either wild boar or jackal, but not both, are in the sanctuary

4. Jackals are in the sanctuary if Nilgais, Leopards, or both are in the sanctuary

If there are no wild boars in the sanctuary, then which one of the following is a kind of animal that cannot be in the sanctuary:

A. Nilgai	**B.** Chinkara
C. Black buck	**D.** Jackal

Q.99 Given A ÷ B means A is father of B, A × B means A is wife of B, A + B means A is the brother of B, A - B means A is the daughter of B.

If, E ÷ F × G + H, then how is H related to F?

A. Brother-in-law	**B.** Brother
C. Father	**D.** Father-in-law

Q.100 Choose the odd one out:

A. FCDE	**B.** UQRS	**C.** KGHI	**D.** PLMN

// Smart Answer Sheet //

Correct — Percentage of students who answered correctly. **Skipped** — Percentage of students who skipped.

Q.	Ans.	Correct / Skipped
1	B	22.59 % / 7.83 %
2	A	39.39 % / 6.13 %
3	D	36.55 % / 8.4 %
4	B	34.85 % / 7.83 %
5	B	38.37 % / 8.17 %
6	C	29.85 % / 12.15 %
7	A	64.25 % / 11.46 %
8	D	15.78 % / 14.19 %
9	B	58.68 % / 11.81 %
10	C	64.47 % / 11.69 %
11	C	65.49 % / 11.47 %
12	A	32.58 % / 12.48 %
13	D	42.34 % / 11.46 %
14	B	38.82 % / 12.14 %
15	B	42.91 % / 10.89 %
16	A	54.26 % / 12.6 %
17	B	40.18 % / 6.93 %
18	C	37.12 % / 12.82 %
19	A	40.64 % / 10.44 %
20	D	61.63 % / 10.11 %
21	A	35.41 % / 12.83 %
22	C	39.39 % / 12.82 %
23	A	23.84 % / 5.79 %
24	B	23.38 % / 10.33 %
25	A	38.14 % / 9.76 %
26	B	43.47 % / 12.83 %
27	C	49.38 % / 5.9 %
28	D	34.62 % / 12.6 %
29	A	24.63 % / 12.6 %
30	C	33.37 % / 13.17 %
31	A	49.72 % / 7.15 %
32	C	47.22 % / 13.28 %
33	A	59.82 % / 10.67 %
34	D	61.75 % / 11.8 %
35	C	56.41 % / 10.67 %
36	B	64.36 % / 10.33 %
37	A	52.44 % / 8.63 %
38	A	71.17 % / 12.94 %
39	A	60.95 % / 8.52 %
40	D	72.76 % / 11.12 %
41	B	55.05 % / 13.96 %
42	D	64.59 % / 12.6 %
43	A	38.59 % / 13.4 %
44	A	71.74 % / 13.5 %
45	A	40.07 % / 6.7 %
46	B	20.54 % / 12.6 %
47	A	44.15 % / 11.13 %
48	C	67.76 % / 12.26 %
49	A	18.39 % / 7.94 %
50	D	36.44 % / 12.48 %
51	C	39.39 % / 10.33 %
52	B	50.51 % / 13.17 %
53	A	61.18 % / 12.6 %
54	A	66.17 % / 11.81 %
55	A	40.64 % / 10.1 %
56	A	73.33 % / 9.76 %
57	B	67.31 % / 12.83 %
58	C	65.27 % / 12.03 %
59	D	61.29 % / 9.08 %
60	A	42.79 % / 13.51 %
61	B	73.44 % / 12.26 %
62	C	43.47 % / 12.15 %
63	A	40.07 % / 10.1 %
64	B	23.95 % / 11.12 %
65	A	49.94 % / 12.6 %
66	C	36.21 % / 11.58 %
67	D	18.62 % / 10.1 %
68	C	57.66 % / 12.49 %
69	D	49.83 % / 13.17 %
70	D	43.13 % / 12.49 %
71	D	53.12 % / 12.49 %
72	B	39.16 % / 12.49 %
73	B	44.61 % / 11.8 %
74	C	53.58 % / 13.28 %
75	B	54.37 % / 5.22 %
76	A	52.44 % / 11.01 %
77	D	56.19 % / 14.64 %
78	A	33.03 % / 12.83 %
79	D	74.12 % / 12.03 %
80	B	62.66 % / 10.78 %

Q.	Ans.	Correct / Skipped
81	A	72.99 %
		14.52 %
82	B	44.04 %
		12.94 %
83	C	51.76 %
		7.26 %
84	A	50.17 %
		11.46 %

Q.	Ans.	Correct / Skipped
85	D	75.37 %
		7.94 %
86	B	33.6 %
		12.48 %
87	C	32.8 %
		12.38 %
88	C	29.28 %
		12.49 %

Q.	Ans.	Correct / Skipped
89	A	35.19 %
		14.3 %
90	B	43.47 %
		13.06 %
91	C	52.89 %
		13.4 %
92	C	18.27 %
		13.97 %

Q.	Ans.	Correct / Skipped
93	D	19.86 %
		12.04 %
94	A	52.1 %
		13.28 %
95	D	27.01 %
		13.17 %
96	C	21.23 %
		11.46 %

Q.	Ans.	Correct / Skipped
97	D	19.86 %
		11.81 %
98	B	33.14 %
		8.29 %
99	A	51.42 %
		13.73 %
100	A	55.96 %
		10.67 %

Ques (1-2):Direction: Question given below has a set of three statements. Choose the alternative where the third statement can be logically deduced from both the preceding alternatives, but not just from one of them.

Q.1 A. Few mathematicians are scientists. Some scientists play. Few Mathematicians play

B. Rabbit is a flower. Some flowers are made of chromoplasts. Rabbit is made of chromoplast

C. No elephant eats grass. All lions eat grass. No lions are

A. A and C only   **B.** B and C only

C. C only   **D.** B only

Q.2 A. Many teachers are not readers. All singers are teachers. All singers are not readers

B. Some giraffes are donkeys. Some giraffes are sheep. Some sheep are donkeys.

C. All locks are keys. Some keys do not open. Some locks do not open.

A. A and C   **B.** B and C   **C.** C only   **D.** B only

Ques (3-4):Direction: Read the following information carefully and answer the question given below.

(i) A is older than S

(ii) M is older than A but younger than K

(iii) K is elder than S

(iv) S is younger than M

(v) G is the oldest

Q.3 Who is the youngest?

A. K   **B.** A   **C.** M   **D.** S

Q.4 Agewise, who is in the middle?

A. K   **B.** A   **C.** M   **D.** S

Ques (5-6):Direction: Read the following information carefully and answer the question given below.

The sum of the incomes of A and B is more than that of C and D taken together. The sum of incomes of A and C is the same as that of B and D taken together. Moreover, A earns half as much as the sum of the incomes of B and D.

Q.5 Whose income is the highest?

A. A   **B.** B   **C.** C   **D.** D

Q.6 Which statement is correct.

A. A earns more than B

B. A earns equal to C

C. C and D together earn half of what A earns

D. None of the above

Q.7 Under Trade marks act,1999 the trademark is granted for?

A. 10 years, but may be renewed from time to time provision of the Act.

B. 5 years, but may be renewed from time to time subject to the provisions of the Act.

C. 20 years, but may be renewed from time to time subject to the provisions of the Act.

D. 15 years, but may be renewed from time to time subject to the provisions of the Act.

Q.8 World Intellectual Property Day is celebrated on:

A. 26th April   **B.** 21st June

C. 23rd September   **D.** 4th August

Q.9 Clause (4) of Article 15 has been added to the Constitution of India by:

A. The Constitution (First Amendment) Act

B. The Constitution (Second Amendment) Act

C. The Constitution (Fourth Amendment) Act

D. The Constitution (Sixth Amendment) Act

Q.10 As per the Constitution of India the sovereignty of India lies with:

A. The Constitution of India

B. The Supreme Court of India

C. The Parliament of India

D. ThePeople of India

Q.11 Article 360 of Constitution of India has been invoked in India:

A. Once   **B.** Twice

C. Thrice   **D.** Never invoked

Q.12 Article 20 and Article 21 has been taken from the purview of Article 359 of the Constitution of India by:

A. TheConstitution (42nd Amendment) Act

B. TheConstitution (43rd Amendment) Act

C. The Constitution (44th Amendment) Act

D. The Constitution (59th Amendment) Act

Q.13 Representation of members in House of People in India is based on:

A. Literacy of State   **B.** Areaof the State

C. Population   **D.** Community

Q.14 The writ of prohibition may be issued, when there is?

A. Anabsence of jurisdiction or access of jurisdiction

B. Violation of principles of natural justice

C. Request to produce the body of the person

D. Both An absence of jurisdiction or access of jurisdiction & Violation of principles of natural justice

Q.15 Article 51A of the Constitution of India provides for the Fundamental Duties of:

A. Citizens of India

B. Public Servants

C. All those who run public and private sectors

D. Prime Minister and his Council of Ministers

Q.16 In the year 2002 the Competition Act was enacted. ThisAct replaces:

A. Consumer protection Act, 1986
B. Prevention of corruption Act, 1988
C. Monopolies and restrictive trade practices Act, 1969
D. Protectionof Civil Rights Act, 1955

Q.17 The power of the President of India issue an ordinance is a:

A. Legislative power   **B.** Executivepower
C. Quasi-judicialpower   **D.** Judicialpower

Q.18 In which landmark judgment did the Supreme Court of India decriminalized homosexuality?

A. Nilabati Behera vs. State of Orissa, 1993
B. Navtez Singh Johar vs. Union of India, 2018
C. Maneka Gandhivs. Union of India, 1978
D. Hussainara Khatoon v. State of Bihar, 1979

Q.19 In which one of the following judgments the Constitutional Bench of the Supreme Court of India, the 'rarest of rare' principle in the award of death penalty was first laid down?

A. Bachan Singh vs. State of Punjab (1980)
B. Gopalanachari vs. State of Kerala (1980)
C. Dr. Upendra Baxi vs. State of UP (1983)
D. Tukaram vs. State of Maharashtra (1979)

Q.20 How many times the President of India can seek re-election to his post?

A. Ones
B. Two times
C. Three times
D. Any number of times

Q.21 ThePresident gives his resignation to the:

A. ChiefJustice
B. VicePresident
C. Speaker of Lok Sabha
D. PrimeMinister

Q.22 Which one of the following does not constitute the electoral college for electing the President of India?

A. Elected members of Lok Sabha
B. Electedmembers of the Legislative Assembly of each state
C. Electedmembers of the Legislative Council
D. Elected members of Rajya Sabha

Q.23 The charge of impeachment against the President of India for his removal can be preferred by:

A. Both Houses of Parliament
B. Speakerof Lok Sabha and Chairman of Rajya Sabha
C. RajyaSabha
D. Lok Sabha

Q.24 Which of the following writs called bulwark of personal freedom?

A. Certiorari   **B.** HabeasCorpus

C. Mandamus   **D.** QuoWarranto

Q.25 For the philosophy underlying our Constitution, the historic 'Objectives Resolution' was moved in the Constituent Assembly on 13th December 1946 by:

A. Jawaharlal Nehru
B. Dr. S Radhakrishnan
C. Dr.B.R. Ambedkar
D. RajendraPrasad

Q.26 The Preamble of Indian Constitution envisages what kinds of justice:

A. Social   **B.** Economic
C. Political   **D.** All of these

Q.27 In which year Right of Children to Free and Compulsory Education, Act was enacted by Parliament of India?

A. 2009   **B.** 2005   **C.** 2008   **D.** 2007

Q.28 Which of the set is said to be the Golden triangle ofIndian Constitution?

A. Articles 14,15, and 16
B. Articles 20, 21 and 22
C. Preamble, Fundamental Right and Directive Principles
D. 14, 19 and 21

Q.29 Basic structure of Constitution can be amended:

A. By simple majority
B. By 2/3rd of majority
C. By special majority and ratification by half of states
D. None of these

Q.30 As per VII Schedule of the Constitution of India, the power to enact laws on residuary matters lies with:

A. State legislature   **B.** Parliament
C. ThePresident   **D.** None

Q.31 SarkariaCommission was concerned with:

A. Judicial reforms
B. ElectoralReforms
C. Centre-StateRelations
D. FinancialReforms

Q.32 Who is equivalent of Attorney General in State?

A. Chief Minister
B. Judge of the High Court
C. AdvocateGeneral
D. Noneof these

Q.33 The name of the Union given in the Constitution is:

A. Hindustan i.e Bharatvarsha
B. India i.e. Hindustan
C. Indiai.e. Bharat
D. Bharatdesh i.e. India

Q.34 Proceedings to be incamera means:

A. Proceedings in private
B. Proceedings recorded in camera
C. Proceedingsin public
D. Noneof these

Q.35 A watch reads 4:30. If the minute hand points towards north east, then the hour hand will point towards the:

A. South -west **B.** North

C. South **D.** South-east

Q.36 X+Y> U+V and Y+U>X+V, then it is definitethat:

A. V>Y **B.** U>V **C.** X>V **D.** Y>V

Q.37 Complete the series:

H	K	Q
C	G	O
E	J	?

A. T **B.** P **C.** N **D.** L

Q.38 Complete the series :

A	D	G
D	I	N
I	P	?

A. V **B.** W **C.** X **D.** V

Q.39 What is the product of all numbers in the dial of a telephone?

A. 1,58,480 **B.** 1,59,480

C. 1,59,450 **D.** Noneof these

Q.40 Five people, A, C, D, F and G are sitting around a table. A is sitting to the left of G. One person is sitting between G and D. C is sitting to the left of A: Choose the correct option:

A. Fis sitting between G and D

B. Fis sitting between C and D

C. Fis sitting between A and G

D. Fis sitting to the right of D

Q.41 One card is drawn from a pack of 52 cards. What is the probability that the card drawn is either a black card or a queen?

A. $\frac{1}{2}$ **B.** $\frac{15}{26}$ **C.** $\frac{7}{13}$ **D.** $\frac{1}{52}$

Q.42 Find the average of prime numbers between 20 and 50.

A. 37.6 **B.** 35.8 **C.** 39.8 **D.** 40.5

Q.43 The average of five consecutive numbers is 16. Find the smallest of these numbers.

A. 14 **B.** 8 **C.** 12 **D.** 20

Q.44 The 26 2nd Law Commission of India report deals with:

A. Abolition of death penalty

B. 2015 Model Bilateral Investment Treaty

C. Amendment of Arbitration and Conciliation Act 1996

D. ElectoralReforms

Q.45 The principle of quantum merit is applicable when?

A. Thecontract is divisible, and some parts areperformed

B. When the contract is indivisible and something in relation to contract is done

C. Both The contract is divisible, and some parts are performed and When the contract is indivisible and something in relation to contract is done

D. Whenan act is done graciously

Q.46 The President of the India can consult the Supreme Court of India:

A. When a question of law of public importance arises

B. To seek advice before he impose emergency in any state

C. Against any decision taken by the Prime Minister and his council of ministers

D. In order to do complete justice when a death penalty convict seeks clemency from the President

Q.47 What kind of damages are available for breach of contract?

A. Vindictive Damages

B. LiquidatedDamages

C. UnliquidatedDamages

D. All of the above

Q.48 Fraudoccurs when:

A. An act is done with the intention to deceive another party

B. Active concealment of facts

C. Both an act is done with the intention to deceive another party & active concealment of facts

D. Noneof these

Q.49 The three lists in the Seventh Schedule of the Constitution of India represent:

A. Principle of Division of power

B. Principle of Separation of Power

C. Doctrine of Cooperative Federalism

D. Rule against non-arbitrariness

Q.50 Anagreement in restraint of marriage is:

A. Void **B.** Voidable **C.** Illegal **D.** Valid

Q.51 'A' threatens his wife and son to commit suicide in case they did not execute a deed in his favour. This will amount to:

A. Coercion **B.** Undueinfluence

C. Noneof the above **D.** Both the above

Q.52 'A' agrees to sell his house to 'B', 'A' has two houses. The agreement is:

A. Void **B.** Valid

C. Voidable **D.** Both Void and Valid

Q.53 Non est factum means:

A. Document executed under fraud

B. Document executed under misrepresentation

C. It is not my deed

D. None of the above

Q.54 A' agrees to Pay 'B' Rupees 1000 if it rains today, 'B' will pay him Rupees 1000 if it does not rain. Which kind of agreement is this:

A. Wagering Agreement

B. ContingentAgreement

C. VoidableAgreement

D. None of the above

Q.55 Caveat Venditor means:

A. Buyer beware

B. Sellerbeware

C. Manufacturer beware

D. None of the above

Q.56 In which of the cases the relationship of principal and agent exists:

A. Relationship between partners

B. Relationship between husband and wife

C. Relationship between employer and employee

D. Both Relationship between partners & Relationship between employer and employee

Q.57 Capacity to contract relates to:

A. Ageof parties to contract

B. Competence of the parties to enter into contract

C. Intention of the parties to enter into contract

D. None of the above

Q.58 When both the parties are under a mistake of fact essential to the contract, the contract is:

A. Voidable

B. Void

C. Doesnot affect its validity

D. None of the above

Q.59 The essential characteristic of a tort is, violation of:

A. Right in personam (a right available only against some determinate person or property)

B. A contractual right

C. Right in rem (a right vested in some determinate person and available against the world at large)

D. None of the above

Q.60 The doctrine of 'double jeopardy' enshrined in Article 20 (2) means:

A. No one can be prosecuted and punished more than once for the same offence

B. One can be prosecuted several times for the same offence

C. Punishment once awarded cannot be enhanced in appeal or revision

D. One can be prosecuted more than once, but punished only once

Q.61 Under the Indian Penal Code, 1860 dislocation of tooth constitutes the offence of:

A. Simple hurt

B. Grievoushurt

C. Assault

D. None of the above

Q.62 The term used to describe an accused who seeks pardon from the court by agreeing to testify against all others involved in the crime is:

A. Hostilewitness

B. Approver

C. Accomplice

D. None of the above

Q.63 A First Information Report (FIR) for a cognizable offence may be lodged by:

A. Victim

B. Familymember of the victim

C. All of these

D. Police officer

Q.64 Malimath Committee is associated with reforms in the field of:

A. Education

B. CriminalLaw

C. LabourWelfare

D. Domesticrelations

Q.65 In taking and recording evidence,the language of every Court within the State other than the High Court shall be:

A. Hindi

B. English

C. Determined by the respective State Government

D. Hindior English

Q.66 Theessentials of a valid custom are:

A. Antiquity

B. Certainty

C. Consistency

D. All of the above

Q.67 The doctrine of 'Transferred Malice' is contained in which Section of the IPC,1860?

A. Section34

B. Section 139

C. Section301

D. Section304A

Q.68 Whichof the following is an inchoate crime?

A. Public nuisance

B. Riot

C. Criminalattempt

D. Culpablehomicide

Q.69 Theft and Extortion are listed under the IPC as offences against:

A. Public order and tranquillity

B. Body

C. Property

D. All of the above

Q.70 Which of the following is not an essential ingredient ofCriminal Breach of Trust?

A. Misappropriation/conversion

B. Entrustment

C. Negligence

D. Dishonestintention

Q.71 On 9th March 2018, a Constitution Bench of the Supreme Court of India confirmed that the right to die with dignity is a fundamental right while allowing passive euhanasia and living will. This judgment is known as:

A. P.Rathinam v. UOI,

B. CommonCause v. UOI

C. JusticeKS Puttaswamy v. UOI

D. SupremeCourt Advocates-On-Record Association v. UOI

Q.72 The word 'plagiarist' refers to a person who?

A. Is aprofessional boxer

B. Uses language and thoughts of another author without authorization and the representation of that author's work as one's own, without crediting the original author

C. Is called by courts to give testimony in cases relating to fingerprints

D. Is a collector of old and antique stamps of different countries

Q.73 In which of the following cases was the judgment popularly known as Jallikattu verdict pronounced?

A. Gauri Maulekhi vs. UOI

B. Nair, NR and others vs. UOI

C. AnimalWelfare Board of India vs. A. Nagaraja

D. Federation of Indian Animal Protection Organisation vs. UOI

Q.74 Abhiram Singh vs. CD Commachen (2017) is a judgment of the Supreme Court dealing with which of the following issues?

A. Proper and adequate access to public places for visually disabled persons

B. Compensation to Uphaar tragedy victims

C. Linkage of IT returns with Aadhaar

D. Seeking votes in the name of religion amounts to a corrupt practice

Ques (75-76):Direction: In question four alternatives are given for the Idiom/Phrase under in the sentence. Choose the alternative which best expresses the meaning of the Idiom/Phrase.

Q.75 Flog a dead horse means:

A. Tobeat a horse to death

B. Crueltyto animals

C. Waste effort on something when there is no chance of succeeding

D. To try to get work out of someone who is already exhausted

Q.76 'Achillesheel' means:

A. A painful soot

B. A weak point

C. A food disease

D. A Kind of fungus

Q.77 Choosethe correct spelling:

A. Survellience

B. Surveillance

C. Surveilance

D. Surveilence

Q.78 What do you mean by "candidate losing the deposit" after the poll result is announced?

A. A defeated candidate who fails to secure more than one sixth of the valid votes polled in the constituency will lose his security deposit

B. A defeated candidate who fails to secure more than one fourth of the valid votes polled in the constituency will lose his security deposit

C. A defeated candidate who fails to secure more than one third of the valid votes polled in the constituency will lose his security deposit

D. A defeated candidate who fails to secure minimum 600 valid votes polled in the constituency will lose his security deposit

Q.79 The anti-defection law in India is contained in:

A. The IV Schedule of the Constitution of India

B. The VII Schedule of the Constitution of India

C. The IX Schedule of the Constitution of India

D. The X Schedule of the Constitution of India

Q.80 The electoral college that elects the Vice President of India comprises of:

A. Members of both Houses of Parliament

B. Elected members of both Houses of Parliament

C. Elected members of both Houses of Parliament and State Legislative Assemblies

D. Elected members of both Houses of Parliament and State Legislative Assemblies and Legislative Councils

Q.81 Whoamong the following is famous for Bharatnatyam?

A. Sonal Mansingh

B. Sonal Mansingh

C. MadhaviMudgal

D. Yamini Krishnamurti

Q.82 Who among the following is the First Iraqi National to have received the Nobel Peace Prize?

A. Najiba Ahmed

B. NadiaMurad Basee Taha

C. ReemAlasadi

D. JennaKrajeski

Q.83 Which of the following is correct?

A. FIFA, 2014 - Brazil, FIFA, 2018 - Russia & FIFA, 2022 - Qatar

B. FIFA, 2010 - South Africa, FIFA, 2018 -Russia & FIFA, 2022 - Qatar

C. Both FIFA, 2014 -Brazil, FIFA, 2018 -Russia & FIFA, 2022 - Qatar & FIFA, 2010 -South Africa, FIFA, 2018 -Russia & FIFA,2022 -Qatar

D. None of the above

Q.84 Bt.in 'Bt. Brinjal' is:

A. Bacterium

B. Vrius

C. Antibiotic

D. None of the above

Q.85 Who authored the book 'Indian Philosophy'?

A. CharlesDickens

B. William Shakespeare

C. ShashiTharoor

D. Sarvepalli Radhakrishnan

Q.86 Who is the Director General of International Atomic Energy Agency (IAEA)?

A. Mohamed Elbardei

B. General Rafael Mariano Grossi

C. MahmoudMekki

D. LutherRangreji

Q.87 Ageneral offer is an offer which?

A. Contains all the essentials of a valid contract

B. Canbe accepted by anyone

C. Cannotbe termed as a contract

D. None of the above

Q.88 Who is the first Indian woman appointed as Judge of ITLOS (International Tribunal for the Law of the Sea)?

A. Indira Banerjee

B. RumaPal

C. FlaviaAgnes

D. NeeruChadha

Q.89 'Properrespect is shown to National Anthem by standing up when the National Anthem issung. It will not be right to say that disrespect is shown by not joining inthe singing.' It has been held in:

A. BijoiEmmanuel vs. State of Kerala

B. SuryaNarain vs. U.O.I

C. Ram JawayaKapur vs. U.O.I

D. Keshavananda Bharati vs. U.O.I.

Q.90 Two young persons, A & B fight with each other. A was having a blade with which 'A' inflicts injury on the face of B leaving a scar on the cheek of B. A is guilty of offence of causing.

A. Grievoushurt

B. Grievous hurt by rash or negligent act

C. Simplehurt

D. Simplehurt by rash or negligent act

Q.91 The right to protect one's own person and property against the unlawful aggression of others is known as:

A. The right of private defence

B. Volentinon fit injuria

C. Anact done by the consent of the other

D. None of the above

Q.92 The first Constitutional Amendment was challenged in thecase:

A. SankariPrasad vs. UOI

B. Sajjan Singh vs. State of Rajasthan

C. both Sankari Prasad vs. UOI & Sajjan Singh v. State of Rajasthan

D. None of the above

Q.93 Which of the following are included as fundamental duties under the Constitution of India?

I. To abide by the Constitution and respect for its ideals and institutions

II. To uphold and protect the Sovereignty, Unity and Integrity of India

III. To ensure the rule of law in the country

IV. to safeguard public property and to abjure violence

A. I, II, IV

B. I, III, IV

C. I, II, III

D. None of the above

Q.94 General exceptions are laid down in the Indian Penal Code in:

A. Chapter VI

B. ChapterIV

C. ChapterIV and VI

D. ChapterVIII

Q.95 The Right of private defence of the body extends to thevoluntarily causing of death, if the offence which occasions the exercise ofright is:

A. Anassault with the intention of kidnapping or abducting

B. An assault reasonably causing an apprehension that simple injury will be caused

C. An assault with intention of escaping with stolen property immediately after the theft

D. Of arresting a person who is running away after having committed an offence of voluntarily causing hurt

Q.96 Which of the following laws has not been amended by the Criminal Law (Amendment) Act, 2018?

A. Protection of Children from Sexual Offences Act (POCSO), 2012

B. Sexual Harassment of Women at Workplace (Prevention, Prohibition and Redressal) Act, 2013

C. IndianPenal Code, 1860

D. CriminalProcedure Code, 1973

Q.97 Z' takes away a golden chain of his wife which was given by her father as Stridhan, without her consent, and gifts it to his girlfriend. 'Z' is guilty of:

A. Notguilty of theft as the chain was their joint property

B. Not guilty of theft as the property was temporarily taken away

C. Guiltyof theft

D. Guilty of criminal misappropriation

Q.98 Who among the following is the current member of the International Law Commission from India?

A. Nagender Singh

B. P.S. Rao

C. Aniruddha Rajput

D. Dalbir Bhandari

Q.99 Which provision of the Constitution of India prohibits employment of children below the age of fourteen years to be employed in factories?

A. Article 23

B. Article 17

C. Article 27

D. Article 24

Q.100 Who won the Gold Medal for India in the Women's 10 metre air pistol event at the XXI Commonwealth Games, 2018?

A. Manika Batra

B. Punam Yadav

C. Pooja Sahasrabudhe

D. Manu Bhaker

// Smart Answer Sheet //

Correct Percentage of students who answered correctly. **Skipped** Percentage of students who skipped.

Q.	Ans.	Correct / Skipped	Q.	Ans.	Correct / Skipped	Q.	Ans.	Correct / Skipped	Q.	Ans.	Correct / Skipped	Q.	Ans.	Correct / Skipped
1	C	21.67 % / 2.91 %	17	A	61.67 % / 8.33 %	33	C	86.67 % / 8.33 %	49	A	51.67 % / 8.33 %	65	C	62.08 % / 8.34 %
2	C	22.5 % / 6.67 %	18	B	77.08 % / 8.34 %	34	A	61.67 % / 8.75 %	50	A	61.25 % / 8.33 %	66	D	59.17 % / 8.75 %
3	D	63.75 % / 7.5 %	19	A	76.25 % / 9.17 %	35	B	38.33 % / 6.67 %	51	A	46.67 % / 8.75 %	67	C	30.83 % / 10.0 %
4	C	56.25 % / 7.92 %	20	D	77.08 % / 8.34 %	36	D	37.5 % / 8.33 %	52	A	46.25 % / 8.75 %	68	C	33.33 % / 8.75 %
5	B	24.17 % / 8.33 %	21	B	84.17 % / 5.83 %	37	A	50.83 % / 7.92 %	53	C	37.08 % / 8.34 %	69	C	42.92 % / 8.75 %
6	C	8.33 % / 8.34 %	22	C	71.67 % / 7.5 %	38	B	60.0 % / 8.33 %	54	A	50.83 % / 7.92 %	70	C	54.58 % / 8.75 %
7	A	47.08 % / 8.75 %	23	A	80.83 % / 7.92 %	39	D	53.33 % / 9.17 %	55	B	55.42 % / 9.16 %	71	B	40.0 % / 8.75 %
8	A	49.58 % / 8.75 %	24	B	74.17 % / 8.33 %	40	A	62.5 % / 8.75 %	56	D	50.42 % / 8.75 %	72	B	56.25 % / 8.33 %
9	A	39.17 % / 8.33 %	25	A	79.17 % / 6.25 %	41	C	30.42 % / 8.75 %	57	B	54.17 % / 8.33 %	73	C	45.83 % / 6.67 %
10	D	75.83 % / 8.34 %	26	D	87.08 % / 8.34 %	42	B	37.92 % / 8.75 %	58	B	50.0 % / 8.75 %	74	D	22.08 % / 7.92 %
11	D	67.92 % / 8.75 %	27	A	37.92 % / 9.16 %	43	A	42.92 % / 7.5 %	59	C	40.42 % / 8.75 %	75	C	57.08 % / 9.17 %
12	C	45.42 % / 8.75 %	28	D	68.33 % / 8.34 %	44	A	25.0 % / 8.33 %	60	A	82.92 % / 8.75 %	76	B	51.25 % / 9.17 %
13	C	79.58 % / 8.34 %	29	D	62.92 % / 7.08 %	45	B	8.33 % / 7.92 %	61	B	66.67 % / 8.33 %	77	B	60.0 % / 8.33 %
14	D	63.75 % / 8.33 %	30	B	62.5 % / 8.75 %	46	A	61.25 % / 8.33 %	62	B	38.33 % / 7.92 %	78	A	48.75 % / 8.33 %
15	A	86.25 % / 7.5 %	31	C	70.83 % / 7.92 %	47	B	49.58 % / 7.5 %	63	C	66.67 % / 9.16 %	79	D	70.83 % / 8.75 %
16	C	57.5 % / 8.33 %	32	C	75.42 % / 8.75 %	48	C	71.25 % / 8.33 %	64	B	35.42 % / 8.75 %	80	A	25.83 % / 8.34 %

Q.	Ans.	Correct		Q.	Ans.	Correct		Q.	Ans.	Correct		Q.	Ans.	Correct		Q.	Ans.	Correct
		Skipped				Skipped				Skipped				Skipped				Skipped
81	D	33.75 %		85	D	44.17 %		89	A	51.25 %		93	A	59.17 %		97	C	74.58 %
		7.08 %				8.33 %				8.75 %				8.75 %				8.34 %
82	B	27.08 %		86	B	24.17 %		90	A	53.33 %		94	B	69.58 %		98	C	27.08 %
		8.34 %				9.16 %				8.34 %				8.34 %				8.75 %
83	C	45.42 %		87	B	68.75 %		91	A	77.5 %		95	A	63.75 %		99	D	57.5 %
		7.5 %				9.17 %				9.17 %				7.5 %				9.17 %
84	A	52.08 %		88	D	30.0 %		92	A	48.75 %		96	B	26.67 %		100	D	35.0 %
		8.75 %				8.75 %				8.33 %				8.33 %				8.33 %

Ques (1-4):Direction: Read the following passage carefully and choose the best answer to the question out of the four alternatives.

Civil and political rights and socio-economic rights do not exist in. a state of antagonism. The conditions necessary for realizing or fulfilling socio-economic rights do not postulate the subversion of political freedom. The reason for this is simple. Socio-economic entitlements must yield true benefits to those for whom they are intended. This can. be achieved by eliminating rent-seeking behaviour and by preventing the capture of social welfare benefits by persons who are not entitled to them. Capture of social welfare benefits can be obviated only when political systems are transparent and when there is a free flow of information. Opacity ensures benefit to those who monopolize scarce economic resources. On the other hand, conditions where civil and political freedoms flourish ensure that governmental policies are subject to critique and assessment. It is this scrutiny which sub-serves the purpose of ensuring that socio-economic benefits actually permeate to the underprivileged for whom they are meant. Conditions of freedom and a vibrant assertion of civil and political rights promote a constant review of the justness of socio-economic programmes and of their effectiveness in addressing deprivation and want. Scrutiny of public affairs is founded upon the existence of freedom. Hence civil and political rights and socio-economic rights are complementary and not mutually exclusive.

Q.1 According to the passage, assertion of rights _______.
A. Is frowned upon
B. Must be discouraged
C. Promotes just social policies
D. Is desirable

Q.2 Which of the following statements best conveys the idea of the passage?
1. Civil and political rights and social and economic rights are opposed to each other.
2. Political freedom must be compromised to realize rights.
3. Existence of criticism of government is a proof of vibrant assertion of civil and political rights.
4. Transparency ensures equitable distribution of resources.
Choose the correct code:
A. 2 and 4   B. 1 and 2   C. 1 and 3   D. 3 and 4

Q.3 According to the passage capture of social benefits

_______.
A. Ensures accountability
B. Must be discouraged to ensure equitable distribution of resources
C. Is an evil necessity
D. Should be encouraged to maintain free flow of information

Q.4 Opacity means:

A. Ostensible   B. Transparent
C. Unclear   D. Opal like

Q.5 A is the mother of D and sister of B. B has a daughter C who is married to F. G is the husband of A. How is G related to D?
A. Son   B. Father   C. Uncle   D. Husband

Q.6 If the price of a book is first decreased by 25% and then increased by 20%, then the net change in the price will be:
A. 30   B. 20   C. 10   D. 40

Q.7 Which among the following is correctly matched?
A.   Indian Law Institute - Bhopal
B.   Central Institute of Indian Languages - Chandigarh
C.   Film and Television Institute of India - Chennai
D.   National Insurance Academy - Pune

Q.8 Which among the following languages was added to the Eighth Schedule of the Constitution of India, 1950 through 92nd Amendment Act of 2003?
A. Manipuri   B. Nepali
C. Maithili   D. Konkani

Q.9 Britishers established Fort St. George as a trading outpost of East India Company in:
A. Varanasi   B. Chandigarh
C. Chennai   D. Jaipur

Q.10 Which among the following cities does not have a bench of the National Green Tribunal?
A. Ahmadabad   B. Chennai
C. Pune   D. Kolkata

Q.11 Which among the following was chosen as the Oxford Dictionaries Word of the Year in 2017?
A. Vape   B. Post-truth
C. Emoji   D. Youth quake

Q.12 Which amongst the following is a committee constituted to inquire into allegations of corruption in Indian Premier League?
A.   Satyajit Ray Committee
B.   Shyam Benegal Committee
C.   Justice Mukul Mudgal Committee
D.   Justice Khosla Committee

Q.13 In India, the National Voter's Day is celebrated on:
A. 25th December   B. 25th January
C. 17th March   D. 17th January

Q.14 If A >B, B>C and C>D, then which of the following conclusion is definitely wrong?
A. D< A   B. C< B   C. A< D   D. B< A

Q.15 Who won the Gold Medal for India in the Women's 10 meter air pistol event at the XXI Commonwealth Games, 2018?

A. Manika Batra   **B.** Punam Yadav

C. Pooja Sahasrabudhe   **D.** Manu Bhaker

Q.16 In a class of 45 students, one of the student ranks 20th. When two more students take admission then his rank gets one place down. What is his position from the bottom?

A. 28   **B.** 26   **C.** 25   **D.** 27

Q.17 Which Schedule of the Constitution of India, 1950 prescribes the forms of oaths or affirmations for constitutional functionaries?

A. Sixth Schedule   **B.** Second Schedule

C. Fifth Schedule   **D.** Third Schedule

Q.18 Which provision of the Constitution of India, 1950 deals with legislative powers of the President?

A. Article 123   **B.** Article 73

C. Article 139   **D.** Article 59

Q.19 Which provision of the Constitution of India prohibits employment of children below the age of fourteen years to be employed in factories?

A. Article 23   **B.** Article 17

C. Article 27   **D.** Article 24

Q.20 Who among the following is the current member of the International Law Commission from India?

A. Nagender Singh   **B.** P.S. Rao

C. Aniruddha Rajput   **D.** Dalbir Bhandari

Q.21 The product of the ages of X and Y is 240. If twice the age of Y is more that X's age by 4 years, what is the age of Y?

A. 18   **B.** None of these

C. 12   **D.** 16

Q.22 Two numbers are in the ratio of 3:7. If 5 is subtracted from the numbers, the ratio becomes 4:11. The numbers are:

A. 18,42   **B.** 12,28   **C.** 9,16   **D.** 21,49

Q.23 Direction: In question four alternatives are given for the Idiom/Phrase under in the sentence. Choose the alternative which best expresses the meaning of the Idiom/Phrase.

"Do unto others as you would have them do unto you" means:

A. People tend to want whatever they don't have.

B. Don't do mean things to people.

C. If someone offers you a gift, don't question it.

D. Don't trust other people to do important things for you.

Q.24 Who headed the group of experts on Privacy constituted by the Planning Commission?

A. Justice Arijit Pasayat

B. Justice M.B. Shah

C. Justice M.N. Venkatachalia

D. Justice A.P. Shah

Q.25 Who amongst the following judges of the Supreme Court of India never served as a High Court judge?

A. Justice A.M. Khanwilkar

B. Justice Uday Umesh Lalit

C. Justice Kurian Joseph

D. Justice Abhay Manohar Sapre

Q.26 In which of the following judgments did the Supreme Court of India set aside thepractice of talaq-e-biddat i.e., triple talaq?

A. Fazlunbiv. K. KhaderVali

B. Mohd. Ahmed Khanv. Shah Bano Begum

C. Bai Tahirav. Ali Hussain Fissali Chothia

D. Shayara Banov. Union of India

Q.27 The name of the largest river island of the world located in India is:

A. Cijuli   **B.** Pajuli   **C.** Khajuli   **D.** Majuli

Q.28 In which state the Sasan Ultra Mega Power Project is located?

A. Tamil Nadu   **B.** Uttar Pradesh

C. Madhya Pradesh   **D.** Maharashtra

Q.29 Identify the correct statement:

A. Only taking of dowry is prohibited under law.

B. Only giving of dowry is prohibited under law.

C. Dowry is legally allowed with the consent of involved parties.

D. Giving as well as taking dowry is prohibited under law.

Q.30 The recently launched 'LaQshya' programme is aimed at:

A. Reducing malnutrition in children below ten years of age

B. Reducing maternal mortality rates

C. Elimination of tuberculosis by 2025

D. Improving quality of life in rural areas

Q.31 X is wife of Y. Y is uncle of Z. B is sister of Y. How is B related to X?

A. Sister-in-Law   **B.** Cousin

C. Brother   **D.** Uncle

Q.32 A judge of the Supreme Court of India after retirement can practice in:

A. None of the these

B. High Court

C. National Green Tribunal

D. Supreme Court of India only

Q.33 Four tests—French, Hindi, English and Sanskrit are to be conducted on four consecutive days, not necessarily in the same order. The English test is held before the test which is conducted after Hindi. Sanskrit test is conducted exactly after two tests are held. Which is the last test held?

A. French   **B.** Sanskrit   **C.** Hindi   **D.** English

Q.34 The headquarters of the World Trade Organization is located in:

A. Geneva   **B.** London

C. New York   **D.** Nairobi

Q.35 First UNESCO mixed heritage site of India is:

A. Kangchendzonga National Park

B. Kaziranga National Park

C. Dachigam National Park

D. Bharatpur Bird Sanctuary

Q.36 Renu, Sheena, Heena and Seema are sitting around a table. Renu is just right to the Sheena. Heena is left to Seema. Who amongst the following facing each other?

A. Renu – Sheena
B. Renu – Seema
C. Sheena – Seema
D. Heena – Renu

Q.37 If B is coded as 2 and RATE is coded as 44 in a code language, how would you code NATION in that code language?

A. 74
B. 75
C. 72
D. 73

Q.38 There are two groups of birds. If one bird moves from first group to the second group, the number of birds in the second group becomes double of the first group. If one bird moves from second group to the first group, the number of birds in both the groups becomes equal. How many birds were there in group 1 and 2 initially (respectively)?

A. 9,5
B. 5,7
C. 7,5
D. 5,9

Q.39 Hari's commute never bothered him because there were always seats available on the train and he was able to spend 40 minutes comfortably reading newspapers. Ever since the train schedule changed, the train has become extremely crowded, and by the time the doors open at his station, there isn't a seat to be found. Which of the following inference is correct?

A. Hari's commute is less comfortable since the train schedule changed

B. Many commuters will complain about the new train schedule.

C. Hari is likely to look for a new job closer to his home.

D. Hari would be better off taking the bus to work.

Q.40 European Court of Human Rights is located in:

A. Hamburg
B. Strasbourg
C. Luxembourg
D. St. Petersburg

Q.41 'Earth Hour' is a global initiative of the:

A. UN Development Programme
B. Earth Day Organization
C. World Wide Fund for Nature
D. UN Environment Programme

Q.42 Arrange these mountain ranges from North to South:
1. Satpura
2. Nilgiri
3. Vindhvas
4. Aravalis

A. 1432
B. 4312
C. 4132
D. 4123

Q.43 Which of the following is/are principal organ/s of the United Nations?
1. International Court of Justice
2. United Nations Development Programme
3. United Nations Economic and Social Council
4. United Nations Environment Programme.

A. Only 1
B. All of these
C. 1, 2 and 4
D. 1 and 3

Q.44 Who among the following can attend the meetings of both Houses of Parliament while being not a member of either House?

A. Solicitor General of India
B. Attorney General of India
C. Chief Election Commissioner
D. Comptroller and Auditor General of India

Q.45 Who among the following is known as the 'Frontier Gandhi'?

A. Maulana Abul Kalam Azad
B. Maulana Shaukat Ali
C. Sir Syed Ahmed Khan
D. Khan Abdul Ghaffar Khan

Q.46 Who among the following was not conferred Bharat Ratna?

A. Atal Bihari Vajpayee
B. Nelson Mandela
C. Homi J. Bhabha
D. Khan Abdul Ghaffar Khan

Q.47 Who among the following was not a member of the Constituent Assembly of India?

A. Lakshmi Sehgal
B. Rajkumari Amrit Kaur
C. Hansa Mehta
D. Sarojini Naidu

Q.48 Who amongst the following did not serve as the Chairman of the Law Commission of India?

A. Mr. M.C. Setalvad
B. Justice B.P. Jeevan Reddy
C. Justice A.P. Shah
D. Justice V.R. Krishna Iyer

Q.49 Direction: Fill in the blanks with an appropriate word.
"Behind the eight ball" means ________.

A. In safety
B. In extravagance
C. In comfort
D. In trouble

Q.50 Who is the author of the book titled "Why I am a Hindu"?

A. Rakesh Sinha
B. Shashi Tharoor
C. Gopal Krishna Gandhi
D. Justice R. Banumathi

Q.51 Inter-state river water disputes in India are to be decided by:

A. Central Water Commission
B. None of the these
C. High Courts
D. Ministry of Water Resources

Q.52 Direction: In question four alternatives are given for the Idiom/Phrase under in the sentence. Choose the alternative which best expresses the meaning of the Idiom/Phrase.
What is the meaning of ex facie:

A. Making the face down

B. Beside the face of it

C. Behind the face it

D. On the face of it

Q.53 Who proposed the idea of Constituent Assembly of India in 1934?

A. Dr. B.R. Ambedkar

B. S.N. Mukherjee

C. Dr. Rajendra Prasad

D. M.N. Roy

Q.54 Which of the following is explicitly prescribed as a Directive Principle of State Policy under the Constitution of India?

A. All of the these

B. Promotion of co-operative societies

C. Participation of workers in management of industries

D. Organization of village panchayats

Q.55 Which of the following rivers does not flow into the Bay of Bengal?

A. Godavari

B. Periyar

C. Kaveri

D. Krishna

Q.56 Which of the following smart cities has become the India's first city to run on 100% Renewable Energy during Daytime?

A. Chandigarh

B. Puducherri

C. Gwalior

D. Diu

Q.57 Which of the following does not fall in the List I—Union List of the Seventh Schedule to Constitution of India?

A. Naval, military and air force works

B. Public health and sanitation

C. Sanctioning of cinematograph films for exhibition

D. Banking

Q.58 Which of the following is not placed at Hague?

A. Permanent Court of Arbitration

B. International Tribunal for the Law of the Sea

C. International Court of Justice

D. International Criminal Court

Q.59 Which of the following is not a Fundamental Duty under Article 51A of the Constitution of India?

A. To value and preserve the rich heritage of our composite culture

B. To safeguard public property and to abjure violence

C. To respect and propagate political values

D. To cherish and follow the noble ideals which inspired our national struggle for Freedom

Q.60 Which of the following statement best explains the phrase 'Devil's Advocate'?

A. Expressing contentious opinion

B. Expressing discontentment

C. Arguing for the sake of argument

D. Arguing for the guilty

Q.61 Which of the following fundamental right is not available to a foreigner in India?

A. Freedom of Speech and Expression

B. Right to Life and Liberty

C. Right to equality

D. Right against Ex post facto laws

Q.62 Direction: In the following question, there is a certain relation between two given words on one side::

Choose the suitable words to be put on the other side from the given alternatives.

Glutton : Willpower ::________ :________

A. Platoon : Squad

B. Charlatan : Hoax

C. Savant : Gumption

D. Coward : Courage

Q.63 Direction: In the following question, there is a certain relation between two given words on one side. Choose the suitable word to be put on the other side from the given alternatives.

Inflexible: Limber :: Failure:

A. Achievement

B. Expunge

C. Trouble

D. Murmur

Q.64 Find out which part of the sentence given below has an error:

Demi has not completed her homework, isn't it?

A. her homework

B. No fault

C. isn't it

D. has not completed

Q.65 Find out which part of the sentence given below has an error:

My Mother asked me that what I was doing.

A. that what I was doing

B. asked me

C. My mother

D. No fault

Q.66 Direction: In the following question, four words have been given of which three are alike in some way and one is different. Choose the odd one out.

People who are bald are generally happy. Asif is bald. Therefore, Asif is happy.

A. Can't be determined

B. False

C. Probably true

D. True

Q.67 Direction: In the following question, four words have been given of which three are alike in some way and one is different. Choose the odd one out.

The presence of calcium in milk makes it white. Egg is white. Therefore, egg also contains calcium:

A. TRUE

B. Can't be determined

C. FALSE

D. Probably true

Ques (68-69):Direction: In the following question, four words have been given of which three are alike in some way and one is different. Choose the odd one out.

Q.68 Identify the odd one out

A. Tree

B. Leaf

C. Branch

D. Stem

Q.69 Identify the odd one out.

A. RAM = 18113

B. SUA = 19211

C. HOP = 81516

D. MAP = 13115

Q.70 Choose the correct collective noun:

A ____of ships

A. Army   **B.** Fleet   **C.** Belt   **D.** Pack

Q.71 Choose the correct collective noun:

A ____of baboons

A. Herd   **B.** Congress

C. Pack   **D.** Meeting

Q.72 Choose the word that is nearest in meaning to the given word:

Abrogate

A. Revoke informally   **B.** Revoke formally

C. Accept informally   **D.** Accept formally

Q.73 Choose the word that is nearest in meaning to the given word:

Extol

A. Glorify   **B.** Dishonour

C. Provoke   **D.** Announce

Q.74 Choose the most appropriate option to fill in the blanks:

I have never seen _______painting before.

A. as beautiful   **B.** so beautiful

C. such a beautiful   **D.** any beautiful

Q.75 Choose the most appropriate option to fill in the blanks:

They ______learning classical music next year

A. will have been   **B.** will be

C. will   **D.** will have to

Q.76 Fill in the missing word:

Insect: Disease :: War:?

A. Army   **B.** Victory

C. Destruction   **D.** Weapon

Q.77 Fill in the missing word:

Distance : Meter :: Force : ?

A. Dioptre   **B.** Joule   **C.** Watt   **D.** Newton

Q.78 Arrange the words given below in a meaningful sequence:

1. Chaitra 2. Falgun 3. Magh 4. Bhadrapad 5. Aashadh

A. 1,2,5,4,3   **B.** 1,2,3,4,5   **C.** 1,3,4,2,5   **D.** 1,5,4,3,2

Q.79 Direction: In the following question a statement is given, followed by two conclusions. Give answer:

Statement:

In a one day cricket match, the total runs made by a team were 300. Out of these 240 runs were made by bowlers.

Conclusions:

I) The opening batsmen were bowlers.

II) 80% of the team consists of bowlers.

A. Both Conclusions I and II follow

B. Neither Conclusion I nor II follows

C. Only Conclusion II follows

D. Only Conclusion I follows

Q.80 Complete the series:

BAY, EDV, HGS, KJP,____?

A. NMQ   **B.** NMP   **C.** NMM   **D.** NMO

Q.81 Complete the series:

REF, SGH, ______, UKL

A. TIJ   **B.** VJT   **C.** MNT   **D.** VXZ

Q.82 Complete the series:

BCB, DED, FGF, HIH,____?

A. IJI   **B.** JHJ   **C.** JKJ   **D.** HJH

Q.83 Complete the series:

53, 53, 40, 40, 27, 27,____?

A. 12   **B.** 14   **C.** 53   **D.** 27

Q.84 Complete the series:

E64, ______, K16, N8, Q4

A. H32   **B.** G23   **C.** F32   **D.** J23

Q.85 Complete the series:

70, 68, 66, 63, 61, 59, 56, 54,____?

A. 52   **B.** 51   **C.** 50   **D.** 53

Q.86 Complete the series:

192, 48, ______, 3

A. 11   **B.** 13   **C.** 12   **D.** 14

Ques (87-90):Direction: Apply the principle to the facts and choose the most appropriate option.

Q.87 Principle 1:

When a person voluntarily consents to infliction of some harm upon himself/herself, he/she cannot complain for the harm suffered and his/her consent acts as a good defence against him/her.

Principle 2:

The consent may be express or implied.

Facts:

The plaintiff was a spectator at Formula One Car race. Despite due care by the organizers, there was a collision between two cars during the race and one of the cars was thrown among the audience, gravely injuring Hasan. Hasan was paralyzed waist down due to this injury.

Decision:

A. Organizers are liable to compensate Hasan as even though he agreed to take the risk of being injured, he did not agree to be paralyzed.

B. Organizers are liable to compensate Hasan as he did not expressly consent to being gravely injured.

C. Organizers are liable to compensate Hasan for the harm caused to him, as he did not voluntarily agree to be gravely injured.

D. Organizers are not liable to compensate as Hasan impliedly took the risk of injury. The danger of car collision is inherent In Formula 1 Car Race. The possibility of spectators being injured by such collision is foreseeable.

Q.88 Principle:

If the offeror has prescribed a particular mode or manner of acceptance, the acceptance must be made in the prescribed manner only. In the event of the acceptor not following the prescribed mode of acceptance, no valid contract comes into existence.

Facts:

Arora Enterprises made an offer to buy desks from Bharucha Co. Ltd. According to the terms of the contract, the acceptance was to be made through e-mail. Bharucha Co. and Ltd. sent the acceptance through post. Arora Enterprises received this letter but entered into contract with Abdulla Enterprises. Bharucha Co. Ltd. sued Arora Enterprises for breach of contract.

Decision:

A. Bharucha Co. Ltd can successfully sue Arora Enterprises as it has conveyed its acceptance and fulfilled essential conditions required by contract.

B. Arora Enterprises can be sued as it entered into contract with Abdulla Enterprises after receiving the acceptance of Bharucha Co. Ltd.

C. Arora Enterprises cannot be sued, as the acceptance was invalid.

D. The acceptance is valid as what is necessary is that the acceptance must reach the offeror.

Q.89 Principle:

A contract to do an act, which, after the contract is made becomes impossible is void when the act becomes impossible.

Facts:

Sheela owned a two storey building. She agreed to lease the property to Harleen for a period of 1 year for a rent of fifty thousand rupees per month. The contract was signed by both the parties on April 30, 2015. It was agreed that the lease period would start from May 5, 2015. On May 3, 2015, a massive fire broke out and the building was completely destroyed.

Decision:

A. The contract is void as the subject matter of the contract has ceased to exist.

B. The contract is void as the fire broke out two days before the start of the lease period.

C. The contract is valid as the performance of the contract does not depend on the existence of the subject matter of contract, i.e. the building.

D. The contract is valid as it was already signed before the fire broke out.

Q.90 Principle:

Unreasonable interference with a person's use or enjoyment of land constitutes nuisance.

Facts:

A brick grinding machine was installed by Mihir adjoining the premises of George who was a medical practitioner. The dust from the machine used to enter George's medical chamber and cause inconvenience to the patients.

Decision:

A. George cannot sue Mihir for nuisance as every nuisance is not inconvenience.

B. George cannot sue Mihir for nuisance as Mihir has a right to use his property as he deems fit.

C. George cannot sue Mihir for nuisance as the use of land by George was not illegal.

D. George can sue Mihir for nuisance as the dust interfered with the physical comfort of George and his patients.

Q.91 One who studies elections and trends in voting is known as:

A. Demagogue   B. Odontologist
C. Psephologist   D. Numismatic

Q.92 Right to Property is a:

A. Fundamental Right
B. Not recognized in India
C. None of these
D. Legal Right

Q.93 'Operation Cactus' recently in the news refers to:

A. Indian army's cross border strike in Myanmar
B. India's nuclear project in Pokhran
C. India's military intervention in Maldives in 1988
D. India's Surgical Strikes on terror launch pads in PoK in 2016

Q.94 Recently the UN General Assembly passed a resolution rejecting the Israeli claim of Jerusalem as its new capital. Which among the following countries voted against the resolution to support the Israeli claim?

A. Guatemala   B. India
C. Cuba   D. Sri Lanka

Q.95 Fundamental Duties were added in the Constitution of India on the recommendation of:

A. Malimath Committee
B. Santhanam Committee
C. Sarkaria Committee
D. Swaran Singh Committee

Q.96 Murugappa Gold Cup is related to which of the following sports?

A. Wrestling   B. Swimming
C. Kabaddi   D. Hockey

Q.97 The President of India can be impeached on the ground of:

A. Both Violation of the Constitution of India and Proved misbehaviour or incapacity
B. Proved misbehaviour or incapacity
C. Violation of the Constitution of India
D. None of these

Q.98 The Vice-President of India may be removed from his office by:

A. Resolution of the House of the People and duly approved by President.
B. Resolution of the Council of States and agreed to by the House of the People.
C. Resolution of the Council of States only.
D. The President of India upon the advice of the Council of Ministers.

Q.99 As per the XIV Finance Commission Report how much is the State Governments' share in taxes?

A. 42%   B. 40%   C. 41%   D. 44%

Q.100 Under the 'Adopt a Heritage' project, which corporate house has signed MoU to maintain historic site "Red Fort"?

A. Larsen & Tourbo
B. Dalmia Bharat Ltd.
C. Tata Motors
D. Tata Consultancy Service

// Smart Answer Sheet //

Correct Percentage of students who answered correctly.　　**Skipped** Percentage of students who skipped.

Q.	Ans.	Correct / Skipped	Q.	Ans.	Correct / Skipped	Q.	Ans.	Correct / Skipped	Q.	Ans.	Correct / Skipped	Q.	Ans.	Correct / Skipped
1	C	46.6 % / 2.61 %	17	D	75.39 % / 6.29 %	33	A	59.16 % / 5.76 %	49	D	35.6 % / 6.28 %	65	A	62.83 % / 6.28 %
2	D	34.03 % / 2.62 %	18	A	59.16 % / 4.71 %	34	A	74.87 % / 4.71 %	50	B	67.02 % / 5.23 %	66	C	41.88 % / 5.24 %
3	B	28.27 % / 3.14 %	19	D	73.3 % / 4.19 %	35	A	42.41 % / 4.19 %	51	B	28.27 % / 6.28 %	67	B	29.84 % / 6.81 %
4	C	43.46 % / 3.14 %	20	C	29.84 % / 7.33 %	36	B	56.54 % / 2.62 %	52	D	46.6 % / 7.33 %	68	A	52.36 % / 7.33 %
5	B	75.39 % / 5.76 %	21	C	27.75 % / 6.28 %	37	D	64.92 % / 6.28 %	53	D	74.87 % / 5.76 %	69	D	51.31 % / 7.33 %
6	C	50.26 % / 4.19 %	22	D	42.93 % / 2.1 %	38	B	45.55 % / 3.14 %	54	A	81.68 % / 4.18 %	70	B	60.21 % / 6.81 %
7	D	19.9 % / 6.28 %	23	B	48.17 % / 4.19 %	39	A	63.87 % / 4.19 %	55	B	45.55 % / 4.71 %	71	B	29.32 % / 6.81 %
8	C	54.45 % / 7.33 %	24	D	26.7 % / 3.14 %	40	B	31.94 % / 6.8 %	56	D	28.8 % / 6.8 %	72	B	52.36 % / 6.8 %
9	C	50.79 % / 5.75 %	25	B	24.61 % / 6.28 %	41	C	24.61 % / 5.76 %	57	B	52.36 % / 5.76 %	73	A	31.94 % / 6.28 %
10	A	37.7 % / 6.8 %	26	D	62.83 % / 2.09 %	42	B	21.99 % / 6.81 %	58	B	54.45 % / 5.24 %	74	C	86.39 % / 2.09 %
11	D	34.03 % / 6.28 %	27	D	53.4 % / 6.29 %	43	D	46.07 % / 6.29 %	59	C	75.39 % / 6.29 %	75	B	73.3 % / 4.19 %
12	C	55.5 % / 6.28 %	28	C	24.61 % / 6.8 %	44	B	80.1 % / 3.15 %	60	A	24.08 % / 6.81 %	76	C	79.58 % / 6.81 %
13	B	66.49 % / 5.76 %	29	D	84.29 % / 6.29 %	45	D	68.59 % / 6.28 %	61	A	58.64 % / 5.76 %	77	D	67.54 % / 6.28 %
14	C	72.77 % / 4.72 %	30	B	16.75 % / 2.62 %	46	C	41.88 % / 4.19 %	62	D	38.22 % / 5.24 %	78	D	26.18 % / 6.8 %
15	D	42.41 % / 6.28 %	31	A	83.25 % / 7.33 %	47	A	25.65 % / 6.29 %	63	A	57.59 % / 4.71 %	79	B	41.88 % / 5.24 %
16	D	34.55 % / 3.15 %	32	A	60.21 % / 3.14 %	48	D	30.37 % / 3.14 %	64	C	47.64 % / 7.33 %	80	C	70.16 % / 6.8 %

Q.	Ans.	Correct	Skipped
81	A	81.68 %	6.28 %
82	C	84.29 %	2.62 %
83	B	78.53 %	4.19 %
84	A	80.63 %	3.14 %

Q.	Ans.	Correct	Skipped
85	A	73.82 %	5.76 %
86	C	59.16 %	6.81 %
87	D	68.59 %	5.23 %
88	C	64.92 %	5.24 %

Q.	Ans.	Correct	Skipped
89	A	59.69 %	5.76 %
90	D	71.73 %	6.28 %
91	C	39.27 %	6.8 %
92	D	83.77 %	6.28 %

Q.	Ans.	Correct	Skipped
93	C	23.04 %	6.8 %
94	A	16.23 %	6.28 %
95	D	80.1 %	6.81 %
96	D	38.22 %	6.28 %

Q.	Ans.	Correct	Skipped
97	C	47.64 %	6.81 %
98	B	43.98 %	6.81 %
99	A	29.32 %	3.66 %
100	B	36.65 %	6.28 %

// Notes //

// Notes //